Universalist Hopes in India and Europe

Universalist Hopes in India and Europe

The Worlds of Rabindranath Tagore and Srečko Kosovel

ANA JELNIKAR

OXFORD
UNIVERSITY PRESS

OXFORD
UNIVERSITY PRESS

Oxford University Press is a department of the University of Oxford.
It furthers the University's objective of excellence in research, scholarship,
and education by publishing worldwide. Oxford is a registered trademark of
Oxford University Press in the UK and in certain other countries.

Published in India by
Oxford University Press
YMCA Library Building, 1 Jai Singh Road, New Delhi 110 001, India

ISBN-13: 978-0-19-946090-8
ISBN-10: 0-19-946090-6

Typeset in Minion Pro 10.5/13
by The Graphics Solution, New Delhi 110 092

For William Radice

'Ours is essentially a tragic age, so we refuse to take it tragically. The cataclysm has happened, we are among the ruins, we start to build up new little habitats, to have new little hopes. It is rather hard work: there is now no smooth road into the future: but we go round, or scramble over obstacles. We've got to live, no matter how many skies have fallen.'

—D. H. Lawrence, *Lady Chatterley's Lover*, 1928

Contents

Acknowledgements

This book has grown out of the research conducted for a PhD degree at the School of Oriental and African Studies (SOAS) under the mentorship of William Radice. It is to him that I owe my foremost words of gratitude. I will remain forever indebted to him for opening the doors of the world of Tagore scholarship and Bengali studies for me, and for setting such an inspiring example of combining rigorous scholarship with creative literary work. This book is my own attempt at turning literary interest into academic research and I wish to thank the following institutions and individuals who enabled me to carry the project through the various stages to its completion.

I gratefully acknowledge the financial support received from the Arts and Humanities Research Council (AHRC) fee-only doctoral award for the second and third years of my research, as well as a fieldwork grant, and the supplementary maintenance grant received from the Slovenian Ministry of Culture for postgraduate studies abroad. At the same time, without further financial assistance from both my parents, whose all-round support surpasses any words of acknowledgement, I would have had to struggle incomparably more with the practical realities of life. The one-year Ad Futura grant to join the Science and Research Centre of Koper, University of Primorska, has allowed me to continue my research in modern Indian cultural history, while facilitating my transition back to Slovenia. The one individual who has been hugely supportive in this is Lenart Škof, one of the few Slovene scholars pursuing research on India-related subjects, and to him I would like to extend a special word of thanks. The Indian Council for Cultural Relations Tagore Fellowship for 2011–12 not only sustained me through another year, but also gave me a year-long opportunity to live in Kolkata researching the theme of hospitality in relation to Tagore's ideas and creative writing at the Department of Bengali, Presidency University. Special thanks go to Debapriya Bhattacharya for his support throughout. In this period, I benefited immensely from conversations I had with various scholars, often combined with invitations to their homes. Heartfelt thanks go to Swati Lal and Ananda Lal whose warm household I have come to associate over the years with the best of Bengali hospitality and cosmopolitan intellectual rigour. With Nandini Bhattacharya, I engaged in hours of stimulating conversation and I wish to thank her for hosting me at West Bengal State University as well as introducing me to the English Department staff there, including Anupama Choubey, whose help with Bengali sources has been invaluable to me ever since. I am grateful to Debashish Raychaudhuri and his family, including the brilliant Rabindrasangeet singer, Rohini Raychaudhuri, who kindly collaborated with me alongside her father at a literary event exploring connections between India and Slovenia that was hosted by the Slovene Embassy in India with the Honorary Consul of the Republic of Slovenia in Kolkata. Amit Chaudhuri's sharp insights on Kosovel's poetry at the same event and his fresh approach to Tagore that liberates him from the national iconic status have been very important for my work. Equally important have been my frequent collaborations with the wonderful poet and translator Stephen Watts, not only for sharpening my ability to appreciate poetry in general, but also for enhancing my sensibilities as a translator; not to mention the stimulus exuding from his own appreciation of both Bengali and Slovene literatures.

I also want to thank Sanjukta Dasgupta and Chinmoy Guha for hosting me at the Department of English, University of Calcutta, and giving me the opportunity to engage with the students there on the topic of this book, as also to Jolly Das, Saptarshi Mallick, Kalapi Sen, and Pinaki De for having me at their Department of English at Raja Peary Mohan College for a guest lecture, but then also extending their invitation to a guided tour of the Uttarpara Joy Krishna Public Library, allegedly the first public reading library in Asia, as well as a day trip to Chandannagar—both unforgettable experiences. Opportunities to discuss my work with Rosinka Chaudhuri, Sibaji Bandyopadhyay, and Kamalika Mukherjee at the Centre for Studies in Social Sciences have also been invaluable. Kamalika's friendship and her help in always getting me the needed materials have made all the difference to my research. Supriya Chaudhuri and Sukanta Chaudhuri have also offered generously of their time to engage with my ideas as well as given me opportunities to participate in events and conferences at Jadavpur University. I have been fortunate enough to have met and had various opportunities to talk to Malashri Lal, Jasodhara Bagchi, Radha Chakravarti, and Fakrul Aklam. There is nothing better than good intellectual engagement turning into friendship. The intellectual rigour, support, and friendship of Ketaki Kushari Dyson and that of her husband, Robert, has been invaluable over the years. My stay in Santiniketan and Kolkata would not have been half as pleasant and stimulating if it were not for the times and conversations I had with Kathleen O'Connell and now sadly late Joe O'Connell, as well as those with Martin Kämpchen, Imre Bangha, Christine Kupfer, Deen Chatterjee, and Uma Das Gupta. Kalyan Bagchi and his wife spent hours with me discussing Tagore's universalism at their home in Santiniketan. My research undertaken at the Rabindra-Bhavana Library in Santiniketan was greatly facilitated by the assistance of Swati Ghose, and I would also like to thank Hana Basu for her help as a translator of some of the Bengali sources. The friendship of a number of individuals, especially of my Bagan Para neighbour Arpita Saha (Choton) and of Keya and Satish from Purva Palli, has sustained me through the more trying times in Santiniketan. Monjita Mukharji and Jayani Bonnerjee have made me feel at home in Kolkata and their friendship as well as the sharing of our joint PhD lives still back in London alongside the many discussions on our respective topics since have enriched my understanding of Bengali literature and culture. The work of Benjamin Zachariah on the intellectual history of Indian nationalism has been of key importance in my own engagement with the problematic, and having the opportunity to meet him in Kolkata and further being invited to give a talk at the Department of History, Presidency University, while he was there, has allowed me to explore these issues further and that has no doubt influenced my own work.

Even prior to the submission of my thesis I had had the privilege of the drafts of my Tagore chapters being read by Uma Das Gupta,

Kalyan Bagchi, Ketaki Kushari Dyson, Parimal Ghosh, Joseph O'
Connell and Kathleen O'Connell, and Amina Yaquin. My handling
of the unwieldy subject of universalism was critically responded
to by Projit Mukharji, Polly Pallister-Wilkins, and Maja Petrović-
Šteger, and the response of the examiners Antony Copley and Zoran
Milutinović provided me with excellent pointers as to improving the
work for publication. All their incisive comments, including those of
the anonymous reviewers, are gratefully acknowledged. In the latter
stages of preparation of the manuscript, I have relied on the always
sharp insights of Carool Kersten, whose tireless support and friendship throughout the entire project bears no parallel. Many walks and
talks with Mara Malagodi on subjects academic and non-academic
have always produced fresh insights.

   I amply acknowledge the institutional support I have received from
the Research Centre of the Slovenian Academy of Sciences and Arts
(SASA) in getting me through the revisions stage of my manuscript.
Furthermore, the intellectual support of Nataša Gregorič Bon, Maja
Petrović-Šteger, Borut Telban (of the Institute of Anthropological and
Spatial Studies, SASA, Slovenia), and Nataša Rogelja (of the Slovenian
Migration Institute) as well as their friendships have helped me
overcome the doubts and hurdles in completing the manuscript. The
ongoing seminars with the project team at the Science and Research
Centre Koper at University of Primorska Research Institute have been
truly inspiring and have encouraged me to sail more philosophical
waters. Carlos Pascual has pushed me to grapple more critically with
writing style and narrative structure and I hope some of his efforts
finally got reflected in the work. And last but not least, I want to thank
Aljaž Kovač who kindly read the full manuscript, assuming the role
of a 'general reader'.

   As for the Kosovel part of the book, I have benefited greatly from
my discussions and collaboration with Iztok Osojnik and the annual
Golden Boat International Poetry Translation Workshop we co-founded
and ran for a number of years. My Kosovel co-translator and friend,
Barbara Siegel Carlson, has probably come to read the book in all its
different stages, and I thank her for her always incisive comments
and her ceaseless enthusiasm and support of my work over all these
years. I am also deeply grateful for the editorial and critical comments
of David Brooks, Sinan Gudžević, and Peter Svetina, all of whom

keenly engaged with the Kosovel chapters and made suggestions for improvements. The opportunities to discuss Kosovel with Dubravka Djurić and Miško Šuvaković at their Belgrade home, and with Ravel Kodrič at a Kosovel seminar in Slovenia have also been invaluable. Meta Kušar's always original take on Slovene poetry has been an inspiration for many years now. Informal conversations with Dragica Sosič and Pavle Skrinjar, people who have had close acquaintance with members of the Kosovel family and have privileged insight into his personal background, have no doubt been some of the highlights of my research. I thank them for the time they have ungrudgingly given me, and for enabling me to access Kosovel's personal library. I would also like to thank the staff at the Ljubljana's Slavonic Library (Slovanska knjižnica), and National and University Library of Slovenia (Narodna Univerzitetna knjižnica) in Ljubljana, as well as the National Library of Serbia (Narodna Biblioteka Srbije) for their kind assistance. The opportunities to present my work on Kosovel and Tagore at various conferences at home and abroad and give lectures on the topic have all importantly helped give shape to the present book. The more recent exchanges and collaboration with scholars of Indian religions and philosophies in Slovenia—Tamara Ditrich, Ana Bajželj, Tina Košir Mazi, Mia Dora Prvan, and Lenart Škof— as well as Lora Tomaš from Croatia have also generated something of a strong wish for Indian Studies to acquire a more substantial and permanent presence in the Slovene academic environment.

Ana Jelnikar
Ljubljana, April 2015

Note on Translation

Where published translations of Slovene source texts in English were available, I have used and accredited these accordingly. All remaining translations from the Slovene language are mine. If they have not been published in their own right in English, I give the title of the source text in the original with a translation in brackets, in all other instances I simply refer to the English title.

Introduction

Tagore and Kosovel—Framing an Unusual Encounter

Thou hast made me known to friends whom I knew not. Thou hast given me seats in homes not my own. Thou has brought the distant near and made a brother of the stranger.

—Tagore, *Gitanjali: Song Offerings*, 1912, poem no. 63

In the early decades of the twentieth century, two remarkable individuals who lived worlds apart spoke up in strikingly similar voices. At first sight, theirs is a strange alignment—also a bold one. For who would dare put a towering poet-philosopher on par with a budding, however talented, writer whose life was cut short just as his artistic voice was beginning to gather momentum. And yet, this is not the first time that Rabindranath Tagore and Srečko Kosovel have been caught between the covers of the same book. If you were to pick up the primer from my early school days in what was then still Yugoslavia, you would find both the Slovene poet and the Bengali writer amidst its pages. While, no doubt, this education policy was spurned by Tito's involvement—along with that of Nehru, Nasser, and Sukarno—in the Non-aligned Movement in the 1960s, which opened up Yugoslavia to the Global South, the interest in Tagore amongst Slovenes has an altogether longer—and a more personal—history. This book is the first to explore the various facets of that history.

***

In the 1920s, at the height of Tagore's reputation in continental Europe, Srečko Kosovel (1904–1926) penned these lines:

> In green India among quiet
> trees that bend over blue water
> lives Tagore ...[1]

Almost a century later, for the occasion of the centenary of the publication of Tagore's English *Gitanjali: Song Offerings* (1912), William Radice, one of Tagore's foremost translators into English, used these four lines as an epigraph to his translation of the award-winning collection of poems, in itself a real act of literary excavation and creative restitution that brings the 'real' English *Gitanjali*[2] to the reader for the first time. Srečko Kosovel would never have thought it possible that one day the opening lines of his most explicit tribute to the Indian contemporary he read and admired so much, the poem 'In Green India', would share book space with the Laureate. Indeed, it would be hard to think of a bigger compliment to the then barely known poet who looked to Tagore convinced that there was no one greater than him on the horizon at the time. Thrown about on the rough seas of the post–Great War Europe, the young poet was only too eager to jump into Tagore's 'Golden boat'—incidentally the title he borrowed from his Indian 'mentor' for his first collections of poems.

Despite his absurdly short life—he died aged twenty-two—Kosovel left behind an impressively large and diverse body of work that

[1] 'In Green India', translated by Ana Jelnikar and Barbara Siegel Carlson, in Kosovel (2010a), p. 97.

[2] This new translation, done from the source Bengali poems, is unique in that it restores the original sequence of the poems as Tagore had intended them for publication before the manuscript was edited by W. B. Yeats and others. It also restores the diversity of the original poems' styles and forms, the musicality and rhythm, as well as the overall conception that Yeats's editorial interventions had tampered with.

continues to attract critics and scholars, as well as general readers at home and abroad. Gaining due recognition only decades after his premature death, he is today considered Slovenia's foremost avant-garde poet of the interwar period as well as a lyricist of great sensitivity and beauty. Not unlike Tagore, he is celebrated as a national icon, with street names, institutions, and various associations carrying his name. Even though in recent years, Kosovel's international reputation has been given a boost by new, quality translations, it can be safely assumed that most people picking up the new 'authoritative' English translation of *Gitanjali* would not have heard of Srečko Kosovel, and may wonder why such an 'obscure' poet has been chosen for the epigraph.

Radice's rationale for selecting these lines stems from seeing in Kosovel a 'divinely gifted' poet who genuinely empathized with Tagore, unlike, say, Yeats, who 'did not see Tagore as an individual, as a man in a specific time and place who felt and thought and suffered'. The poem 'In Green India' is seen to capture in 'its imagery with haunting lucidity Tagore as a man in a time and a place'.[3] This is no small claim, and this volume offers to explore and possibly vindicate this claim. For here is a response to Tagore that does indeed fall outside the more familiar 'standard' appropriations of the Indian poet in Europe and elsewhere as a mystic and guru. So what was it then that made Kosovel respond so heartily, and with such urgency, to his older Indian contemporary if it was not, or not just, the transcendental allure?

To be sure, intuition and creative imagination will have a part to play in the exploration of this little-known meeting of minds. For it is clear that India's best-known poet for over a century now and Kosovel lived worlds apart. One wrote in Bengali and English, and the other in Slovene. They never met, and it was only Kosovel who knew of Tagore, and not the other way around. And yet, as contemporaries during the volatile 1920s, they were surprisingly close to each other in their aspirations and their aesthetic–moral vision, more so than to the majority of their own compatriots. I will therefore compare, confront, and align these two writers' engagements with the particulars of their time and place from their respective backgrounds, cutting across a

---

[3] Radice (2012), p. lxxix.

number of contexts. They were kindred spirits precisely in that they shared both a particular view of the world and a strikingly similar worldview. Kosovel, barely out of his teens, and reading Tagore in freshly minted translations in a number of European languages, felt a strong—indeed vital—connection with the older Indian poet. This connection was motivated as much by questions of aesthetics as it was by a pressing need to understand and address issues of perceived common concern.

Kosovel *identified* with Tagore through the experience of political and cultural subjugation, when after World War I, and following the dissolution of the Austro-Hungarian Empire, Italy claimed control over a sizeable portion of Slovene-populated territory, subjecting it to harsh assimilatory politics. Without equating the two poets' situations or statures in any way, Kosovel will be seen to share—from this structurally similar positioning as a subjugated 'other'—a whole set of preoccupations with Tagore.

KOSOVEL READS TAGORE

When in 1925, only a few months before his untimely death, Kosovel was getting his first manuscript ready for publication, he decided to give it the title *Zlati čoln* ('The Golden Boat'). In a letter to his friend and associate, Ciril Debevec, he wrote: 'I am going to call it *Zlati čoln*, why, I'll tell you.'[4] If Debevec ever did get to hear of his friend's reason, the revelation has been lost to history, and the snippets of information that have survived in Kosovel's notes and letters do not tell us, in so many words, that he was alluding to Tagore's collection of poems of that title, or its eponymous poem, 'Sonar tari'.[5] Would he have read the poem or the collection? Not likely,

[4] Letter dated 10 September 1925, Kosovel (2006), p. 246. All translations of Kosovel's letters, notes, and journals are mine.

[5] The collection is also mentioned in letters to some other friends, at around the same time. For example, in a letter to Ivo Grahor, on 31 August 1925: 'The collection will bear the title "*Zlati čoln*". Do you agree?' (Kosovel 2006, p. 239); and to Fanica Obidova a day later, further stating that had he the time and will, he would have sent the manuscript to her (Kosovel 2006, p. 241).

as neither had by then appeared in English (or in other European languages), but he must have known of Tagore's writing *Sonar tari*, since the collection was mentioned in the press coverage following the Nobel Prize. In any case, there is ample evidence telling us that Kosovel was an enthusiastic reader of Tagore (in Slovene, Croatian, and German translations), and that Tagore occupied an important place among the writers and thinkers he admired. In fact, the Indian poet stands out as one of the writers most frequently referred to in Kosovel's collected works: his poetry, prose pieces, essays, letters, and notes.[6] Presumably then, the choice of the same title was no mere coincidence, but a direct allusion to the Indian poet—an act of homage from one poet to another.

It is nothing short of extraordinary—and wonderfully serendipitous—that in 2008, within a few months of each other, two books of selected poems came out independently of each other in English translation in Britain, bearing the same title, *The Golden Boat*. One brought us new translations of Tagore's poetry and the other, those of Kosovel.[7] That the publication histories of these two poets, whose writings extend back in time by more than a century, with Tagore having a long and complicated English career to his name and Kosovel practically none, should have converged in such a way is, of course, pure coincidence. Beyond the commendable fact that poetry in English translation has become richer by a contribution from the world of Bengali and Slovenian letters, respectively, there would be nothing obvious to link the two books, nor the two poets, were it not for the same title. It is precisely this connection and the intriguing symbolism of the phrase 'the golden boat'—presumably meaning different things to the two writers—that compelled me to undertake this piece of research.

One of the tasks at hand was then to trace the ideas and lessons Kosovel imbibed from Tagore and see how he related them to his

[6] A cursory glance at the index pages of his *Collected Works* (henceforth abbreviated as *CW*) reveals that Tagore gets a mention over fifty times. Leo Tolstoy, another figure Kosovel admired, is referred to thirty times and Romain Rolland, fifteen.

[7] See Tagore (2008a), translated by Joe Winter, and Kosovel (2008b), translated by Bert Pribac and David Brooks.

particular context. Were there suggestions in Kosovel's writings that could be attributed directly to Tagore? Why did Kosovel feel drawn to the Indian poet in the first place? How did he incorporate and assimilate what he read into his own poetic and intellectual horizon? In what way did this serve his preoccupations and interests? And, finally, were there correspondences or deeper unities connecting the two contemporaries?

Although Kosovel scholars have invariably noted Tagore alongside other important writers and thinkers that Kosovel read, beyond a mere mention of this fact, or at most a few paragraphs or pages stating the obvious, the topic has not been researched in its own right.[8] Albeit a small piece in the mosaic of Tagore's international reputation, its significance can be said to extend beyond its arcane literary, historical value.

The existing tools for analysing the ways in which Tagore was appreciated across Europe, all too often simply blurred with 'the West', can only take us so far in understanding this particular cross-cultural response. Coming from the so-called margins of Europe as opposed to the strong Western European imperial metropoles, the response is inflected with preoccupations and concerns which cannot be subsumed under the more familiar power–knowledge nexus of the orientalist paradigm instituted by Edward Said's book *Orientalism* (1978) as a way of reading how the Western world perceived 'the Orient'.

The question of a theoretical framework within which to make sense of responses that do not fall neatly (not that many do) within the ubiquitous Said-inspired model of Western perceptions of the Orient presents itself forcefully when we come to the 'subalterns' of Europe itself, those who have been, like the once-colonized countries, delegated to 'an imaginary waiting room of history', the 'not-yet' of political modernity.[9] A differentiated view of Europe is certainly in order here, as is a consideration of the symbolic geographies of Europe

---

[8] The only more extensive engagement with the topic to date exists in the form of an undergraduate thesis in Slovene, see Erzetič (2010). For a mention in published works, see Ocvirk (1977), pp. 1008–11, 1020–1; Šrimf (1981/82); Tokarz (2004), p. 173; (2013), pp. 15, 146–7, 175, 220–1, 224, 237; Vrečko (2011), pp. 34, 164, 275, 429, 526, 533; Zadravec (1986), pp. 349–52, 360–2.

[9] D. Chakrabarty (2007), p. 8.

that strive to separate the insiders from the outsiders through ideological constructions of Eastern-ness and Western-ness.

Therefore, in thinking about the many different responses to Tagore coming from within Europe itself, we might ask: what of the fellow poets and like-minded individuals who endorsed Tagore's literary and intellectual credentials outside the confines of an imposed or self-styled mystic identity? Or, who looked to Tagore from a strongly felt sense of identification or sympathy derived from perceiving a common cause with the poet, rather than from the need of having to assert an intractable (cultural) difference and, ultimately, superiority?

Argued differently, in as much as Kosovel's response to Tagore, itself emblematic of a host of no doubt other similar European responses, known and unknown to us, is still seen to operate within the twentieth-century orientalist discourse of 'Otherness', then we must at least acknowledge that the strategy of othering need not always—indeed often it did not—serve the interest of politico-cultural hegemony. A study which has brought orientalist discourse from under the decades-long shadow of Said's seminal work, giving the phenomenon a brighter face by refusing to see it invariably as a mask for racism and rationalization of colonial domination, is that of J. J. Clarke's *Oriental Enlightenment: The Encounter between Asian and Western Thought* (1997). In striving to 'recover a richer and often more affirmative orientalism, seeking to show that the West has endeavored to integrate Eastern thought into its own intellectual concerns in a manner which, on the face of it, cannot be fully understood in terms of "power" and "domination"', Clarke goes on to identify a counter-hegemonic cultural dimension to this phenomenon. In this, 'Eastern thought', by which he means philosophies of India and China, served as a 'corrective mirror' to Europe, undermining its imperialist ideologies and orthodoxies.[10] The talk of crisis or sickness besetting Western civilization and of the need to turn to 'the East' for cure which characterized the more subversive strain of twentieth-century orientalist discourse, will provide one meaningful framework from within which Kosovel's response can be made sense of.

In contrast to Tagore's more famous cross-cultural literary encounters, most notably with Yeats, Ezra Pound, and André Gide, the case

---

[10] Clarke (1997), p. 27.

of Kosovel follows a one-way trajectory. Sadly, the young poet died just months before Tagore travelled to former Yugoslavia on his longest European tour, stopping in Zagreb (Croatia) and Belgrade (Serbia) in November 1926, but not in Ljubljana (Slovenia), where Kosovel lived and worked for the most part of his short life. Tagore, we can safely assume, would not have heard of the Slovenian poet, who was then only just beginning to emerge as a literary figure of a 'national' standing. Certainly, Kosovel wielded neither the influence nor the power of established poets à la Yeats, whose laudatory introduction to Tagore's English *Gitanjali* (1912) travelled far beyond the English-speaking world and set the tone to the chorus of worldwide adoration for the Indian poet. So perhaps the value of looking at his response lies precisely in that Kosovel is a representative of what Leela Gandhi, in her suggestively titled book *Affective Communities* (2006), has dubbed 'western "non-player[s]" in the drama of imperialism', but whose 'minor' discourses are nevertheless a variation on the larger theme of anti-imperialism shared internationally by a small intellectual elite in the first decades of the twentieth century.[11]

Furthermore, in the absence of direct historical links also between the two poets' respective countries, we are led to adjust the comparative angle to consider correspondences and relations which are *not* primarily guided by direct impact or exchange, but are the outcome rather of negotiating a common—virtual—space of global modernity. Partha Mitter's concept of 'virtual cosmopolis' to denote a shared, worldwide corpus of modern ideas, as well as ideas on modernity, with which the metropolitan elites from both 'centre' and 'periphery' of the (pre-)industrialized world were grappling, sometimes through channels of direct personal contact, but largely through the printed medium[12]—will provide another relevant framework for linking the two writers across their vastly different cultural and geopolitical spaces, and take us beyond the more conventional model of direct influence. While personal relations and networks, realized in practice through travel and correspondence, were crucial for creating worldwide

[11] Gandhi (2006), p. 1.
[12] Mitter (2007), pp. 11–12. I discuss this further in Chs 3 and 6, p. 125 and pp. 272–3 respectively.

platforms of solidarity in the early decades of the twentieth century, they were not, as Kosovel's example will show, essential.

TAGORE *AND* KOSOVEL

It soon became apparent to me that Tagore and Kosovel both had a very strong sense of participating in a historical era, shaped by what is now commonly referred to as the first wave of globalization. Between 1870 and World War I, in some ways 'foreshadowing our own time', as Adam K. Webb puts it, 'international commerce flourished and bound far-flung corners of the world together. Industrial development and modern habits of mind made their first inroads into traditional societies. By the time Europe's own imperial confidence collapsed into war and revolution, the old civilizations of Asia had already undergone a half century or so of transformation.'[13]

Imperialism, migration, and technological advances had all contributed towards an expanded international context, whereby individuals and cultures could no longer live in complete ignorance of each other. Both poets saw themselves as writing on the threshold of a new era, stressing the need to understand local problems in a global perspective, and seek solutions in worldwide cooperation. Painfully aware of the historical realities of their time, in which a handful of Western European powers had brought an overwhelming part of the globe under imperial control, they deplored the fact that the meeting of cultures had come largely on the back of conquest and colonization, rather than in the spirit of free exchange, but argued, against the odds, for a non-hierarchical dialogue between cultures. How to resist foreign impositions and yet not bar oneself from the discoveries of the modern age, whether in science, technology, economics, politics, art, or literature? How to adjust creatively and retain agency as opposed to imitating slavishly or conforming unthinkingly? What are the implications of global expansion for cultural identities? These were questions that preoccupied both Tagore and Kosovel. So rather than seeing Kosovel's reading of Tagore merely in terms of direct influence, it is possible to understand some of their shared concerns as a result of being exposed to the same globalizing forces of capitalism and imperialism and of

[13] Webb (2008), p. 189.

intuiting common goals arising out of the consciousness of inhabiting one world as opposed to separate cultural enclaves.

It must, however, be acknowledged that the onslaught of modernity on tradition was more distressing in Asia than in Europe, since the new impulses got identified with an alien civilization. Kosovel's 'in-between' status within Europe, though perhaps muting the question of Westernization, does not, however, make it irrelevant. Once again, a differentiated view of Europe is essential to my analysis. The comparison certainly brings to the fore common questions of civilizational identity, particularly against the new climate of self-questioning in Europe after World War I, when the high noon of imperialism had passed and challenges to colonialism could no longer be ignored. Imperialist wars had collapsed the world, as Tagore put it, into the biggest 'orgy of evil',[14] and Europe, as Kosovel kept reiterating, was 'in crisis'. Many intellectuals and avant-garde artists of the 1920s raised a vocal protest against aspects of European civilization and its self-proclaimed certainties. And it would seem that their protest was not unrelated to the emergence of new colonial writers and their presence in the avant-garde circles in the West, whose own concerns posed a challenge to European cultural authority and contributed to the 'volatile new cosmopolitan climate'.[15] Cultural and aesthetic influences appear to have moved in two directions as nineteenth-century forms were being superseded by more revolutionary modernist aesthetics. That Kosovel's avant-garde poetics is visibly indebted to his reading of Tagore, himself a forerunner of postcolonial modernism, is a case in point.

Linn Cary Mehta has made an important observation when comparing a number of poets of decolonization from Asia, Africa, Latin America, and the Caribbean that poetry of the early twentieth century 'stands at the fulcrum of the world literary tradition', meaning that from that point onwards 'the world [could] no longer be divided into two literary hemispheres, into the European and non-European … or into first-world and third-world literature'.[16] As in politics and economics so in literature, she sees the aesthetic changes of the period

[14] Tagore (2002i [1932]), p. 660.
[15] Boehmer (1995), p. 123.
[16] Mehta (2004), p. 2.

as portending to 'a new "world order"'.[17] The sort of cross-fertilization and internationalism that characterizes the poetry of decolonization, and which predates their respective countries' political independence, would also seem to be self-consciously motivated by the idea that it was from within one's own tradition that one worked towards a 'universal' tradition, opening one's language, whether a vernacular or an adopted—and adapted—colonial tongue, for the experience of 'the other'. Kosovel's aspirations for an ideal 'universal artist', as he noted in his journals, someone who in the manner of his descriptions would not be 'patriotically local' but *humanly universal*, can be productively related to his search for a form that would capture the larger concerns of his age.[18] To align him with other thinkers and poets of resistance and decolonization is one way in which his poetry can be opened up to fresh interpretations, an approach that is largely validated through his reading of Tagore, but also through his frequent expressions of solidarity with the colonized the world over.

This brings us to a key notion that I see as underlying Kosovel's particular response to Tagore—that of *situational identification*. The term itself comes from Patrick Colm Hogan, who uses it to suggest the forging of sympathies between individuals and shared inspirations derived from a sense of shared predicaments. Or, as he puts it: 'We develop an immediate sense of intimacy with someone as we intuit shared feelings, ideas, references, [and] expectations.'[19] The colonial framework provided one such situational-identification context for worldwide solidarities. Elleke Boehmer has spoken pertinently of *cross-colony* identifications (in the context of anti-colonial nationalist movements), whereby ideas are transferred and adapted laterally across geographical space at the same historical time from structurally similar, yet specific, material conditions. The 'contact zone' of cultural exchange conventionally located between the colonial centre and its periphery is thus relocated *between* peripheries themselves.[20] What emerges is a more unwieldy picture of ideas travelling multilaterally, from various 'centres', as opposed to unilaterally spreading out from

---

[17] Mehta (2004), p. 15.
[18] Kosovel, 'Journal XV', emphasis author's, *CW* 3, p. 750.
[19] Hogan (2004), p. 26.
[20] Boehmer (2002), p. 2.

the (Western) centre to the (non-Western) margins, as the conventional influence model would have us believe.

And once the flow of ideas is recognized as polycentric and also inherently dialogic; spatial constructs such as 'East' and 'West' also become increasingly problematic. 'Modern civilization', as Debraj Bhattacharya has argued, is a global phenomenon enabled by a communication revolution and characterized by 'the emergence of a network of metropolises as a product of the worldwide spread of capitalism'.[21] Its history must therefore be understood through a connected history of world metropolises, as much of Calcutta, Bombay, Cairo, and Shanghai, as those of London, Paris, and New York. Indeed, a metropolis like Calcutta, even though it stood outside the industrialized world, was 'more in tune with ideas associated with modernity than the countryside or small towns of Europe or America',[22] or, for that matter, the rest of colonial India. Distinctions between 'East' and 'West' are thus made redundant, superseded arguably by more problematic and trenchant divisions between those who have access to modern forms of knowledge and those who do not, an issue that will be addressed once I consider Tagore's and Kosovel's efforts as educators.

Two notions that can thus helpfully frame our comparative analysis are *cross-colony situational identification* and *shared* or *global modernity*. The first is useful in that it rotates the focus from the conventional centre–periphery paradigm to one that connects different peripheries, but the second concept dispenses the core–periphery paradigm altogether and opens up a more radical methodological perspective that deals with specific regions or cultures as continuously enmeshed in processes of multilateral transfer, exchange, and interaction. These processes, needless to say, complicate identity discourses along national or regional lines. How Tagore and Kosovel each negotiated global modernity from their respective regions, taking over some of its impulses and certainties, while questioning others, including its metropolis-centric bias, will also be considered in the course of this book.

As I do this, it will become clear that the particular story of Tagore and Kosovel belongs to a distinct interwar context of intellectual,

---

[21] D. Bhattacharya (2008b), p. 243.
[22] D. Bhattacharya (2008b), p. 263.

literary, social, and political associations linking South Asia to the wider world that has recently been theorized as the 'internationalist moment'[23]—a 'moment' in which 'individuals journeyed across the terrain of internationalist engagements, geographically and intellectually, while promiscuously drawing from … diverse ideologies [that] were not seen as mutually exclusive or opposed to one another, but were seen as converging and complementary routes towards a suprapolitical project that aimed at transforming the future of humanity and, in fact, humanity itself'.[24] In this the broad-ranging intellectual exchanges rarely observed the boundaries of states, nations, and cultures in ways that we tend to assume. From the vantage point of today, it is good to be reminded that between the Russian Revolution and the beginning of World War II, in the period that had begun on the hopeful note that humanity would create a new future for itself but ended in another world war, the nation-state was *not* universally acknowledged as the ordering principle of human societies.

Following on from this, and by engaging the aspirational worlds of Tagore and Kosovel, my concern will be to furthermore restore to the intellectual histories of the period a strain of early-twentieth-century discourse of (non-hegemonic) universalism that has largely been overlooked by postcolonial scholarship and cultural studies in general. This is largely due to the overly suspicious, negative take on all notions of 'universality' by a field that arose out of the poststructuralist turn in theory. Paradoxically, it is also due to an overly homogenizing and essentialist reverse take on 'Europe'.

UNIVERSALISM REVISITED

As I have already suggested, the broad structural presence of European imperialisms provides a framework that makes it possible to identify individual voices across space and time that carry a strikingly similar message. Often it may not even be a question of direct influence or borrowing or, for that matter, situational identification, but a case of a parallel voicing of ideas against the backdrop of similar subjugating

---

[23] Raza, Roy, and Zachariah (2014b).
[24] Raza, Roy, and Zachariah (2014a), p. xii.

forces. It is against these forces, which pit the colonizer against the colonized, the suppressor against the suppressed, and burden the relationship with various binaries of racial imagination, that both Tagore and Kosovel came to propound a universalist stance. Their 'larger search for liberation'[25] brought them into a fraught relationship with nationalism as a dominant ideological and political force of their time. They both strove to define an alternative identity for themselves and their compatriots, one that would resist foreign domination without succumbing to nationalist exclusivism. But could nationalism ever be anything but exclusive? It may have been the main legitimizing force for conducting anticolonial resistance on the road to political independence, but was it legitimate?

Indeed, there are certain paradoxes that present themselves here: Tagore, for example, was an important figure in the Indian nationalist struggle, for a time in the lead of the Swadeshi[26] movement in Bengal, but was he a nationalist? Kosovel's attitude towards his native region's Italian occupiers was almost benign, as was Tagore's to the British. And yet both wrote from a strong awareness of their countrymen's status as a subject people and were powerful spokesmen for their disenfranchised peoples. What were their attitudes to the question of nation, nationality, and nationalism in relation to anti-imperialism? What, in turn, was the 'universal' they reached for by way of transcending categories of nation and ideologies of nationalism they found so problematic? Was this a category that supposedly already existed, or was it a category in the making—an open-ended concept? And if open rather than determined, descriptive rather than prescriptive, then how was it to be created?

Both nationalism and universalism are notions as well as sets of practices that do not lend themselves to any one single interpretation

---

[25] Said (1994), p. 265.
[26] The Swadeshi movement began as an anti-partition movement in 1905 when the British partitioned Bengal into two separate provinces, allegedly for administrative reasons. Led by Aurobindo Ghose, Bipin Chandra Pal, and Brahmabandhab Upadhyay, amongst others, the movement soon acquired the contours of a direct struggle against British rule and is considered to be the first mass popular nationalist movement under the new middle-class leadership that had developed under the British rule. I discuss the movement and Tagore's role in it in more detail in Ch. 2, pp. 78–81.

or approach. They will continue to fuel heated discussions across humanities and social sciences as to their relevance and meaning. My interest is primarily in 'universalism' as a departure from 'nationalism' in the precise context of anti-imperialist struggles. This is the embattled triangle of -isms that I will be exploring in relation to Tagore and Kosovel, as I historicize their particular stances.

In order to derive an enabling notion of universalism, so that Tagore's and Kosovel's intellectual orientations can be analysed with more precision, some understanding of the arguments that have 'split' theorists into anti- and pro-universalist camps is in order. This will be dealt with in the first, more theoretical, chapter. Starting from the negative evaluation of universalism (understood in the singular) from within the postcolonial studies, where it is rejected as a totalizing imperialist discourse carrying a distinct Eurocentric or ethnocentric stigma, I want to ask: Is universalism perforce a hegemonic and totalizing ideology rooted in a fictitious universality of certain races, classes, nations or some such other category? When articulated in opposition to imperialism and its totalizing discourses, is it still hegemonic? Had we not better assume the existence of multiple universalisms, and if so, are there modalities that may be defensible? Or, is it even possible, as Edward Said argued in relation to humanism, to be critical of universalism in the name of universalism and fashion a different kind of universalism that is not ethnocentric but truly cosmopolitan?[27]

Tagore's and Kosovel's examples will certainly allow us to break with the monolithic conceptualization of Universalism as an exclusive site of imperialist control. In this respect it is important to acknowledge from the outset what the historian Sugata Bose was led to conclude with respect to the social, political, and cultural history of the Indian Ocean during the age of European imperialisms and anticolonial nationalisms. His conclusion carries a sense of more general applicability:

> A discerning historical investigation makes clear … that universalism was hardly a quest over which European modernity had any kind of monopoly. Local, regional, and national cultures in different parts of the globe were not just jealous guardians of their own distinctiveness, but

[27] Said (2004), pp. 10–11.

also wished to participate in and contribute to larger arenas of cultural exchange. In this process the lines that separated the large constructs of East and West, Asia and Europe, as well as the smaller communitarian categories came to be transcended in myriad ways.[28]

The sense of intellectual entitlement unrestricted by artificial geopolitical boundaries as well as the need to belong to a larger universe is no doubt one key aspect that connects the two writers across their continents. Since Tagore is the poet and thinker from whom Kosovel took inspiration, and not the other way around, the first half of the book (in number of words if not in chapters) is therefore devoted to him. Understanding Tagore's main preoccupations and ideas, particularly those Kosovel imbibed from the works that were available to him in translation, will in turn enable us to reflect more sharply on Kosovel's own thinking, as I come to locate it in the particular context of the place and time in which he lived. Though the initial impetus behind this study was to understand Kosovel's fascination with Tagore—the reasons behind it, its relevance, and the manner in which the young poet 'translated' Tagore's ideas for his own goals—the fact that these two writers and intellectuals also had much in common prevented me from relegating Tagore to a mere 'influence'. Ultimately, this book is a study of how *both* writers, from their respective 'margins', responded to the historical predicament of European imperialism by reaching out to some kind of 'universal' ideal. Therefore, I wish to accord equal weight to both of them.

I should, however, state from the start that my analysis of Tagore's universalism is based primarily on his non-literary writings: his essays (both in translation and in original English), foreign addresses, lectures, and letters, with a focus on what Kosovel himself is known to have read. The socio-political thought of Tagore will take precedence over Tagore the poet and creative writer on these pages, but the focus shifts once we come to consider Kosovel's universalist bent. Internationalism and universalism are closely related to the modernist shift occurring in Kosovel's poetic idiom, and much is to be gained also in seeing intellectual and social commitment in literary terms, where language, and how language is handled, becomes a

---

[28] S. Bose (2006), p. 270.

crucial site of resistance. I have thus intentionally reserved the larger part of poetry analysis for the Kosovel section of the book, barring a close reading of one or two of Tagore's key poems, in which case I read them with assistance also in the source language. Not wanting to make a virtue out of what is an obvious linguistic limitation, it is nonetheless worth acknowledging that Tagore's international reputation was based more on his English writings than on his Bengali ones. Further translations took place through this medium. Moreover, the *performative* nature of Tagore's internationalism, by which I am thinking of its didactic content, that is, his 'message' of universalism and humanism intended to be put across on an international plane, demanded that it be conveyed in an international language. Tagore certainly knew how to use a 'foreign' language as an enabling medium in the service of an authentic dream of a new—more 'universal'—Indian identity. In fact he will be seen as astonishingly free of anxieties that would subsequently overlay this aspect of the colonial encounter.[29]

Tagore was in fact a bilingual writer who also translated his own works into English. This creativity should not be dismissed or overlooked, not least because it exerted such an important influence on so many people across the world. Moreover, as one historian has noted, 'almost forty per cent of his writing is in English', many of his essays written directly in the language.[30] But the most encouraging fact is that in recent decades Tagore's existing English writings have been continuously expanded through new translations by the twin efforts of

---

[29] Writing on the vexed question of the English language as a foreign imposition and thus a form of cultural colonialism that censors the true identity of the colonized, Slavoj Žižek provocatively turns the argument on its head:

> The true victory over colonization is not the return to any 'authentic' pre-colonial existence, even less any 'synthesis' between modern civilization and pre-modern origins—but, paradoxically, the *fully accomplished loss of these pre-modern origins*. In other words, colonialism is not overcome when the intrusion of the English language as a medium is abolished, but when the colonizers are, as it were, beaten at their own game—when the new Indian identity is effortlessly formulated in English, i.e., when English language is 'denaturalized', when it loses its privileged link to 'native' Anglo-Saxon English speakers. (Žižek 2014, emphasis author's, p. 169.)

[30] U. Das Gupta (2006), p. xv.

translators and editors both in India and Britain, thus making more of his works accessible also to readers who are not familiar with Bengali.

Tagore was foremost a poet and creative writer, but he was also a mature thinker, even philosopher, who exerted a 'considerable influence as a cultural mentor and socio-political critic on national and international scales', and this area, as noted by Joseph T. O'Connell and Kathleen M. O'Connell, 'remains challenging for further research'.[31] This is ultimately the challenge taken up in this book as Tagore's 'mentorship' is explored for the first time in relation to one Slovenian poet, and the two writers seen to hold out universalist hopes from their respective geographic locations that in many ways still ring true today.

[31] J. T. O'Connell and K. M. O'Connell (2008), p. 946.

1   Universalism

Balancing Domination and Liberation

How to be free from arrogant nationalism is today the chief lesson to be learnt. Tomorrow's history will begin with a chapter on internationalism, and we shall be unfit for tomorrow if we retain any manners, customs, or habits of thought that are contrary to universalism.

—Tagore, 'The Unity of Education', 1921

Man is not a house made perfect. Man grows like a tree.

—Kosovel, [Notes]

This chapter conceptually engages the topic of universalism by gradually coming to it from the perspective of nationalism. The cue is provided by Tagore's citation above, which posits 'universalism' as a goal underpinning all future social progress. It is a progressive project-in-the-making that must involve leaving behind 'arrogant nationalism' via an endorsement of 'internationalism'. To what extent this leaves the position of nationalism entirely incompatible, or in conflict, with universalism, of course, remains to be seen. What is certain is that universalism (also not without its set of problems) is inextricably linked to the 'deeply problematic enterprise'[1] of nationalism.

---

[1] Said (1994), p. 258.

I have suggested that Tagore's and Kosovel's notions of universalism emerged against their respective backdrops of political and cultural domination. In fact both Tagore and Kosovel thought and wrote from the embattled middle ground between strategies of nationalism (readily available at the time) and universalism (less so) as alternative forces to counter foreign rule. Therefore, both concepts must be engaged, and I will do so in the precise context of anti-colonial/imperialist resistance or liberation struggles, with which both poets were deeply concerned, to determine if and how nationalism and universalism relate to—and depart from—each other. The idea is to derive a workable, however tentative, definition of 'universalism' when we come to examine the two writers' individual struggles and their respective answers.

NATIONALISM AND A LARGER SEARCH FOR LIBERATION

Historically, nationalism has resonated powerfully with ideas and practices that signified anything from the most brutal repression to national emancipation and political independence. In the words of Isaiah Berlin: 'Nationalism is responsible for magnificent achievements and appalling crimes.'[2] It has stood at both ends of the colonial–anti-colonial spectrum—as a means of enforcing domination or as a force to counter subjugation. Many theorists of nationalism in fact insist that a vital distinction has to be maintained between imperialist nationalism(s) and the anti-colonial and the imperialist varieties. Simon During, for example, wants us to bear in mind that 'nationalism has different effects and meaning in a peripheral nation than in a world power'.[3] More resolutely, Peter Hallward contends: 'What determines the validity of any particular nationalist engagement is the nature of the *relation* involved (the nationalism that encourages imperialist aggression has *nothing* in common with the nationalism that resists it).'[4] The subtext in both instances is that nationalism, when in the service of an anti-colonial struggle, is justifiable, necessary, and good, while nationalism harnessed to imperialist aggression that subjugates

[2] Berlin (1997), p. 251.
[3] During (1990), p. 139.
[4] Hallward (2001), emphasis author's, p. 129.

other people is not—indeed it cannot be. The same means are valorized differently when put to different ends. Insofar as nationalism can be linked to both 'a mode of freedom'[5] and imperialist aggression, it is essential to interrogate—as Tagore and Kosovel did—the limitations of nationalisms in both cases, even as their *difference* in relation, effects, and meaning need not be denied. We should also try not to remove 'nationalism' as a concept from people's actual lived experience of it.

Anti-Colonial Nationalisms

To delimit what is a variously construed subject with multiple meanings, it must once again be stated that the nationalism that primarily concerns me is one that, broadly speaking, developed in response to imperialism and is referred to variously as 'anti-colonial nationalism', 'resistant nationalism', 'anti-imperial nationalist resistance', or even simply 'anti-colonialism', though the latter is highly misleading in that it conflates 'anti-colonial' with 'national', and not *all* anti-colonialisms were nationalist.[6] In fact, as this study will show, some were decisively not.

This conflation of anti-colonialism and nationalism has been part of an ongoing problematic of the historiography of nationalism in the context of 'national' liberation movements precisely because of the particular valorization—and subsequent naturalization—of nationalism and nationhood as *the* legitimizing framework for countering colonial subjugation and making claims for an independent collective political existence. Once the language of legitimacy becomes nation-centric—in Europe roughly from mid- to late-nineteenth century, and in India in the last quarter of the nineteenth century—then 'liberation' is legitimized by the 'national', so the 'national' becomes even harder to discard. Anti-colonialism must perforce be 'nationalist'.[7]

Historians and theorists, on the other hand, seem to overall agree on the fact that the modern idea of the nation, the nation-state, and the

---

[5] During (1990), pp. 138–9.

[6] On this point see, for example, Boehmer (2002), p. 11.

[7] On this, see Zachariah (2011), pp. 16ff., whose book *Playing the Nation Game: The Ambiguities of Nationalism in India* provides a lucid and consistent interrogation of the meta-narratives of nationalism that have informed the various historiographical perspectives on nationalism in the context of India.

language of nationalism are of Western origin.[8] Greatly consolidated by the European Enlightenment thought, the grammar of nationalism became the linchpin 'to actualize in political terms the universal urge for liberty and progress'.[9] The colonial expansion of European nation-states across the globe, however, denied to *others* what it claimed for itself: the principles of people's rights to self-determination and personal liberty. But with territorial expansion came also the rhetoric of cultural (and political) self-determination—the genie was out of the bottle—and Boehmer aptly notes 'a certain poetic justice' in that colonial rule 'produced the conditions for its own delegitimization'. For any number of twentieth-century anti-colonial opposition movements, nationalism thus became 'the platform for mobilizing against the occupying power in the name of a common culture, language, or history'[10]—those doctrinal components of nationalism as they were invented by the liberal nineteenth-century European writers.[11] This neat, but far from benign, equation that affiliates a people with a language, a territory, and eventually a nation-state as the crowning momen was, for example, readily assimilated into a cultural nationalism by the Slovenes under the Austro-Hungarian empire in the late nineteenth century, even as the forging of the 'national' language required standardization of a variety of Slovene dialects spoken by communities dispersed across a number of provinces.[12] How problematic this modern formula can be, and more so in contexts characterized by great diversity and scale, was quite apparent to Rabindranath Tagore, who sounded a clear 'no' against nationalism

---

[8] This is not to forget that the first 'nationalisms', as Benedict Anderson argues in his influential study *Imagined Communities* (1991), originated in the Americas in the form of various Creole-led anti-colonial movements in the second half of the eighteenth and the first half of the nineteenth centuries, predating 'populist' nationalisms of Western Europe, which in turn predated nationalisms in Asia and Africa.

[9] P. Chatterjee (1993 [1986]), p. 2.

[10] Boehmer (1995), pp. 104–5.

[11] How different is the context presented by India, or South Asia more generally, will be taken up later, when I discuss the problematic of language and 'mother' tongue in Ch. 2.

[12] On the point about language, see Rusinow (2003), p. 19.

and the nation-state as an option for India, saying this was essentially an alien concept.[13]

In the context of Third World anti-colonial nationalisms, it is Partha Chatterjee who has brought our attention to the inherent contradiction, and therefore weakness, of anti-colonial nationalisms that comes from the fact that while they challenge the colonial claim to political domination, they at the same time accept the 'very intellectual premises of "modernity" on which colonial domination was based.'[14] Being thus a 'derivative discourse' (a European import), its suitability for peoples seeking to contest the ideological tenets that ostensibly justified their subjection rendered it highly problematic.

On the other hand, Chatterjee's conceptual 'formula'—as he calls it in his subsequent book *Nation and Its Fragments* (1994) on the subject—for reading anti-colonial nationalisms, decisively opposes the conventional narratives of nationalism, which, in aligning nationalism too strictly to a political movement, fail to see the *autonomous creative* moments of anti-colonial nationalist resistance that much preceded 'the political battle with the imperial power'.[15] Contra such scholars who have allegedly reduced nationalism to a political movement, Chatterjee, with backing historical evidence, proceeds to make a case for an 'anticolonial nationalism' (in the singular) that 'creates its own domain of sovereignty within their own colonial societies well before it begins its political battle with the imperial power'.[16] The novelty of this 'culturalist' argument, however, seems overstated.[17]

---

[13] I discuss this in detail on pp. 93–8 in Ch. 2.

[14] P. Chatterjee (1993 [1986]), p. 30. Although Chatterjee draws his theoretical conclusions from his specific study of anticolonial nationalism(s) of the nineteenth- and early twentieth-century Bengal and India, his contribution to the debate on 'Third-World' nationalism holds a more general theoretical application.

[15] P. Chatterjee (1999 [1994]), p. 6.

[16] P. Chatterjee (1999 [1994]), p. 6.

[17] In fact, in *Imagined Communities*, Anderson makes a rather similar claim: 'Nationalism has to be understood, by aligning it not with self-consciously held political ideologies, but with large cultural systems that preceded it, out of which—as well as against which—it came into being, (1991, p. 19). The argument that the most powerful form of nationalism to have developed in resistance to colonial domination was cultural nationalism that preceded

But more than to this, Chatterjee objects to Anderson's theory of nationalism that (allegedly) posits the historical experiences of nationalism in Western Europe, Americas, and Russia as *the* sole suppliers of 'a set of "modular" forms' for all subsequent nationalisms in Asia and Africa.[18] For an author of the derivative-discourse theory who went on to convey the essential(ist) mark of 'Third-World' nationalisms—or for someone who unambiguously states, 'Whether of the "good" variety or the "bad", nationalism was entirely a product of the political history of Europe'[19]—the objection seems in the first instance baffling, even self-contradictory. However, the real butt of Chatterjee's critique is not the Western origin and spread of nationalism, but the all too familiar Eurocentric denial of agency to Asia and Africa, their confinement to being mere 'consumers of modernity'—that is to say those whose imaginations were once and for all colonized.[20]

For Chatterjee, then, nationalist thought in the colonized world constitutes a *different* but *dominated* discourse.[21] His 'formula' rests on a dichotomy between 'the spiritual' and 'the material' realms, confined respectively to the 'inner' and 'outer' domains, the former bearing 'the "essential" marks of cultural identity' and the latter relating to matters of 'state-craft, science and technology'.[22] With this distinction, he shows how anti-colonial nationalists were able to concede a large measure of founding influence to 'the West' in the outer material and political arena, while claiming prior and ongoing sovereignty in the inner spiritual domain (as represented by religion, home, women, family, and peasants). Chatterjee proceeds to read the social reform period in India as one with two distinct stages: after the early

---

the political struggle has been made by any number of theorists since then, as also before. See, for example, During (1990, p. 139) and Hobsbawm (1992, p. 10), who stated unambiguously of both European and colonial nationalisms that 'some form of national culture pre-existed the state'.

[18] B. Anderson (1991), p. 5.

[19] B. Anderson (1991), p. 4.

[20] B. Anderson (1991), p. 5. I agree with Neil Lazarus in that Chatterjee's own tangle with 'area specialists' can at times lead him to overstate the arguments of Benedict Anderson. See Lazarus (1999), pp. 128–33.

[21] On this, see Bose and Jalal (2003), p. 122.

[22] P. Chatterjee (1999 [1994]), p. 6.

stage informed by the influence of colonial authorities as traditional institutions are reformed, there comes 'a strong resistance to allowing the colonial state to intervene in matters affecting "national culture"'; this second stage already constitutes the story of anti-colonial nationalism as a *cultural* mo(ve)ment, in which, according to Chatterjee, the colonial state is 'kept out of the "inner" domain of national culture'.[23] This is not to say that that so-called spiritual domain is left intact, but to underline the nationalists' preoccupation 'to preserve the distinctness of one's spiritual culture' as a fundamental feature of anti-colonial nationalist struggle. Put differently, the projections of a future independent 'nation' meant creating 'a "modern" national culture that is nevertheless not Western'.[24]

While Chatterjee undoubtedly has arguments for stressing how the most creative results of the nationalist imagination in Asia and Africa are posited not on an identity but on a *difference* with the 'modular' forms propagated by the modern West,[25] there is something of a 'difference-seeking distortion'[26] to be noted there. The need to separate the 'indigenous' from the 'foreign', along with the question of 'authenticity', and then to identify and assert 'India's unique cultural difference' was indeed something that dominated the psycho-political life of many colonial intellectuals, and in its residual nationalist form it seems to have survived well into the postcolonial era.[27] The affective pull of nationalism is strong.

Chatterjee's representation of anti-colonial (nationalist) thought is unbalanced also in that it privileges *one* type of response to the challenge of 'Western modernity'—his dichotomous 'formula' is based primarily on the nationalist thought of the late nineteenth-century Bengali novelist Bankimchandra Chatterjee—to the exclusion of

[23] P. Chatterjee (1999 [1994]).

[24] P. Chatterjee (1999 [1994]).

[25] P. Chatterjee (1999 [1994]), emphasis author's, p. 5.

[26] See Bose and Jalal (2003), p. 112. The discernible 'nationalist' shift perceived in Chatterjee's writing in his second book dealing with the problematic of anti-colonial nationalisms should perhaps be read in the context of India's economic (neo-)liberalization of the early 1990s and a reaction against the onslaught of global capitalist dynamics.

[27] See Zachariah (2011), pp. 8–10.

many other responses, even within Bankim's own Hindu middle class. Indeed, not all anti-colonial intellectuals followed this dynamics. Not everyone felt the need to fight the colonial present by fashioning myths about a pristine pre-colonial past alongside authentic and untouched realms of the present, or by creating 'illusions about *our* past and denouncing *their* modernity'.[28] The more imaginative intellectual engagements in fact 'consciously transgressed the frontier between "us" and "them"'.[29] We must bear this critical insight in mind when we consider Tagore's (as well as Kosovel's) responses to foreign rule.

Furthermore, to carve out a space for 'our modernity' as opposed to 'their modernity',[30] or of the colonial world versus 'the West'—what another critic sees as having become somewhat of 'an academic orthodoxy' for much of recent Indian scholarship—is not only historically untenable but also imposes the experience of one segment of colonized society, the male middle class, on the experiences of all other segments. It also ignores significant contributions of those who in fact belonged to 'both blocs' and whose intellectual and social pursuits were driven by a search for 'a sense of belonging within a larger universe'.[31]

The imaginative content of anti-colonial modernity that Chatterjee also celebrates would seem to emerge precisely out of transcending boundaries rather than re-asserting them.[32] But the anxieties about the 'derivativeness' of Indian nationalist thought, and prescriptions about what qualifies as an 'authentic' Indian response, in other words, the problem of *nationalist* readings of nationalism itself, are clearly

[28] Bose and Jalal (2003), emphases authors', p. 112.

[29] Bose and Jalal (2003), p. 113.

[30] The reference to 'our modernity' refers to the Srijnan Halder Memorial Lecture that Chatterjee delivered in Bengali on 3 September 1994 in Calcutta subsequently published in his translation as 'Our Modernity', in P. Chatterjee (2010), pp. 136–52.

[31] See D. Bhattacharya (2008a), pp. 7–9.

[32] Of course, the boundaries were not only horizontal, that is, between 'the colonizer' and 'the colonized', but also vertical: between the elites and subalterns, not to mention the countless other divisions along the lines of caste, religion, and gender. I address the vertical limitations of nationalism with respect to Tagore's anti-nationalist re-conceptualizations of society in the following chapter.

ghosts that continue to haunt the debate on anti-colonial resistance. It is therefore all the more urgent to decouple anti-colonialism from nationalism, and make it available at least for those cases when anti-colonialism was decisively *not* nationalism. Tagore and Kosovel will help us do that.

Resistance at Its Best

Whatever there may be to level against Chatterjee's 'formula', one cannot but support his intellectual pursuit of challenging complacent assumptions that most, if not all, creative solutions are West-generated. Bose and Jalal, for example, also share this fundamental insight, but they go further in identifying alternative responses outside the set parameters of difference and domination, holding up Tagore as exemplar of this particular strain of anti-colonialism. The question remains, however, whether they go far enough.[33]

Another impassioned intervention in the historiography of Third World nationalisms, one that takes historians to task for not paying due attention to the many different strands of nationalist thought across the once colonized world, is that of Edward Said.[34] Fully acknowledging the 'abuses of statism, national chauvinism, and reactionary populism', Said urges us to consider whether that was *all* the anti-imperial nationalisms in India, Africa, and the Arab world had yielded.[35] With reference to such 'towering figures' as C. L. R. James, Pablo Neruda, Frantz Fanon, Amílcar Cabral, and Rabindranath Tagore, to some extent also W. B. Yeats, Said identifies 'a fair number of nationalists who are wholehearted supporters of the national movement itself', and yet whose writings possess 'a clear, if paradoxical,

---

[33] I agree with Bose and Jalal that 'the more imaginative strands of anti-colonial modernity fashioned a cultural and political space where there was no necessary contradiction between nationality and human community' (2003, p. 123), but that some anti-colonial intellectuals may have jettisoned 'nationality' altogether, establishing direct links between the individual and the universal, is rarely conceded.

[34] Elsewhere, I disagree with Said, but in this respect, I recommend his entire chapter 'Resistance and Opposition' in *Culture and Imperialism*, 1993, his sequel to *Orientalism*.

[35] Said (2001), p. 425.

antinationalist theme'.[36] Whether Tagore can justifiably be considered a nationalist, or how far he was a wholehearted supporter of the national movement itself, of course, remains to be seen. Said's point, however, was to underline that 'at its best, nationalist resistance was always critical of itself'.[37] The fact that Said was ultimately unable to disentangle 'resistance' from 'nationalist' is of course symptomatic of the all too apparent difficulty to think and feel *beyond nationalist frames*, to borrow from the title of Sumit Sarkar's book, especially in the context of liberation struggles.[38] But even if Said's conclusion is wrong,[39] the various stages in his thinking towards a more 'universalist' perspective are instructive enough to warrant more attention.

Within the allegedly underappreciated emancipatory strain of anti-colonial resistance, Said wants 'to consider the intellectual and cultural argument' that emerged out of such resistance, and pay attention to the 'new and imaginative reconceptions of society and culture'[40]—precisely what awaits us with respect to Tagore's and Kosovel's writings. The self-critical component that Said identifies as the mark of (nationalist) resistance at its best essentially means a 'pull away from separatist nationalism towards a more integrative view of human community and human liberation'.[41] For him, it constitutes 'an *alternative* way of conceiving human history'. Building on this premise, Said develops his theory of liberation, what he refers to as 'a larger

[36] Said (2001), pp. 425–6.

[37] Said (1994), p. 264.

[38] There is indeed a tendency to look more sympathetically at the nationalism of national liberation struggles as opposed to metropolitan nationalisms, as seen from the citations (During; Hallward) at the beginning of the chapter. On this, see also Zachariah (2011), introduction and ch. 1, pp. 1–78.

[39] Michael Collins (2012, pp. 4–6) is quite right in stating that Said's lumping together of all these poets and intellectuals into the 'nationalist ranks' obfuscates more than it helps to elucidate. Indeed: 'To be clear, Rabindranath Tagore was not a nationalist in any analytically useful sense of the word' (p. 15). This is a rare statement in the literature on Tagore, and a truly emancipatory one, for it allows us to bring Tagore into a fresh historical focus, beyond the limits of both postcolonial and subaltern paradigms, and their respective imperial–national and elite–subaltern dichotomies.

[40] Said (1994), pp. 263–4.

[41] Said (1994), emphasis mine, p. 260.

search for liberation'[42]—a phrase I will appropriate for designating anti-colonialism that was *not* nationalism.

There is a clear progression in the phases of nationalist resistance that make up Said's liberation theory, evidently inspired by Frantz Fanon's charting of the stages in the nationalist struggle.[43] It is a movement that is best described as one *beyond* nationalism. Liberation as 'the new alternative' requires what Fanon described as 'a transformation of social consciousness beyond national consciousness'.[44] This, for Fanon, need not mean abandoning one's sense of national selfhood, but it does mean overcoming 'the emotional self-indulgence of celebrating one's own identity'.[45] It meant leaving the *nativist* position behind so as to embrace 'a more generous pluralistic vision of the world'.[46]

Négritude is by far the most well-known example of nativism, but nativism in the strict sense implies any essentialization of human identity evoked as much by *Algerianness, Indianness, Bengaliness, Slovenianness* as by the valorizations of 'the Negro'. What this suggests is that opposition to coercive colonial politics with its suppression of people's language(s) and culture(s) will always—at least to begin with—express itself in some form of nativism: a more or less narrow counter-assertion of an essentialized identity—'us' versus 'them'.

Romantic idealizations of the past, a return to 'roots', a pre-eminent search for lost 'authenticity' and, above all, in Boehmer's apt formulation, 'a strenuous defence of the virtues of native culture'[47]—are all part and parcel of assertive self-definitions aimed at overcoming foreign humiliation and re-establishing a sense of cultural integrity. These strategies are readily available in all cultures that have had to deal with colonial or other oppression. Yeats's Celticism is an

---

[42] Said (1994), p. 265.

[43] Frantz Fanon (1925–1961), the Martinique-born psychiatrist, who went on to join the Algerian liberation struggle, is somewhat of a favourite among the theorists of anti-colonial resistance, considered to be one of the foremost thinkers of the twentieth century on issues of decolonization and psychopathology of colonialism.

[44] Fanon (1963 [1961]), p. 203.

[45] Said (1994), p. 277.

[46] Said (1994), p. 277.

[47] Boehmer (1995), p. 100.

illustrative example that comes to mind as a nativist enterprise of this kind—a form of Irish négritude. Tellingly too, Yeats's valorization of 'the Celt' converges with the stock attributes ascribed to 'the Oriental', so that simplicity, naturalness, spirituality, innocence, and so on, become tropes of anti-imperialist struggle in one discourse and tools of oppression in another, attesting to the fact that nativism is but racism reversed.[48] Even as it serves the purpose of reviving the self-esteem of a downtrodden collective, ultimately it cannot but fail to challenge imperialist structures: 'To accept nativism is to accept the consequences of imperialism, the racial, religious, and political divisions imposed by imperialism itself.'[49]

The movement that Said describes as one from 'nationalist' to 'liberationist' anti-imperialism thus requires a fundamental shift in perspective and (self-)consciousness. It requires a jettisoning of binary oppositions that comes with the knowledge that identities, like cultures, are never fixed or homogeneous but fluid and hybrid, and that the 'history of all cultures is the history of cultural borrowings ... common experiences, and interdependencies'.[50] Therein lies the revolutionary energy for displacing hierarchies rather than solely reversing them, and for transgressing boundaries in favour of a more open 'system of mobile relationships', a system that will inaugurate—as Nigel C. Gibson remarks, also with reference to Fanon—'a new human reciprocity'.[51]

Gibson's analysis of Fanon's grappling with the nationalist problematic is further instructive in that it differentiates between *three* types of (anti-colonial) nationalist thought and politics, rather than the commonly theorized two. So, besides 'a moderate and conformist nationalism' (dubbed nationalism 1) and 'a militant nationalism' (nationalism 2), the former being the prerogative of the nationalist elites who, guarding their own interests, remain subordinate to external powers, and the latter belonging to national liberation groups such as the National Liberation Front (*Front de Libération National*, FLN), wanting genuine independence—there is 'nationalism 3'. This 'unique conception of nationalism', in contradistinction to the other

---

[48] On this, see Innes (2002); Jelnikar (2008).
[49] Said (1994), p. 277.
[50] Said (1994), p. 261.
[51] Gibson (2003), p. 181.

two, refuses to be bound by the simple logic of the colonizer versus the colonized. Its ambition is (r)evolutionary in the true sense of the term in that it demands 'the complex transformation of the colonized, not the simple departure of the colonizers'.[52] Only on the threshold of such a transformation will, Fanon portends, *new* humanity flourish, and this *new* humanity will be grounded in what Said, taking inspiration from Fanon, has developed into his theory of *liberation*: 'Liberation is consciousness of self, "not the closing of a door to communication", but a never-ending process of "discovery and encouragement" leading to true national self-liberation and to universalism.'[53]

The recasting of the anti-colonial struggle in psychological terms; its transposition into the domain of both individual and collective self-consciousness, marks a crucial step on the path to larger liberation. For what lies at the heart of *liberation, nationalism,* or *new human-ism,* is 'consciousness of self' as the precondition and consequence of (national) *self*-liberation leading to universalism. Gibson puts it thus: 'This "self" which does not close the door to communication develops by undergoing mediation (and therefore self-negation) and only then embraces the other in mutual recognition.'[54]

The communication between the 'self' and the 'other' through openness and self-negation holds the potential of resolution on a higher plane of mutual recognition, whereby the other is embraced as part of a larger self-definition. In the context of India, Ashis Nandy has written pertinently that the cultural forces unleashed in the colonial encounter not only 'fractured the personality of every sensitive exposed Indian' but they also 'set up the West as a crucial vector within the Indian self'.[55] The other does not have to forever remain an external menacing presence but can become an integral part of the enlarged self.

The liberationist anti-imperialism promoted by Said in opposition to, or as a departure from, nationalist anti-imperialism—and the tension between the two never quite disappears—has since been advanced by several other postcolonial critics. Neil Lazarus, for example, similarly underscores the role of 'Third-World' intellectuals

---

[52] Gibson (2003), pp. 79–80.

[53] Said (1994), p. 282.

[54] Gibson (2003), p. 189.

[55] Nandy (1983), p. 89.

in creatively contesting received forms of knowledge by what he refers to as a 'fundamentally *universalistic* gesture' of their intellectual practice. It is a gesture 'directed through and beyond the nodal point of the nation to a proleptic space of *internationalism*'.[56] The inspiration, once again, comes from Fanon's famous proposition that '[n]ational consciousness, which is not nationalism, is the only thing that will give us an international dimension'.[57] The national and international in this dictum, for all the efforts to displace the former, remain closely bound to each other. 'It is at the heart of national consciousness that international consciousness lives and grows.'[58] The 'beyond' here is only ever possible 'through' the 'nodal point' of the nation.

This brings us to the question of internationalism. The internationalism invoked in the lines above, to reiterate, is routed via national(ism). Such an understanding of internationalism, referring to inter-state relations and links that state actors with varied interests forge between themselves, has come to dominate contemporary usage of the term, but is inadequate for our case study. The 'internationalism' that concerns us is *non-statist* in character; of a kind that disregards the interests of states and strives for solidarities and unities in a far more 'promiscuous' a manner.[59] The internationalism of the pre-World War I and interwar period, fuelled by proletarian energies, would be a paradigmatic case in point (and relevant for understanding Kosovel's sense of solidarities and aspirations). Another problem of the term 'inter*national*' is that it implies too bounded a primary entity. It is here that Homi Bhabha's deconstructive manoeuvre, his interrogation of the imagined unity of the nation, is worth invoking, as the final attempt to go beyond the nation.

The '*inter*national dimension' that Fanon speaks of—even as he is unable to resolve the tension between nationalism and (international) anti-colonialism—has been posited by Bhabha as much within the 'margins of the nation-space' as 'in the boundaries *in-between* nations and peoples'.[60] The *ambivalent* margins of the nation-space make it difficult, if not impossible, for national culture to be located in any

---

[56] Lazarus (1999), emphasis author's, p. 141.
[57] Fanon (1963 [1961]), p. 247.
[58] Fanon (1963 [1961]), pp. 247–8.
[59] See Zachariah (2011), pp. 264–5; Raza, Roy, and Zachariah (2014).
[60] Bhabha (1990), emphasis author's, p. 4.

precise or bounded manner: 'it is neither unified nor unitary in relation to itself, nor must it be seen simply as "other" in relation to what is outside or beyond it'.[61] The boundary itself is 'Janus-faced', so that 'the problem of the outside/inside must always itself be a process of hybridity, incorporating new "people" in relation to the body politic...'[62] It is this 'ambivalent nation-space' that Bhabha then signposts as 'the crossroads to a new transnational culture', which in its thrust is, he insists, 'anti-nationalist'.[63]

The resolution of the 'national' questions clearly rests on a paradox apparent from such designations as Said's 'anti- or post-nationalist nationalists',[64] or Bhabha's 'anti-nationalist, ambivalent nation space', which convey the need to transcend a restrictive category but at the same time also retain it. Is it at all possible then to go beyond the nation?

TOWARDS UNIVERSALISM

The arguments put forward by Chatterjee, Said, Bose and Jalal, Lazarus, and others, insist on discriminating between a variety of nationalisms, retaining in sight a strain that can be linked to freedom and liberation as well as creativity and imagination. The question, however, arises as to what extent the debate on nationalism in which there is a manifest need to discriminate between 'good' and 'bad' nationalism, between forms that are 'true' because they are self-critical and inclusive and those that are 'false' because they are communalist and exclusive, is itself steeped in a nationalist perspective? And whose nationalism are we referring to when talking about nationalism?

In the next part of the chapter, I will attempt to go beyond nationalism by introducing a notion of 'universalism', even as it should be apparent by now that nationalism will keep coming back to haunt our discussion. Moreover, the terminological and conceptual tangle— 'the tug-of-war over a word'[65]—that characterizes the discussion on nationalism is no less present in the debates on universalism.

---

[61] Bhabha (1990).
[62] Bhabha (1990).
[63] Bhabha (1990), emphasis author's.
[64] Said (1994), p. 270.
[65] Appiah (2005), p. 242.

Universalism as a concept has a long and varied history, longer than anything nationalism can hope to aspire for. Whether part of the heritage of religious thought across the globe—and we can go to the Gospels or the Upanishads for universalist thinking—or a central piece of modern-day secular ideologies, the notion, as it is crops up in discussions today, is a highly embattled one. With claimants and rejecters across the board of social, political, and cultural theory, it has been engaging philosophers, historians, and literary critics alike. An entry point that lends itself in relation to the two poets, whom I approach, schematically speaking, as thinkers and poets of decolonization, or rather liberation, is to balance universalism between the opposite ends of domination and liberation: universalism-as-hegemony and universalism-as-emancipation. For indeed, some reject universalism on the basis that it is hegemonic and others uphold it with precisely the opposite argument that universalism amounts to a liberationist, emancipatory idiom. With further distinction between 'true' and 'false' modes of universalism we enter the already familiar territory of distinctions designed to re-appropriate an existing concept anew.

I will start by looking at the debate on universality and universalism that has been animating postcolonial theorists, since this will introduce some of the key issues surrounding the concept, demonstrating primarily the grounds for its critique. It is within this field (and cultural studies more broadly), especially the more theoretical strain informed by poststructuralist thought, that universality, at least initially, came under severe attack, perceived not only as anachronistic but also as dangerous.[66] Over the last decade or so, however, the pendulum of critique, even among the postcolonial critics, seems to have swung back in the opposite direction. In Amanda Anderson's words:

> One of the more remarkable developments in contemporary cultural criticism has been the surge of interest in the idea of and history of universalism.... Partly in reaction of the excesses of identity politics, and partly in response to the political and ethical impasses of a strictly negative critique of Enlightenment, a number of theorists have begun to

[66] Gayatri Chakravorty Spivak, one of the foremost postcolonial theorists, for example, leaves little scope for debate: '[T]here can be no universalist claims in the human sciences' (Hallward 2001, p. 176).

re-examine universalism, asking how we might best combine the critique
of partial or false universals with the pursuit of those emancipatory ideals
associated with traditional universalism.[67]

There have indeed been several notable contributions, arguing
staunchly for the need to retain the category of universality. 'The
attempt to dismiss [the notion of the universal] *theoretically*, and
in general, places one in an impossible position,' writes Nicholas
Harrison, further saying it is necessary 'to protect at once a certain
notion of the universal'.[68] Similarly, Neil Lazarus claims it is 'vital
to retain the categories of [both] "nation" and "universality"'.[69] And
Patrick Colm Hogan makes a related claim for the need to defend universality, saying that 'genuine universalism is the only way in which we
can recognize the common humanity and thus the shareable value of
distinct instatiations'.[70] If universalism stands in such need of defence,
we might start by asking what the problem with universalism is.

What Is Wrong with Universalism?

Over the last few decades universalism has been subjected to rigorous
criticism on a number of related counts. Bill Ashcroft, Gareth Griffiths,
and Helen Tiffin (the famous trio of the postcolonial classic *The Empire
Writes Back* [1989]),[71] for example, have disqualified the concept
altogether as a potential emancipatory tool in their edited volume *The
Post-Colonial Studies Reader*[72] as well as in their glossary of essential
concepts, *Post-Colonial Studies: The Key Concepts*.[73] For critics who
proclaim in the introduction to the glossary that they will explain 'the
most important terms and concepts in English in postcolonial theory
by providing an insight into their genesis and by offering an account

---

[67] A. Anderson (1998), p. 265.
[68] Harrison (2003), emphasis author's, p. 153.
[69] Lazarus (1999), p. 143.
[70] Hogan (2000), p. xvii. See also a special issue of the feminist journal
differences, which came out in spring 1995, in defence of universalism. Lazarus
et al. (1995); Balibar (1995).
[71] Ashcroft, Griffiths, and Tiffin (1989).
[72] Ashcroft, Griffiths, and Tiffin (1995).
[73] Ashcroft, Griffiths, and Tiffin (2002).

of *the range of meanings* with which they have been deployed'[74]—the treatment of the concept of 'universalism/universality' is strikingly univalent, formulated strictly in negative terms.

Notions of universality, according to Ashcroft and his co-authors, are grounded in the essentialist assumption that 'there are irreducible features of human life and experience that exist beyond the constitutive effects of local cultural condition'.[75] Such a universalist premise, with its reliance on common humanity and the idea that members of different cultures share 'fundamental cognitive, emotive, ethical, and other properties and principles',[76] to draw, in part, on Hogan's definition of universalism—and he, unlike the authors of the glossary, would not discard the notion of common humanity or human nature altogether— is bound to work against a vital recognition of cultural difference. Why the authors object to what they call 'the myth of universality' is therefore not just because, in their view, universal features of humanity are pure fiction, part of the old nineteenth-century liberal-humanist vocabulary, but also—and foremost—because such ostensibly universalizing notions level out cultural differences by working to impose on others what is in fact local masquerading as 'universal'.[77] In short, universalist assumptions are reductive and essentialist. Moreover, they are closely linked with totalizing imperialist ambitions:

> The assumption of universalism is a fundamental feature of the construction of colonial power because the 'universal' features of humanity are the characteristics of those who occupy positions of political dominance.[78]

What impels the authors' anti-universalist stance is the view that universalism is by definition a hegemonic discourse, projecting Western values embedded in Western interests as *the* way to be. It is presumptuous at best and totalitarian at worst. Indeed, no one would want to dispute the historical link between this mode of universalism and the project of (neo-)imperialism, and it is not difficult to see

[74] Ashcroft, Griffiths, and Tiffin (2002), emphasis mine, p. 2; entry found on pp. 235–7.
[75] Ashcroft, Griffiths, and Tiffin (2002), p. 235.
[76] Hogan (2000), p. xv.
[77] Ashcroft, Griffiths, and Tiffin (2002), p. 235.
[78] Ashcroft, Griffiths, and Tiffin (1995), p. 55.

why (a particular notion of) universality and universalism would be at odds with the postcolonial vocabulary concerned with difference, the specific and the particular; but this argument seems a little too rash in its categorical rejection of universality simply because of the abuses history has put it to.

Without getting ourselves too entangled in the discussion, the philosophical dimensions of which are in any case beyond the scope of this chapter, let us consider the question that seems to fuel much of the contention surrounding universalism, namely the question whether one upholds the notion of universals or not. There are, of course, various dimensions to this question and these get progressively more complex. Appiah, for instance, who also does not object to the older argument of evoking human essences, believes in 'such a thing as a universal human biology ... biological human nature ... shaped by more than 99 percent of our genes that we all share'.[79] Universality at the level of human species apart, cross-cultural research also points to 'some basic mental traits that are universal', that is to say, found in every human population.[80] Language—if it is a mental trait—would certainly be one. Though there is no doubt a great deal of variety amongst cultures, pro-universalists would point out that there is also much that is shared between societies, not least because of the shared problems of our human condition. Appiah offers a sample list, based on Donald Brown's research in his study *Human Universals* (1991):

> ...practices like music, poetry, dance, marriage, funerals; values resembling courtesy, hospitality, sexual modesty, generosity, reciprocity, the resolution of social conflict; concepts such as good and evil, right and wrong, parent and child, past, present, and future.[81]

If one then need not be too sceptical about the existence of universals, one should not get too optimistic either, for 'a shared biology or a natural human essence does not give us, in the relevant sense, a shared ethical nature'.[82] It is precisely in the realm of human values that the assumptions of universality become more problematic and where

[79] Appiah (2005), p. 252.
[80] Appiah (2007), p. 96.
[81] Appiah (2007), pp. 96–7.
[82] Appiah (2005), p. 252.

consequently much of the pro- and anti-universalist argumentation takes place. Though, even here, pro-universalists have been adamant in saying that the historicist and relativist positions need not be incompatible with a notion of universals.

Let us, however, come back to our discussion of universalism being linked to imperial hegemony. While one can understand that universalism has been made suspect because of the historical legitimacy lent to imperialism by 'three of the most powerful universalist ideologies of the West, Christianity, Liberalism, and Marxism', we must also note that 'there is no straightforward argument demonstrating that universalism is necessarily imperialist'.[83] Indeed, when the major novelist and theorist of postcolonial literature Ngũgĩ Wa Thiong'o refers to himself as 'an unrepentant universalist',[84] it can only be presumed that there must be more to universalism than meets the postcolonial eye of Ashcroft, Griffiths, and Tiffin. Ngũgĩ's universalism—and his political imagination engages an unremitting call for 'a plurality of centres all over the world' and the 'possibilities of opening out the mainstream to take in other streams'[85]—has little in common with the absolutist pretensions of the imperialist brand. In fact, Ngũgĩ himself acknowledges the dangers of such lofty a type of universalism that posits a transcendent, ahistorical subject that Ashcroft and company so rightly object to:

> Coming from that part of the globe, called, for lack of a better word, the Third World, I am suspicious of the uses of the word and the concept of the universal. For very often, this has meant the West generalising its experience of history as the universal experience of the world … what is Western becomes universal and what is Third World becomes local … One historical particularity is generalised into a timeless and spaceless universality.[86]

Ngũgĩ's own *universalist* aspirations must then be of a *different* order. Hogan aptly dubs it 'particularist universalism' to suggest 'the deep compatibility of universalism and particularism'.[87] It is something that

---

[83] P. B. Mehta (2000), p. 622.
[84] Thiong'o (1993), p. xvii.
[85] Thiong'o (1993), pp. 11, 8.
[86] Thiong'o (1993), p. 25.
[87] Hogan (2000), p. xvii.

Ngũgĩ himself explicitly subscribes to—'the universal is contained in the particular just as the particular is contained in the universal'[88]—to on the one hand overcome the isolation of particular cultures while on the other posit the very particularities of cultures as a basis for their overcoming. His universalist ideal envisages a world where:

> the wealth of a common global culture will ... be expressed in the particularities of our different languages and cultures very much like a universal garden of many-coloured flowers. The "flowerness" of the different flowers is expressed in their very diversity. But there is cross-fertilisation between them. And what is more they all contain in themselves the seeds of a new tomorrow.[89]

Ngũgĩ is just one among the many postcolonial intellectuals—Jameson would call them 'cultural intellectuals' to denote their double engagement with both 'poetry and praxis'[90]—who, according to some critics, are unafraid to ground their position in the 'older categories of universalism and true humanism'.[91] But this position, in my view, is strongly motivated by the idea that a 'true' humanism and universalism needed to be reclaimed for the whole of humanity, and what will make it 'true' is precisely this act of reclaiming, projected into the future— 'a new tomorrow'. If colonization is essentially dehumanizing—and Amié Césaire called it 'thingification'[92]—then to close the gap between a human being and another human being, the colonizer and the colonized, one requires to, as Tagore put it, 'awaken their humanity by our own'.[93] It is on this conviction that Fanon urged for a 'new

[88] Thiong'o (1993), p. 26.

[89] Thiong'o (1993), p. 24. Ngũgĩ's Afro-centric position in the language debate on the other hand is impelled rather by anti-universalist sentiments. The close association Ngũgĩ perceives between language and culture, the former seen as a cultural reservoir of the latter, leads him to ultimately reject the language of the colonizer as a legitimate language for creative expression, and sees this as a necessary step in 'decolonizing the mind'. While cross-fertilization is an option, in this case there is a strict limit set on universality. For further discussion, see Lazarus (1993); Mazrui (1993).

[90] Jameson (1986), p. 75.

[91] Childs and Williams (1997), p. 61.

[92] Césaire (1972), p. 21.

[93] See Tagore (1961d [1908]), p. 138.

humanism' to be defined at the Congress of Black Artists and Writers in Rome in 1959. Or, as he wrote more famously in 1961 towards the end of the Algerian war for independence: 'This new humanity cannot do otherwise than define a new humanism both for itself and for others.'[94] He felt that the only way out of the 'absurd drama' others had 'staged' round him was to break out of the racialized binarism of the colonial imagination, and, 'through one human being ... reach out for the universal.'[95]

Clearly then, universalism cannot be exhausted by the definition found in the two postcolonial compendiums referred to above. To see it solely as a grand Western imperialist narrative geared to dominate 'the Other' is to ignore a major strain of universalist thought launched in opposition to imperialism, or for that matter independently of it, and commit the mistake of what Nicholas Harrison has called a 'tendentious "definition" of universalism/universality.'[96] Such a reading fails to acknowledge, or distinguish between, the diverse universalist discourses which straddle both ends of the imperialist–anti-imperialist divide. Ironically, by viewing the concept as being solely in the domain of Western modernity, this point of view perpetuates the very hegemonic drive of Western discourse it purportedly seeks to undermine.

Furthermore, to frame the intellectual legacy of modernity as a divide between the West claiming to be universal and the non-West striving to be different, is to endorse a model that is ultimately disabling, because, if nothing else, it is false. It seems what Kenan Malik said speaking in the aftermath of 9/11 needs to be said time and again:

> The Western tradition is not Western in any essential sense, but only through an accident of geography and history. Indeed, Islamic learning provided an important source of both the Renaissance and the development of science. Many of the ideas we call 'Western' are, in fact, universal, laying the basis as they do for greater human flourishing.[97]

---

[94] Fanon (1963 [1961]), p. 246.

[95] Fanon (1986 [1952]), p. 197. Of course, it needs to be said here, that Fanon advocated violence in his theory of liberation, seeing it as a necessary step in opening up a space for dialogue between the colonizer and the colonized. Neither Tagore nor Kosovel found (counter-)violence justified.

[96] Harrison (2003), p. 153.

[97] Malik (2002). At the conference, *After 11 September: Fear and Loathing in the West*, held at the Bishopsgate Institute in London on 26 May 2002.

He is also right in pointing out that many radicals of the past century, whether from the Global South or not, understood that the problem of imperialism was not in it being a Western ideology, but in it being 'an obstacle to the pursuit of the progressive ideals that arose out of the Enlightenment'.[98]

Eurocentrism: False or Pseudo-Universalism

The sceptical, anti-universalist position discussed so far, which is grounded in the more general opposition to Enlightenment humanism, has since met with several objections. The pro-universalist camp, prominently Marxist in orientation, has been at pains to point out that this critique rests on a terminological as well as a conceptual muddle: on mistaking Eurocentrism for universalism. The very opening paragraph of Samir Amin's thought-provoking book *Eurocentrism* lays bare the threads of this argument:

> Eurocentrism is a culturalist phenomenon in the sense that it assumes the existence of irreducibly distinct cultural invariants that shape the historical paths of different peoples. Eurocentrism is therefore anti-universalist, since it is not interested in seeking possible general laws of human evolution. But it does present itself as universalist, for it claims that imitation of the Western model by all peoples is the only solution to the challenges of our time.[99]

Hence, the real basis of the anti-universalist attack, following Amin, is not universalism at all or, for that matter, the universalist pretentions of European Enlightenment, but its Eurocentric ideological appropriation (a part and parcel of the capitalist mode of production). If modern culture's claim is that it is founded on humanist universalism, then in its Eurocentric variant, it undermines its own claim. Without negating the purchase of the founding idea, Amin sees the challenge in having to elaborate 'a universalism liberated from the limits of Eurocentrism'.[100]

Kwame Appiah has defended universalism along similar lines: 'It is characteristic of those who pose as antiuniversalists to use the term

---

[98] Malik (2002).

[99] Amin (1989), p. vii.

[100] Amin (1989), pp. 114–16.

universalism as if it meant *pseudo-universalism*, and the fact is that
their complaint is not with universalism at all. What they truly object
to—and who would not?—is Eurocentric hegemony *posing* as universalism'.[101] Over a decade later he felt compelled to reiterate the same point:

> But, of course, Hume's or Kant's or Hegel's inability to imagine that
> an African could achieve anything in the sphere of 'arts and letters' is
> objectionable not because it is humanist or universalist but because it is
> neither. What has motivated this recent antiuniversalism has been, in large
> part, a conviction that past universalism was a projection of European
> values and interests. This is a critique best expressed by the statement
> that the actually existing Enlightenment was insufficiently enlightened; it
> is not an argument that Enlightenment was the wrong project.[102]

Two related claims appear to underlie these arguments. One is that
the term 'universalism'/'universality' be unhinged from its associations
with the Eurocentric notional imputation and be subjected to a new
appraisal. And the second is that the project of Enlightenment, by laying the moral and legal foundations for equality and respect among *all*
human beings, was not a misplaced project, even as it clearly remains
an unfinished one. The question therefore is not whether to reject
universalism but how to further its pursuit. This takes us to the heart
of today's political and philosophical debate, which I can only hope
to address cursorily in these pages. I will briefly outline three major
arguments underpinning the resurgent interest in universalism and
the growing belief in its necessity as a theoretical concept.

The first argument relates to the reality of the contemporary world
that is poised precariously between the various pulls of 'global integration' on the one hand and 'sociocultural disintegration' on the other.
It is given credence by the political philosopher Seyla Benhabib in
her advocacy of 'a pluralistically enlightened ethical universalism'.[103]
Because today we live in a global situation that is 'creating real con-
frontations between cultures, languages, and nations', with people's

[101] Appiah (1992), p. 58.
[102] Appiah (2005), p. 250. See also pp. 219–20 and 258–9. For the same
type of argument, see also Lazarus et al. (1995), pp. 78–9; Hallward (2001),
pp. 177–9.
[103] Benhabib (2002), p. 36.

lives being encroached upon in a number of ways, we have, she argues, 'a *pragmatic imperative* to understand each other and to enter into a cross-cultural dialogue'.[104] Insofar as this global 'community of interdependence ... resolves to settle issues of common concern to all via dialogical procedures in which all are participants', we will have 'a moral community'. The 'all' she refers to is indeed 'all of humanity', not because she wants to 'invoke some philosophical essentialist theory of human nature, but because the condition of planetary interdependence has created a situation of worldwide reciprocal exchange, influence, and interaction'.[105]

The second argument similarly posits a universalist outlook as being mandated by the situation of global interdependency, but this time the category commanding the discovery of possible general laws that govern societies is that of the capitalist economic system. 'The global purchase of actually existing capitalism obliges us to develop concepts adequate to its systematicity', write Lazarus and his collaborators, in large part joining hands with Amin.[106] Imposed on a worldwide scale, capitalism, as it were, 'created a demand for universalism as much at the level of scientific analysis of society as at the level of elaboration of a human project capable of transcending its historical limits'.[107] In striving to fashion the latter, these critics make it imperative to take on the false universalism espoused by bourgeois culture (that is, capitalist ideology that in great part overlaps with the Eurocentrism as Amin defines it), but rather than adopting an anti-universalist stance, whether of the ideological left or right, they opt for a *radicalized* universalist position. They refuse to surrender the concept of universality either to the bourgeois ideologues or concede theoretical ground to contemporary post-theories with their proclamation of the death of the universalist ideal and the attendant categories of 'reason', 'truth', and 'logic'. Instead they forward a kind of third position from which they can defend the 'universalistic claims of scientific knowledge' against 'various counter-enlightenment attacks'.[108] Again, they would say, it is too little enlightenment, not too much, that is the problem.

[104] Benhabib (2002), emphasis author's.
[105] Benhabib (2002).
[106] Lazarus et al. (1995), p. 103.
[107] Lazarus et al. (1995).
[108] Lazarus et al. (1995), pp. 77–8.

Lastly, instead of laying the perspective of universality aside as an antiquated totalitarian framework, pro-universalists argue that some sort of a universal dimension must be retained so as to avoid the pitfalls of cultural relativism, of ending up with cultural enclaves or mutually sealed-off impenetrable worlds. Appiah's complaint with anti-universalism seems justified when he says that anti-universalism 'protects difference at the cost of partitioning each community into a moral world of its own'.[109] Such a strict relativist or particularist position is of course historically and empirically indefensible. Cultural interpenetration is a fact of history. This is no less true of today when, as sociologist Ulrich Beck argues, it is necessary that we accept and work with our 'intercultural destiny':

> [T]here are no separate worlds (our misunderstandings take place within a single world). The global context is varied, mixed, and jumbled—in it, mutual interference and dialogue (however problematic, incongruous, and risky) are inevitable and ongoing.[110]

If universalism is problematic because, through its promotion of what is shared between cultures and individuals, it can obliterate particularities—and insensitivity to difference can acquire malicious forms indeed—there is also much cause for concern when cultures are defined strictly along the lines of difference. The former would accept 'the other' only in terms of sameness, but in the latter the supposed incommensurability of cultures precludes any meaningful dialogue or understanding. The difference-seeking or particularist approach is also inherently inconsistent, since 'upholding differences among groups typically entails the erasure of differences within groups'.[111] Its tendency is to homogenize identity on both ends of the cross-cultural divide. Some critics have become highly sceptical of the whole concept of 'cross-cultural difference'. If not altogether abandoned, it should at least be restricted in the way it is used within contemporary cultural theory, since it commits, what Appiah has rightly called, a 'characteristically modern mistake': the assumption that 'international difference ... is an especially profound kind of something called "cultural

109 Appiah (2005), p. 249.
110 Beck (2004), pp. 436–7.
111 Appiah (2005), p. 254.

difference"[112] Insofar as one argues that the differences existing among societies, groups and individuals profoundly complicate what we think of as cross-cultural understanding, one should also remember that often the differences and the difficulties are no less true from *within* societies themselves.[113] Indeed, no one would dare suggest that dialogue or agreement, particularly when distances between beliefs, experiences, and practices are substantial, come easily—historical record testifies to the opposite—but this, true universalists will go on saying, is no reason to stop trying.

New Universalism: Striving for the Unattainable?

From the discussion so far, it is clear that cultural relativists are as vulnerable to charges of essentializing as are universalists. Writing from their own historically and culturally contingent positions, universalists may elevate what is local and specific to the status of the universal, but cultural relativists, with their predilection for difference, can succumb to reification and particularistic closures. Both positions are equally undesirable, not least because they form the extreme ends of the relativist–universalist divide.

Can there be a third position? A way of engaging the positive aspects of both universalism and relativism?[114] Is it possible to conceive of the relation between the particular and the universal outside the either/or matrix, and have an alternative to both a universalism that eliminates difference and to a particularism that rejects the possibility of developing any general principles? For indeed, the universalism that concerns us, and which has been dubbed by the various theorists I have been referring to as *new, genuine,* or *progressive* universalism to mark it off from the old-style imperialist, or the new-style neo-colonial, brands, recasts the terms of this debate along the premise that similarity (what is shared, universal) and difference (what is local, particular) are not incommensurable but mutually dependent and constitutive (think of Ngũgĩ's 'particular universalism' mentioned earlier). They are parts

---

[112] Appiah (2005).

[113] On this see Benhabib (2002), p. 25.

[114] I take a cue from Beck's helpful analysis here, where each of the contended '-isms' (nationalism, universalism, relativism, and ethnicism) is seen to have 'two faces'. Cf. Beck (2004).

of the same continuum. Hence, universalism, as Hogan emphatically notes, is 'not at all a matter of everyone having the same culture', but rather it provides the only rationale for 'all cultures being preserved in their uniqueness'. Respect for different cultures, he concludes, 'is not the antithesis of universalism, but a *consequence* of universalism'.[115]

Point taken, but this still leaves the question of (new) universality unanswered. Hogan's vital recuperation of the term is quite unambiguously grounded in the belief in universal humanity: 'All people share universal feelings, propensities, rights, and our various cultures all develop out of these shared feelings, propensities, rights'.[116] No doubt many will not share his optimism for what some would see as a 'Western' discourse of human rights. But Hogan will not concede to the unproductive relativist–universalist binary that he sees as false; rather he wants to rethink the idea of universality through an essentially psychological framework. To explain away the conceptual tangle discussed in the previous section, he sees *false* universality as an outcome of the psychological mechanism of *projection*. According to him, in contrast to 'the unself-conscious assumption that everyone thinks the same ways I do', (true) universalism 'involves a self-conscious effort to understand precisely what is common across different cultures—empirically, normatively, experientially'.[117] In that sense he acknowledges the subjective, tentative nature of (true) universality, which can always turn against itself 'when anti-universalist tendencies arise, consciously or unconsciously'.[118]

Others have been more explicit in refracting the category of universality in the prism of humanity's patently darker side. Writing in the wake of growing nationalist unrests in France, Eastern Europe, and elsewhere in the 1990s, Julia Kristeva, for example, wrote:

Yes, let us have universality for the rights of man, provided we integrate in that universality not only the smug principle according to which 'all

---

[115] Hogan (2000), emphasis author's, pp. xvii–xxiii. The danger of this type of argument is that evocations of 'culture' and respect for different 'cultures' can all too easily rest on essentializing assumptions about what it is that constitutes a particular 'culture'.

[116] Hogan (2000).

[117] Hogan (2000), p. xvi.

[118] Hogan (2000).

men are brothers' but also that portion of conflict, hatred, violence, and destructiveness that for two centuries since the *Declaration* has ceaselessly been unloaded upon the realities of wars and fratricidal closeness and that the Freudian discovery of the unconscious tells us is a surely modifiable but yet constituent portion of the human psyche.[119]

What is conveyed much more forcefully here is the need to see the human condition as a complex of abstract—but vital—principles and destructive, if modifiable, tendencies. What, in her view, makes universality an enabling concept is the recognition gleaned from psychoanalysis that strangeness—or 'the Other'—is to be confronted, and reckoned with, within our own selves: '[L]et us know ourselves as unconscious, altered, other in order better to approach the universal otherness of the strangers that we are—for only strangeness is universal.'[120] Giving due validity to this proposition, according to Kristeva, would be a step in the direction of not always having to consolidate one's sense of (important) self in opposition to an outside other.

A similar argument has been drawn upon so as to salvage another embattled, and relevant, concept—that of multiculturalism. Ashis Nandy, for example, writing against the context of tremendous violence of the twentieth century, has suggested that multiculturalism 'should not invoke an inventory of cultures, but a multilayered self, in which the others are telescoped into the self, so much so that the self cannot be described without the others'.[121] Such interpenetration between self and other radically destabilizes notions of bounded and pure identities, and suggests a relationship between the particular and the universal that is deeply intertwined and open-ended.

In contrast then to the old universalism which rests on the false dichotomy between 'us' and 'them', new universalism is altogether less sure about identities:

[119] Kristeva (1993), p. 27.

[120] Kristeva (1993), p. 21.

[121] Nandy (2002), p. 272. In an earlier publication, the sentence runs: '[Multiculturalism] should not invoke an inventory of cultures, but a multi-layered self, constantly in dialogue with others, conceptualised not as distant strangers but as alien fragments of the self' (Nandy 2002, p. 223). The question to ask here would be, at what point does something which initially is seen and felt to be 'alien' ceases to be 'strange' but becomes an integral part—as opposed to an *alien* fragment—of the self.

When we pose the question 'Is Universalism ethnocentric?' do we take account of [the] complex global dialogue across cultures and civilizations? ... The question 'Is Universalism ethnocentric?' presupposes that we know who the 'West and its others', or in Tzvetan Todorov's famous words—'Nous et les autres'—are (1993). But who are we? Who are the so-called others? Are they really our others?[122]

This is not to say that differences do not exist or are unimportant, but it is to realize that differences are, in the words of another French philosopher, 'already abundant in one and the "same" individual'.[123] Alan Badiou's famous interpretation of the universalist outlook of Saint Paul plays on the ambiguities of the construction of difference: 'For although it is true, so far as what the event constitutes is concerned, that there is "neither Greek nor Jew", *the fact is* that there are Greeks and Jews.'[124] One could even maintain that there is nothing but differences. It is precisely at this crucial juncture that universality then comes into its own as something that moves beyond established and evident differences, rendering them as momentarily irrelevant. This, essentially, is an act of love:

> Nevertheless, these fictitious beings, these opinions, customs, differences, are that to which universality is addressed; that toward which love is directed; finally that which must be traversed in order for universality itself to be constructed.[125]

If in the traditional understanding universality was posited as 'a judgement', a foundation or a fixture, it is now perceived as a moment of 'becoming indifferent to difference'. Universality thus becomes a category that is constantly in the making, always yet to be achieved. To create something universal—what Badiou terms 'an event', 'a truth'—means to go beyond evident differences, not in the sense

---

[122] Benhabib (2002), p. 25.

[123] Badiou (2005), p. 11.

[124] Badiou (2003), emphasis author's, p. 100.

[125] Badiou (2003), p. 100. See also Badiou's book on love, where the identity cult is seen as antithetical to love and needing to be challenged by it. 'When the logic of identity wins the day, love is under threat' (translated by Peter Bush, Badiou and Truong 2012, p. 98).

of enacting another particularist closure but rather in the sense 'of maintaining a noncomformity with regard to that which is always conforming us'.[126] The 'always' here is, needless to say, historically, culturally, and personally contingent. For indeed, once we move away from the theoretical, and admittedly rather abstract, discussion of universalism and locate Tagore's and Kosovel's ideas and practices of 'universalism' in their respective historical contexts, it will become clearer that the particular histories of universalisms are integrally linked to the histories of production of difference (the difference, for instance, between 'Slavs' and 'Italians', or 'East' and 'West', and so on).

To be sure, there is a paradox at the core of the debate on 'universality' and 'universalism'. The political theorist Ernesto Laclau has explained it thus: '[U]niversality is incommensurable with any particularity [and] yet cannot exist apart from the particular'. Or, put differently: '[T]he particular exists only in the contradictory movement of asserting a differential identity and simultaneously cancelling it'.[127] The paradox, Laclau further insists, must remain unsolved if hegemonic closure is to be avoided. For the minute it is solved, it would mean that 'a particular body [has] ... been found that [is] ... the *true* body of the universal'. But 'democratic' interaction is made possible precisely because the universal does not have any fixed, necessary content, so that different groups can compete to 'give their particular aims a temporary function of universal representation'.[128]

When Chinua Achebe, in his essay on colonialist criticism, proclaimed, 'I should like to see the word *universal* banned altogether from discussions of African literature until such a time as people cease to use it as a synonym for the narrow, self-serving parochialism of Europe, until their horizon extends to include all the world',[129] the source of his grievance was self-evident enough. And yet—what ironically defeats the purpose of Ashcroft, Griffiths, and Tiffin, who included Achebe's essay in their postcolonial compendium as evidence of his anti-universalist stance—Achebe does not, if we read

---

[126] Badiou (2003), p. 100.

[127] Laclau (1992), p. 89.

[128] Laclau (1992), p. 90. See also the collaborative book on the subject by Butler, Laclau, and Žižek (2000).

[129] Achebe (1995), p. 60.

his quote carefully, throw the notion of universality altogether out of the window. True, we might argue, he may as well have done, for when will our horizon ever extend to include the whole world? But to say that is to miss the point. Any critique of *false* universalism is possible only against an invocation of—to borrow from Lazarus and his co-authors—'the regulative ideal of genuine universalism'.[130] In other words, behind the manifest false universality there is such a thing as genuine, true universality. Posited on this fine line between 'false' and 'genuine', it is always in danger of turning against itself. To evoke it is to evoke its limitations and the self-conscious effort to transcend them. Any articulation of the universal is inherently anti-universalist. So rather than as an actuality, universality is there as a receding goal: 'The universal emerges out of the particular not as some principle underlying and explaining it, but as an incomplete horizon, suturing a dislocated particular identity.' The *new* universal is 'the symbol of a missing fullness'.[131] Its evocation remains crucial, because it is regulative.

Where the strain of nationalist thought discussed in the first half of the chapter converges with universalism is in the point where nationalism is in fact transcended and overcome, not in the sense of negating any one particular identity, but in the sense of laying it open to new dimensions and multiple interactions. If Fanon was right in saying that the fight for a national existence is a founding moment which sets 'a culture moving and opens to it the doors of creation', he was also right in stressing that 'a people is not simply a dominated people'.[132]

> There's no end to it
> so who's to say the last word?
> What came as a blow
> Will later glow as a fire…[133]

So run the lines of one of Tagore's songs written in 1914. A notion of universality/universalism that I have traced in this chapter is

---

[130] Lazarus et al. (1995), p. 88.

[131] Laclau (1992), p. 89.

[132] Fanon (1963 [1961]), pp. 244, 150.

[133] A song from *Gitali*, translated by Ketaki Kushari Dyson, Tagore (2010a [2003]), pp. 262–3.

emphatically an open-ended and above all a *creative* concept. Instead of a definite cultural content, the 'universal' in this perspective is given flexibility. As such it runs counter to oppressive constructions of sameness or prescriptive norms for humanity at large that inform imperialist and hegemonic agendas. It is with such a notion in mind that I wish to approach Tagore's and Kosovel's own articulations of 'universalism' and their projects of liberation, as I situate them within their respective histories.

2 Rabindranath Tagore

From Swadeshi *to* Vishvakabi

I remember the time when the word 'national' first came to be propagated in Bengal. I awoke one morning to find on all sides national paper, national fair, national song, national theatre. Everything was in the shadow of a national fog.[1]

But one is not fully entitled to anything one cannot give away.[2]

Rabindranath Tagore was born in 1861, three years after the British Crown had taken over the administration of India from the East India Company, and died in 1941, six years before India gained political independence from the British rule. His entire life was lived under colonial rule, and yet throughout he would reiterate with undiminished conviction that there was one 'great fact' about his age, and that was 'the meeting of human races'.[3] The arrival of the British was for Tagore 'a human fact',[4] and the ownership of the subcontinent an open, even possibly, an irrelevant, question.

---

[1] Tagore, 'Nabyobanger Andolon' ('The New Bengal Movement'), translated by Uma Das Gupta, 1890.

[2] Tagore, translated by Swapan Chakravorty, Tagore (2001f).

[3] Tagore (2002c [1921]), p. 76.

[4] Tagore (2002d [1922]), p. 104.

How do we understand such a positioning against the more depressing historical fact of India's colonization? Do we take it as symptomatic of what Bengal's 'first' novelist Bankimchandra Chatterjee saw as a distinctive trait of Indian psyche, their indifference to the question of rulership, and lack of desire for liberty? Was that, as Bankim argued, the root cause of their subjugation?[5] Does it reveal a betrayal, or a lack, of nationalist consciousness or is it rather, as I intend to argue, a radical critique of, and an alternative, to it?

In this chapter, I will extract a line of thought in Tagore's (then still evolving) response to the British presence in India that is a *double* critique of both imperialist culture and its anti-colonial, nationalist derivation, but without surrendering an anti-colonial, intellectual position. Tagore gave his anti-colonialism a broader base, envisioning it as *a larger search for liberation*, leading on to universalism.[6]

It would be impossible to attempt anything close to a comprehensive account of eighty years of Tagore's life with reference to his numerous initiatives, aspirations, and achievements.[7] But key personal and historical factors that helped shape Tagore's theory and practice

[5] P. Chatterjee (1993 [1986]), pp. 54–5.

[6] The phrase 'larger search for liberation' was used by Edward Said (1994), p. 265. See Ch. 1, pp. 27–31.

[7] For this I can refer the reader to a number of existing biographies of Tagore in English, the most comprehensive and critical of them being Dutta and Robinson (2003). See also Kripalani (2001 [1986]), first published in 1986, for a more personal and subjective appreciation of the man. Krishna Kripalani was a teacher at Santiniketan and close associate of Tagore for many years (from 1933 to the Tagore's death in 1941), and edited the journal *Visva-Bharati Quarterly* that Tagore first founded and edited himself. For a short and concise biography focusing primarily on Tagore's social work as educationist and rural reformer, see U. Das Gupta (2004). With a more precise focus on the poet as educator, see primarily O'Connell (2002) and the new expanded edition (2013). For an original take on Tagore's life and thought through the centrality of music, his poetry, and songs, see Som (2009), and for a biographical take on Tagore that portrays him as a profoundly self-critical and lonely figure, see Bhattacharya (2011). For the most authoritative and comprehensive Bengali biography of Tagore and works, see the nine volumes of Prasanta Kumar Pal. Volume 9 (cf. Pal [2003]), which covers year 1926, however, does not state anything about Tagore's visit to Yugoslavia that year.

of liberation are in order. My main concern is to critically highlight those aspects of Tagore's cultural and historical background that were crucial in (*a*) his emerging out of his boyhood seclusion as a relevant public—for a short time also 'nationalist'—voice, and (*b*) which led to his subsequent withdrawal from the political arena, disillusioned as he became with the ideology and politics of nationalism, both of which he came to reject in no uncertain terms.

CHANGING TIMES

The nineteenth century was a time of enormous social change and unrest as the Bengali society had to negotiate European influences under the increasing pressures of the British East India Company's tightening of the colonial machinery. The English-educated, urban Hindu middle class, to which Tagore belonged, were eager to engage with diverse materials made available through British Orientalism, the spread of English education, and the advent of print culture in the first half of the nineteenth century and, in the process, they not only came to articulate a new religious, historical, and national consciousness, but also produced new science, art, and literature. Bengali poetry and prose flourished in this period.

The seismic shifts notwithstanding, the more recent and finely tuned historical perspectives have assessed the nature of this change in terms of both novelty *and* continuity of 'Indian culture' under the colonial rule. Paying more attention to Indian initiative, agency, and creativeness of response—how imported ideas were reshaped in the indigenous setting and given a new distinct sensibility and purpose— the newer narratives of India's interactions with 'the West' stress how a new indigenous culture evolved out of the inherited traditions, and are interested in exploring the *nature* of that change.[8]

The 1820s and 1830s are seen as the period that kick-started the so-called Bengal Renaissance, characterized, as the name suggests, by heightened intellectual ferment and creativity.[9] Besides major

---

[8] See, for example, Bose and Jalal (2003), p. 77; Ray (2001), p. 63.

[9] The line of analysis interested in the *creative* aspect of the phenomenon is to date best represented by Subrata Dasgupta's cognitive approach (cf. 2006, 2011). I discuss this in more detail in the next chapter, pp. 133–4.

achievements spanning literature and science, nineteenth-century India was also the time when questions of radical social and religious reform were first brought to the agenda, as public debate became 'a new dimension of sociability'. The educated Indians, even though excluded from the country's government, 'created for themselves a public arena where the issues of the day were discussed'. Tracts, pamphlets, journals, newspapers, texts, and translations were published and circulated, creating a print culture that was not very different to that which was being spawned in Europe at around the same time.[10]

For Tagore, as well as for other key figures of the Bengal Renaissance, Western-derived rational thinking stimulated the questioning of every aspect of life as they knew it. Issues of social welfare, human rights, and justice came to the fore. Addressing the abuses in Indian society, a number of men set out with the aim to reform time-honoured social practices, of which the caste system was one. Rammohun Roy (1772–1833), appealing to reason, but also seeking sanction in religious books, perhaps in part to satisfy his own religious needs and in part to silence his critics, raised a stark protest against the practice of *sati* (the custom of a widow's self-immolation on her husband's funeral pyre), and played a key role in it being outlawed in 1829. Iswarchandra Vidyasagar (1820–1891) led a campaign for legalizing widow remarriage in the 1850s. Child marriage, education for women, agrarian reforms, these and other issues all came up for heated debate, as various reformers made efforts to distinguish convention from tradition. In an essay titled 'The Changing Age' (1933), Tagore, looking back on this period, wrote of 'revolutionary changes' in received modes of thought and attitudes: 'This is evident in the proposition that those whom social usage has decreed to be untouchables should be given the right to enter temples.'[11] We do not have space here to discuss the many different causes that were being championed,[12] let alone debate the question of the implementation of these in social reality, something that has subsequently led to various attempts to disqualify what is also known as 'the Indian

[10] B. Metcalf and T. Metcalf (2010), p. 89.
[11] Tagore (1961l [1933]), p. 344.
[12] See Susobhan Chandra Sarkar (1970), the classical text on this.

Awakening'.[13] Despite these attempts—and the standard narrative arc of the renaissance runs from Raja Rammohun Roy to Rabindranath Tagore[14]—the dimension of a more creative strain of Bengali/Indian intellectuals' response to the problem of alien cultural 'imposition' and colonial modernity should not be downplayed.

Among the early responses to English education and culture that was first to reach the city of Calcutta—the then commercial and political centre of the British rule in the subcontinent—three broad strands tend to be identified. The first is exemplified by the Young Bengal group that was based at the Hindoo College in Calcutta (established in 1817, in large part through Indian initiative, as the first English language higher education institution in India). Under the tutelage of the hugely charismatic Calcutta-born teacher of Anglo-Portuguese origin, Henry Louis Vivian Derozio (1809–31), the group's young members became enthusiastic takers of the new ideas from the British. At the same time, they derided 'irrational' Hindu ways, broke taboos through eating beef and drinking alcohol and flaunted their newly acquired tastes through Western dress.[15] Opposing them

[13] The very idea of the Bengal Renaissance has presented a fierce bone of contention among scholars, ever since it was met with a radical Leftist critique in the 1970s and 1980s. Was it a renaissance? How, if at all, does it compare with the Italian Renaissance? What was its significance in the social, religious, and political spheres? These were some of the issues debated, with the suggestion that since many of the issues debated in theory failed to be resolved in practice, it meant that the phenomenon was a failure and inherently weak. See, amongst others, R. K. Das Gupta (2003); Ray (2001), pp. 6–9, 29–66; Raychaudhuri (2002); Sarkar (2005).

[14] Omissions of certain figures in this standard narrative, however, seem inadvertent, also untheorized. For example, Kazi Nazrul Islam (1899–1976), considered the foremost Muslim modern poet-intellectual of Bengal, who rose to prominence in the 1920s as a major dissenting voice, opposing not only the British colonial government but also religious bigotry (Hindu and Islamic) does not at all figure in the Renaissance literary studies literature. On this see Priti Kumar Mitra (2009, pp. 14–15).

[15] See Bose and Jalal (2003), p. 81. Tagore alludes to the Young Bengal group in his essay 'Bengali National Literature' (1895): '... the earliest people to learn English proved an unnecessary nuisance to those around them, resolving that wine, meat, and volubility were the chief ingredients of civilisation' (Tagore 2001f., p. 185).

and their fierce denunciation of contemporary Hindu practices was the Dharma Sabha, a conservative society founded and led by Radha Kanta Deb (1784–1867). In contrast, its members rallied support for Hinduism and objected to colonial government's interference in matters of domestic and family life. This led them to launch a campaign against Bentick's abolition of sati in 1829. This kind of revalorization of 'tradition', as some historians suggest, should be seen in its proper context as a reaction against the oppressive regime and colonial humiliation.[16] Similar objections to British-sponsored reform were to recur among nationalists at the end of the century.[17] If these two strands of response give a sense of two extremes spanning an uncritical acceptance of everything British to an outright rejection thereof, then there is a fair amount of middle ground where the two ends meet and feed into each other.[18] The third strand in the standard narrative thus covers the in-between space, presenting a more measured way of trying to come to terms with ideas from the colonizer's quarters. It is typically exemplified by the figure of Rammohun Roy: 'The most creative strand was led by Rammohun Roy, who attempted to adapt elements from all that he considered best in Indian and Western learning.'[19] Interestingly, what is said of Roy, Tagore himself would have affirmed of the reformer and scholar, who was a close associate of his father and grandfather, over seventy years earlier. In Roy, according to Tagore, modern India found a true synchronizer of 'East'

[16] For example, Nandy (2005c). What had previously been infrequent occurrences of sati increased in number after the introduction of the legislation to outlaw the practice; see Bates (2007, p. 50).

[17] B. Metcalf and T. Metcalf (2010), p. 89.

[18] Of course, to present the Young Bengal and Dharma Sabha in terms of strict opposition between 'Westernization' and 'traditionalism' or revivalism is to simplify the complexities of both strands of response. Deb and his followers, for example, supported English education and patronized Hindu College; see B. Metcalf and T. Metcalf (2010), p. 88. In matters of literature, Rosinka Chaudhuri (2002) has, for example, linked a body of early nineteenth-century poetry written by Indians *in English* to the very beginnings of the formation of a 'national' consciousness in India, going against the later-day nationalist assumptions. Henry Derozio's sonnet 'To India, My Native Land' is a case in point.

[19] Bose and Jalal (2003), p. 81.

and 'West'. Let me cite a substantial chunk from Tagore's centenary address on Roy—delivered on 18 February 1933, at the Senate House in Calcutta—for the tribute tells us as much about Tagore's own aspirations for the modern age as it does about Roy's.

> Rammohun was the only person in his time, in the whole world of man, to realize completely the significance of the modern age. He knew that the ideal of human civilization does not lie in the isolation of independence, but in the brotherhood of interdependence of individuals as well as of nations in all spheres of thought and activity…. His attempt was to establish our peoples on the full consciousness of their own cultural personality, to make them comprehend the reality of all that was unique and indestructible in their civilization, and simultaneously, to make them approach other civilizations in the spirit of sympathetic co-operation…. In social ethics he was an uncompromising interpreter of the truths of human relationship, tireless in his crusade against social wrongs and superstition, generous in his co-operation with any reformer, both of this country and of outside, who came to our aid in a genuine spirit of comradeship…. Deeply versed in Sanskrit, he revived classical studies, and while he imbued the Bengali literature and language with the rich atmosphere of our classical period, he opened its doors wide to the spirit of the age, offering access to new words from other languages, and to new ideas.[20]

The casting of Roy as 'the universal man' who personifies the ideal of the new age in terms of interdependence of individuals and nations, self-awareness and cooperation, the need to address and eliminate social ills and, finally, openness to new ideas directly corresponds with Tagore's own preoccupations with, and imaginings of, what 'modern' India should be like a good half a century later.[21]

The point is also to see Tagore in an extended historical context as someone who had important predecessors (and whom he recognized

---

[20] Tagore (2002j [1933]), p. 668.

[21] Such historical imaginings are of course never neutral, and this kind of a 'progressive reading of Indian history' (Collins 2012) and its personalities can be traced forward in time to India's first prime minister, Jawaharlal Nehru. See Collins (2012), p. 28, and also note 20 on p. 167. For understanding how and why the latter-day Brahmo community, with Tagore's father in the lead, retrospectively attributed the founding role of the Brahmo Samaj to Roy, who to this day is routinely referred to as 'the father' of modern India and the first reformer, see Hatcher (2006).

as such) as opposed to an extraordinary lone voice emerging out of thin air, a perception encouraged by his iconic status. The early nineteenth-century history of the colonial encounter provided an important backdrop for Tagore's own social concerns over half a century later, as the 'old' India had already entered the high noon of Empire, and the relations between the British and the Indians became significantly more strained.

For indeed, around the time of Tagore's birth, the atmosphere surrounding the relations between the British and the Indians had tensed considerably. The first major rising against the British rule, the Sepoy revolt—or the uprising—of 1857,[22] was crushed and the traditional ruling classes were more or less destroyed. The government of India came under the direct control of the British Crown. The subsequent changes in the British policies on India, and administrative measures taken 'disrupted the inter-racial relationships, led to the import of brides for the British population, to the psychological fear of the native and resulted in harsh exclusionary policies'.[23] Anti-British sentiments were on the rise.[24]

Tagore's family took an active part in all aspects of social change that revolutionized nineteenth-century colonial Bengal, providing major stimulus to the young Rabindranath. Born as the fourteenth, effectively the youngest, child into 'a cultural hothouse'[25] that nurtured

[22] Historians have now warned against presenting the year 1857 in exceptionalist terms, stressing the fact that throughout the long nineteenth century, the British had to face continual uprisings of one sort or another. Pax Britannica in India was a myth. What was unique of the events of 1857 was 'their scale'; see Bayly (1988), cited in Bates (2007), pp. 56ff.

[23] Jain (2006), p. 24.

[24] In his assessment of the British rule in India, Tapan Raychaudhuri, sees the rebellion of 1857, in which both sides had exercised great brutality, as creating a legacy of racial hatred that cast a shadow over all aspects between the ruler and the ruled for decades to come. Mutiny, according to him, is an inaccurate description of an event that had multiple and complex causes and was the result of 'accumulated anger of many sections of the population in north and central India—dispossessed princes, disgruntled soldiers and a harassed peasantry from whom the Company's army was largely recruited' (1999, p. 161).

[25] Dyson (2003), p. 23.

arts and sciences, music and dance, philosophy and religion, and whose many members themselves became distinguished writers, musicians, and painters, Tagore had, no doubt, a highly privileged upbringing, and his many talents were encouraged to flourish. The 'patrician' family background does not in itself provide a straightforward link between the family members (of whom Tagore was to become the most famous) and their intellectual vanguardism in the Hindu social and religious spheres, in the same way that it would be hard to argue that financial independence automatically leads to independence of mind.

Foremost a poet, Tagore was fond of the river metaphor to capture the changing times that were both a break with and a continuation of India's cultural and religious traditions. 'My ancestors came floating to Calcutta upon the earliest tide of the fluctuating fortune of the East India Company', he wrote, thus describing his forefathers back in the early seventeenth century, who had settled in Gobindapur, one of the three fishing villages that later became the city of Calcutta.[26] Building on the river metaphor, he would reiterate: 'My family had broken from the mainstream well before I was born.'[27] He must have been referring to the occasion when, a long time ago, two ancestors, the Brahmin brothers Kamadev and Jayadev, lost their caste from having smelt Muslim food—or so the legend goes. Thus outside the dominant fold of orthodox Hindu society even before the arrival of the British, the Tagores were in a better position to experiment with new ideas. 'Thanks to our seclusion, my family enjoyed a certain freedom,' acknowledged Rabindranath, noting also that this freedom found direct expression in their family dialect, which the Calcuttans referred to as 'Thakurbari-r bhasha', meaning the language of the

[26] Tagore (1961k [1926]), p. 289. It was a man called Panchanan Kushari who joined the leading traders of the time in supplying provisions to foreign ships sailing up the river Ganges, and thus laid the foundation stone in the family's thereafter continuing lucrative associations with the British. It was then too that the name Tagore first came into being. Since the family were Brahmins, the low-caste local population would address them with the respective term 'Thakur' (Sir), taken by foreign merchants to be their family name. Once 'Thakur' was anglicized, it became Tagore; see Kripalani (2001 [1986]), pp. 1–4.

[27] Translated by Devadatta Joardar and Joe Winter, Tagore (2006a [1904–40]), pp. 77–8.

Tagore household.[28] This was an important foundation for the poet's art of moulding a language for his own self-expression, as was the family's insistence on using Bengali on all occasions and not yield to the trend of adopting English.

Tagore framed the family's heterodox status in *positive* terms of freedom to build their own world with their own thoughts and 'energy of mind'.[29] Significantly too, he saw the family's 'code of life' as being 'composed of three cultures, Hindu, Muslim and British', a point he would translate into a plural, inclusive, and essentially open conceptualization of India.[30] And, staying faithful to his riverine idiom, he spoke of 'the currents of three movements' meeting 'in the life of our country' at the time of his birth, identifying them in turn as religious, initiated by Rammohun Roy and later revived by his father Debendranath Tagore (1817–1905); literary, with Bankimchandra Chatterjee (1838–1894) as a pioneer in modernizing the Bengali literary idiom; and national, which gave rise to a political movement in protest against the British rule.[31] I will explore all these in relation to the 'national' problematic, for both the literary and the religious movements were heavily underpinned with the newly discovered nationalist sentiments, as I position Tagore's own views vis-à-vis these sentiments.

Literature and Nation: Languages Lost and Found

To anybody brought up on the notion of a 'mother tongue' and a close alliance between a language and a (cultural) identity, the linguistic map of the early nineteenth-century colonial Bengal would be anything but straightforward. There were several languages in close competition and interaction with each other, each having a distinct social function. The early nineteenth-century scheme of linguistic practice of an educated middle-class Bengali would have been something like this:

> An ordinary Bengali householder would speak to his family and friends and in the bazaar in one of the local Bangla dialects.... But dealing with political authority, for instance regarding landholding or revenue, called

---

[28] U. Das Gupta (2006), p. 8.
[29] Tagore (2002e [1925]), p. 8.
[30] Tagore (1961k [1926]), p. 290.
[31] Tagore (2002e [1925]), p. 3.

for the consistent and skilful use of Persian. Religious ceremonies—a constant part of the householder routine—involved the mandatory use of Sanskrit.... Any transaction with colonial power required knowledge of English.[32]

Under increasing institutional pressures of colonial rule, this 'linguistic repertoire'[33] was to undergo substantial changes. We need to understand that language in pre-colonial India was much more part of a flexible register of occasion and identity, as opposed to an ideologically bounded entity located on a map and codified in dictionaries, grammar books, and literary canons. By the time Tagore began his writing career in the latter part of the nineteenth century, the linguistic map had long been simplified with English taking over the administrative function of Persian (Tagore's grandfather and Rammohun would still have been part of the Persianized elite, as they still worked under the aegis of the Mughal Empire).[34] Sanskrit was to remain the 'high' language used for the occasions of worship and marriage, as well as high literary cultivation amongst the Hindus, while English entrenched itself as the language associated with law, administration, and external trade, in other words, with modern forms of power and knowledge. At the same time, Bengali—or Bangla—of the nineteenth century, wedged as it was between the two spheres of influence, and crucially prompted by new and rising nationalist tendencies, began selectively negotiating with both Sanskrit and English to eventually emerge as 'an entirely new kind of high Bangla'.[35]

With the arrival of a new 'international' candidate on to the linguistic stage in India, the challenge facing *modern* Bengali was to develop into a language that was sufficiently differentiated and flexible to be a language of both worship and science, what had previously been a more exclusive domain of Sanskrit and English. But if Bengali at

[32] Kaviraj (2003), p. 538.
[33] Lelyveld (1993), p. 201.
[34] It was after Thomas B. Macaulay's 'Minute on Education' (1835), that English came to replace Persian as the official language of the government and the higher courts, but Bengali and Urdu continued to be important at the lower levels of the administration across eastern and northern India (cf. Bose and Jalal 2003, p. 84).
[35] Kaviraj (2003), p. 533.

that point in time already had a history of being a language in the religious context, through the translations of the Ramayana and the Mahabharata, the Upanishads, the narrative poems (Mangalkavyas), the Bhakti movements, *kirtans* and Baul songs—in the realm of science, it tread entirely new ground. Sudipto Kaviraj, for example, has shown how English syntactic forms and expressions related to the scientific worldview had percolated into Bengali and were naturalized with astonishing rapidity, affecting a substantial break with the traditional syntax.[36]

The challenge for modern Bengali, however, also meant—and this is more relevant to our point—acquiring 'the capacity to produce a high literature',[37] a decisive marker of modernity. In a remarkably short period of experimentation, literary Bangla went from Vidyasagar's proto-nationalist project of Sanskritizing the language, through Bankimchandra's championing (at least for a while) of 'a mixed language for literature' to Tagore's mature and highly complex Bangla freed of 'unpractical classicism'.[38]

The obvious point then to be made here is that the creation of modern Bengali (literary) language involved complex transactions with at least two different literary worlds and aesthetic grammars. As different authors drew on these resources—in line with their own convictions, sensibilities, and agendas—what emerged was inevitably 'a distinctively Indian/Bangla species of the literary modern'.[39] Tagore's response to the linguistic impulse of his age, according to one critic, yielded a poetry in which 'the *Upanishads* and Kalidasa, Vaishnava lyricism, and the rustic vigour of the folk idiom, are so well blended with Western influences ... that generations of critics will continue to wrangle over his specific debt to each of them'.[40] As will be seen, Kosovel too responded to a variety of literary models and resources available to him as a committed enthusiast, taking his language forward in sensibility and formal innovation, presenting a rather similar problem to his critics.[41]

[36] Kaviraj (2003), pp. 546–7.
[37] Kaviraj (2003), p. 542.
[38] Kaviraj (2003), pp. 544–5.
[39] Kaviraj (2003), p. 558.
[40] Kripalani (2007), p. 282.
[41] Discussion of concrete texts to demonstrate the dynamics of relating to 'internal' and 'external' literary traditions is reserved for Kosovel's creative

The nineteenth century in Bengal and India was then—in the words of Amit Chaudhuri—'a time of radical crossings-over in language'.[42] Furthermore, bi- or multilingualism was not simply the case of having command over more than one language but of having more than one language inscribed into the very language of choice for creative expression, which in Tagore's case remained Bengali. Common assumptions that link hybridity with postcolonial uses of English and delegate vernacular languages of the erstwhile colonized countries to a sphere of some sort of authenticity are indeed grossly oversimplified.

In the same way that the evolution of modern Bengali language can be understood by situating it at the crossroads of English and Sanskrit, modern Bengali literature too emerged out of complex negotiations with these two linguistic and literary spheres. This brings us to our next point. If Persian was lost as the language of law and power and superseded by English, it was only with the adoption of English that the Bengali colonial middle class of barristers, advocates, schoolteachers, lecturers, doctors, and civil servants—the *bhadralok* (meaning genteel, cultured people), who sought to distinguish themselves from both the traditional brahmanical elite as well as from their colonial masters[43]—got the idea of writing in their 'mother-tongue'. This, in turn, provided a major stimulus for the literary efflorescence that ensued.

One of the more remarkable characteristics of the nineteenth-century *Bangla sahitya* (Bengali literature) was precisely its 'excitement about the present'.[44] And this excitement was overwhelmingly due to 'the discovery of nationalism'. J.G. von Herder's idea of literature in the 'mother tongue' hitched to that of 'the nation' was to capture the imagination

---

writing. For more on how Tagore drew on narratives and characters from the Sanskrit high classical tradition but handled the subject matter in experimental modern ways; see Chaudhuri (2008), p. 79; Kaviraj (2003), pp. 558–9.

[42] 'The Flute of Modernity: Tagore and the Middle Class', in Chaudhuri (2008), p. 73.

[43] This internally diverse but outwardly rather exclusive group was the first indigenous governing class—many literary persons of the time were administrators (Bankim, for example, was a district magistrate)—to experience power while being cut off from its source (cf. Chaudhuri 2008, pp. 81–2).

[44] Datta (2003), p. 220.

of Bengali writers and intellectuals no less than it would grip, in another part of the globe, the Slovene intelligentsia in the latter part of the nineteenth century. In the Bengali scenario, however, English became something of an intimate rival:

> What provided a palpable proof of the power of this relationship (between literature and nation) was the speed with which Bangla sahitya rectified its asymmetrical relationship with English, the language of the colonial masters.[45]

Bengali writers who had initially adopted English for their creative expression, most famously Michael Madhusudan Datta (1824–73), would now convert to writing in Bangla, becoming more and more convinced of the expressive power of their own language. With Bengali works being published—and sold—in England for the first time, there was also a growing sense that Bengali language had an international future at hand.[46] Tagore's winning of the Nobel Prize in Literature in 1913, largely for his own English translations of poems and songs from the original Bengali,[47] was to enable Bengali literature scale previously unimaginable heights of international acclaim. But the fact that a disconcerting number of reviewers in Britain, and elsewhere, did not even know, nor were they interested in knowing, that Tagore was a *Bengali* writer, someone who wrote poetry and creative prose in Bangla,[48] undercut the aspirations for Bengali's international future, as it also foreshadowed the anxieties

---

[45] Datta (2003), p. 221.

[46] Bankimchandra Chatterjee's novel *The Poison Tree: A Tale of Hindu Life in Bengal*, translated by Miriam S. Knight, for example, was published in London by T. Fisher Unwin in 1884. See Datta (2003), p. 221.

[47] Strictly speaking, and as recently argued by Michael Collins, Tagore did not receive the Nobel Prize exclusively for the small volume of 103 poems of his English *Gitanjali: Song Offerings*, but also on the basis of his other works, *The Gardener* (1913), *Lyrics of Love and Life* (1913), *Glimpses of Bengal Life* (1913). The committee apparently even had access to Tagore in the original Bengali (cf. Collins 2012, pp. 57–8).

[48] See Kundu, Bhattacharya, and Sircar (2000) for the various newspaper responses, where some critics even thought that the *Gitanjali* was originally written in English.

about the hegemony of English that inform the language debate in India to this day. Nonetheless, the optimism for, and the excitement over, the potential of Bangla sahitya to earn 'its nation widespread recognition'[49] (and the conflation of Bengali with 'nation' should not be missed here) was running strong towards the end of the nineteenth century, and this optimism was closely linked to notions that seek in literature a repository for nationhood. The recent and mixed origins of the Bangla sahitya, however, did not make it an easy site to possess or to control,[50] and its heterogeneity was not easily reconcilable with the dictates of a nationalism that sought its legitimacy in notions of pure and ancient origins (provided, ironically, by British Orientalism).

Tagore, for one, seemed unperturbed by the mixed origins of modern Bengali literature, a product of the 'East–West' encounter that had led to the adoption of literary genres and forms previously unknown to the Bengali world of letters (the novel, the essay, the pamphlet). In any case, it was in Bengali literature that he identified the primary vehicle for the spread of English education. Moreover, Bengali literature was an essential and willing 'accomplice' in the vitalizing project of furthering the circulation and production of new knowledge, both 'ancient' and 'modern' that came with the new medium of English. In 1895, in a lecture entitled 'Bangla Jatiya Sahitya' ('Bengali National Literature'), as if to appease the mounting anxieties of his compatriots, Tagore spoke thus:

> [I]t is not as though English education has spread through the English language. Its real support is now Bengali literature. Bengalis had once helped establish English rule in India; in today's India, Bengali literature is the principal help in furthering the dominion of English ideas and knowledge. It was when English ideas found easy passage through Bengali literature, at home and outside, that we consciously began to seek freedom from a blind servility to English culture. English education is now inextricably fused with our society; we have thus acquired the

---

[49] Datta (2003), p. 221.

[50] Women provided a much easier site, as Datta (2003) points out. For the discussion of women becoming the privileged site in nationalist discourses as the preserve and embodiment of the 'inner' domain untouched by colonialism, see, amongst others, Chatterjee (2002), T. Sarkar (2001), and Sinha (1995).

right to judge freely what in it is good and what evil, what is major and what minor.... English education has vitalised the Bengali mind, and reliance on the Bengali mind has invigorated that education itself.[51]

The case was thus put forward for assimilating imported ideas. The strong sense of entitlement to the ideas, regardless of their origins; the need for discriminating between critical engagement as opposed to blind acceptance; and finally an acknowledgement of the synergy developed between the two ideational realms—all give Tagore's analysis a pragmatic confidence grounded in seeing *both* spheres of contact as equally legitimate and in need of close cooperation. This confidence mixed with idealism, which Tagore clearly possessed, was, more generally, the lot of the *earlier* nineteenth-century intellectuals responding to the colonial encounter.[52] For indeed 'since the beginning of the century, English could be seen as forming a part—undoubtedly a highly problematic and internally conflicted one—of a cultural continuum with Bengali.'[53]

It is therefore not surprising to see Tagore in his speech on Bengali national literature evoking, once again, his predecessor Roy and singling him out as the key figure behind the vital push towards a more open, tolerant, and inclusive modernity through the endorsement and development of prose—the most suitable medium, according to Tagore, for imparting education and disseminating knowledge, and one that Bengali literature sorely needed. For at the heart of literature, Tagore pointed out, as its etymological root *sahit*—meaning together—in the word *sahitya* suggests, is the idea of union. Literature can therefore provide the channel through which ideas, languages, and individuals can come into contact with one another and unite across time and space.[54] In this, prose was needed as much

---

[51] Translated by Swapan Chakravorty, Tagore (2001f [1895]), pp. 185–6. The lecture was delivered at the annual meeting of the Bengal Academy of Literature, founded in 1893 and later known as Bangiya Sahitya Parishad.

[52] For a while at least, nineteenth-century Bengali intellectual circles thrived on 'that distinctive combination of utilitarianism, strong positivism and social evolutionism', as they engaged with various European philosophers and social theorists, from John Stuart Mill, August Comte to Herbert Spencer and articulated their critical social commitments (cf. Bhatt 2001, p. 28).

[53] Datta (2003), p. 229.

[54] Translated by Swapan Chakravorty, Tagore (2001f [1895]), p. 179.

as poetry, since it was well suited to 'discourse on all matters to all people'[55] and therefore relevant to the new temperament of the age as Tagore perceived it. Raja Rammohun Roy is accredited with laying the ground for Bengali prose through his Bengali translations of religious texts (Vedantasutras, Brahmasutras, and the Upanishads). This impulse that was to usher in 'a new age' of modernity in Bengal, Tagore understood as coming from Rammohun's 'genuine respect for [the common people]' whom he did not think 'unworthy' of having access to this storehouse of knowledge.[56] Tagore can be seen here to continue the discourse that was begun by Bankimchandra in the 1870s for the need of a 'popular literature' in Bengal that would cut across the divide between the elites and the common people.

This was another vital component to what Datta has termed 'situated universalism',[57] where the heterogeneity of one's (literary) identity was evolved and created through the other, be it the colonizer or the lower strata of one's own society. But as culturo-religious nationalism was gathering momentum from 1870s onwards, the self-assured heterogeneity of the literary and linguistic space began to be displaced by the quest for a different confidence—a strong Bengali, Hindu identity. For inasmuch as the confidence and idealism of the new Bengali middle class was spurred by the spirit of nationalism, it was also affected by communal pride. Theirs was a 'bounded heterogeneity', and Bangla sahitya was not without its outward limits.[58]

Bankim's own novels in the wake of his indigenist turn[59] were highly influential in articulating a didactic aesthetic of Hindu

---

[55] Translated by Swapan Chakravorty, Tagore (2001f [1895]), p. 182.

[56] Translated by Swapan Chakravorty, Tagore (2001f [1895]), p. 183. It is precisely these kinds of arguments that have led scholars, for example Van Biljert (2003), to draw close parallels between Indian modernity and European Reformation.

[57] Translated by Swapan Chakravorty, Tagore (2001f [1895]), p. 229.

[58] Translated by Swapan Chakravorty, Tagore (2001f [1895]), p. 223. Literary histories of the time, an incredibly important genre for fashioning notions of the past, were largely silent on Muslim literary figures. For Muslim literary modernity, see N. Bose (2011).

[59] Bankim's writings tend to be seen as falling into two distinct phases: his earlier writings visibly demonstrating a humanist and reformist bent with narratives of social and gender equality, and his later ones ostensibly

nationalism with the idealization of the 'motherland' and the 'Hindu nation', portrayed as at once long-suffering and resilient. It would be unfair, however, to lay the blame for what was effectively an anti-universalist turn entirely at Bankim's doorstep. From the way in which these notions were quickly internalized, it seems more accurate to regard his input as fulfilling a pressing social need:

> The speed with which alali bhasha [a variety of idioms taken from colloquial speech, which Bankim had initially introduced as a vital component of modern literary Bengali] was snuffed out can only be explained by the sort of Bengali identity that was seen as desirable. This had little in common with alali bhasha. Its association with the lowly speech of women folk—accentuated by its ability to articulate the registers of street language—did not fit in with the desire to acquire a high status for Bengali.[60]

The need to acquire a high status for Bengali was matched by, or rather reflected in, Bankim's struggle in his later novels to represent 'an ideal national subject'. With the privileging of religion over literature as the main source of collective identity—mainly because the devotional aspect of religion offered a sense of 'a purer ideality', which was not unnecessarily complicated with questions and doubts[61]—this ideal of the national subject was conflated with the Bengali Hindu identity, now articulated in opposition to, rather than through, the other (the British *and* the Muslim). This also held profound implications for intercultural relationships. The positive belief in mutual intelligibility and appropriability of cultures was overwritten by an emphasis on impenetrable boundaries and incommensurability of India and 'the West' as two irreducibly particularistic traditions. Situated universalism was to become a thing of the past. Or was it?

It is precisely in this setting of the 1880s that Tagore made his entry on to the Bengali literary scene as someone whose views and convictions

---

championing a Hindu exclusivist nationalism pitted against the Muslims and accompanied by a muting of his earlier writings on gender equality; see Bhatt (2001), pp. 26ff.

[60] Datta (2003), p. 226.

[61] Datta (2003), pp. 230ff.

continued to support the 'liberal universalism' of former times. His distance from the revivalist, cultural, nationalist project can already be gleaned from an essay he wrote in the 1890s. One of the enterprises that (romantic) nationalism launched was collecting proverbs, folk tales, songs, and nursery rhymes. This was one way the English-educated Bengalis strove to address the widening gap between the rural and urban cultures, a concern Tagore was to share. The idea was to try and bring the 'low' oral and folk traditions within the fold of 'high' elite culture. Here are Tagore's opening lines to his essay on nursery rhymes, a form that most considered unworthy of serious literary scrutiny:[62]

> For some time now, I have been collecting the rhymes current in Bengali in which women divert children. These rhymes may have a special value in determining the history of our language and our society; but to me, their simple natural poetic strain seems more worthy of regard.[63]

Although Tagore can see the importance of the nationalist enterprise of raising awareness about folk culture—the 'special value' of nursery rhymes for the 'history of our language and our society'—no sooner does he acknowledge this agenda, than he removes himself from the historical interest in them to articulate a purely literary admiration for what he calls 'simple' and 'natural' in them. The significance of what may seem an inconsequential shift in focus has been pointed out by Amit Chaudhuri, who aptly underscores here Tagore's privileging of the literary (the poetic, the expressive, the intangible) over the more authoritarian field of the discursive and the linear.[64] Tagore, in his essay, 'is not speaking up for Bengali nursery rhymes as an Indian nationalist but as a modern'; what interests him is not 'national identity and its prestige, but the realm that lies beyond justification.'[65]

[62] I am tempted to see in Tagore's enthusiasm for the nursery rhymes, that were probably composed by women and passed on orally down the generations, his bringing in, through the back door, the feminine component that Bankim had introduced into 'high' literary Bengali with *alali bhasha* but then erased.

[63] Translated by Sukanta Chaudhuri, Tagore (2001e [1894]), p. 100.

[64] Datta, too, points out that 'Tagore emphasized the autonomy of the literary' (2003, p. 240).

[65] Chaudhuri (2008), p. 23.

In this section, we have tried to understand not just the hybrid—and cosmopolitan—context of the 'Bengal Renaissance', and Tagore's place in it, but also the hybrid context out of which modern Bengali language and literary 'high' culture emerged. The new vernacular culture that Tagore confidently envisioned was intended to be cosmopolitan, not parochial, and this is reflected as much in his refashioning of Bengali as it is in his endorsement of English (further discussed in the next chapter). Of course, this is not to suggest that the parochial and the cosmopolitan in relation to the vernacular fall neatly on the side of pre- and post-Tagore era (or, for that matter, pre- and post-colonization age), any more than they can be seen as totalizing forces of any one culture at any one given time. Cosmopolitanism had better be seen as one of the tendencies existing within a given culture; more precisely as 'a mode of literary (and intellectual, and political) communication' that stimulates an awareness beyond one's immediate environment.[66] Certainly cosmopolitanism was not newly discovered either by Tagore or the modern Bengali intelligentsia; they were merely 'rearranging and redirecting a much older tradition of linguistic and cultural versatility'.[67] This relocation, however, was at once an expansion (through appropriations of European-derived forms) and a narrowing from the twin sources of Sanskrit and Arabic–Persian cosmopolitan literary spheres to a more exclusively Sanskrit-based orientation. Towards the end of the nineteenth century, the Bengali literary high culture whose history was once rooted in 'lively transactions' between the Hindu and Islamic literary traditions, also transformed under the colonial impact 'to become a more solidly Hindu sphere'.[68]

Reform, Revival, and Worldliness

Those who wish to sit, shut their eyes,
and meditate to know if the world's true or lies,
may do so. It's their choice. But I meanwhile
with hungry eyes that can't be satisfied
shall take a look at the world in broad daylight.[69]

[66] Pollock (2000), p. 539.

[67] Kaviraj (2003), p. 531.

[68] Kaviraj (2003), p. 531.

[69] 'Against Meditative Knowledge', translated by Ketaki Kushari Dyson in Tagore (2010a [2003]), p. 118.

This poem, written in the 1890s, is just one illustrative example of a number of poems Tagore wrote at around the same time, which, in a similar vein, refute the philosophy of renunciation of the influential Shankara, the eighth-century philosopher and theologian of Vedantic monism, in favour of a full participation in worldly affairs.[70] Tagore in this poem also, in something of a rebellious tone, lays out his intention—and right—to look at the world critically ('in broad daylight') with eyes that will not be sated easily, if at all. The premium he puts on a fresh—and independent—way of seeing the world is obvious.

In this, Tagore is again a disciple of Rammohun Roy, who in 1822 started a reform movement that promoted monotheism based on the Upanishads, opposing ritualistic practices of the Hindu orthodoxy, and which Tagore's father Debendranath, after an intense spiritual experience beside his dying grandmother, revived decades later. The Brahmo Samaj—a society worshipping 'a universal and formless Divinity that informs all life and being', the Brahma[71]—as it was renamed in 1843, continued Roy's opposition to idol worship and the caste system of the Hindu orthodoxy, though Debendranath was more a religious rather than a social reformer. In this he differed from the movement's 'founder' Roy as he also differed from him on some of the finer points of religious interpretation.[72] However, Debendranath's instrumental role in passing on the love of the Upanishads to his son Rabindranath, who daily recited its verses as a young boy and drew on their wisdom throughout his adult life, cannot be overstated.[73]

Roy's attacks on ritual formalism were underpinned by his non-dualistic—Advaita—reading of the Vedanta. Central to his reworking of Upanishadic Hinduism was the belief that 'the individual human soul is also of the same substance with the indivisible unity of the godhead (Brahma)'.[74] In arguing for the essential unity of the self

[70] See, for example, 'Renunciation' from the same collection *Chaitali* (Chaitra Harvest, 1896) as the poem cited above, or the poems 'On the Doctrine of Maya' and 'Play' from *Sonar tari* (The Golden Boat, 1894), in Tagore (2010a [2003]), pp. 113, 104.

[71] Kripalani (2001 [1986]), p. 7.

[72] Collins (2012), pp. 29–31; Sartori (2008), pp. 114–16.

[73] For Debendranath's influence on his son in this respect, see Hatcher (2011).

[74] Sartori (2008), p. 78.

with the Supreme Soul, Roy evoked Shankara, but he departed from Shankara's theology in at least one crucial sense. For Shankara, the spiritual discipline of direct contemplation of the Supreme Soul was a path available only to the Brahman renouncer (*sannyasi*), but for Roy it presented 'a universal path of salvation.'[75] If nothing mediates between the individual and the Universal then it follows that nothing should stand in the way of the relation between individual man and universal humanity. The revolutionary thrust of this proclamation is evident in that it cuts out the mediators (religious institutions and the self-serving priestly caste) and institutes the *individual* in a direct relationship to universal truth.[76]

If spiritual and intellectual independence of the householder—and Brahmo universalism is also not without its limits—was of central concern to Roy, the other aspect reflected in Tagore's poem and one that can also be traced back to Roy is the idea of worldliness that is not incompatible with a spiritual search. Tagore, unlike his own father, could not accept the negation of worldliness as the condition for individual emancipation and release: 'Deliverance is not for me in renunciation/I feel the embrace of freedom in a thousand bonds of delight.'[77]

Tagore is often seen to have combined in his outlook the temperaments of both his worldlier grandfather, 'Prince' Dwarkanath,[78] and

[75] Sartori (2008), p. 80.

[76] In function, this is essentially indistinguishable, Sartori argues, from the way British liberals used anticlericalism and anti-Catholicism to speak up for freedom of conscience and the individual right to pursue rational self-interest. It is also what lends validity to seeing in Roy's reinterpretation of Advaita Vedanta 'a doctrine of liberal egalitarianism'; see Sartori (2008), pp. 81–2.

[77] Poem no. 73, Tagore (2004a [1912]), p. 191.

[78] Tagore's grandfather, Dwarkanath Tagore (1794–1846), is considered to be India's first major industrialist. He was an astute businessman under whom the family fortune was made through acquiring large agricultural estates in Bengal and Orissa. He was also a lavish entertainer of his European friends (for which he earned himself the title 'Prince'). A close friend of Rammohun Roy, he stood on the side of social reform and unorthodoxy. He generously supported public charities, and many cultural and educational institutions such as the Hindoo College (later Presidency College), the Asiatic Society of

his more spiritually inclined father, Debendranath, known, in contrast, as the 'Maharshi', meaning the great seer. But the entrepreneur-meets-sage model also reflects a more fundamental impulse underlying Brahmoism—the need to combine spirituality with worldliness.

Brian A. Hatcher has written pertinently that what lay at the core of Brahmo theological vision was the theme of the 'godly householder'—someone who is after 'spiritual comfort and worldly happiness'.[79] The ideal was thus no longer the ascetic renouncer of classical Hinduism, the samnyāsin, who turns his back upon the world, but the brahmanistha grhastha—the godly householder who engages with life's affairs and whose personal experience becomes the ultimate arbiter of religious truth.[80] 'The trick is to remain in touch with ultimate reality while engaged in one's worldly affairs'.[81] Worldliness thus becomes a central part of the rational spiritual practice of the householder. Individual property—that universalist category of capitalist modernity[82]—is an interesting case in point.

For Tagore, private property and spiritual welfare did not need to be in conflict, provided there was an observed social ethics and responsibility to private ownership. A man who owned a number of houses could hardly be averse to private ownership per se. According to him, property was something fundamentally linked to 'human nature'—'a medium for the expression of our personality'.[83] At the same time, recognizing the 'tendency towards extravagance' also as being 'natural in man', he understood that property could easily become 'anti-social' and 'intensely individualistic', a vehicle not for 'social ethics' but for ostentatious display of wealth, begetting envy, irreconcilable class

---

Bengal, and the National Library of Calcutta owe something to Dwarkanath's financial assistance. In defiance of Hindu strictures that forbade sea travel, Dwarkanath journeyed to Europe twice, met Queen Victoria in England and Max Müller in Paris, and like Rammohun Roy some years before him in Bristol, he too died away from India, in London, a decade before the Revolt of 1857 (cf. Kripalani 2001, pp. 4–8).

[79] Hatcher (2008), p. 99.
[80] Hatcher (2008), p. 25.
[81] Hatcher (2008), p. 99.
[82] On this, see Sartori (2008), pp. 231ff.
[83] Tagore (2002g [1930]), p. 623.

divisions and conflict.[84] Still, he was far from agreeing with those who thought that eradicating property could be a path to achieving freedom and social equality (the lecture on wealth and welfare was delivered in 1930). For Tagore, the ideal was that the house as property comes second to the household as a field of spiritual discipline, and this ideal he located within the larger Hindu tradition: 'the home of the Indian has never been looked upon as his castle, the place where he is lord and master'.[85] In the Hindu scheme of things, the household is something to be given up eventually. Tagore will extrapolate this argument to mount a further criticism against mastery and ownership also of territory, women, and nation.

The ethics of worldly responsibility Tagore is seen to be uphold- ing in his attitude towards property is, no doubt, part of the bigger picture of Brahmo theology that strove to reconcile the worldly and the earthly with the divine purpose, thereby legitimizing a claim to worldly goods and earthly life through a kind of spiritualization of materiality and sociality. Tagore's own religio-ethical outlook, his spiri- tual concerns (often expressed in his writings as a search for 'truth') and this-worldly orientation and social engagement (a vital part of his universalism) can be seen to fall within this paradigm, even as Tagore pushed against the limits of Brahmo reformism, particularly on the question of marriage and women.[86]

In seeking a return to the original philosophical monotheism of the Vedas and the Upanishads, Brahmo universalism, on the other hand, owed something to Protestant Christianity (the Unitarians in particular).[87] Thus Meenakshi Mukherjee, for example, sees in it

[84] Tagore (2002g [1930]), p. 624.

[85] Tagore (2002f [1925]), p. 525.

[86] The question of women's choice and desires, for example, the need for women to develop their autonomy on their own terms, rather than under the paternalistic, however benevolent, gaze of their husbands, finds powerful expression in a number of Tagore's short stories, most famously 'The Wife's Letter'. On the question of women in relation to Tagore's novel *Home and the World*, see T. Sarkar (2003).

[87] Again, for the parallels between Christian Reformation and the nineteenth-century Indian intellectual rediscovery and reinterpretation of Vedanta, and on how Hindu (Vedanta) religious modernity became the first vehicle of ideological modernity, see Van Biljert (2003, 2009).

'the most palpable institution through which both the religious and social impact of the West was mediated'.[88] She cannot overstate its significance for shaping Bengali bhadralok culture in the nineteenth-century colonial Bengal. Similarly, Amit Chaudhuri, in line with David Kopf's study of the movement, understands it as 'the most powerful intellectual movement to shape modern, secular India'. This is because:

> In place of a varied, polyphonic, amorphous heterogeneity [of the Hindu gods and goddesses], there was now a unifying, all-encompassing meaning that was capable of accommodating and subsuming what it had replaced; and if this was Brahmo Samaj's reworking of the Hindu religion, it was also Nehru's concept of what India as a nation-state should be.[89]

Certainly, the unity in diversity paradigm[90] that emerges from this reworking of Hinduism exacted a strong hold on Tagore's own socio-cultural imagination—though Tagore found himself ill at ease with the factionalism of the movement and its sectarian community—but he did, as Kopf argues, always return to the universalist philosophical Brahmoism with its bent on reform.[91] In fact, as a Brahmo, Tagore was somewhat of a square peg in a round hole, having stopped school at thirteen and never having pursued the Brahmo professional line of Calcutta intelligentsia ostensibly cut off from the masses.[92] Moreover, the 1866 schism in the movement—Tagore was only five then—between the larger tradition of Brahmo universalism with its reformist propensities advocated, in a radical way, by Keshub Chandra Sen (1838–1884), who enacted the split, and the Adi ('original') Brahmo Samaj's more nationalist leanings and loyalty to their own Hindu culture led by Tagore's father, can be seen as reflected in Tagore's own

---

[88] Mukherjee (2001), p. xii.

[89] A. Chaudhuri (2008), p. 76.

[90] Similarly, the 'unity in diversity' paradigm has since been identified by, for example, Amartya Sen, as the core element of what he calls 'classical nationalism' of Indian anti-colonial thought, and expressed, most influentially, by Jawaharlal Nehru in his *Discovery of India* (Sen 1996, pp. 13–20).

[91] Kopf (1988), p. 297.

[92] Kopf (1988), pp. 292–3.

struggle, at various periods in his life, to position himself between the modernizing alternatives of nationalism and universalism.[93]

This struggle is most memorably fictionalized in the novel *Gora* (1910), in which the eponymous hero undergoes a change from an aggressive Hindu nationalist to an individual freed of abstract, sectarian identifications, who is willing to subject reality to close critical scrutiny, against which an idealized tradition or imagined community cannot bear up. When Gora finds out that he is an orphan of Irish parents who were killed in the Revolt of 1857, and not a Hindu, the myth of pure identities explodes in his face. This marks the end point of his arduous self-searching journey and the beginning of a new, non-sectarian, identity: 'Today I am free,' says Gora famously at the end of the novel, 'Today I have become an Indian—Bharatvarshia. In me there is no hostility towards any community, Hindu, Muslim or Christian. Today I belong to every community of this Bharatvarsha, I accept everyone's food as mine.'[94] But the novel does not just offer a critique of reactionary Hindu ideology. In its quest for an *alternative* modernity, which is neither 'Western' nor purportedly pre-colonial, it also targets 'the sanitized modernity of Brahmo Samaj.'[95] The main characters of the novel, all part of the English-educated Bengali elite, fall within two camps split between a Hindu and a Brahmo household. The forte of Tagore's novel is precisely that it complicates these positions and refuses to see them in simple binary terms.

Within the framework of reactive cultural nationalism evoked by Kopf and located within Adi Brahmoism, to come back to the ideological split within the Brahmo Samaj, we can more readily appreciate why Tagore's father, unlike his own father, never travelled to the West (but travelled extensively in India); why he refused to read letters if

---

[93] Against Sen's zeal for Christianity, Debendranath's group argued for the authority of Hinduism. The various disputes allegedly led to exclusivist conceptions of 'Hindu nationalism', where Hinduism was seen as the basis of national unity in India. For more on the arguments about Hinduism in relation to Christianity and the controversy about whether Hinduism has the resources for universal ethics or not, see Bhatt (2001), pp. 23–6.

[94] Translated by Radha Chakravarty, Tagore (2009), pp. 505–6.

[95] M. Bhattacharya (2003), p. 133. For an excellent analysis of the novel from the perspective of nationalism and identity, with a focus on gender, see R. Chakravarty (2013), pp. 62–76.

they were written in English, and preferred to keep the British and Europeans at bay; and why his orientation was almost exclusively towards raising Bengalis' awareness of their own Hindu cultural heritage.[96] This brings us to the next section dealing more explicitly with cultural and political nationalism, and Tagore's role in it.

Swadeshi and Partition

As nationalist fervour was gathering momentum in the late nineteenth and early twentieth century, the search for a distinctive Indian identity found an outlet in the so-called swadeshi (literally 'of our own country') enterprises. Under Debendranath, the young Tagores stood firm on the question of language in the face of the rising trend of adopting English by the English-educated middle class: Bengali was to be used and cultivated in all affairs of social and personal contact.[97] In his autobiography, *My Reminiscences* (*Jibansmriti*), Tagore lauded this fact, and as an educator, he invariably championed Bengali as the primary language of education on the grounds of it being the natural vehicle capable of engaging the child's whole mind and experiential world. The foundation of education must be in the mastery of one's 'mother tongue', both as a vehicle of creative thought and as a tool of precise (scientific) reasoning.[98] In the realm of politics also, Tagore insisted that the language used at Provincial Conferences (annual political meetings) should be that of the province and not English, as was the common practice. He was concerned about the communication gap between the English-educated leaders and their public.[99] Apparently at the Bengal Provincial Conference in 1895, Tagore pushed for the

[96] See Radhakrishnan and Roychowdhury (2003), p. 30.

[97] Parimal Ghosh identifies this as one aspect of the more general bhadralok cultural position: 'true culture and enlightenment could not be attained through the neglect of one's native language or through aping' (2008, p. 274).

[98] Translated by Surendranath Tagore, Tagore (2003b [1917]), pp. 71–2. See Tagore's first essay on education, 'The Vicissitudes of Education' [1892], where he sets forth a plea for accepting Bengali as a medium of instruction in schools at all stages of education, from primary to university level, in Tagore (1961a [1892]).

[99] Poddar (2004), pp. 50–1.

Bengali language to be used instead of English, but his suggestion was met with stiff opposition: no one, it turned out, was capable of making a speech in Bengali. Tagore then offered to simultaneously translate the conference proceedings. Afterwards, one of the leaders remarked: 'Rabi Babu, your Bengali was wonderful, but do you think that your *chashas* and *bhushas* (meaning peasants and the common people) understood your mellifluous language better than our English?'[100]

In his autobiography, Tagore furthermore writes how his brothers had been awakened to a pronounced nationalism in dress, literature, and music, leading the way in writing patriotic poems and songs.[101] Besides such cultural nationalism, the Tagores also participated in the economic swadeshi, which advocated self-help and self-reliance, intended to rouse the inherent strength of the people or *atmashakti*. On the positive side it fostered the production and consumption of indigenous goods and on the negative it led to the boycott of British products and services. Long before the swadeshi cry was raised throughout the province as a summons to boycott the British goods and schools, the Tagores promoted swadeshi enterprises. As early as 1867, the Hindu Mela, a 'political-cum-cultural festival' was founded by a Brahmo nationalist to bring the attention of the urban bhadralok to the indigenous rather than imported products and bolster national pride. The Mela became an annual event with the support and involvement of the Tagores.[102]

Tagore's elder brother, Jyotirindranath, seems to have been the most reckless and romantic in his schemes to defy foreign rule. Within the Mela, he set up a secret society on the model of the Carbonari, the secret revolutionary groups of the early years of Italian Risorgimento, of which a thirteen-year-old Rabindranath became a member. With the chanting of Vedic hymns, the discussions conducted in whispers and the secret manufacture of matchsticks—an enterprise Tagore gently mocks as one that failed to generate any fire—the society provided more of a romantic release than a consequential political force to resist foreign rule. It was short-lived, not unlike another one of Jyotirindranath's daring schemes in which he established,

---

[100] Rathindranath Tagore (2003 [1958]), p. 17.

[101] Tagore (2003b [1917]), pp. 169–70.

[102] See Radhakrishnan and Roychowdhury (2003), p. 30.

and for a while ran, a steamer line in competition with the British companies—a venture which floundered badly and brought him close to bankruptcy.[103]

With this we begin to appreciate the kind of stimulus and emotionalism Rabindranath was exposed to in his youth as he himself was beginning to emerge in public as a relevant voice, for the most part supporting—and in sympathy with—much of the assertive cultural nationalism of his family. Aged fifteen, he delivered a fiery, anti-British poem at the tenth anniversary of the Hindu Mela and publicly denounced the British Raj for consigning India to a deplorable state of degradation. His gesture coincided with a Durbar held in Delhi in the honour of Queen Victoria, who was just declared 'The Empress of India' (1 January 1877). The country on the other hand was being ravaged by a famine.[104]

Two decades later, in 1896, he inaugurated the singing of 'Bande Mataram' (Hail to the motherland) at the Calcutta session of the Indian National Congress. In what he would later see as a highly problematic poem, written by Bankimchandra Chatterjee for his novel *Anandamath* (1882), India is likened to the Hindu goddess Durga, and its slogan became the rallying cry of the nationalists during the Swadeshi movement.[105] The first half of Tagore's life seems to disprove the predominant image of the poet as someone high above politics, even in the narrow sense. And it was in the Swadeshi movement proper, as it reached its highpoint around 1905–6, that Rabindranath threw himself wholeheartedly into politics.

Opposition to British rule, as we have seen, was expressed in the form of religious, cultural, and social movements. The Indian National Congress—when it was founded in 1885 by a British civilian—although providing a political platform, was 'an extremely moderate annual

---

[103] See Poddar (2004), pp. 8–12.

[104] See Radhakrishnan and Roychowdhury (2003), pp. 30–1.

[105] Eventually Tagore came to dispute the appropriateness of this song for the National Congress because of its strong Hindu bias that would alienate the Muslims and prevent fostering a sense of unity between all communities in India. In a letter to Subhas Chandra Bose in 1937, he wrote: 'The novel *Anandamath* is a work of literature, and so the song is appropriate in it. But Parliament is a place of union for all religious groups, and there the song cannot be appropriate', in Dutta and Robinson (2005, p. 487).

meeting of mostly Hindu politicians'. This fact alone had the consequence of alienating some Muslims.[106] For a long time, the chiefly Hindu Bengali professional middle class that had grown up under the British rule, were loyal supporters of the government, seeing in it the guarantee of its own survival. But with economic opportunities shrinking in the latter part of the nineteenth century and the promises of the rulers failing to materialize, this began to change.

When in 1905 Lord Curzon made the move to partition the province of Bengal into eastern and western parts, his decision gave rise to 'the very first large-scale popular anti-colonial movement since 1857'[107]—the Swadeshi movement. For the first time too, Indian politics saw the emergence of organized urban terrorism. A time of great political turmoil, affecting all segments of society including the rural areas, the Partition of Bengal in 1905 and its aftermath came to occupy something of a landmark in Tagore's life. Many of his most compelling literary works arose out of his engagement with this particular moment in India's history.

Though the official argument for the partition was administrative—the province of Bengal was too large to be efficiently run—and despite there being genuine administrative considerations, the real reason was political, aimed at undermining growing nationalism in Bengal (the Bengali intelligentsia were the most articulate political voice at the time) through the policy of divide and rule. While at Dacca, Lord Curzon planted the seed of separatism by evoking a Muslim-dominated separate province and the unity this would grant the Muslim population.[108] When the partition was formally announced in July 1905, this drew a cry of protest from the politically conscious, Hindus and Muslims alike.[109] Tagore became deeply involved. His son Rathindranath writes:

[106] Bates (2007), p. 110.

[107] Bates (2007), p. 110.

[108] S. Sarkar (1973), pp. 9–18. The Muslims were promised greater opportunities for education and jobs; the Chittagong port of East Bengal was to be made to rival the port of Calcutta. For more on this, see S. Chakravarti (2013), p. 153.

[109] On Muslim swadeshi leaders and Hindu–Muslim relations, see S. Sarkar (1973), pp. 79–82.

> Father took an effective part in the agitation that followed the partition of Bengal. It almost appeared as if one day he emerged out of his seclusion to become overnight the high priest of Indian nationalism. In songs and poems and in trenchant addresses on the public platforms he bitterly attacked Curzon's policy of divide and rule.[110]

It was clear that the ideologues of the partition had overlooked the sense of unity that had come to exist among the Bengalis. On the one hand there were the growing economic disaffections (aggravated by repeated famines and epidemics in the 1890s), and the particularistic interests of the landed gentry and English-educated Hindu intelligentsia,[111] which fuelled the fires of the anti-partition movement, but on the other there was the existence of 'something like a common culture' (the in-bred social hierarchies and regional differences notwithstanding) sustained by literary and folk traditions that made protesters instinctively react against the imperialist tactics to drive a wedge between a people who shared the same language.[112] This common culture (a blend of Hindu, Buddhist, Muslim, and folk elements) is also what provided Tagore with a source of inspiration for his own vision of India. The rich Bhakti tradition, the Baul songs, and medieval Vaishnava poetry, with their emphasis on the oneness of human experience, transcending caste and religion, were all important sources for his reinterpretation of India's past and articulation of a possible future.[113]

The movement itself consisted largely of upper-caste Hindus, many of whom were, like Tagore's family, zamindars with vested interests in

---

[110] Rathindranath Tagore (2003 [1958]), p. 61.

[111] 'Zamindars and landlords, who often had connection with the professional middle classes, resented the fact that now they would have to maintain two "kucharees", one in Calcutta, and other in Dhaka, which would be the capital of the new province. This would entail greater expense and hassle. Even more important, there was the fear that the Permanent Settlement, which had hitherto worked in favour of the landlords, might be revised. Those in the legal profession feared that the Dhaka High Court might overshadow the Calcutta High Court, while academicians based in Calcutta did not welcome the proposal to set up a new University in East Bengal' (Chakravarti 2013, p. 153).

[112] S. Sarkar (1973), pp. 22–5.

[113] Cf. Tagore (2002a [1912]).

the land worked by lower-caste Hindus and Muslims.[114] It must be understood that Bengali bhadralok were the first enthusiastic takers of English education, securing for themselves a privileged position throughout upper India. A new mood of confidence was in the air, derived also from a sense of pride in India's heritage as well as contemporary achievements in arts and sciences, not to mention events abroad, particularly the unexpected Japanese victory over Russia in 1905, which 'blew up the myth of European superiority'.[115] Tagore is said to have taken his pupils at Santiniketan for an impromptu victory parade for the occasion.[116]

The famous opening lines of the Japanese art historian Okakura Tenshin's *The Ideals of the East* (1902) that 'Asia is one'—the manuscript was completed during his stay at the Tagore's family mansion Jorasanko—were also a timely evocation of pan-Asian solidarity vis-à-vis the West.[117] With the influence of the Irish devotee of Swami Vivekananda, Sister Nivedita, who took up the cause of India's freedom with great zeal, confidence in the potential of their own civilization was on the rise. All in all, 'by 1905 the sense of identity was strong enough for partition to provoke widespread anger and lead to a genuine patriotic outburst'.[118]

For a period of three months, Tagore was practically at the forefront of political agitation, composing patriotic songs—seen as his most enduring contribution to the movement and said to be free of jingoism or incitation to hatred or violence[119]—delivering lectures, publishing

[114] See Poddar's analysis of Tagore's anti-imperialist stance from the perspective of the interests of the propertied class dependent on the colonial system. Though a rigorous and important analysis, Poddar's perspective does at times feel overdetermined by the class perspective.

[115] S. Sarkar (1973), p. 8.

[116] Mishra (2012), p. 224. Tagore's son, for example, wrote about the event: 'On the day the Treaty was signed we lit a big bonfire in the middle of our football field and sang songs all night long to celebrate the awakening of Asia' (Rathindranath Tagore 2003 [1958], p. 58).

[117] On this see Bharucha (2006).

[118] S. Sarkar (1973), p. 23.

[119] Poddar (2004), p. 98. The song that subsequently became the national anthem of Bangladesh ('Amar Sonar Bangla') was composed at this time, and what became the national anthem of India ('Jana Gana Mana') was written for the Indian National Congress meeting of December 1911 in Calcutta.

articles, as well as, at one point, heading a huge procession of *rakhi bandhon*[120] through the streets of Calcutta, singing 'Let the lives and hearts of sons/And daughters of my country/Be one'. When the boycott of British goods was announced, Tagore read an article titled 'Abastha o byabastha' (literally 'the situation and the remedy') in which it is clear he supported the strategy, though for him it was not a move intended to 'harm the English', but a means for his countrymen and women to strengthen themselves and through sacrifice come closer to one another.[121] In this paper, Tagore also suggested the setting up of a parallel government.[122] It is therefore not true to maintain, as critics have often done in outlining Tagore's political thought, that he was against the boycott and non-cooperation from the start.[123] It would be truer to say that his position shifted and evolved in response to concrete political developments, and his ideas adjusted accordingly.

If initially Tagore stood more or less united with the founding impetus of the movement that came from strong dissatisfactions with the moderate and abortive politics of the National Congress, the English-educated political elite alienated from the masses, and therefore sought an alternative in a people's movement building on atmashakti, he withdrew all his support once patriotic passions—to which he himself had contributed significant fuel with his songs and

[120] 'Rakhi' is a thread bracelet tied around one's wrist as a symbol of friendship and brotherhood.

[121] From an abstract quoted in Poddar (2004), p. 95.

[122] Sisirkumar Ghosh (2005), p. 8.

[123] 'Boycott' was the name of an Irish estate manager to whom Irish tenants refused to pay taxes, and the word was derived from this aspect of the Irish struggle against British landlords and rulers. The boycott of foreign goods was an extremely important aspect of (economic) swadeshi, since India at the time had little industry and most manufactured goods were imported from Britain. For Britain it made economic sense to keep India in the state of 'agricultural backwater of industrial Britain, supplying raw materials and consuming the finished products', something that did not escape nationalist leaders at the time. Also Bengal could claim for itself 'a proud heritage of manufacturing in earlier ages', particularly of Bengali textile. Swadeshi, therefore 'promised to restore something of the lost economic glory and manufacturing capactity' that cultural and professional achievements compensated for only partially, again see Chakravarti (2013), pp. 154-5.

lectures—took a violent turn. Although he was never to give up his belief in the need to build on self-reliance and autonomous self-development—a belief that in his case predated the political movement by at least two decades—in around 1907 he was to radically re-evaluate some of the ideas that became linked with the emphasis on atmashakti or self-strength/reliance and which, for a short period, also informed his own thinking.[124]

The call for self-reliance and a revival of indigenous institutions became tied up with the use of traditional Hindu symbols and concepts. Stoking up religious sentiments was seen as an effective means of bridging the gulf between the educated and the common people and of galvanizing Bengal into action. The anti-colonial nationalism thus became distinctively Hindu-oriented, and its recourse to a perceived glorious past—a general feature of nationalisms—assumed the form of Hindu revivalism.[125]

Sarkar observes that Tagore's writings between 1901 and 1906 visibly demonstrate a hold of revivalist ideas on his mind, from an attempt to defend some of the time-honoured practices in Hindu society (including caste and sati) to the glorification of India's past and a romanticization of the traditional village, and sees them in an obvious relationship with the political turmoil of the period.[126] It was indeed in this period that Tagore, in defiance of Brahmo reformist

[124] Tagore was on the side of 'constructive swadeshi' in the movement, promoting a trend towards self-development, building on education and promoting indigenous industrial enterprises. But there were also the political extremists who either resorted to boycott or passive resistance in addition to self-help efforts, or those who became terrorists (cf. Sarkar 1973, p. 33). On his own lands as a zamindar he was active in social work with the tenants and had at one time invited some of the revolutionary leaders to take part in his village upliftment work. Their disinterest irritated him as did the gap between the rhetoric and real work (cf. S. Chakravarty 2013, p. 157).

[125] S. Sarkar (1973), p. 48.

[126] S. Sarkar (1973), p. 54. The most discussed essay from the point of view of its revivalist undercurrent, already in Tagore's time, is his 'Swadeshi Samaj', where *samaj* (commonly translated as 'society') is romanticized as the locus of true Indian social polity, and India's future seen to rest in a revival of a truly benevolent Hindu samaj (cf. Tagore 1961b). For further insight, see Bharucha (2006), pp. 55–62; S. Sarkar (1973), pp. 52–7.

precepts, and possibly under the influence of his more conservative father, married off his daughters, aged twelve and fifteen in the traditional Hindu way.[127]

But once Tagore saw concrete outcomes of the alignment of nationalism with Hindu revivalism, particularly as it pushed the frontiers of moderation and entered the sphere of militancy, he would have nothing more to do with the movement. The Hindu–Muslim riots that broke out in parts of East Bengal in the early months of 1907 made him withdraw from every national committee in one day, shocked as he was that 'Muslims were being attacked in the name of swadeshi'.[128] To the consternation of many, he left Calcutta to retreat at Santiniketan for a time of 'deep introspection and auto-critique'.[129] For a period of nine months his political voice went quiet, but when he re-entered the public domain, his views marked a decisive break with his earlier swadeshi writings.

In a series of new essays of 1907–8, he put forth a stringent critique of Hindu social traditions, and urged for the country 'where people are doomed to perdition for drinking water from the hands of a neighbour, where one's caste is to be preserved by insulting that of another' to reassess itself and reform its practices.[130] Of great worry to Tagore became also the communal problem, which he would keep addressing throughout the remaining part of his life. On the one hand, he urged both Hindus and Muslims to overcome their differences by addressing 'defects in their own character', believing that external forces cannot by themselves turn the two communities against each other, unless internal dissensions are already there. And this was combined with a strong appeal to a shared human identity, since the riots threw into sharp relief that using religion as an arbiter of an individual's politically viable identity will lead to disunity and incapacitate a truly 'national' movement:

> The fact remains that we live in the same land, sharing common joys and sorrows. We are human beings; our failure to unite is a shame, a sin. We

---

[127] Kopf (1988), p. 294.

[128] U. Das Gupta (2004), p. 4.

[129] S. Sarkar (2002), p. 119.

[130] Tagore, 'Byadhi o pratikar' (The disease and the cure), cited in Poddar (2004), p. 110.

(Hindus and Muslims) are the children of the same motherland. If in full recognition of this God-given compulsion we do not step forward to jointly shoulder the vicissitudes of the land, then fie on our humanity.... Our sin is England's main strength.[131]

But on the other hand, Tagore had the perspicacity to link Hindu–Muslim dissensions with social and economic issues. He wrote of the disparity between the English-educated, Hindu majority and the larger proportion of low-income Muslims, and recognized the need to secure an adequate share of 'the posts and prestige of government' also for the Muslims, if concord was to be established and jealousies abated.[132] Seeing that colonialism had introduced a new major division into the society, Tagore spoke of the importance to turn to the villages and try and bridge the gap between the educated and the masses that were being left out of the transformation. This concern was already present in the Hindu Mela, but Tagore was now able to delink it from its culturo-religious affiliation and give it a new dimension in his concern for the welfare of everyone, regardless of caste or religion. This involved a profound questioning of a freedom struggle based on swadeshi or top-down Hindu nationalism.

In the novel *The Home and the World* (*Ghare Baire*, 1915–16)—in many ways a sequel to his earlier political novel *Gora* (1910)—Tagore explores the fascination with the more violent strand of nationalist politics through the domestic drama of a love triangle. Set against the background of the Swadeshi movement, and written in the midst of World War I, the story revolves around the aristocratic housewife Bimala, who finds herself in an emotional quandary, caught as she is between her enlightened, self-effacing zamindar husband Nikhilesh and his charismatic friend, the fiery and manipulative nationalist leader Sandip. Bimala's dilemma is as much a personal one as it is suggestive of a political choice she has to make between conflicting ideological stances.[133]

Sandip's usurpatory tactics in the novel—his mantra being 'I want, I want,[134] and wanting in his worldview justifies taking—are

[131] Poddar (2004).
[132] Tagore (1961c [1908]), pp. 105–6.
[133] Cf. Shohini Ghosh (2003), p. 84.
[134] Translated by Sreejata Guha, Tagore (2005a), p. 76.

counterpoised to Nikhilesh's concerns for the welfare of his disad-
vantaged Muslim tenants who cannot afford to practise swadeshism.
Nikhilesh, no doubt voicing Tagore's own evolved outlook, proclaims:
'I want greater things than swadeshi. I do not want a lifeless post, I
want a living tree. My work will take time.'[135] The question of personal
freedom is brought into sharp relief against a nationalism that stifles
individuality. 'The country is not just this land and soil, it is also the
people,' is the answer given to overzealous youths by Chandranathbabu
(Nikhilesh's one-time teacher and a voice of compassionate reason in
the novel) who have come to demand banishment of foreign goods
from the market.

> Have you ever bothered to spare these people a second glance? Today,
> suddenly you have woken up to the fact that you must decide what they'd
> eat and what they'd wear. Why should they tolerate that and why should
> we let them tolerate that?[136]

Clearly, Tagore understood how the colonial political economy had
created unequal dependencies among the different groups in a hierarchical society and how it was often the economically weak who
were more dependent on the colonial system than the better-off. For
them to follow a nationalism imposed from the above was not just a
curtailment of freedom but an existential impossibility:

> You have the money and if you use a few paise more to buy homespun
> goods, they don't come and stop you. But what you want them to do is
> sheer abuse of power. They are caught in the fray of life every single day
> of their lives, struggling to just stay afloat—you cannot even imagine the
> value of a few paise to them—you have nothing in common with them.[137]

This is a strong indictment of 'a nationalism' which, as Ashis Nandy
writes, 'steam-rollers society into making a uniform stand against
colonialism, ignoring the unequal sacrifices imposed thereby on the
poorer and the weaker'.[138] Rather than coercing a top-down 'solution',

---

[135] Translated by Sreejata Guha, Tagore (2005a), p. 138.
[136] Translated by Sreejata Guha, Tagore (2005a), pp. 107–8.
[137] Translated by Sreejata Guha, Tagore (2005a), p. 108.
[138] Nandy (2005b), p. 19.

Tagore's answer advanced constructive work and education, while urging his middle-class compatriots to break out of their insularity and establish contact with the masses:

> Come down into the midst of the people of our country, spread out a network of multifarious welfare activities, expand the scope of your work, broaden it in all directions—so that high and low, Hindus and Muslims and Christians, all without exception can come together, mingling heart with heart, effort with effort.[139]

In the post-swadeshi era, Tagore moved on to advocate patient and sustained constructive work in a few villages to the southwest of Santiniketan. 'There is not the slightest doubt in my mind,' he wrote in 1910, 'that, if any enterprise is to succeed in this country, then the best thing is to start it single-handed on a very modest scale and gradually build it up ... [t]hat is the natural method'.[140] Often regarded as a hopeless idealist, Tagore, one could argue, was in fact staunchly realist, even pragmatist, in his pursuit of ideals: 'I alone cannot take responsibility for the whole of India. But even if two or three villages can be freed from the shackles of helplessness and ignorance, an ideal for the whole of India would be established'.[141] His pleas for constructive work fell largely on deaf ears, regarded as politically inexpedient and a betrayal of his initial enthusiasm for the nationalist movement.

Let us sum up what has been said so far. With the help of Sarkar's chronological assessment, Tagore's prose writings vis-à-vis the turbulent Swadeshi years has helped us understand that Tagore's evolving attitudes towards the national movement were inextricably linked to the movement's developments, and that his position was far more embattled than readings which put him on a timeless pedestal care to portray. Caught between the contradictory pulls of 'modernist' and 'traditionalist' ideas—an ideological conflict that runs throughout the nineteenth century—Tagore is seen to return 'to a basically anti-traditionalist and modernist approach', now underpinned by

---

[139] Tagore, 'Path o patheo' (Ways and means), cited in Sarkar (2002), p. 84.

[140] U. Das Gupta (1991), p. 128.

[141] U. Das Gupta (1991), p. 128.

explicitly stated universalism.[142] If in his swadeshi writings, Tagore dreamt of a synthesis through Hinduism, he now looked towards a broadly defined humanist ideal where barriers of caste and religion separating individuals were pulled down. Indeed, after his break with the nationalists, his vision of India is no longer tied to a Hindu imaginary or glorification of the past but is projected into the future as 'India united on a modern basis transcending all barriers of caste, religion and race'.[143] Such an advocacy of a 'new' India does indeed admit of liberal and secular interpretations, but one should not forget the more poetic and therefore distinctly Tagorean aspect to his evocation. In this, India is not so much a geographical fact, even less so a political one, but an 'Idea' that is 'against the intense consciousness of the separateness of one's own people from others'. It stands rather 'for the co-operation of all peoples of the world'.[144] It is at this point we see Tagore move outside existing perceptions, defining his dissent in starkly individualist terms, to be considered next.

Deterritorializing 'the Nation'

One of the points Tagore would persistently make in his essays and addresses from 1908 onwards is that the arrival of the British in India, though an entirely new chapter in India's history, was not in itself a revolutionary break with it. He pointed out that over millennia various races and peoples had come to occupy and inhabit the geographical space that comprises India's territory. To that end he wanted Indians to recognize that the history of the subcontinent did not belong to one particular race but was recreated time and again through the contributions of various races, the Dravidians and the Aryans, the ancient Greeks, the Persians, and the Muslims. Now that the 'the turn of the English' had come, he said, the Indians had neither 'the right nor the power to exclude this people from building of the destiny of India'.[145] The question of the ownership of the

[142] S. Sarkar (1973), p. 52.
[143] S. Sarkar (1973), p. 85.
[144] Tagore, letter to C. F. Andrews, 13 January 1921, in Andrews (2002), p. 110.
[145] Tagore (2001a [1917]), pp. 423–4. This idea is most famously captured in the poem 'Pilgrimage to India' ('Bharat Tirtha'), written in 1910, see in Tagore (2004b), p. 200.

subcontinent was for Tagore quite irrelevant. 'Whether India is to belong more to the Hindu or to the Muslim, or whether some other race is to achieve a greater supremacy—that is not the problem with which Providence is troubled,' the poet told his students in 1908 in an address later published as 'East and West'.[146] In the same essay, the following striking lines emerge:

> Who are we to say that this country is ours alone? In fact, who is this 'We'? Bengali, Marathi, or Punjabi, Hindu or Muslim? Only the larger 'We' in whom all these—Hindu and Muslim and British and whoever else there be—must eventually unite, shall have the right to determine what is India and what is of the outside.[147]

This quotation completely undermines any conventional idea of *ownership* of a given territory, as it questions the idea of the 'nation' as something already out there, or achieved. It also raises the key question of unity and boundaries. With Homi Bhabha, the '*inter*national dimension' that comes through Tagore's open-ended pluralist 'We', can be seen to fall as much within the 'margins of the nation-space' as 'in the boundaries *in-between* nations and peoples'.[148] The unity Tagore here speaks of is not a fantasy projection of a homogenizing oneness, but an acknowledgement of already existing cultural heterogeneity from which it is then possible to extrapolate an essentially deteritorrialized and open-ended notion of 'India'. The diversity of peoples, languages, and cultures that is India's reality, the 'ambivalent nation-space' in Bhabha's language, is but 'the crossroads to a new transnational culture' suggested by Tagore's 'larger "We"'. This fundamental acceptance of hybridity, which predates the arrival of the British, matched with a reluctance to re-purify oneself for strategic anti-colonial purposes, lies at the core of Tagore's anti-nationalist *and* anti-colonial ideological thrust.

If ownership and territoriality were ultimately inconsequential, what was of consequence to Tagore was that India had throughout her unfolding history, in her own way, succeeded in accommodating diverse races, cultures, and creeds. She may have been flawed

---

[146] Tagore (1961d [1908]), p. 130.

[147] Tagore (1961d), p. 133.

[148] Bhabha (1990), p. 4. See Ch. 1, pp. 32–3.

in dealing with 'the race problem', but in struggling with this 'great difficulty', she tried 'to make an adjustment of races, to acknowledge the real differences between them where these exist, and yet seek for some basis of unity'. India's caste system, Tagore ventured to say, is the outcome of her 'spirit of toleration'. To incredulous Western listeners, he submitted Europe's record of dealing with the indigenous populations in America and Australia to suggest that caste-regulated toleration when pitted against 'the spirit of extermination' that was Europe's solution to the problem of 'race-conflict' left little room for high moral ground.[149] At the same time, Tagore would critique India's model of inclusion-through-hierarchization as a means of attaining social cohesion. He objected to the rigid boundaries set up on racial or other grounds, whereby people's lives were narrowed—'their minds crippled'—so as to fit them into social forms.[150] He deplored India's 'tyrannical social restrictions'.[151] To him the question of political freedom, and hence who ruled India, came second to pressing social issues. India's 'real goal' was 'moral and spiritual freedom for the individual in society'.[152]

Moreover, Tagore was already thinking in terms of a world community, so that the problems plaguing India were not seen as entirely different to those facing the rest of the globe: 'The world-wide problem today is not how to unite by wiping out all differences, but how to unite with all differences intact.'[153] If India, with all its diversity, was, in a sense, 'the world in miniature', then, Tagore felt, the manner in which she deals with the problem could offer a more comprehensive solution, so much so that if India could create a basis of social cooperation instead of exploitation and conflict, she would be in a position to 'infuse the sap of a fuller humanity into the heart of modern civilization'.[154]

How do we read Tagore's allocating India a central place in the unfolding of human civilization? Interpreting some of the same quotes

---

[149] Tagore (2001a [1917]), pp. 459–61.
[150] Tagore (2001a [1917]), p. 419.
[151] Tagore (2001a [1917]), p. 463.
[152] Tagore (2001a [1917]), p. 463.
[153] Tagore (1961e [1911]), p. 146.
[154] Tagore (2001a [1917]), pp. 443, 459.

that set forth Tagore's 'multicultural' reading of India's history, Collins aptly observes that: 'What becomes clear is not simply that Tagorean philosophy is grounded in the ideal of universal man, but that India itself, its civilisation and its history, lies at the centre of an unfolding historical ideal.'[155] Is this the confidence of the *new* humanists who have set out to improve on the failings of the modern Western civilization or is it symptomatic of reactive cultural self-assertiveness, bordering on chauvinism? However we choose to see it, I would suggest to read Tagore's arguably proto-nationalist sentiments here in parallel with his iconoclastic insistence that the British too—or anybody else for that matter—had a part to play in fulfilling the idealistic vision of the changing age. For the 'India' Tagore had in mind, was an India open to all.

Tagore, once again, sought to assert the foundations of his country's complex identity so as to re-imagine India *and* the world—as well as India *in* the world—along open and non-sectarian lines. If ownership and territoriality were categories that needed transcending with respect to 'the nation', this was because Tagore's political philosophy was poised, in no uncertain terms, against the nation-state. His most stringent critique of the cult of the nation came with his lectures on nationalism, published in 1917 as *Nationalism*.[156]

One precept of Western modernity that Tagore refused to accept as an unproblematic given was the nation-state with its ideological corollary of nationalism. To reiterate, for Tagore, the basis of unity for a collective had to be social, rather than political. This led him to distinguish between 'the nation', consistently written out as 'the Nation' (upper case) and taken to mean the nation-state—possibly to stress the universalizing aspect of the concept as well as the dimensions of evil he came to associate with it—and the less restrictive idea of collectivity as embodied in his notion of 'society', which stood for the expression of higher moral and spiritual aspirations of human beings.

Tagore defined 'the Nation' in terms of population welded into a political and economic union for the purpose of commercial self-interest. It was 'the aspect of a whole people as an organized power'

---

[155] Collins (2012), p. 96.
[156] I discuss this book in relation to Kosovel's ideas on nation, nationhood, and nationalism in Ch. 5, pp. 244–7.

and as such an abstraction, subject to impersonal laws.[157] Its objectives were utilitarian and ignoble: efficiency and competition were placed in the service of material greed and power. The supreme ideals were to accumulate and hoard and not expand growth and social development.[158] Nation-states generated wars and resulted in colonialism. Society, on the other hand, had no such ulterior motive but was based on 'natural regulation of human relationships' through individual ties and sensibilities so that the ideals of life could be developed through mutual cooperation.[159] Professionalization versus socialization of a people, organized and mechanical versus natural and human—these are the opposite poles between which Tagore's thinking moves, as he points out that Indian languages have no word for nation and that 'India of no nation' should resist adopting this aspect, or modular form, of modernity.[160]

While Tagore urged Indians to accept what he called 'the spirit of the West' and heed the ideals of social justice and human rights,[161] he condemned in no uncertain terms the politicized and commercialized aspect of the modern civilization that had sprung up from Europe—its 'political civilization' based upon exclusiveness and 'always watchful to keep at bay the aliens or to exterminate them'.[162] Through the cult of nationalism—'its paraphernalia of power and prosperity, its flags and pious hymns, its blasphemous prayers in the churches, and the literary mock thunders of its patriotic bragging'[163]—the Nation exploited mass psychology by legitimizing people's instincts of self-aggrandizement, and imbuing them with an irrational pride in their race and hatred of others. Tagore warned that it is not the crowd but the individual who thinks, and pride tends to lead to moral blindness.[164]

Two things need to be underlined here. First is that Tagore's tirade against 'the Nation' was emphatically global (his lectures on

[157] Tagore (2001a [1917]), p. 421.
[158] Tagore (2001a [1917]), p. 448.
[159] Tagore (2001a [1917]), p. 422.
[160] Tagore (2001a [1917]), p. 429.
[161] I discuss this in more detail in the next chapter, see p. 115.
[162] Tagore (2001a [1917]), p. 440.
[163] Tagore (2001a [1917]), p. 429.
[164] Tagore (2001a [1917]), p. 455.

nationalism targeted nationalisms in Japan, India, and the West), and second that his target of critique was not specifically the British government but 'the government by the Nation' as it 'affects the future of all humanity'.[165] Anti-British sentiments or anti-Western attitudes therefore made little sense to Tagore, whose butt of critique was not the people but the system. 'Our government,' he explained, 'might have been Dutch, or French, or Portuguese, and its essential features would have remained much the same as they are now'.[166] Anticipating thus the postcolonial critiques of the nation, he foresaw the danger that an 'alien government' may take the shape of 'our own countrymen',[167] as one elite substitutes another. He was also rightly suspicious of the nationalists' motives: 'Your main motive is hatred of the foreigner, not love of country'.[168] Unlike the latter-day Marxists, Tagore did not place his trust in a simple change of system or turnover of classes as a way of addressing historical wrongs and anticipating future salvation.[169] His search for liberation was altogether more ambitious, because in refusing to surrender to a position of victimhood, it demanded moral introspection and adjustment on the part of everyone.

Nationalism was endemic to the world, and Tagore condemns every variety of it, including the anti-colonial one. Some saw in this an inadvertent apology for British imperialism, but Tagore could not have been fiercer in denouncing imperialism too. Reading *Nationalism* carefully, we see that for Tagore imperialism and nationalism were two sides of the same coin, or—as Kopf had put it in line with Tagore's own rhetoric—'two faces of the same monster'.[170]

Another problem of the nation-state in Tagore's view is that it deludes people into thinking they are free, but having political freedom

[165] Tagore (2001a [1917]), p. 423.

[166] Tagore (2001a [1917]), p. 424. Tagore, in his polemic with Gandhi in 1921, said 'Alien government in India is a kind of chameleon. Today it is seen in the guise of the Englishman, tomorrow it may take the form of some other foreigner, and the following day, its malignity unabated, it will bear the semblance of our own countrymen' (Tagore 1961j, p. 255).

[167] Tagore, 'The Call of Truth', rejoinder to Gandhi, 1921, in S. Bhattacharya (2005), p. 71.

[168] S. Bhattacharya (2005), p. 70.

[169] See on this, Kopf (1988), p. 305.

[170] Kopf (1988), p. 305.

does not automatically guarantee freedom; it merely ensures power. 'Not merely the subject races,' he would declaim, 'but you who live under the delusion that you are free, are every day sacrificing your freedom and humanity to the fetish of nationalism, living in the dense poisonous atmosphere of world-wide suspicion and greed and panic'.[171] Only those willing to extend freedom to others are themselves free.[172] The nation-state, though ostensibly holding up the values of freedom, undermines those very values in its treatment of 'others'. It creates 'huge organizations of slavery in the disguise of freedom'.[173] In the Swadeshi movement too, Tagore saw how easily *real* freedom is sacrificed in the cause of political freedom.

In the final instance, Tagore's social philosophy moved outside the framework of freedom being tied to political and territorial sovereignty. There is something patently exclusivist in upholding the ideals of human justice and freedom and then confining them to closely guarded territorial units. In this, Tagore can be seen to reject the dominant Western notion of citizenship linked to the nation-state and offered as *the* way in which people gain equal status and freedom.[174] The cataclysmic events of World War I, against which Tagore wrote *Nationalism*, were for him proof enough of the ultimate self-destructiveness of the organized modern nation. He sought to understand the deeper logic behind why people are driven to kill each other:

> If you want me to take to butchering human beings, you must break up that wholeness of my humanity through some discipline which makes my will dead, my thoughts numb, my movements automatic, and then from the dissolution of the complex personal man will come out that abstraction, that destructive force, which has no relation to human truth, and therefore can be easily brutal or mechanical.... Turn a tree into a log and it will burn for you, but it will never bear living flowers and fruit.[175]

[171] Tagore (2001a [1917]), pp. 426–7.

[172] For more on freedom in connection with independence, underpinned by Upanishadic philosophy, see discussion on pp. 118–20 in the next chapter.

[173] Tagore (2001a [1917]), p. 462. See also Tagore's play, *Red Oleander* (*Rakta-karavi*, 1926), which mounts a strong defence of freedom against a terror-projecting power on the one hand and a soul-wrecking conformism on the other, Tagore (2001j [1924]).

[174] See Purkayastha (2003), pp. 49–50.

[175] Tagore (2001a [1917]), p. 432.

What terrified Tagore was 'an abstraction', which was 'ready to ignore living reality',[176] as he put it elsewhere, and the 'Nation' to him was such an abstraction. He compared it to a powerful anaesthetic that dulled one's sense of moral responsibility and could easily lead to terrible crimes.[177]

Taking lessons from nature, Tagore observed that all living things are easily hurt and therefore require protection. What truly protected human beings in his view were spiritual ideals that were vitally connected with life.[178] He acknowledged that in human relations, self-love and self-interest do have a part to play, but as essentially baser traits, they remain dangerously incomplete if not counterbalanced by 'higher instincts of sympathy and mutual help'.[179] While self-respect is important, it cannot be allowed to degenerate into egoism. We have seen how in his Swadeshi days he made a powerful appeal to his people to stand together in self-respect and self-reliance, but he would not tolerate chauvinism and violence.

'Man in his fullness is not powerful, but perfect [and] when we are fully human, we cannot fly at one another's throats; our instincts of social life, our traditions or moral ideals stand in the way'.[180] And these ideals, he would further argue, owned no geographical boundaries, and were part of the spiritual heritage of both 'East' and 'West'.[181]

As can be more readily appreciated now, Tagore had to withdraw from a nationalist ethos to re-imagine a world guided by relationships different to those mandated by self-interest and 'national self-seeking'. At the core of his moral philosophy was the belief that 'men are so closely knit that when you strike others the blow comes back to yourself'.[182] This led him to predict the eventual demise of nation-states and nationalisms in anticipation of a time when human beings will

---

[176] Tagore, in a letter to C. F. Andrews, in which Tagore polemicizes with Gandhi's Non-cooperation Movement, calling it 'political asceticism', in S. Bhattacharya (2005), p. 58.

[177] Tagore (2001a [1917]), p. 434.

[178] Tagore (2001a [1917]), p. 446.

[179] Tagore (2001a [1917]), p. 454.

[180] Tagore (2001a [1917]), p. 431.

[181] Tagore (2001a [1917]), p. 442.

[182] Tagore (2001a [1917]), p. 447.

be reborn in the freedom of their individuality.[183] Given that these predictions have not yet come true, it is perhaps necessary to see his utopian construction of samaj in its proper place as 'a politics of hope'.[184]

Indeed, the strength of Tagore's position lies in that he spoke up for *individual* rather than national rights, and held on to the values of universalism in the face of fierce nationalist pressures. We are reminded once again of Gora's painful transition, where 'Indianness', in Bharucha's cogent analysis, meant a birth of 'an inner self ... ready to embrace the universe' rather than 'a politically determined self'[185] circumvented by caste, creed, and—we might add—nation.

The fact that Tagore opposed British rule, but was not anti-British, that he rejected anti-colonial nationalism as a viable stand against British imperialism, is what made him amenable to charges of denationalized Anglophilism, or insufficient patriotism, or even imperialism—unstated assumptions that also inform also more recent writings.[186] The idea that you had to be a nationalist in order to be anti-colonial/imperialist has also made scholars reluctant to uncouple Tagore from the designation 'nationalist'.[187] Tagore's 'nationalism' is obligatory, as it were. Of course, a paradox presents itself here. How can the *foremost builder of a national culture*, as Partha Chatterjee has referred to Tagore recently, be at one and the same time also 'one of the most vociferous critics of nationalism'? [188]

My question here is why do we have to presume that Tagore was a builder of a *national* culture in the first place? It is clear that Tagore's wholesale repudiation of the modern idea of the nation-state, which

[183] Tagore (2001a [1917]), p. 435.

[184] Bharucha (2006), p. 109.

[185] Bharucha (2006), p. 64.

[186] The problem seems to lie in the assumption, as identified by Sarkar, that 'the entire field of early-twentieth-century Bengal (and Indian) history was, or should have been, occupied by the single colonial/anti-colonial binary' (S. Sarkar 2002, p. 117).

[187] See, for example, two recent engagements with Tagore's views on nationalism and his standing as a 'nationalist'—Mukhopadhyay (2013) and Indra Nath Choudhuri (2013).

[188] P. Chatterjee (2011), emphasis mine, p. 116.

Chatterjee takes fully on board, presents 'a serious problem' to him.[189] In his view, Tagore's critique of the nation (state) is that it is at once too one-sided and too absolute, seen 'from a rather narrow and limited angle', for there are aspects of nation building that cannot simply be dismissed as 'mechanical' or 'interest-driven', the point Tagore indeed harps on in his critique of the nation state. This time with an explicit nod to Benedict Anderson, Chatterjee contends: 'It is striking how much of our personal and even intimate lives—our habits and desires—are shaped by the literature, art, music, or advertising produced within the imagined community of the nation.'[190] Though he takes Tagore's 'trenchant critique of nationalism' seriously, he fails to see how Tagore's political thinking could be relevant to the 'purposes of contemporary postcolonial world',[191] beyond it being an 'attractive' *aesthetically* motivated intellectual critique of modernity, propelled by an 'urge for universality'.[192]

It would be hard to disagree with Chatterjee that Tagore's political thinking cannot be made sense of from within a Marxist framework of critical thinking, nor with the assumption that Tagore's project for an alternative community in two or three villages premised on interpersonal bonds of cooperation and mutual help, could realistically offer a viable alternative to the large imagined community of the nation. Yet while these might all be considered serious problems, the question remains, why would Tagore even have wanted an alternative to something he did *not* ultimately acknowledge as legitimate or desirable. It seems to me that the problem lies elsewhere: in the difficulty to nowadays think of Tagore's 'political thinking' from outside the limits of a 'nationalist' framework or the dictates of the 'nation game'.[193] I do not for a moment believe that Tagore was self-consciously, or intrinsically, a 'builder of a *national* culture',[194] a culture he thought dangerous,

---

[189] P. Chatterjee (2011), p. 116.

[190] P. Chatterjee (2011), p. 109.

[191] P. Chatterjee (2011), p. 122.

[192] P. Chatterjee (2011), p. 108.

[193] For how nationalist frameworks have become the meta-narrative of so much of academic and intellectual pursuit as well, see previous chapter, pp. 21–3.

[194] Emphasis mine.

since 'India' for him was emphatically a 'no-nation'.[195] Rather I see him agreeing with the following statement of a historian who has been most rigorous in identifying the nationalist bent of (Indian) historiography itself:

> [I]t is futile to search for a serviceable nationalism that is less than exclusionary or oppressive; nationalisms draw boundaries of inclusion and exclusion, impose belonging and non-belonging, and police these. Nationalism, even when it is a search for unifying factors, ends up squeezing or coercing identities towards neat formulations that inevitably exclude.[196]

Indeed, whether serving imperialist aggression or liberation movements, for Tagore nationalist ideologies resulted in social exclusion, entrenched hierarchies, and led to violence.

Tagore knew full well that his alternative to anti-colonial nationalism was out of tune with the prevalent mood of his times, alienating as it did both the extremists and the orthodox. Like Nikhilesh at the end of *The Home and the World*, he too must have felt pangs of abandonment but resolved to carry on with his self-designated path:

> My trial is hard indeed. Just when I want a helpmate most, I am thrown back on myself alone. Nevertheless, I record my vow that even in this trial I shall win through. Alone, then, shall I tread my thorny path to the end of this life's journey.[197]

The novel ends tragically in the midst of communal violence with Nikhilesh's life hanging in the balance and with the young Amulya dead—'He took a bullet in the chest. He is no more',[198] a sinister foreboding of Gandhi's fate at the hands of extremism. Its author, however, carried on with the work of education of the Hindu and Muslim tenants in his family's agricultural estates, a project he later developed into the Sriniketan rural upliftment programme based on promoting

---

[195] P. Chatterjee (2011). See also Bharucha's retort to Chatterjee's politically realist critique of Tagore's views on nation (2006, pp. 105–11). For Chatterjee's earlier contributions to the debate, see also his other works (2003, 2004).

[196] Zachariah (2011), pp. 250–1.

[197] Tagore (2005a), p. 197.

[198] Tagore (2005a), p. 211.

agricultural economy.[199] The start of Tagore's project more or less coincided with Gandhi's launch of the Non-cooperation Movement, the next mass anti-colonial nationalist movement after Swadeshi had gone into decline in around 1908. Tagore found himself once again reiterating his belief in a constructive programme, this time directly at odds with the basic principle of non-cooperation and the boycott of British goods and institutions. Ultimately, he was unable to accept the negative tenets of non-cooperation (which to him was a form of 'political asceticism'), and in his polemic with Gandhi (further discussed in the next chapter), it is clear that Tagore harboured no illusions about the 'anti-political'[200] choice he had taken, the only choice suited to his temperament and convictions:

> If you cannot keep step with your countrymen at the great crisis of their history, never say that you are right and the rest of them are wrong; only give up your role as a soldier, go back to your corner as a poet, be ready to accept popular derision and disgrace.[201]

Love of 'India'

From all that we have said, it would be wrong to assume that Tagore's pull-out from active political life and his subsequent tirade against nationalism spelt the end to his anti-imperialist politics or his protest against the Raj. Even in his post-Swadeshi years, Tagore never strayed far from the political concerns of India, despite his preferred vocation as a poet. He was always the first to speak up publicly should an occasion demand it. His resignation of knighthood after the British had gunned down an unarmed gathering of people in the Jallianwala Bagh massacre in 1919 is certainly a case in point.

[199] For more on Tagore's rural reconstruction programme, see U. Das Gupta (1991, 2009) and S. Sen (1989).

[200] E. P. Thompson writes about Tagore's 'anti-politics' as an alternative to the irreconcilable polarity of nation and no-nation, finding concrete expression in Tagore's concerns for social welfare and education, and 'civil society'. Tagore's idea 'that power should not be matched by the organization of anti-power, but should be ignored' lies at the core of Thompson's argument; see Thompson (1991), pp. 14ff.

[201] Letter from Tagore to C.F. Andrews, March 1921, published in *The Modern Review*, May 1921, cited in S. Bhattacharya (2005), p. 56.

Part of the complexity of Tagore's response to colonialism is precisely in that he was able to make important distinctions between nationalism and anti-imperialism (you could be anti-imperialist without being nationalist), and as some critics would have it, also between nationalism and patriotism, distinctions that would not have existed in the minds of most Indians in his day. Ashis Nandy, who has contributed significantly to this debate, asserts that Tagore's was the ideology of 'patriotism' rather than nationalism. It was the poet's undeniable *Bharatchinta* or *swadeshchinta* (literally 'thinking about India or one's own country', terms borrowed from Arabinda Poddar) that, Nandy argues, underpinned his version of 'universalism' and can be seen to convey an 'idea of patriotism without "nationalism"'. In other words, 'patriotism', unlike nationalism, is not incompatible with higher laws of humanity and can transcend political and geographical barriers.[202]

We might be getting ourselves into an irresolvable conceptual tangle here, but, in my view, we would be missing something important if we reduce Tagore's particular configuration of *anti-nationalist anti-imperialism* to a kind of self-reflexive 'patriotism' that has 'a built-in critique of nationalism'.[203] While it is no doubt necessary to reconcile Tagore's tirade against nationalism with his love of 'India', I wonder if 'patriotism' is the right term. Amartya Sen rightly points out that 'Tagore's censure of patriotism has been a persistent theme in his writing'.[204]

Certainly, in Tagore's usage of the word in his English writings, patriotism does not stand apart from nationalism. We have seen already in *Nationalism* that both the cult of the nation and that of patriotism are reviled indiscriminately, used more or less synonymously, and both are seen as abstract, impersonal constructs to be resisted. There is also ample evidence in Tagore's political novels (which Nandy takes up for detailed analysis) to show that 'patriotism' did not really stand apart from 'nationalism' in Tagore's conceptual world. In *Four Chapters* (*Char Adhyay*, 1934), for example, Atin, allowing himself to be recruited for the revolutionary cause by Ela, a beautiful woman he is in love with, cannot accept that Ela has pledged allegiance to

---

[202] Nandy (2005b), pp. 80–5.
[203] For other similar responses to Nandy, see Bharucha (2006), pp. 80–3; S. Sarkar (2005), pp. 117, 128–9.
[204] A. Sen (2005a), p. xix.

her country and is not free to act on her own feelings for him. He condemns her patriotic betrothal in no uncertain terms: 'This pledge of yours was a crime and, every day you keep it up, you commit a fresh outrage against your own nature.'[205] Moreover, the ideology of 'country' is seen to be a fake imposition and a curtailment of freedom: 'What right have you, let me ask, to deliver me up to the country, or to any one else? ... the place you've assigned me, calling it country—which after all is nothing but a country of your band's own make—whatever it may mean to others, it's nothing but a cage for me.'[206] Two chapters later we read: 'The patriotism of those who have no faith in that which is above patriotism is like a crocodile's back used as a ferry to cross the river.'[207] Tagore's profound scepticism of patriotism on the grounds of its violation of what is human and personal is, if anything, a recurrent theme in these novels, where the main protagonists rediscover their selves through ties of love and intimate relationship, away from all abstractions.

If the nation-state was one precept of modernity Tagore refused to accept as a given, patriotism, I would say, was another. We have seen that he differentiated between the idea of a nation/a people/a community and the political organization of the nation-state, introducing the looser alternative of 'society' to stand in for the former. Tagore's 'India' too was an essentially open concept, subject to free and voluntary associations between individuals and cultures, and thus uncircumscribed by politico-geographical borders:

> I love India, but my India is an Idea and not a geographical expression. Therefore, I am *not* a patriot—I shall ever seek my compatriots all over the world. You are one of them and I am sure there are many others.[208]

Perhaps he was unwittingly harking back to the old Sanskrit cosmopolis that Sheldon Pollock has reconstructed for us as a world extending from today's Afghanistan to Java and from Sri Lanka to Nepal, and created by voluntary circulation of traders, literati,

[205] Tagore (2002k [1934]), p. 37.
[206] Tagore (2002k [1934]), pp. 44–5.
[207] Tagore (2002k [1934]), p. 77.
[208] Tagore, letter to C. F. Andrews, 1921, emphasis mine, in Andrews (2002), p. 119.

religious professionals, and freelance adventurers, where it would not be in the slightest bit odd to find, for example, a Chinese travel-ler studying Sanskrit grammar in Sumatra in the seventh century.[209] Certainly for Tagore it was not acceptable to have communication, love, or creative aspirations bound by geopolitical boundaries. Rather, he would stress that Indians will 'truly gain their India by fighting against the education which teaches them a country is greater than the ideals of humanity'.[210]

Was Tagore's renunciation of knighthood then primarily an act of 'patriotism'? Are we not missing something vital, if we put down his outrage to 'patriotic' concerns, or to 'nationalism', as Harish Trivedi does when he writes that Tagore's response to the Jallianwala Bagh massacre constitutes 'the most decisive nationalist act of his whole life'?[211] Insofar as an Indian of considerable standing sides with his countrymen voicing their protest against the aggressive ruler through this gesture, it can arguably be seen as a patriotic act, albeit one imposed from the outside through interpretation. But if we take into account Tagore's rationale behind his protest, which he expressed explicitly in terms of what is humanly acceptable or not,[212] then his resignation has less to do with his wounded sensibility as an Indian, and more with the fact that the act of opening fire on a defenceless crowd is an insult to humanity, the measuring rod of Tagore's moral compass. That this was a protest mounted in the name of humanity rather than any patriotic motivation or political capital-making is also evident from Tagore's subsequent refusal to give support to having a memorial built at Jallianwala Bagh.[213]

Since morality cannot be delimited by group loyalty or made sub-ordinate to race or nationality, Tagore did not stop short at India's own door. Throughout his long career, he would condemn countless atroci-ties the world over. He spoke against Japanese imperialist attack on the Koreans, African slavery, and as in his essay 'The Changing Age' (1933),

---

[209] Pollock (2000), pp. 603, 599.

[210] Tagore (2001a [1917]), p. 456.

[211] Trivedi (1995), p. 59.

[212] See Tagore's letter to the viceroy in which he repudiated his knight-hood, in Dutta and Robinson (2005), pp. 223–4.

[213] See Mahalanobis (1985), pp. 13–14.

he condemned 'the horrors of European rule in the African province of Congo', the treacheries of opium trade in China, the strangling of the youth movement in Iran, and the list could go on.[214]

As for his 'patriotism', we need to consider the Bengali word for it: *deshprem*, which literally means the love of land or place. Far less abstract a notion than 'patriotism' (i.e. love of country/nation), for which Tagore harboured deep distrust, and like nationalism perceived it as an undesirable import, deshprem suggests rather more local and therefore intimate ties with a particular place and community. Perhaps then it is Tagore's deshprem, at once more local and 'universal', that lay at the core of his love of 'India', which cannot be subsumed under the more conventional patriotic love of country:

> Swadeshi, Swarajism, ordinarily produce intense excitement in the minds of my countrymen, because they carry in them some fervour of passion generated by the exclusiveness of their range. It cannot be said that I am untouched by this heat and movement. But somehow, by my temperament as a poet, I am incapable of accepting these objects as final. They claim from us a great deal more than is their due. After a certain point is reached, I find myself obliged to separate myself from my own people, with whom I have been working, and my soul cries out: The complete man must never be sacrificed to the patriotic man, or even to the merely moral man. To me humanity is rich and large and many-sided.[215]

In the final analysis, Tagore's anti-colonial dissent was shaped by holding on to moral values rather than a protest mounted for superficial and immediate gain. There is nothing dogmatic about this view, except for the belief that meaningful change can only ever come about from critical introspection by individuals and societies at large. The bias towards one's own country implicit in patriotism and nationalism was for Tagore an obstacle to the larger goal of freedom from race-consciousness, but he also understood the very human and deep-seated nature of that bias, and was not himself always above it.[216]

[214] Tagore (1961l), p. 349.

[215] Tagore, letter to C. F. Andrews, 14 January 1921, in Andrews (2002), pp. 91–2.

[216] The most notable example of this is Tagore's belligerent response to Edward Thompson's well-intended biography of the poet. See Trivedi (1992), pp. 17–36.

His continuous struggle remained thinking and working outside the narrow constraints of identity politics. Tagore, as we have seen, could turn the pluralism of modern society inward, revealing an essentially multifaceted nature of the individual. Around the time of his last birthday in 1941, he penned the following lines, which, to my mind, convey a basic tension of Tagore's life and philosophy: a tension between someone eager to embrace the many, kaleidoscopic possibilities of the modern world, while at the same time feeling himself to be out of bounds, reluctant to draw fast and secure boundaries of any kind.

> This life of mine's been nurtured by a river.
> In its arteries flow
> the gifts of mountain-peaks.
> Its fields have been shaped by many alluvial layers.
> Mysterious vital juices from diverse sources
> have spread themselves in harvests upon harvests.
> From the east and the west networks of song-streams
> lull its sleep and wake.
> Ambassadres of the cosmos, that river,
> she who brings the far near, bids us greet
> the unknown at our doorsteps—it was she
> who wove the day of my birth. And for ever
> On her streams, untied, my mobile home
> drifts from bank to bank.
> I am an outcast. I am a vagabond.
> Boundless bounty piles my birthday plate
> again and again with food, making no bones about it.[217]

The next chapter considers in more detail Tagore's post-Swadeshi era, an era which culminated in 1913 with the reception of the Nobel Prize in Literature and which launched Tagore overnight as a *vishvakabi* ('world poet'). Tagore's subsequent personal experience of the wider world, including the East-Central part of Europe (taken up in the final Tagore chapter), will be seen as inseparable from his emboldened 'world' vision that broke with the nationalist imaginary and telos. How he defied nationalistic assertions of the self, and what, more precisely are the contours of his universalism, is what I explore next.

---

[217] No. 28, from *Janmadine*, 1941, translated by Ketaki Kushari Dyson.

3 The Individual and the World

Ideas Set Free

The seedlings that were reared within narrow plots must now be transplanted into the open fields. The seeds must pass the test of the world-market, if their maximum value is to be obtained.

—Tagore, 'Eastern University', *Creative Unity*, 1922

Truth does not know of East and West.

—Tagore, 'Ideals of Education', 1929

Nothing gets destroyed in the cosmos. Least of all ideas. If life gave them birth, they were born for life, not death.

—Kosovel, in a letter to Fanica Obidova, 1925

After an intense personal involvement with the Swadeshi movement in 1905 and the disillusionment that followed, Tagore, as we have seen, underwent a shift in attitude that can best be described as a turn away from nationalism towards universalism. Universalism, however, had been there all along—as part of Tagore's upbringing, rooted in his family and wider social history. It is evidenced amply in Tagore's earlier writings, and while it is important to see his intellectual growth in terms of this shift, universalism for Tagore was not a novelty. What was new was his overcoming—and complete disavowal—of nationalism.

At one level, therefore, this was a rejection of a politics of identity that splits people along the lines of nation, religion, caste, ethnicity, race, gender, or any other, which for Tagore served the goals of social exclusion, hierarchy, and violence. At another level, it meant the adoption of a global outlook that objected to the ownership of ideas in the sphere of knowledge. So rather than interpreting intellectual products of various groups or peoples along racial or hereditary lines, it saw them as part of human heritage at large.[1] This was essentially an argument for agency and creativity in a colonized setting where the cultural choice presenting itself seemed overwhelmingly determined by the either/or logic: either to assimilate an 'alien' modernity (and effectively conform), or return to the spurious 'authenticity' of pre-colonial roots and origins (shutting oneself off from modern-day developments). Tagore understood this to be the prevalent, but intolerable, choice and sought out possibilities, intellectually and practically, that would deconstruct this binary logic and make way for an alternative form of modernity. I will first consider Tagore's intellectual arguments that reposition 'India' and the individual vis-à-vis the world, then move on to consider how these informed his very practical answers to the challenges of colonial modernity by looking at his educational efforts at Santiniketan to finally outlining the specific contours of his brand of universalism. For one of the first things to realize about Tagore's universalism is, as has been pointed out, that it is neither 'placeless' nor 'vague'.[2]

COLONIAL AMBIVALENCE

The nature of colonial rule has been subjected to diverse interpretations, varying from emphasis on economic and political subjugation to interpretations focusing on the cultural hegemony of the imperial power over the dominated society. The cultural focus of anti-colonial critique was given an unprecedented boost with the publication of Edward Said's *Orientalism* (1978). But the extrapolation of cultural conquest from a political one, often interpreted to be the subtext of Said's thesis, has been widely criticized since.[3]

---

[1] On this, see also Hogan (2003), pp. 16–17.

[2] Hogan (2003), p. 11; see also S. Tagore (2006), p. 21.

[3] See, amongst others, Ahmad (2006), pp. 159–219; Porter (1994 [1983]); Young (1990). For a debate of these issues in relation to India, see Raychaudhuri (2007).

The simple theoretical model of domination and conquest on the part of the colonizer and passive acquiescence on the part of the colonized has now been superseded by an acknowledgement that under colonialism the movement of ideas was not a matter of one-way traffic but worked both ways, and that the encounter produced initiatives and ideas that were subsequently novel to both sides. It was a matter of 'transaction', 'an interactive, dialogic, two-way process ... involving complex negotiation and exchange', to borrow from Harish Trivedi's important intervention from within the field of postcolonial studies.[4] And yet, we are made to wonder how obsolete the old model actually is when reading Trivedi's piece on Tagore in the very same book *Colonial Transactions.*

Here the argued-for agency approach upheld in the introduction is strikingly at odds with the author's conclusions about 'the greatest Indian writer of the colonial age', who, according to the author, was but 'a child of his English-Liberal times and upbringing in both what he gave and what he received, poetically as well as politically'. It is indeed surprising to have Trivedi regard Tagore's achievements in terms of the poet's 'largely acquiescent individual pulse'.[5] This almost seems to resurrect some of the orientalist ghosts of the British press at the height of Tagore's fame in England, when the Indian poet was conceived mainly as a product of the strength and vitality of British rule and civilization in India.[6] The close convergence Trivedi then observes between English liberal thought (seen as the ideological foundation stone of British imperialism) and Tagore's own intellectual stance—Tagore had 'internalis[ed] an idealised version of the English Liberal conceptualisation of its imperial project'—also makes him regard Tagore's '"apolitical" internationalism and universalism' to be entirely of a coherent piece with British imperialism. And it is this—predictable—conflation of universalism with imperialism (discussed in Chapter 1), combined with a monolithic approach to the subject, that I want to challenge with respect to Tagore, notwithstanding the

---

[4] Trivedi (1995), p. 1.

[5] Trivedi (1995), p. 64.

[6] '[U]nder the strong shield of our Empire', wrote one reviewer, 'the genius of this Bengali singer found itself and flourished' (*Pall Mall Gazette*, 10 May 1915, in Kundu, Bhattacharya, and Sircar 2000, p. 197).

question that if Tagore, as Trivedi suggests, was but a mouthpiece for the colonizers' ideologies, what then was so 'artistically compelling'[7] about his response? We must indeed take cognizance of the 'complex negotiations and exchange' of the colonial encounter, to follow Trivedi's own precepts, if we are to get a fairer sense of Tagore's anti-imperialist, universalist intellectual position.

To begin with, rather than seeing him as a child of English liberal times, I suggest we see him as a child of *ambivalent* colonial times, for every culture under foreign domination finds itself in 'an ambivalent position' as regards the foreign culture.[8] The power inequality between the colonizers and the colonized puts a severe strain on the transfer and exchange of knowledge. In the eighty years of Tagore's life, the encounter between Britain and India 'came close to a clash of civiliza- tions and had to be resolved piecemeal by adjustments at various levels of Indian life'.[9] One particular aspect of the colonial ambivalence that Tagore addresses time and again in his writings relates precisely to the question of freeing up intellectual transactions and moving beyond the 'colonizer'–'colonized', 'foreign'–'indigenous' dichotomy. Regarding this to be an imperative of his age, Tagore speaks from a deeply felt historical and existential dilemma pertaining to subjugated societies in general. Berlin captures the dilemma spot on:

> it may happen that the foreign culture has made a deep impress upon my own, and even when, in some respects, it has made inroads upon it, distorted it, and partially enslaved my own civilisation, yet once I have tasted it, I cannot expel it from my system without great damage, cannot reject or blind myself to what is true and good or delightful or noble merely because it comes from the wrong quarter.[10]

How one could resist colonial onslaught and humiliation without jeop- ardizing one's own humanity or surrendering one's own individuality— be it through disallowing it to change and grow (as in isolationism) or through violation of humanity's basic principles (as in violence and terrorism)—shaped a large part of Tagore's questioning and concerns.

[7] Trivedi (1995), p. 64.
[8] Berlin (1997), p. 158.
[9] U. Das Gupta (2006), p. 1.
[10] Berlin (1997), p. 158.

In the wide spectrum of responses generated by the British rule in India, Tagore's evolving position eventually stood out in its conviction that the colonial situation be used creatively to the long-term advantage of the Indian people (and he was not thinking merely of the elites) over and above the historical fact of colonial rule and its injustices. The man himself is probably the most celebrated proof of 'the great flowering of writers, poets and thinkers' who have come to represent 'the creative response of Indians coming to terms with, and shaping, changes in their history and identity'.[11] I begin by exploring the poet's reading of the impact of 'the West' on the making of the *nava yuga* (new age), incidentally one of the indigenous terms for what subsequently became known as 'the Bengal Renaissance'.[12]

The *Nava Yuga*: 'East' Meets 'West'

In the previous chapter, we have already seen how Tagore framed the founding moment of *nava yuga* in terms of India's contact with Europe.[13] Prefiguring many of the contemporary debates, he himself stressed both the novelty and identity of Indian culture in the wake of the colonial encounter—in the Fanonian sense of setting a culture moving in both self-critical introspection and branching out to the world. Essentially, to reiterate, he celebrated what he referred to as the 'great fact of this age'—the coming together of different 'races' and worldviews.

[11] N.C. Chaudhuri (1987), p. 158.

[12] The term 'new age' was first deployed by the Bengali historian Shivanath Shastri at the beginning of the twentieth century in his Bengali work of history entitled *Ramtanu Lahiri and Bengal Society in His Time* (1903). When this was translated into English in 1907 by Roper Lethbridge, it was subtitled 'A History of the Renaissance in Bengal'. The term soon gained currency and was extended to include all India in what became known as 'Indian Awakening'. Charles Freer Andrews, James Cousins, Sri Aurobindo—all contributed important works on the topic and made the term 'Renaissance' stick until the 1970s and '80s when it met with a radical Leftist critique (cf. S. Tagore and S. Ray 2003a, p. 30). For further insight into the revisionist Marxist, subaltern, and postmodernist history of the phenomenon, see, among others, A. Das Gupta (2003), pp. 327–39; S. Sarkar (2005), pp. 95–105; R. K. Ray (2003), pp. 6–9, 29–66; and T. Raychaudhuri (2002), pp. 345–62.

[13] See the subsection entitled 'Changing Times', on pp. 54 ff.

The human races have been exposed to each other, physically and intellectually. The shells, which have so long given them full security within their individual enclosures, have been broken, and by no artificial process can they be mended again.[14]

This for Tagore was an irreversible fact of global modernity that required everyone to make a mental and moral readjustment. It meant our countries had 'to harmonize our growth with world tendencies ... to prove our worth to the whole world not merely to admiring groups of our own people ... to justify our own existence'. Problems which had previously been of local make were now affecting much larger areas. Solutions could no longer be found 'in the seclusion of our own national workshops' but had to be sought in cooperation with different cultures, through intercultural negotiations.[15]

However much Tagore deplored the fact that the meeting of cultures had come largely on the back of commercial exploitation and imperial conquest, he wanted to move beyond the static and oppositional view of civilizations and stress the limitless potential for everyone—the colonizer and colonized alike—to realize a new, more consummate, identity. For the dilemma facing the modern world, and potentially affecting everyone, was straightforward enough, even when a viable solution was not: different peoples had irretrievably come together and could either fight each other till death or they could try and find the 'true basis of reconciliation and mutual help'.[16]

What was the source of Tagore's optimism and high expectations with regard to India in relation to the nava yuga? It was India's contact with Europe (through the British), Tagore declared, that had awakened her to the 'great gift of knowledge in its universal aspects', both in the world of science and that of politics. The former, he pointed out, advanced 'the universal laws of cause and effect', the cornerstone of scientific inquiry, and the latter put forward the idea that 'all men [are] equal before the Law'.[17] Both were revolutionary propositions. Therefore, if modernity, at one level, meant a pursuit of universal freedom based on a growing and shareable body of open

---

[14] Tagore (2002c [1921]), p. 71.
[15] Tagore (2002c [1921]), p. 71.
[16] Tagore (2001a [1917]), p. 461.
[17] Tagore (1961l [1933]), pp. 343–4.

and generally applicable knowledge, then Tagore, I dare say, was its foremost supporter.

The context of colonial subjugation, of course, glaringly undermined the verities promised by the political discourse of universal human rights established by the Enlightenment philosophers, but it did not, Tagore argued, reduce the value of the ideals of freedom and individual liberty. 'If, today, we challenge our rulers with demands which we would not have dreamed of presenting to the Mughal Emperor,' he wrote, 'it is because of the ideal voiced in the words of the poet: "a man's a man for a' that."'[18] There is significance in the fact that Tagore linked this 'novel point of view' with the domain of poetry (the above lines are taken from Robert Burns) rather than the realm of politics, drawing a vital link between creative practice and social change.[19] From reading English literature, he asserted, Indians had gained 'the will to break man's tyranny over man'.[20]

But how, one might ask, did Tagore resolve the tension existing between the ideals voiced in literature and the reality of men running empires (by 1870s the belief in the benevolence of the British Empire had become more or less untenable)? Here we see Tagore introducing a distinction that allowed him to hold on to his faith in 'the British character' as culled from literature (but also experienced personally),[21] while, at the same time, condemn the 'British conqueror'.[22] The 'boro ingrej' (great Englishman) was thus set off against the 'chotto ingrej' (the little Englishman) in his book *Kalantar* (literally 'the changing age'), in the same way that 'the spirit of the West' was seen to be at loggerheads with 'the Nation of the West' in his book *Nationalism*. Such distinctions, however over-simplistic they may at first seem, are in fact good strategies for gaining a more balanced and discerning

[18] Tagore (1961l [1933]), p. 345.

[19] This is something I will be discussing in much greater depth with reference to Kosovel in Ch. 6.

[20] Tagore (1961l [1933]), p. 346. For the impact the romantic poets had on Tagore's creative imagination, see also 'The Poet's Religion' in *Creative Unity*, in Tagore (2002d [1922]), pp. 1–30.

[21] For Tagore's—not always easy—friendships with the English (Rothenstein, Andrews, Thompson), see correspondence volumes: Andrews (2002), U. Das Gupta (2003), and Lago (1972).

[22] Tagore (1961l [1933]), p. 347.

sense of a conflicting reality, since they resist seeing one side of the opposition as altogether bad and projecting the other as entirely good.

Certainly Tagore understood the dangers of attitudes that would lean either too heavily towards infatuation with the West (blinded by the display of imperial power) and dismiss out of hand all native traditions or, at the opposite extreme, reject the West wholesale and find an emotional outlet in chauvinism:

> The reaction of disillusionment is just as unreal as the first shock of illusion. We must try to come to that normal state of mind, by which we can clearly discern our own danger and avoid it, without being unjust towards the source of that danger.[23]

Tagore's was going to be 'the difficult middle path' or 'the narrow causeway' that was to avoid both the trends of 'radical modernism' and 'proud and gloomy traditionalism'.[24] Understanding 'the natural temptation' to retaliate and 'pay back Europe in her own coin', Tagore implored his countrymen to resist imitating Europe in her worst features—'her behaviour to people whom she describes as yellow or red, brown or black'. By the same token he insisted that Indians acknowledge their own record of 'treating with utter disdain and cruelty men who belonged to a particular creed, colour or caste'.[25] Or, as he put it in another, earlier, essay: 'These faults of the English hurt us only because we have them ourselves.'[26] Following the Amritsar massacre, which made him renounce the knighthood, he administered what could only have tasted as bitter medicine to a wounded nation: 'Let us forget the Punjab affair, but never forget that we shall go on deserving such humiliation over and over again until we set our house in order.'[27] There is no end to such and similar exhortations to self-analysis in Tagore's post-Swadeshi writings—what Nandy has aptly identified as Tagore's ability to transform, at times of most acute crisis,

---

[23] Tagore (2001a [1917]), p. 450.
[24] Berlin (1997), pp. 160–5.
[25] Tagore (2001a [1917]), p. 450.
[26] Tagore (1961g [1917]), p. 194.
[27] Tagore, letter to C. F. Andrews, 7 September 1920, in Dutta and Robinson (2005), p. 237.

the 'passionate self–other' debate into a 'self–self' debate.[28] 'Do not mind the waves of the sea, but mind the leaks in your own vessel.'[29]

If Tagore described the imperial face of Europe as based on exclusiveness and discrimination, he also recognized that this trait had a corresponding Indian face in caste distinctions. Whether a Brahmin was exercising his inviolable rights against a member of the lower caste or an officer of the British Empire was victimizing his subjects, both stood accused of abusing humanity. On the same principle that Indians were challenging British authority, they also needed to rise up to the authority of their own cruel indigenous practices. Political freedom could not be built on 'the quicksand of social slavery'.[30] Clearly, this was a double-speared critique, grounded in a universalist ethos or—with Said—a larger search for liberation.[31]

Insofar as Tagore acknowledged his debt to the European Enlightenment thought, he also brought the scriptural sources of Vedantic thought, particularly the classical Upanishads, to bear on the modern concepts of universal human rights and respect for all individuals. The notion of universal ethical principles has a counterpart, as pointed out by Hogan, in the fundamental principles of *sadharanadharma*, or 'universal dharma'.[32] Complex a notion as *dharma* is, attempts to bring it close to Western understanding have translated the concept into 'ethical duty' that provides 'the pattern of life'. From the Sanskrit word meaning 'nature', dharma relates to things behaving in the way they behave because of what they are (that is, it is the dharma of fire to burn, water to flow, and so on).[33] Or, as Tagore had put it in his book *Sadhana* (1913):

> *Dharma* is the innermost nature, the essence, the implicit truth, of all things. *Dharma* is the ultimate purpose that is working in our self. When

---

[28] Nandy (2005b), p. 82.

[29] Tagore, letter to C. F. Andrews, 7 September 1920, in Dutta and Robinson (2005), p. 237.

[30] Tagore (2001a [1917]), p. 462.

[31] Said (1994), p. 265. See Ch. 1, pp. 27–31.

[32] Hogan (2000), p. 309.

[33] Hogan (2000), p. 309.

any wrong is done we say that *dharma* is violated, meaning that the lie has been given to our nature.[34]

In relation to human agents it implies duty and tells me what I should do with respect to the various binding social links, for example as wife, daughter, son, teacher, warrior, householder, and so on. Though classical texts on dharma distinguish several types of dharma, in popular Hinduism and common practice the notion tends to get reduced to the hierarchical doctrines of familial dharma and caste dharma (*varnadharma*). In contrast to these types of dharma that vary from individual to individual and situation to situation and are governed by distinctions of caste, stage of life, and so on, there is sadharanadharma or *manavadharma* ('human dharma'), in other words, universal dharma applicable to all individuals and binding for all.[35]

The two most important principles of universal dharma are those of truth and *ahimsa* (commonly translated as 'non-violence' but more precisely meaning 'restraint from infliction of pain').[36] When violence is commissioned or sanctioned by a specific dharma, these principles of sadharanadharma can be invoked to dispute it. In principle sadharanadharma should have higher authority over varnadharma, though even in theory this is not always the case. It was precisely these principles of truth and ahimsa that individuals like Tagore and Gandhi evoked, as they strove to re-actualize India's heritage in modern conditions of economic and social exploitation. Placing these ideals at the core of their anti-colonial dissent, they found themselves, their differences notwithstanding, opposing not only the colonizers but also the colonized. For '[w]hat makes colonialism wrong is not any difference between Indians and English ... [but] that it purveys violence and untruth, which is adharmic for any agent and any object'.[37] Though sadharanadharma must necessarily place one on the side of the oppressed in any existing—world and societal—hierarchy, blind as it is to group demarcations and loyalties, it counteracts the rule of might anywhere, pushing beyond the colonial binary logic.

[34] Tagore (2002b [1913]), p. 79.
[35] Hogan (2000), p. 214. See ch. 7 of the book *Orthodoxy and Universalism: Rabindranath Tagore's Gora*, pp. 213–55.
[36] Hogan (2000), p. 216.
[37] Hogan (2003), p. 16.

While this is one aspect of Hindu universalism upon which Tagore could draw for addressing societal wrongs, there is also the Vedantic principle that all individual souls are ultimately identical in Brahman, not to mention that it was in the Upanishads that Tagore discovered his philosophy of the One in the Many.[38] It is in the concept of life as the manifestation of the divine in a multitude of forms that Tagore embeds his defence of cultural diversity.

Tagore's liberal views and humanistic ideals no doubt owed much also to his high regard for the Buddha and Buddhist humanism, its teachings of non-violence and compassion, its anti-casteism and objection to outward ritualism and superstitions, as well as its overall emphasis on restoring human rights to the dispossessed. There is no dearth of resources within India's many traditions for opposing a system that privileges a few over the many—Tagore's distaste for (political) violence had obvious roots—and Tagore can be seen to dig deep into and across the religious and literary possessions of his land to come up, for example, with an essentially universalist reading of religious personalities such as the Buddha, Nanak, Kabir, and Chaitanya. This is understandable also because the historical evolution of Bengali literary culture is closely connected to a number of anti-Brahmanical heterodox religious experiments, starting with Buddhist poetical compositions, *caryapadas,* to the *padavali* poetry of the medieval Vaishnava tradition,[39] which Tagore held in high regard and which informed both his poetic and spiritual sensibilities.[40] As a teenager, he is known to have imitated the medieval Vaishnava hymns on the Krishna–Radha theme under the pseudonym Bhanusingha, passing off his *Bhanusingher Padavali* as the work of a medieval poet who wrote in Brajabuli, an older literary language. He was apparently delighted that his songs had fooled

---

[38] See also U. Das Gupta (2003), pp. 88–100. In an intriguing essay on Tagore's reading of the classical Sanskrit poet Kalidasa, entitled 'Two Giant Brothers: Tagore's Revisionist "Orient"', Amit Chaudhuri argues that Tagore gives the ideals of Western Enlightenment and humanism, compromised through their compulsion to dominate and colonize, a truer and more humane source in India's antiquity (A. Chaudhuri 2008, pp. 122–39).

[39] On this, see Kaviraj (2003), pp. 514–29.

[40] On Vaishnava strains in Tagore's philosophy, see O'Connell (2011).

an authority on Bengali literature and were taken as an authentic literary discovery from medieval Bengali poetry.[41]

When we consider that Tagore brought this enormous intellectual heritage to bear on modern concepts of humanism that contact with European thought had exposed him to, especially the writings of the English liberal tradition, it becomes absurd to see in him someone who had supposedly surrendered his individuality. Rather, one might suggest with philosopher K. C. Bhattacharya that in some cases 'the foreign ideal is ... in our own ideal' or, even if that is not the case, one is obliged to accept 'the guru or teacher ... when he is found to be a real guru, whatever the community from which he comes'.[42] Tagore understood this and did not shy away from claiming as his own any thought or belief system which he felt would further his own aspirations, regardless of its origins. He could certainly make a virtue out of 'borrowing', which in any case need not be imitation:

> The sign of greatness in great geniuses is their enormous capacity to borrow, very often without their knowing it; they have an unlimited credit in the world market of culture. Only mediocrities are ashamed and afraid of borrowing, for they do not know how to pay back their debt in their own coin.[43]

Individuality, Freedom, and Interdependence

We have already established that for Tagore the question of political freedom was secondary to the question of social and spiritual freedom for the individual, and that the former by no means guarantees the latter. In Tagore's books, claiming something for oneself without being prepared to extend it to others negates that very thing and can only lead to spiritual failure.

[41] See on this, A. Chaudhuri (2008), p. 79.

[42] K.C. Bhattacharya (1984), p. 390. This line of argument also informs Amartya Sen's approach to the 'colonial encounter'. In his book *The Argumentative Indian* (2005b) he shows that the traditions of rationality, science, scepticism have a long lineage in India and that the Enlightenment secular values that have found political expression in 'Nehruvian' democracy are not accidental or a gift from the West. For an extension of this debate, see also 'Argufying: On Amartya Sen and the Deferral of Indian Modernity' (A. Chaudhuri 2008, pp. 100–8).

[43] Tagore (2002c [1921]), p. 71.

Tagore believed in the essential interrelatedness of all phenomena derived through his personal sense of 'the infinite being' which runs through all and unites the individual's mind with the outer world.[44] One particular doctrine that repeatedly crops up in his writings is the Upanishadic ideal that we realize ourselves through others. 'He who sees all beings in his own self and his own self in all beings, he does not remain unrevealed,' which is to say, 'to remain confined within oneself is to extinguish oneself, but to realize oneself in others is to reveal oneself'.[45] This was essentially a religious argument grounded in the Vedantic principle that all individual souls are ultimately identical in the Absolute, but Tagore knew how to turn a religious argument into a secular tool of social emancipation. The self and the other were not enemies, merely different expressions of the same Infinite Being. This grounded Tagore's faith in the possibility of attaining peace and harmony in human affairs, even when differences often seemed insurmountable.

Indeed, Tagore could never conceive of the individual as strictly separate from other fellow beings or the environment. His individual, as pointed out by Purkayastha, is not the Cartesian isolated or atomized individual, but rather 'one nucleus within a web of relationships'. Embroiled thus in multiple ties and associations, where lines between one's self-interest and duty towards others get blurred, Tagore's individual must also be distinguished from the liberal version of the rational, self-interested individual, or the communitarian model of the autonomous individual whose allegiance is to community bonds.[46]

Tagore's notion of 'unity of soul' or 'oneness' with the 'Infinite Self' that underlies his politics of hope and social ethics can, of course, come across as rather abstract to the uninitiated. But Tagore insisted that this knowledge is not an outcome of metaphysical speculation but a matter of lived experience and thus accessible to everyone. 'The principle creative forces, which transmute things into our living

[44] Tagore (2002c [1921]), p. 98. The most important exposé of these ideas is to be found in Tagore's Hibbert lectures, delivered in Oxford in 1930 and published as *The Religion of Man* (1931). Cf. 2002g, pp. 85–9.

[45] Tagore (1961i [1921]), p. 244. Or, from an earlier essay: 'He alone has attained truth who has seen himself in all and all in himself' (Tagore 1961g [1917], p. 185).

[46] Purkayastha (2003), p. 59.

structure, are emotional forces.'[47] It is perhaps best to approach his concept of unity through the 'phenomenology of love',[48] because in Tagore's moral universe, love, as opposed to animosity and hatred, is constantly explored and evoked as a potent force for social change.

> Through the help of logic we never could have arrived at the truth that the soul which is the unifying principle in me finds its perfection in its unity in others. We have known it through joy of this truth. Our delight is in realizing ourselves outside us. When I love, in other words, when I feel I am truer in someone else than myself, than I am glad, for the One in me realizes its truth of unity by uniting with others, and there is its joy.[49]

Here is a man guided by a fundamental belief that there is an inherent impulse in us, beyond instrumental reason and self-interest, for 'creative, active love, which leads us to bonds of unity with our fellow men'.[50] Through relations of affection we extend ourselves beyond ourselves, and this, Tagore wrote time and again, is a matter of experiencing *joy*, the joy where 'all separateness disappears, no feeling of pride remains, and there is nothing in the way of our intimacy with the meanest, the weakest thing'.[51] Love, for Tagore, occupies a more central place in the human condition compared to antagonism.[52] This also explains his concern for both the 'colonizer' and the 'colonized', as well as his distancing from the nationalist project which he felt was driven primarily by hatred of the foreigner and not by love of one's own people.[53]

Following on from Tagore's understanding of the individual, we can more easily appreciate what Tagore meant by freedom, when in

---

[47] Tagore (2001b [1917]), p. 352.

[48] Collins (2012), p. 76.

[49] Tagore (2001b [1917]), p. 373.

[50] Collins (2012), p. 157.

[51] Translated by Surendranath Tagore, Tagore (1936),

[52] See Purushottam Agrawal's essay on Kabir's ideal of love (2011). Agrawal rightly notes a lack of a discourse of love in contemporary social thought as well as a reluctance to give love a space in thoughts of social change. It is always hatred that is seen as all-important in the formation of social forces, while love's importance is acknowledged only as a personal impulse.

[53] I have discussed this in more detail in Ch. 2, p. 95.

Religion of Man (1931), he asserted—in his not uncommon para-doxical mode—that 'only a perfect arrangement of interdependence gives rise to freedom'.[54] Freedom's true ambience, in other words, is interdependence and not independence, and for Tagore 'the history of the growth of freedom is the history of the perfection of human relationship'.[55] Put differently, individuals and societies will grow in freedom by improving interpersonal relationships, and superiority, Tagore submitted, is with those who 'have the power to cultivate understanding and co-operation'.[56] Understanding and cooperation are two essentials for taking part in a multicultural world, and it is time for us to explore Tagore's practical answers to cultivating both.

Education for Sympathy and Joy[57]

Tagore was above all a poet, and he would say so of himself, but alongside the twenty-five volumes of published poetry (other seg-ments of creative writing include two thousand songs, fifteen plays, ninety short stories and eleven novels), he devoted forty years of his life to an experiment in education. The poet's becoming an educator in the very practical sense tells us something about how Tagore had to translate his ideas in the world of everyday reality. As early as 1894 he wrote in a poem: '[H]e who, submerged in self, / Turns from the world, has not learnt to live', admonishing the poet and asking the poet to engage with 'every day's tasks', and stop playing 'a tetherless truant boy'[58]—lines that no doubt reflect his own emergence from the state of seclusion he experienced as a young man, when his father had delegated to him the responsibility of running the family estate. His subsequent work on education and development in rural Bengal certainly bears out his commitment to improve the lives of others.

We will therefore gain most by considering Tagore's evolving uni-versalist philosophy alongside his educational efforts at Santiniketan,

[54] Tagore (2002h), p. 189.

[55] Tagore (2002h), p. 190.

[56] Tagore (2001a [1917]), p. 454.

[57] An earlier digest version of this and the following two sections of the chapter, informs my paper 'Tagore's Universalist Sparks: A Creative Approach' (Jelnikar 2012).

[58] Tagore, 'Now Turn Me Back', translated by Sukanta Chaudhuri, in Tagore (2004b), pp. 95–9.

relating them further to his conscious pursuit of travel (in the next chapter). We would indeed be missing a crucial component to Tagore's universalism if we excluded from the discussion his many practical initiatives and not see the link between them. These initiatives were not, as is often presumed, confined only to his class. Or, rather, when they did originate in a more circumscribed way, as was the case with the Santiniketan School when it was first founded in 1901, they soon grew to overcome the initial limitations, which were in any case more practical than ideological in nature. I want to suggest that Tagore's half-a-lifetime-long educational efforts were his practical answer to the goal of strengthening cooperative ties of interdependence between variously placed individuals and groups. Put differently, they were his *post-political* answer to imperialism and isolationism.

Kathleen O'Connell, in her study of the poet as educator, highlights the transition from the poet's early *brahmacharyashram* model based on the ancient Hindu forest hermitage and a master–disciple relationship, to an international university Visva-Bharati, the motto of which—*Yatra vishvam bhavatyeka nidam* (literally 'where the world becomes one nest')—conveys its global and democratic ambitions. While the former brahmacharyashram model was to a large extent a product of its time informed by the nineteenth-century Hindu revivalism and must be seen, the author contends, as part of the nationalist education movement, the vision and aspirations underlying the latter moved far beyond the nationalist agenda. In fact, the first visible markers of a more universalist outlook, reflected in co-education, interaction with the rural community, commitment to non-sectarianism, coincided, predictably, with Tagore's disillusionment with nationalist politics. O'Connell further links this shift to the advent of World War I (for Tagore the most palpable proof of nationalism gone viral), as well as Tagore's trips to England, America, and the Far East. With these, she maintains, 'the scope of his educational vision broadens further in an attempt to activate co-operation and cultural understanding between different regions of India, the Far East and the Western world'.[59]

When Tagore founded Visva-Bharati in 1921 at Santiniketan, the new international seat of learning (where Satyajit Ray, Indira Gandhi,

---

[59] O'Connell (2002), p. 64.

and Amartya Sen would receive part of their education) was decisively fostered in terms of a 'comprehensive' identity. At the same time that it was to be made into 'a seat of Indian cultures', it was also 'to acquire an international persona'.[60] With respect to 'Indian education', Tagore announced, 'we shall have to collect together treasures of Vedic, Puranic, Buddhist, Jaina, and Islamic minds. We shall have to find out how the Indian mind has flown along these different channels' so as to 'feel her identity in her diversity'. He considered it essential to derive a perception of the Indian self in 'this extended and interlinked way'.[61]

Recognizing Indianness in such an inherently plural way and seeing cultures as nourished through a wide network of traditions—the school would also make a point of celebrating the anniversaries of Buddha, Christ, Mohammed, Chaitanya, Rammohun Roy, and others—encouraged broader identifications and made it harder for people to see themselves as strictly different or separate. On the practical side, Tagore introduced educational activities, such as working in the villages with Hindus, Muslims, and the tribals, specifically targeted at breaking down religious bias and caste prejudices.[62] Personal contact overriding narrow abstract identifications was one way of promoting understanding. Each student was to realize this through their own experience. Learning by doing was a central tenet to Tagore's education: 'The idea,' as noted by Mulk Raj Anand, 'had to be an act.'[63] Or, put differently, 'Tagore wanted his students to climb trees and not just study them.'[64] Education of the senses was seen as a prerequisite to abstract thinking and impersonal knowledge, and it was through the direct and sensual encounter with the natural environment that students were encouraged to relate to the world spiritually and experience 'the oneness of creation', and not see it as a mere instrument for rational, utilitarian purposes.[65]

[60] U. Das Gupta (1982/3), p. 382.

[61] Tagore, cited in U. Das Gupta (1982/3), p. 383. See also his essay, 'The Centre of Indian Culture', 1919, in Tagore (1961h), pp. 223–5.

[62] O'Connell (2002), p. 104.

[63] Anand (1988), p. 84.

[64] Sartori (2008), p. 182.

[65] Sartori (2008), p. 182.

If the school initially set out to resurrect the wealth of Indian heritage (with the aim to instil a sense of self-worth in the students), this was seen as a preliminary step for accepting other cultures and building a strong relationship with 'the world'. Taking part in a multicultural world required a mature sense of identity, so roots were important, and in Tagore's school they were nourished not least through having Bengali as the medium for learning, with English being merely a taught language like Sanskrit.

Tagore wanted Indians to capitalize on what he saw as 'the great opportunity for the creation of new thought by a new combination of truths'. With this in mind, he urged for 'all the elements of [Indian] culture to be strengthened' so as not to 'resist the culture of the West, but to accept it and assimilate it'.[66] Once again, he laid out the familiar intermingling-of-traditions argument, India's past record of absorbing outside influences, to suggest there is no need to distrust a culture just because of its foreign character.

> In our music, our architecture, our pictorial art, our literature, the Muslims have made a permanent and precious contribution. Those who have studied the lives and writings of our medieval saints, and all the great religious movements that sprang up in the time of Muslim rule, know how deep is our debt to this foreign current that has so intimately mingled with our life.[67]

This was also Tagore's timely reminder to the Hindu nationalist that 'India's history is not the story of the Hindu alone'.[68]

Even if Visva-Bharati never quite achieved Tagore's ambitious goal of collating the materials from the various strands of Indian culture down through the ages, it was nevertheless the first all-India university to consciously pursue a model where the non-Hindu traditions would be systematically integrated.[69] As for the international persona of the university, the staff and students came from different parts of the subcontinent as well as abroad, with subjects such as German and French being taught alongside Persian, Pali,

---

[66] Tagore (1961h [1919]), pp. 222–3.
[67] Tagore (1961h [1919]), p. 223.
[68] Tagore (1961d [1908]), p. 131.
[69] O'Connell (2002), p. 176.

and Hindi, with Tagore himself teaching English literature and some European specialists teaching Eastern thought as well as areas of Western science and art.[70]

There is no doubt that Tagore's own travels contributed significantly to widening his aesthetic and cultural vision and were reflected in his programme for Visva-Bharati, and that in Tagore's time, and years beyond, many an interesting intellectual encounter with wider repercussions emerged from the place itself. Tagore also devoted his own tours to promoting intercultural exchange. To know that Tagore most probably visited the Bauhaus school in Weimar in 1921,[71] and was instrumental in bringing over to India the first exhibition of the original works of the European avant-garde a year later,[72] or that, conversely, in 1930, there was a show of Tagore's paintings at the avant-garde Galerie du Théâtre Pigalle in Paris, alongside an exhibition of African and Oceanic art, is to get an idea of one man's vision and his wherewithal. The enthusiasm generated by both these events moreover attests to what the art historian Partha Mitter has submitted as 'the emerging [early twentieth-century] transnational discourse of global modernity' where a shared corpus of ideas on modernity was being negotiated from multiple localities across the world.[73]

Tagore also sought out individuals who would quite literally transport ideas, initially engaging his family and students to become

[70] For more on the specifics of the curricula and staff, see O'Connell (2002), pp. 186–9.

[71] The documentary evidence on this is inconclusive, as pointed out by Ketaki Kushari Dyson and her collaborators, who did pioneering research not only on the impact of Tagore's colour vision on his work as a creative artist, but also on the profound impact of German expressionism on Tagore's art. See the Bengali volume Dyson and Adhikary (1997) and Kushari Dyson's English article 'Rabindranath Tagore and His World of Colours', published on the website Parabaas. It is however very plausible that Tagore had a role to play in the arrangement of the Calcutta exhibition.

[72] The exhibition was held on 23 December at the 14th annual exhibition of the Indian Society of Oriental Art in Calcutta, and will be discussed further in Ch. 5.

[73] Mitter (2007), p. 65. That Kosovel too, at around the same time, became acquainted with the new artistic direction of the Bauhaus, further substantiates Mitter's thesis and the kind of internationalism that was around in the interwar period. I discuss this in Ch. 6, pp. 301–5.

conduits in this cultural exchange,[74] but eventually, under the aegis of Visva-Bharati, bringing together scholars to share their knowledge or expertise. Indeed, an exchange of views was paramount to education, else 'no education becomes a vital part of ourselves'.[75] All of this was premised on the need to work together in pursuit of the ideal enshrined in Visva-Bharati's constitution: 'To study the mind of man in its realization of different aspects of truth from diverse points of view.'[76] Tagore wrote,

> [At Visva-Bharati, we] must work together in a common pursuit of truth, share together our common heritage, and realize that artists in all parts of the world have created forms of beauty, scientists discovered secrets of the universe, philosophers solved the problems of existence, saints made the truth of the spiritual world organic in their own lives, not merely for some particular race to which they belonged, but for all mankind.[77]

This is a succinct expression of a universalism in which intellectual and artistic achievements are seen to be part of common human heritage. Visva-Bharati, in the final instance, was to become Tagore's universalist ideal translated into practice, a place where knowledge is shared, new possibilities imagined, and where creativity is given free reign not for the benefit of a particular country but for the advantage of anyone and everyone.

In a letter to his son in 1916, in one of the earliest indications of his ambition to expand his educational efforts and found an international university, Tagore lays out his grand vision:

> I have it in mind to make Shantiniketan the connection thread between India and the world. I have to found a world centre for the study of humanity there. The days of petty nationalism are numbered—let the

---

[74] His son Rathindranath, for example, was sent to America, to study for a degree in agriculture at Urbana, Illinois; for his first foreign Japanese student Hory San, who came to Santiniketan to study Sanskrit, Tagore anticipated a trip to the monasteries of Japan and China for the purpose of copying out Sanskrit texts preserved there (cf. U. Das Gupta [1982/3], pp. 382–3).

[75] Translated by Swapan Chakravorty, Tagore (2001f [1895]), p. 188.

[76] Tagore, in U. Das Gupta (2004), p. 69.

[77] Tagore (2002d [1922]), p. 171.

first step towards universal union occur in the fields of Bolpur. I want to make that place somewhere beyond the limits of nation and geography—the first flag of victorious universal humanism will be planted there.[78]

The grandiosity of diction and goal notwithstanding, Tagore is making a serious point here. Insofar as Santiniketan was going to be the nodal point between India and the world, it was also going to be a space 'beyond the limits of nation and geography', rooted but unrestricted by geopolitical boundaries. Furthermore, such an experiment in education presupposed individuals with an open mind and a respectful heart to honour or, as Charles Taylor put it in his influential essay on multiculturalism, the universalist presumption of equal worth of all cultures.[79] As an educator, Tagore strove as much for cultivation of feelings as that of the intellect. Emphasis was on the arts and humanities, on music, painting and sculpture, literature, dance and drama, as

[78] Tagore, letter to Rathindranath, 11 November 1916, Los Angeles, translated by Krishna Dutta and Andrew Robinson, in Dutta and Robinson (2005), p. 179.

[79] See Taylor's essay 'Multiculturalism and the Politics of Recognition' (1992), where he sets forth the presumption that all cultures deserve equal respect, since 'withholding this presumption' of the equal value of all cultures—an anti-universalist gesture *par excellence*—would be 'tantamount to a denial of equal status' (1992, p. 66). The demand for recognition of cultures and acknowledgement of their equal worth lies at the heart of all freedom struggles. On the other hand, it cannot be that all cultures or all cultural products are equally valuable; granting them such recognition would involve repudiating all possible standards of judgement. Thus the above claim can only be upheld as a 'presumption', the validity of which is yet to be ascertained through critical evaluation. The tricky question arising here is: Whose value judgements are we invoking when passing judgements of worth? A critical evaluation deserving of this name, must, at least in some measure, bring about a fusion of horizons. Invoking Hans-Georg Gadamer, Taylor states that 'real judgments of worth suppose a fused horizon of standards ... they suppose that we have been transformed by the study of the other, so that we are not simply judging by our familiar standards'(p. 70). The point is—very much also a Tagorean point—that we owe it to others and ourselves to approach all cultures in a spirit of openness, on the assumption that we may have something important to learn (or not), and in turn re-evaluate our own prefixed notions and judgement.

also on the sciences and practical activities. His was to be education for sympathy and joy, for the experience of love that dissolved boundaries, since the world most needed those who possessed 'the sympathetic insight to place themselves in the position of others'.[80] Our sensitivity to others is demonstrated through our conscious efforts to resist the all too familiar psychological mechanism of projection (the unconscious assumption that everyone thinks the same as I do) which, as shown in Chapter 1, underpins the so-called false or pseudo-universalism, and instead make the effort to understand another's point of view. This is yet another important aspect of Tagore's universalism, which Lalita Pandit has aptly dubbed 'empathic' (that is, based on empathy) and pitted it against the 'annihilating, nonassimilative, separatist universalism' that can only appreciate the Other from the point of view of the hegemonic same, the known and the familiar.[81]

Clearly, Tagore understood the need to try to understand values other than those associated with our own way of life, but he also understood that the demand for the effort to go deep into another culture and extend our imagination makes this a challenging proposition. It presupposes a willingness to be open to intercultural study, alongside a stance of humility from knowing our own limited part in a much bigger human story. It is an attitude that needs cultivating, since it rarely comes naturally to individuals or societies, where concerns with protecting or imposing one's own particular valuables seem to override the willingness to offer them up for an ungrudging critical exchange.

Sonar Tari: Letting Go

It is a rainy day in the monsoon season, the skies are rumbling with thunder, and the speaker of the poem finds himself sitting alone on the bank of the river. He had just completed gathering the harvest as it started to rain. The water is rising, the danger of flooding is imminent, and a boat is spotted in the distance, with an unidentifiable, yet strangely familiar, figure at its helm.

[80] Tagore (2001a [1917]), p. 454. For more on the methods and strategies adopted by Tagore in view of this goal, see O'Connell (2002), pp. 105–9, 126–7; Nussbaum (2006).

[81] Pandit (1995), p. 207.

> Oh to what foreign land do you sail?
> Come to the bank and moor your boat for a while.
> Go where you want to, give where you care to,
> But come to the bank a moment, show your smile—
> Take away my golden paddy when you sail.

The entire harvest is loaded on to the boat, and when the vessel is ready to sail again, the speaker too wants to be taken aboard. The boat however is full.

> On the bare river-bank, I remain alone—What I had has gone: the golden boat took all.[82]

Tagore wrote this gem of a poem, 'Sonar tari', in 1892 when he was looking after the family estates at Shelidah, by the river Padma, an experience which is said to have turned him into a short-story writer, as it exposed him, for the first time, to the dire conditions and terrible hardships endured by villagers.[83] This particular poem has probably generated more critical response than any other, with a controversy breaking out over its meaning and poetic merit when it first came out.[84] There is indeed a lot more to the poem than what its simple narrative implies.

Despite its realistic setting, the poem has an enigmatic, elusive quality about it. It was attacked in its day for being supposedly vague and meaningless. Tagore of course knew how to turn an argument in his favour, and not only provided a meaning to the poem but also took a stand against overwrought grappling after meaning. 'But does one write poetry to explain something? It is a feeling within the heart

---

[82] 'The Golden Boat', translated by William Radice, Tagore (1994a), p. 53.

[83] This interpretation has been widely accepted and seems valid enough. Pankaj Mishra puts it well: 'Proximity to lives in Indian villages helped distinguish his worldview from that of the middle-class intellectuals in Calcutta. It unleashed a love of natural landscape, a regard for the everyday, the domestic and the fragmentary, as well as an insight into the plight of the rural poor' (Mishra 2012, p. 224). For a less romantic take on Tagore's emerging as the short-story writer, however, see Radice (1994b, pp. 1–5).

[84] For further details, see the note to the poem in Chaudhuri (2004), p. 382.

that tries to find outside shape in a poem. When, after listening to a poem, someone says he has not understood it, I am nonplussed. If he were to smell a flower and say the same thing, the reply would be, "There is nothing to understand, it is only a scent".'[85]

The boat, according to Tagore's symbolic reading of 'Sonar tari', stands for the World and Life—the Bengali word *samsar* conjoins the meanings of everyday domestic life with the world at large—floating along the stream of time and receiving the fruits of human labour, but not the individuals themselves. Having loaded the world's boat with the harvest of our entire lives' work, we hope to have a place there too; the world, however, has little consideration for us. The products of our life's toil may survive, our signature, need not.[86]

There is also a more realist side to the poem. Located very precisely in the riverine setting of today's East Bengal—there may have been an actual incident that triggered the poem—the peasant's anxieties over the crops ('flood-waters twisting and swirling everywhere') are genuine and not just metaphorical.[87] What makes this poem compelling is precisely that its more philosophical dimensions are grounded in the ordinary and the everyday, suggested by the small plot of land on which the speaker finds himself alone (*ekkhani choto khet, ami ekela*). The unfamiliar (who is the figure at the helm, addressed with the familiar form *tumi*?) grows out of the familiar, challenging us to rediscover ourselves and our everyday lives against larger historical forces.

[85] Translated by Surendranath Tagore, Tagore (2003b [1917]), p. 270.

[86] In a letter to Bireshwar Goswami, 9 Agrahayan 1313/24, November 1906, translated from the notes to Sonar Tari, Visva Bharati, 1375/1950, p. 203. An excerpt of this letter is translated and published in Sukanta Chaudhuri's edited volume of Tagore's selected poems, for the citation above, see Tagore (2004b, p. 382). The entire letter was translated for me by Swati Ghosh from Rabindra Bhavana in Santiniketan, who also helped me appreciate some of the nuances of the Bengali original, such as the word *samsar*. The meaning of the poem is also discussed in Tagore's address to his students at Santiniketan entitled 'Tori bojhai' (A fully loaded boat), delivered on 4th Chaitra, 1315 B.S.

[87] For drawing my attention to the 'home meaning' of the poem, which tends to be bypassed in 'modern urban interpretations', I thank Ketaki Kushari Dyson. Email correspondence dated 16 July 2008.

There are lessons to be learnt from history, and Tagore, in another—this time indirect—commentary to the poem, offered further insight:

> That Alexander failed to bring the world under the banner of Greece only proves the futility of such designs; Greece's arrogant ambition has no meaning for us today … Greece and Rome have laden the golden boat of Time with the ripe harvests of their culture; that they themselves failed to get into the boat proved no loss, but rather lighted its load.[88]

Was Greece a code word for Britain and its arrogant ambition to bring the world under its banner? And the ripe harvest what Tagore saw as invaluable—'universal'—in British culture? That which, in the final reckoning, will survive in one form or another, eventually rendering Britain's arrogant ambition meaningless?[89]

At its most elemental, however, 'Sonar tari' presents us with a sympathetic portrayal of the human condition, in which separation from our worldly existence is as inevitable as it is painful. The theme is taken up in another poem from the same collection, the poem 'I Won't Let You Go', in which the refrain—'I won't let you go'—resounds throughout, progressively gaining in symbolic significance, from a young girl's non-negotiable refusal to let her father go on one of his journeys to the whole universe joining in with the chorus.[90] The longing and the clinging are at the heart of both poems, even as 'Sonar tari' compellingly suggests the value—the necessity—precisely of letting go.

Certainly, in Tagore's philosophy, disinterested giving is the path to self-fulfilment. William Radice reads the poem as a struggle between the self and the soul, ending ultimately in spiritual failure. The soul is liberated only through self-surrender, but the self-interest tied to the giving of the harvest leads to loneliness and alienation—the poem's resolve.[91] Our sense of self-importance, our clamouring for immortal

---

[88] Tagore (1961d [1908]), p. 131.

[89] Cf. 'The English ideas that our people can truly assimilate—that is the ideas that are universal rather than peculiarly English—survive while the rest decay' (translated by Swapan Chakravorty, Tagore 2001f [1895], p. 189).

[90] Translated by Ketaki Kushari Dyson, Tagore (2010a [2003]), pp. 92–6.

[91] Tagore (1994b), p. 132.

recognition is, in the final analysis, the burden that deserves to be lost to history.

Conjoining the two readings—the worldlier, politico-historical one with the more spiritual, subjective one—the Golden Boat becomes a richly textured symbol. Not only does it stand for the idea of all cultures contributing their harvest to the world's storehouse of knowledge along the river of passing Time—or, one can also imagine the poem exploring the relationship between the author and his/her work, which, once released, acquires a life of its own (Tagore's English *Gitanjali* would be a case in point)—it also, most importantly, challenges us to think of distinct cultural products as being freed of narrow identity associations, stripped bare of all the superfluous self-congratulatory baggage, so that once loaded upon the boat, they can travel freely beyond their origins, being offered and integrated into a much larger arena.

The substance of this interpretation is borne out if we think back to the aims of Tagore's educational project. Visva-Bharati, I want to suggest, is Tagore's 'Golden Boat', connecting distant shores and fusing mental horizons. That *Sonar tari*, in my reading, is a symbol of Tagore's universalist ideal will be further validated when we come to consider Tagore's pursuit of world travel in the next chapter.

Ownership Fallacy: Argument for Creativity

The ultimate ideal for Tagore was, therefore, a world in which members of different cultures would enter into an engaged dialogue with each other in a spirit of empathy, openness, and joy, aware of their limited part in a bigger—evolving—whole. The ability to dissociate ideas from constraining colonial and/or nationalist contexts so as to relate to what one experiences as 'true' in them became a constituent part of Tagore's search for liberation vis-à-vis 'the oppressive present'.[92]

His essayistic writings are awash with statements that test the boundaries of ownership—and provenance—of ideas. A few random examples of these 'universalist sparks', as I am tempted to call them, for they can illuminate the darker corners of racial and sectarian thinking, will suffice:

[92] I allude to the Sudhir Chandra's so entitled study of the Indian response to the West (cf. Chandra 1992).

Should my joy of learning and appreciating literature stop with Bengali literature because I am born a Bengali? Have I not been born to the world? Are not the creations of every philosopher, every poet, every scientist as much for me as for anybody else? Should that realization not make me proud of my place in the world?[93]

Or,

But a river belonging to a country is not fed by its own waters alone.[94]

Or,

Even the most foolish of critics does not dare blame Shakespeare for what he openly appropriated from outside his own national inheritance. The human soul is proud of its comprehensive sensitiveness; it claims its freedom of entry everywhere when it is fully alive and awake.[95]

In such and similar statements I read Tagore's uncompromising defence of individual creativity that admits of no artificial boundaries, and against forces of inequality and hegemony, transcends its own historical, geographical, and political determinations. Tagore is here implicitly arguing for what, in a more recent reappraisal of the Bengal Renaissance—in an approach that helps us think beyond the terms of the colonizer–colonized binary—Subrata Dasgupta has identified as a fundamental aspect of a creative mind: its ability to appropriate and discriminate for its own goals and needs.

Dasgupta's perspective presupposes granting 'the colonized' complete agency. For example, on the vexed question of English education and whether or not Rammohun Roy and others who championed the European body of knowledge were getting too close to surrendering to the colonizer's intellectual position, his argument is refreshing:

Thus, regardless of the intentions or goals of British educational policy-makers, be they Orientalists or Anglicists, the means they adopted for this purpose was to introduce Indians to English literature. Here then

---

[93] Tagore, speech at Visva-Bharati, 1922, translated by Uma Das Gupta, U. Das Gupta (2004), p. 67.

[94] Tagore (1961h [1919]), p. 223.

[95] Tagore (2002b [1920?]), p. 71.

was a creative encounter: Indians consumed the literary works over the centuries by Englishmen; and this in turn led Indians to become producers/creators in their own right; they created for themselves a cross-cultural mentality.[96]

In this respect, his focus on the workings of a creative mind and its cross-cultural responsiveness is a welcome shift from the hegemony of power discourses that have come to dominate the way the phenomenon of the 'Bengal Renaissance' and Tagore's place in it is read. From the perspective of cognitive science, anxieties over denationalized surrender on the basis of class interest or whether Indians are condemned to the state of being perpetual consumers of an 'alien' modernity, are brushed aside as inconsequential. The definition of a cross-cultural mentality is that the confines of one's own culture are transcended and cultural 'origins' of ideas rendered insignificant.

> [O]ne's belief/knowledge space is not fragmented into regions by culture; rather it becomes an integrated, richly connected, network of beliefs, theories, facts, concepts, values. In such a situation the selection, retrieval, and processing of these entities in pursuit of a goal or need is determined solely by the goals and needs, and not by the culture-specificity of the entities. Thus, to possess a cross-cultural mentality … is in part to be able to access, manipulate, and transform the contents of one's belief/knowledge space using one's repertoire of mental actions and procedural knowledge equally fluently, independent of the culture in which these contents originated. It is the goals and needs that dictate the use and processing of the beliefs and knowledge; their cultural roots become virtually transparent.[97]

Indeed, Tagore, whose exceptionally creative life is one big testament to such a cross-cultural mentality, would, for example, claim India's right to self-government and scientific knowledge not because these were some sort of a gift from the British for which one had to be grateful, but because it was in the substance of that knowledge itself that he felt compelled to do so. In other words, his mind—and from the 'universalist sparks' above we see that Tagore explicitly objected to the knowledge space being divided into regions by culture or

[96] Subrata Dasgupta (2006), p. 89.
[97] Subrata Dasgupta (2006), pp. 78–9.

nationality—was responding to the content of knowledge itself, rendering its alleged proprietors insignificant. The goal and need he was pursuing was, for sure, the betterment of India's social, economic, and political situation:

> Just as our right to European science lies in the very nature of science, so our right to English politics lies in the very nature of that politics. A small number of Englishmen might say that it would be better not to give Indian students the opportunity to learn science, but science itself would put those Englishmen to shame by inviting, in a stentorian voice, everyone, of whatever colour or creed, to grow strong by studying it. In a similar way a small, or even a large number of English politicians and journalists might say that it would be better to put all sorts of obstacles in the way of Indian self-government, but English politics would reject that advice by inviting every Indian, of whatever colour or creed, to assert his right in the government of his country.[98]

This is a strong argument for entitlement to, and appropriation of, ideas, if these are believed to have relevance. It enabled Tagore to draw on the advantages of a global modernity while remaining an uncompromising critic of colonial rule and Westernization,[99] and making, as Bhattacharya put it, modernity 'ours' without necessarily carving out a space for 'our modernity'.[100] 'Why should Europe restrict to the lost the standards which she herself has formulated? Does it not bear responsibilities towards all the world?'[101] To shun Europe is to practise exclusivism and arrogance no different to that condemned in Europeans. It is also, Tagore believed, lacking in good sense. He understood that under colonial rule 'it is not easy ... to understand

---

[98] Tagore (1961g [1917]), pp. 192–3.

[99] In the previous chapter, I have shown how Tagore condemned the politicized and commercialized aspect of the modern civilization that sprung up from Europe, but he would hold on to 'universalism' of the new age. He also distinguished sharply between modernization and Westernization. 'Modernism is not in the dress of the Europeans; or in the hideous structures, where their children are interned when they take their lessons ... certainly modernism is not in their ladies' bonnets, carrying on them loads of incongruities. These are not modern, but merely European' (Tagore 2001a[1917]), p. 446).

[100] D. Bhattacharya (2008a), pp. 7–8.

[101] Tagore (1961l [1933]), p. 349.

and accept what is good in Europe', but to understand and accept what is 'good' one must try, for where 'truth' is concerned, divisions between East and West, or Europe and India, are meaningless.[102]

Ideas, like people, travel, and in the process they get transformed. There are no national boundaries in the realm of knowledge, though attitudes formed around certain ideas or subjects are often based on seeing them tied to narrow territorial and culturo-political contexts. They are perceived as though they do indeed come with a national flag attached to them. This is especially true in the context of encounters that come on the back of political suppression and economic exploitation. But if beliefs and knowledge systems are considered outside their real or alleged progenitors and claimants, Tagore argued, we can—and must—relate to them simply for the 'truth' of what they convey and express. Further, we can creatively adapt them to suit our own goals and needs. Ideas not only belong to everyone, but there is also nothing inherently 'Eastern' or 'Western' about them. Indeed, knowing that Rammohun Roy cheered the French Revolution in Calcutta at a time when in England it was fiercely opposed, seen as too subversive of the established ways, is to see the futility of confining ideas within territorial boundaries. Would it then not be more sensible, historically accurate even, to see the French Enlightenment as part of a global heritage rather than Europe's heritage only?[103]

Dynamic Truth and a One-World Perspective

Tagore objected to intellectual proprietorship also because of his sense of, and devotion to, 'truth', which has its locus in the individual but can only realize itself in a creative unity with others and the environment. An emphatic believer in personal contacts and the necessity of sharing between individuals from different walks of life and parts of the world, Tagore also tied his concept of truth to the idea of travel, both physically to foreign lands and mentally across ideational landscapes. In his address to his students in Santiniketan on the eve of his third trip to England in 1912, he spoke of the need to relate the life of their country school to the larger world:

[102] Tagore, 1921, cited in U. Das Gupta (2004), p. 66.

[103] See, on this, D. Bhattacharya (2008a, pp. 6–8). The point about Roy is originally from C. A. Bayly, *The Birth of the Modern World 1780–1914* (2004).

The power to move freely in the realm of truth is not tested until one visits other lands. The petty-souled accept the familiar as the only truth and reject all else as unimportant or unreal. The test of our devotion to truth lies in the ability to push open the doors of the unfamiliar, discover what lies behind and pay homage.[104]

To claim the unfamiliar behind the doors of the familiar sets one on what can only be a never-ending process of truth-discovery. Reality for Tagore is not based in the substance of things, but in the principle of relationship, and we can never be true in our isolated selves. So 'making truth ours' involves 'actively modulating its inter-relations'.[105] Truth in that sense is both historical and contingent, and like Tagore's notion of 'God', it is a 'horizon concept',[106] an inspirational category that can lead to the overcoming of the self. It is poised between the opposite pulls of strict relativism and strict universalism or, as Tagore would have it, the finite and the Infinite. Living truth, for Tagore, is not absolute but an inherently dynamic, subversive of set creeds and institutionalized beliefs.[107] 'In the poet's religion we find no doctrine or injunction, but rather the attitude of our entire being towards a truth which is ever to be revealed in its own endless creation.'[108]

[104] Tagore (1961f [1912]), p. 160.

[105] Tagore (2002h [1931]), pp. 132–3.

[106] The term has been coined by Pabitrakumar Roy (2002), p. 197.

[107] Ulrich Beck says something to a similar effect: 'That truth is not absolute does not mean that there is no truth; it means that *truth* continually required an up-dated contextual definition' (emphasis in original, Beck 2004, p. 437).

[108] Tagore (2002d [1922]), p. 16. How strongly Tagore opposed institutionalized forms of religion is seen in the following lines, taken from his address on Rammohun Roy in 1928:

The moment we narrow down the principle unity that constitutes the essence of religion and give it a local form, it becomes a deadly weapon that cuts us out from the rest of the world. Storm, flood, volcanic eruption, plague—there are many kinds of natural horrors. But in the entire history of man we will find nothing that can compare with the horror that is religion. Man's religion was the greatest enemy of human unity; and it cannot be said that enmity has subsided yet. (Cited in Sayeed 1980, p. 7, originally from *Rabindra Rachanabali*, vol. 11, p. 402.)

With such a dynamic concept of truth centred on becoming a movement, rather than a fixity and a dogma, Tagore's universalism, in my analysis, is not an established code of universal principles—though one can, as critics have done, discern ethical universals such as ahimsa, love, and sympathy with reference to Tagore[109]—but an open-ended proposition, subject to creative transmission between cultures at a world-historical junction when 'real geographical boundaries', as he put it, became but 'imaginary lines of tradition'.[110] In contrast to a universalism that boasts of unity but demands uniformity, Tagore's universalism rejects uniformity but aspires for unity:

> Uniformity is not unity; only those who are different can unite. Nations which wipe out the independence of other nations are the destroyers of interdependence. Imperialist nations swallow up other nations, python-like, and they call it unity.[111]

Tagore's is a difference-sensitive universalism, and though it strives for a whole larger than the sum of its parts, it does not necessitate a loss of individuality or erasure of cultural location. On the contrary, he says: 'Only by admitting the individuality of men in matters in which they are separate can we arrive at their real unity in matters in which they are one.' Paradoxically, synthesis for Tagore 'takes place only when two things remain separate and yet unite'.[112] Differences are absolutely integral to the kind of unity Tagore stood for. His universalism not only admits plurality but is conditioned by it:

> In every man truth has a universal form and at the same time an individual form. That is his personal religion. And in that he is preserving the variety of the world. This variety is an invaluable element of creation. However much I may follow the rule of 'sameness', I can by no means blot out the difference between my form and the form of others.[113]

[109] Samir Dayal, for example, is right in arguing that we need 'to read Tagore's universalist humanism not just as a utopic idealism but as one modelled on the universally accessible, everyday experience of love: lived affect' (2007, p. 180).

[110] Tagore (2001a[1917]), p. 454.

[111] Tagore (1961i [1921]), p. 246.

[112] Tagore (1961i [1921]), p. 246.

[113] Translated by Devadatta Joardar, Tagore (2006a), p. 26.

If this can be seen as an expression of universalism of difference (that is, we are all the same in that we are different), it is essential to understand that 'difference' here is not fixed in any taxonomical manner. Neither is it an empty abstraction, because the 'other' for Tagore is a living soul shaped by his or her own self-constituting activity. The spiritual unity he sought could therefore never be grounded in sameness but rather in harmony connecting various particularities in the world. 'Let us unite, not in spite of our differences, but through them. For differences can never be wiped away, and life would be so much the poorer without them.'[114]

Tagore's unity is conceived as *creative*, involving a perpetual back-and-forth movement between the personal self and that which transcends it. 'Our mind has faculties which are universal, but its habits are insular.'[115] This antithesis between our minds and our habits, the human potentiality and its actuality, is what sets the universalist quest into motion in its twin mechanism of self-correction and fulfilment in what Badiou, to remind ourselves of his definition of universality, submits as becoming indifferent to difference, and resist whatever makes us conform.

From all that has been said regarding Tagore's universalism in its various aspects, I find it difficult to see how Tagore can stand accused of either ahistorical imperialist universalism[116] or, more recently, from the other end, of 'civilizational essentialism', by which the author, Adam Webb, means a belief that 'civilizations as a whole have drastically different essences, and that given those essences they become the building blocks of an alternative world order.'[117] Webb is not convinced of Tagore's universalism, wondering 'about the likelihood of getting to a true universalism if one devotes such energy to the affirmation of distinctiveness', admitting though that in Tagore's case, this is 'a far cry from fundamentalist chauvinism.'[118]

It is true that Tagore would sometimes proceed from the distinctiveness of particular civilizations, positing that different peoples had

[114] Tagore (2002e [1925]), p. 49.
[115] Tagore (2002d [1922]), p. 99.
[116] Trivedi (1995).
[117] Webb (2008), p. 208.
[118] Webb (2008), p. 208.

followed different trajectories in their histories, and so he understood 'all particular civilizations' to be 'the interpretation of particular human experience'.[119] In that sense, he posited different truths and knowledge systems for different peoples and civilizations. A consideration of different perspectives and, by extension, granting others the right to exist and own a separate identity, is, after all, one of the key premises of true universalism. But Tagore, as I have shown, does not essentialize difference; he vectors change into all natural and social phenomena in what is arguably a perpetual production of difference or many-sidedness of truth. Moreover, Tagore was no cultural relativist, and believed that different civilizations—sometimes unfortunately collapsed into notions of 'East' and 'West'—were in some essential way complementary, and had to learn from each other, for 'their different outlooks on life' had given them 'different aspects of truth'.[120]

So, from the opposite end, Tagore would say that truth and knowledge are 'one' and 'universal', and that they are variously expressed in different parts of the world, a little like, as one critic has put it, people having different diets across the globe, suited to their climate and taste, but the principle of nutrition being one.[121] In both cases, however, we are dealing with the concept of 'unity *in* diversity', a concept bandied around so much in paroles and speeches that it has lost much of its appeal and meaning, but nonetheless a crucial pivot around which Tagore's universalist thinking turns. In reality, it was a distant horizon in Tagore's times as it is in our own. Its validity, however, is precisely in that it remains an aspiration and not a prescription.

There are also admittedly passages in Tagore's voluminous writings that can lend themselves to Webb's interpretation. The least attractive ones are to be found in some of his foreign lectures and addresses where Tagore's thinking can indeed slide into essentializations of 'East' and 'West' and comes closest to a version of a spiritual proto-nationalism, intended as a kind of confidence booster for people humiliated by foreign domination and lacking a positive sense of identification.[122] Nonetheless, for the most part, Tagore's discourse

---

[119] Tagore (2001 [1917]), p. 441.
[120] Tagore (2001 [1917]), p. 423.
[121] Masud (1988), p. 76.
[122] I say more on this in the next chapter, p. 166.

reveals a discriminating double concern for both the distinctive features in different peoples and societies *and* an interest and belief in a common or shared humanity underlying those features—what he refers to as 'the unity of the soul', but which, he affirms, must not be an abstraction. 'It is not that negative kind of universalism which belongs neither to one nor to another,' he heeded, 'it is not an abstract soul, but it is my own soul which I must realize in others.'[123]

And certainly Tagore was no proponent of a clash-of-civilization theory that Webb's critique might erroneously suggest. If anything, he was a fervent proponent of a one-world idea. 'There is only one history, the history of man. All national histories are merely chapters in the larger one.'[124] The new age demanded a shift in perspective, and Tagore was among the first to exhort his contemporaries across the globe 'to exert [their] power of love and clarity of vision [and] make another great moral adjustment which [would] ... comprehend the whole world of men and not merely the fractional groups of nationality.'[125]

One example that springs to mind by way of illustrating Tagore's 'personalistic' philosophy that sought commonalities with people from different geographies and histories—is from when the poet visited a Bedouin camp on his travels in Iraq and Persia in 1932. As he sat down to break bread with his hosts, he pondered how 'contrasting the two races, the Beduins and the Bengalis', were, and how differently they had been moulded by their environments, the harsh deserts and the nurturing riverine landscape, respectively, the former posing a stark challenge to the everyday lives of Bedouins. And, yet, despite the fact that their 'hosts' and they were 'of two totally different moulds', it struck Tagore, that here too, as elsewhere, where he was not made conscious of belonging to a different nation or different religion, he had found proof of the universality of 'the language that carries the message of the most profound humanity.'[126]

Tagore's vision was indeed premised on a belief in a spiritual unity of humanity, but having at its core an ideal of freedom rooted in individual self-expression and development, his vision was committed to

[123] Tagore (2001b [1917]), p. 373.
[124] Tagore (2001a [1917]), p. 453.
[125] Tagore (2001a [1917]), p. 455.
[126] Translated by Sukhendu Ray, Tagore (2003a), pp. 110–11.

honouring difference and hence diverse ways of being. Not to belabour an earlier point, unity for Tagore does not issue in uniformity. 'It is God's purpose,' he held, 'that in the societies of man the various should be strung together into a garland of unity,' only to understand how trod-upon this ideal is in practice. Indeed, aggressive promotion of similitude across—and within—cultures was what Tagore recognized to be the dominant, if ultimately doomed, trend in history:

> Repeated efforts, even unto violence and bloodshed, have been made, all the world over, to bring mankind together on the basis of the common worship of a common Deity, but even these have not been successful. Neither has a common God been found, nor a common form of worship.[127]

One-size-fits-all solutions are not only hegemonic, they are also too simplistic. It was this belief that lay at the core of Tagore's disagreement with Gandhi and his injunction that all Indians should devote some of their time to spinning as the solution to India's problems.[128] To those who asked with the same objective of *swaraj*, 'Would not the foreigners be drowned even if every one of our three hundred and thirty millions were only to spit at them?', Tagore submitted that no doubt the prospect was fearsome, but one could 'never get all these millions even to spit in unison. It is too simple for human beings'.[129] Complex problems demand complex solutions, and Tagore's principal concern was with guarding the integrity of personal action and freedom, so it is not surprising that he often found himself disagreeing with Gandhi's more politically operative approach. Any kind of instrumentalization of individuals, as must be clear by now, was anathema to Tagore. What makes humans human is precisely, as Collins has put it, 'the inner sphere of the *creative impulse*—the 'abundance' or 'surplus', that wealth of creative capacity and fund of emotional energy—which takes the human beyond the realms of a mere concern with self-preservation'.[130] This *positive* freedom is what Tagore found himself defending in the

---

[127] Tagore, in S. Bhattacharya (2005), p. 105.
[128] For the *charkha* controversy, see the correspondence between Tagore and Gandhi collected in S. Bhattacharya (2005), pp. 99–128.
[129] S. Bhattacharya (2005), p. 109.
[130] Collins (2012), p. 87.

midst of a nation-wide struggle for gaining political freedom. The fact that in a letter to C. F. Andrews, he called Gandhi 'a moral tyrant' for thinking he had the power to 'make his ideas prevail through the means of slavery'[131]—these words were excised from the sanitized 1928 book *Letters to a Friend*[132]—is an indication of just how far Tagore was prepared to go in defence of personal freedom.

Tagore's and Gandhi's opinions seriously diverged on other issues as well; those concerning non-cooperation and the role of science and technology in modern life, but to see their views in terms of strict opposition would be to simplify matters. There was much by way of common ground between them, both in orientation (opposition to caste and communalism) as well as enterprise, such as setting up an alternative education to the state-sponsored system of colonial education. It is telling that Tagore, at the end of his life, concerned with what would happen to Visva-Bharati after he died, nominated Gandhi as the institution's life trustee. The intensity of their exchange over a period of twenty-five years (and both responded positively to each other's criticism) may also have brought them closer on certain points. Bhattacharya has suggested that Gandhi may have begun to see India's relationship to the world differently as a result of the debates he had with Tagore. Gandhi's famous pronouncement, 'I do not want my house to be walled in all sides and my windows to be stuffed. I want the culture of all the lands to be blown about my house as freely as possible. But I refuse to be blown off my feet by any,'[133] could very well have been Tagore's, for he would similarly state: 'True universalism is not the breaking down of the walls of one's own house, but the offering of hospitality to one's guests and neighbours.'[134] On other points, however, such as the Bihar earthquake in 1934 (Gandhi put

---

[131] Tagore, letter to C. F. Andrews, July 1915, cited in Collins (2012).

[132] Likewise, a number of essays published in *The Modern Review* in which Tagore lays out his more controversial take on the West and India are found to be missing from Sisir Kumar Das's seminal compilation of Tagore's English writings. Collins' historiographical and archival input here is most welcome and timely for gaining a more nuanced understanding of Tagore's unconventional position on empire and modernity.

[133] Tagore, in S. Bhattacharya (2005), p. 36.

[134] Tagore (2002c [1921]), p. 75.

the calamity down to God's punishment for the sin of untouchability, but Tagore could not accept such an unscientific approach), Gandhi was intractable, and Tagore in turn accepted 'the eternal human truth that we are in agreement with some people and with some others we are not'.[135]

Tagore's rapport with Gandhi, to explain this short digression, again demonstrates something of what a universalist orientation requires (and what Tagore strove to implement in practice through education): the respect for another's point of view, the openness to learn from it and, in turn, test one's own belief system and, finally, a measure of humility in knowing that one's view is but *a* view. So part of what it means to be 'a universalist' is to understand that one's own perspective is necessarily limited, provisional and, as Tagore had hoped, subject to revision in the face of new evidence or experience. 'Let us be rid of all false pride and rejoice at any lamp being lit at any corner of the world, knowing that it is a part of the common illumination of our house.'[136] In the final analysis, the idea(l) of the unity of humanity that is at the heart of Tagore's universalist, and some would say cosmopolitan,[137] vision is a locus of intersecting— travelling[138]—traditions and histories, suggesting open-ended possibilities for both personal and collective transformation.

With respect to artistic transformation, Tagore held: 'A current trend in Asian countries is to attempt a fusion of Eastern and Western cultures, and this fusion is pregnant with possibilities.'[139] Part of his confidence and optimism must again be put down to his belief in universal humanity that transcends asymmetrical power relations, but Tagore's resources as a thinker were also ever of the pragmatist: 'We have seen the influence of eastern art on European paintings, but that has not spelt doom for the western art and culture,' so how, he asked, would rejecting Europe 'necessarily reinforce the glory of our heritage'?[140]

---

[135] Tagore, in S. Bhattacharya (2005), p. 99.

[136] Tagore, in S. Bhattacharya (2005), p. 61.

[137] On this see S. Tagore (2008), p. 1080.

[138] Here I am of course alluding to Clifford's challenge to cultures being tied to specific locales, and his proposition that they be seen as 'travel' or a product of 'the wider world of intercultural import–export', (1992, p. 100).

[139] Tagore, in S. Bhattacharya (2005), p. 83.

[140] Tagore, in S. Bhattacharya (2005), p. 85.

In his assessment of Tagore's travel writings,[141] Kaiser Haq has remarked on one aspect of Tagore's personality which comes across as a positive influence in his writings about the world, namely that he was free of the 'cultural cringe' and the *ressentiment* associated with colonial relations.[142] There is indeed little, if anything, in his writings that would suggest a colonial mentality that is dismissive of one's own culture, or, conversely, defensively asserts the unique merits of a 'national' culture. Tagore proposes instead a twin scrutiny of the old and the new, the home-grown and the foreign, so as to derive a higher level of understanding surpassing both. Hence he could be, at one and the same time, the severest critic and admirer of the West, and the severest critic and admirer of India. 'In no country in the world is the building up of *swaraj* completed.'[143]

As the early twentieth-century India, fighting colonialism, underwent a transformation from what Sheldon Pollock has termed 'the culture of Place, *deshi*' to *Swadeshi*, 'our own place', that is, 'national', Tagore, his initial involvement in nationalist politics notwithstanding, tried to dissuade his countrymen from adopting the prefix. The alternative Tagore envisioned and strove for was emphatically deshi in its dynamic relationship to the world. He located resources for a new mode of belonging in what became the place of his foremost attachment. His own creation, as it were, Santiniketan, was to bear out his personal conviction that opposes the patriotic 'idea that our homeland is ours just because we have been born in it' and replaces it with a creative principle in which 'whatever country [man] helps to create by his wisdom and will, devotion and action, becomes his real homeland.'[144] Understandably then,

---

[141] Of Tagore's seven travel narratives, four are now available in English translation. Cf. Tagore 1962, 2003a, 2008b, and 2010b. For more on this critical still underappreciated genre of Tagore's writings, see also Sen (2013).

[142] Haq (2005), p. 369.

[143] Tagore, in S. Bhattacharya (2005), p. 82.

[144] Tagore (1961j [1921]), p. 255. Discussing the same quote, but taken from Partha Chatterjee's translation in *Lineages of Political Society*, Poulomi Saha puts it neatly: 'The distinction between *dés* and *svadés*, country and my own country, is located in the imaginative power of the Sanskrit reflexive pronoun prefix *sva*: the reflexivity of self-making is itself country-making' (2013, p. 7). This is a succinct description of the kind of imaginative practice that remains personal and quotidian even as it gestures towards a larger collectivity.

Santiniketan was conceived as 'somewhere beyond the limits of nation and geography', as he had written in the letter to his son cited earlier.[145]

And finally: 'Whatever we understand and enjoy in human products instantly becomes ours, wherever they might have had their origin,' wrote Tagore to his close associate in Santiniketan, C. F. Andrews in 1921, further stating how he was proud of his humanity when he was able to acknowledge the poets and artists of other countries as his own.[146] This statement quintessentially embodies the aspect of Tagore's universalist philosophy which I have tried to highlight in this chapter, namely setting ideas free in the face of historical forces that threatened to partition the world of knowledge as much as they partitioned the world of people. This was a stance that put Tagore in a subversive relationship with the persisting binaries of 'tradition' and 'modernity', split allegedly between 'us' and 'them', suggesting instead a notion of global modernity sustained through travel and exchange of ideas. It also inaugurated the birth of a 'universal human being' as opposed to a 'colonial subject'.[147] For, as Tagore held, 'True modernism is freedom of mind, not slavery of taste. It is independence of thought, not tutelage under European schoolmasters'.[148] This freedom he claimed for himself (over and above the fact of colonization) and tried to extend to others.

[145] See pp. 126–7 of this volume.

[146] Tagore, in a letter to C. F. Andrews, 13 March 1921, in Andrews (2002), p. 107.

[147] On this point, see A. Chaudhuri (2008, p. 106), who suggested that the answer to the 'confidence and magpie-like instinct towards intellectual entitlement' that gave a distinctive mark to Indian modernity in the nineteenth and early twentieth century need not be seen merely as a province of class elitism, but recognized also as an expression of the ability to translate 'the self from [the fixed identity of] colonial subject to "universal" human being'.

[148] Tagore (2001a [1917]), p. 446.

4 Tagore in Europe

Diverse Responses

After gaining some strength I wish to sail for Europe. I do not know
when exactly I can make it. I have done as much as I could have for this
country. Whether the country accepts it or not, there hasn't been any
dearth of interest on my part. People across the sea want me now—I
have my place there among them. Which is my true homeland? The
piece of land where I was born by accident?

—Tagore, Letter to Monoranjan Bandyopadhyay [1912?]

The world vision and a passion for universalism that Tagore pursued also through travelling—and he travelled possibly more
than any other literary person in his time—transcended narrow
identifications as regards both individuals and ideas. Effectively, he
spent more than a tenth of his lengthy life, close to nine years, touring
abroad and this was long before intercontinental travel became commonplace. From the time of his first foreign trip to England in 1878–9
as a young man of seventeen, sent there to acquire the qualifications
deemed fit for his class (he returned to India without completing any
formal education), and his last foreign tour to Persia and Iraq in 1932
at the age of 71, he undertook as many as twelve world tours.[1] Some

---

[1] Strictly speaking, his tour in Ceylon in 1934 may be regarded as his
last 'foreign' tour.

kept him away from Calcutta and Santiniketan for over a year. From multiple trips to Europe, North America, the Middle East, the Far East, and one to South-East Asia, and to South America—Tagore visited every inhabited continent except for Australia and, perhaps more unexpectedly, Africa (discounting a short stay in Alexandria and Cairo on his return trip from Europe in 1926).

It is not surprising then that travelling features so prominently in his writing, and in the previous chapter I have already noted the value he attributed to it with respect to what became the ideal enshrined in Visva-Bharati's constitution: 'To study the mind of man in its realization of different aspects of truth from diverse points of view.'[2] I have also linked it to Tagore's emphasis on interdependence and cooperation as forces that needed strengthening to fend against the identity politics of nationalism and imperialism. Travel for Tagore was indeed both theory and praxis, a way of engaging the ethical self and broadening moral consciousness. Education in turn became the platform for actualizing this in practice.[3]

This chapter further considers Tagore's rationale for travel, with attention to his endorsement of the English language through which his poetry and ideas could be disseminated. This will lead us to explore his reputation in the West, more precisely, in Europe, after he became an international celebrity. His European reputation and fame was not a monolith, a point made clearer as we move away from the metro-politan centres of Western Europe to consider some specific responses to the Indian poet from Europe's central and eastern peripheries. I highlight the identification paradigm as a way of theorizing a differ-ent mode of relating to Tagore than the more conventional orientalist model allows for, and one which will help us frame both the general Slovenian response to the Indian poet as well as Kosovel's personal appreciation of his Indian contemporary.

PURPOSEFUL TRAVELLER

In his correspondence, Tagore often expresses a craving for the 'wide world', the need to distance himself from his own society and embark

---

[2] Tagore, cited in U. Das Gupta (2004), p. 69.
[3] On this, see Sen (2013).

on some new journey. As he put it in a letter to Edward Thompson: 'For some time past I have been feeling restless. It is the migratory instinct in me. I have a nesting place on the other side of the sea and I feel homesick for the wide world.'[4] Often we see him questioning the notion of 'home' and belonging, envisioning possibilities of new and other, possibly better, 'homes'. At the same time leaving your home is a precondition for realizing you have a home, but having once left it also implies loss, since the home you come back to—provided you *can* come back to it—is already a different home. Tagore's close alignment in creative writing with the wandering Baul sect, his imaginative association with the outcast, the pilgrim, a wayfarer stripped of name and identity—not unlike the character in his poem 'A Person' (1932)[5]—and finally, his valorization of the classical Hindu tenet and virtue to ultimately give up one's home, not only point in the direction of superseding bounded and normative identities, they also suggest a permanently transient and fractured notion of 'home'.

In the previous chapter, we established a close link between Tagore's critique of nationalist and patriotic discourses and his deterritorialized concept of India. His experiment in education too was premised explicitly on the idea of a place that transcends national and geographic boundaries. Travel is, as already suggested, vitally connected to both. And yet, it needs to be said, Tagore, in the final reckoning, was and remained *rooted* or *home-bound*, if not to India as a geographical fact—though ultimately he always returned to Santiniketan, and it is hard to imagine him wanting to settle down permanently anywhere else—then certainly in his commitment to 'India' as an idea of unconditional hospitality to 'the world', the inspirational and aspirational category behind all of his projects.

Tagore's migratory instinct that compelled him to travel was no doubt enhanced by his cosmopolitan upbringing, but it was also the peculiar circumstances he found himself in after the short and abortive

---

[4] Tagore, 13 April 1916, in U. Das Gupta (2003), p. 108.

[5] 'The wayfarer appeared/on the outermost line of my universe,/where insubstantial shadow-pictures move./I just knew him to be a person./He had no name, no identity, no pain,/no need whatsoever of anything./On the road to market on a Bhadra morning/he was just a person.' Thus reads the second stanza of this poem, written in 1932, translated from the Bengali original by Ketaki Kushari Dyson, in Tagore (2010a [2003]), pp. 190–1.

stint with nationalist politics that made him consciously seek out alternative spaces. Once he abandoned the struggle which he had, in the eyes of many, so heroically inspired with his songs and addresses, Tagore, by then already a celebrity in Bengal, found himself intellectually and emotionally isolated in the midst of his own people.[6] In the years just prior to that, between 1902 and 1907, he had also suffered a series of tragic bereavements, losing four members of his immediate family (his wife, his second daughter, his father, and his youngest son). In the best years of his life he was, to quote his biographer, 'reduced to utter loneliness'.[7]

Tagore was to remain unmarried for the rest of his life, and while his amorous attachments will always be enveloped by a shroud of mystery, it is clear he sought intellectual companionship also elsewhere.[8] In his post-Swadeshi period, he was particularly keen to meet people who like himself had fought 'the bondage of nationalism'. One such person was the French writer in exile Romain Rolland (1866–1944), 'an outcast from his own people', according to Tagore, who had been made to 'renounce [his] home-world' in the 'true spirit of a *sannyasin*'.[9] But unlike Rolland who went into self-imposed exile in Switzerland as a foresworn pacifist after World War I broke out and remained there until 1938, Tagore always returned to India, bringing back, as it were, the boons of his travels (his was going to be a self-imposed exile at home). Indeed, once he became sought after by agencies across the

[6] See Kripalani (2001 [1986]), p. 112.

[7] Kripalani (2001 [1986]), p. 114. It is against this history of suffering, loss, and great loneliness that Tagore's *Gitanjali* emerged, a history that did not get communicated through to the Western audiences, according to Dutta-Roy, (2001), pp. 6–66. More recently, loneliness and solitude have been identified as important—even key—elements of Tagore's 'mental environment' and psychological demeanour. Tagore is shown to have attributed his restlessness, his passion for travel to 'a positive desire for solitude', though at the same time, loneliness also pained and irked him; see S. Bhattacharya (2011), pp. 25–6.

[8] For a probing psychological analysis of Tagore's relationship with Victoria Ocampo (1890–1979), an Argentinian woman of letters, as well as a study of a major cross-cultural encounter, see Dyson (1996).

[9] Tagore, 'The Call of Truth', 1921, in S. Bhattacharya (2005), p. 86. For more on the encounter between Rolland and Tagore, see Aronson and Kripalani (1945).

world competing to exploit his cultural capital, Tagore made use of the financial gains 'to support his school in Santiniketan, and in sustaining experiments in agriculture, community development, and banking in Sriniketan'.[10] Tagore's royalties, though incomparably larger than that of any of his contemporaries, were not enough to support the institution,[11] so we can imagine the indispensability of this additional financial injection for a school that was self-funded as opposed to state-funded, and did not collect fees, at least not in the early days.

Privileged globetrotter that Tagore unquestionably was, he was not—this much is clear—a casual traveller. Adopting for himself the role of a mediator between cultures, he shouldered the task in larger-than-life terms of a *mission*, a *calling*, or a *pilgrimage*, to give some of the recurring metaphors that crop up in his writings to describe his adopted role.[12] For Tagore, as suggested in the previous chapter, travelling was about connecting distant banks, and that required leaving 'mental easy-chairs' behind and letting go of excessive attachments to 'home comforts', intellectual or otherwise.[13] Driven by a strong anti-isolationist and anti-parochial commitment, the goal of travel was to get to, as one critic has put it, a 'cosmopolitan space of a freedom of ideas'.[14]

A word or two about Tagore's 'cosmopolitanism'[15] is in order here, since a large number of critics have aligned Tagore's social and political

---

[10] Bharucha (2006), p. 125.

[11] On this see Kaviraj (2003), pp. 551–5.

[12] For the idea of travel as *tirtha* (pilgrimage), a recurring term in most of Tagore's travelogues, and how Tagore refashioned this Sanskritic notion and put it to secular, pedagogical, and ethical use in the context of his time, see Sen (2013).

[13] Tagore (2002d [1922]), pp. 88–9.

[14] Sen (2013), p. 84.

[15] It must be noted that although the two terms 'universalism' and 'cosmopolitanism' have distinct histories, in many ways they bear closely on each other. Notional hybrids such as 'universalist cosmopolitanism' testify to their interrelatedness, cf. Appiah (2005), pp. 219–20, 258–9. In fact, revisions of cosmopolitanism in contemporary social and cultural criticism run in close parallel with similar efforts that have recuperated universalism as a theoretically viable concept. In the same way that theorists of diversity have adopted labels such as 'new', 'genuine' and, 'true' universalism to advance a universalism

thought with a version of 'cosmopolitanism' that respects cultural difference while insisting on some fundamental set of universal values.[16]

At a *prima facie* level, Tagore's cosmopolitan credentials are multiple: a multilingual individual at ease with a number of thought systems, combining their features in his creative work; someone who welcomed 'borrowings' as an inevitable and necessary part of a globalizing world; who argued for a critical re-evaluation of received traditions vis-à-vis other traditions; and of course, someone who was widely travelled and gave this component of his life a practical outlet

---

sensitive to difference and differentiate it from its 'older' hegemonic variety that promotes similitude across cultures, cosmopolitanism too has been given a new lease of life away from largely imperialist associations and negative post-Enlightenment associations (that is, privileged mode of detachment or not belonging, imposed acculturation, etc.) to versatile reconsiderations of its emancipatory and ethical potential. For an analysis of the genealogy of the term and its relationship to universalism, see Anderson (1998). For the term's complex history, see P. B. Mehta (2000), pp. 620–4.

[16] Martha Nussbaum has endorsed Tagore's cosmopolitanism more expressly for the field of education, but her reliance on classical cosmopolitanism has provoked a heated debate (cf. Cohen 1996). Alongside others, and contra Nussbaum's understanding of Tagore's cosmopolitan stance, Saranindranath Tagore, for example, has argued for the need to locate Tagore's cosmopolitanism outside the normative, abstract Kantian understanding of universality, so that particular cultural traditions are seen as a vehicle for understanding and morally relating to others (S. Tagore 2008, pp. 1072, 1074). Tagore, in Saranindranath's reading, becomes a new cosmopolitan of the recent debates. But see also Nussbaum's assessment of Tagore's credentials as a democratic thinker in *The Clash Within* (2007, pp. 82–94). Here, speaking of Tagore's position as an individualist *and* humanist, she comes closer to Saranindranath's understanding: 'Humanism might lead to colorless cosmopolitanism; but if it respected the individual it would move instead in the direction of tactful and sympathetic pluralism' (Nussbaum 2007, p. 90). The emphasis is put on what one other scholar has more recently theorized as 'an alternative model of attachment' and has called 'locally rooted globalism', a model that seeks to balance affective commitments with humanist ideals (Saha 2013, p. 3). On this, see also Louise Blakeney Williams (2007), though her emphasis on the 'nationalist' dimension of Tagore's cosmopolitanism runs, in my view, the risk of limiting the scope of Tagore's ideas.

and a concrete base in his institution in Santiniketan.[17] Of course, one would not wish to suggest any straightforward link between 'cosmopolitanism' and global travel, but in Tagore's case, travelling—of the elite privileged kind—*was* a major component of giving his universalist ideal a concrete face. His efforts were positively directed at what is commonly described as cultivating a 'cosmopolitan consciousness', that is to say 'an awareness of the existence and equal validity of other cultures, other values, other mores' alongside 'elements of self-doubt and reflexive self-distantiation'.[18]

Tagore, on the other hand, had his own views regarding the trends he recognized as the shaping forces of his age. Famously he wrote in his book *Nationalism*: 'Neither the colourless vagueness of cosmopolitanism, nor the fierce idolatry of nation-worship is the goal of human history.'[19] This is possibly *the* formulation which shows Tagore's (cultural) ideal to be poised against rootless or detached cosmopolitanism on the one hand and aggressive nationalism on the other. Be that as it may, for Tagore, it was always direct human contact that substantiated his higher, moral ideals. There is ample evidence in his writings to suggest that it was his personal experience of different people from different cultures which led him to understand that over and above the 'organized humanity of nations', as he put it, there is 'no difficulty in accepting the natural man as one's own'. Seeing and recognizing reality also in human beings outside his immediate environment, and beyond instrumentality of power, allowed Tagore to experience

[17] Part of the shift in the interpretation of 'cosmopolitanism' is based on the pragmatic question of what cosmopolitans do rather than what cosmopolitanism is, taking the focus away from philosophical conceptualizations to actually existing cosmopolitanisms. Cf. Malcomson (1998); Robbins (1998); and with regards to South Asian cosmopolitan practices, cf. Pollock (2000).

[18] Werbner (2006), pp. 497–8. There is clearly significant overlap or traffic in the way the terms 'cosmopolitanism' and 'universalism' are being used in theoretical writing. But there is a sense in which universalism is a more philosophically ambitious term and cosmopolitanism a worldlier concept, the former confined to more theoretical discourses and the latter to more literary and essayistic genres. There can be parity between them, one that suggests complementariness. 'Universalism needs the rhetoric of wordliness that cosmopolitanism provides.' See A. Anderson (1998, p. 272) on this point.

[19] Tagore (2001a [1917]), p. 419.

closeness across cultural divides, and this closeness, he found, was largely reciprocated. It was indeed possible to come into touch with, in his words, 'the Eternal Man amongst unknown humanity in a foreign country'.[20] Was this then the source that fed his optimism about the potential for global understanding?

Tagore's English Career

Alongside the vast advances in communication technology and the spread of the print media, the global character of modernity was enabled through the colonial elites' mastery and adoption of languages such as English, French, and Spanish that were instrumental as vehicles for the transaction of influences. What then must be considered as part of Tagore's complex relationship with the world is his relationship with English. Why did Tagore feel the need to endorse and translate his own work into what was largely seen to be the language of imperialism, the colonizer's tongue, rather than the global lingua franca it has become today?

In Chapter 2, we looked at the complex linguistic map of colonial Bengal to understand and appreciate the multilingual context of the Bengali society and the impact of English on the existing linguistic practices. Although English in India to this day operates as a divisive marker of power, prestige, and social mobility, to reduce its impact merely to that of a cultural conquest would be to simplify matters, in the same way that it would be reductionist to portray the cultural impact of colonialism as solely coercive. The Tagores, as we saw, stood firm on the question of Bangla, but English was endorsed as the language that enabled a wider circulation of ideas and communication both within and outside India (Tagore and Gandhi conducted their communication in English for lack of any other shared language).

This brings us to the question of Tagore's *reaching out* to the metropolitan cultural site through translating his own work so as to make himself known as a poet in the West. Recent scholarship has treated this subject more critically, dispelling some of the assumptions regarding Tagore's sudden eruption into fame in the colonial metropolis to which the poet himself may have lent an authorial voice.[21] As Bikash

---

[20] Tagore (2002i [1932]), p. 659.

[21] See Tagore's letter to his niece Indira Devi, dated 6 May 1913, in Dutta and Robinson, (2005), pp. 117–18. For commentary on it, see Dutt (2001).

Chakravaty has argued, Tagore did not embark the ship at Bombay on 27 May 1912, 'only out of a romantic urge for the beyond ... but also with a definite sense of purpose'.[22] Certainly, Tagore's sense of purpose to reach beyond India for intellectual companionship predates his success as a world-renowned literary figure and is central to his philosophy as well as to his 'lifelong endeavour to create a space of communication and communion between the known and the unknown',[23] but Chakravarty more specifically ties this motivation to Tagore's craving for an English-speaking audience.

By tracing what he calls Tagore's 'English career' to as far back as the 1890s, when the poet first tried his hand at translating one of his own poems into English, and following it through a number of fitful starts until its unexpected culmination in the Nobel prize–winning collection, Gitanjali, Chakravarty highlights a history of the promotion of Tagore's poetry in England that tends to be missing in the conventional accounts of the poet's abrupt rise to fame;[24] a history that Sisir Kumar Das has also identified as being 'the culmination of long and intermittent efforts to present his poetic world to a foreign audience'.[25] But while Chakravarty, noting the efforts of Tagore's devoted friends and associates to assist him in this, lays a lot of emphasis on Tagore's desire for an English audience, Das's reading, on the other hand, shows the poet as initially quite detached from the efforts of his admirers in India (and in England) to translate and present his work. According to him, it was only in response to increasing demands for translations by these admirers, and from being dissatisfied with the existing translations, that Tagore took charge of translation himself.[26] Either way, it seems reasonable to think that when Tagore decided to write or translate his works into English, 'he did so because he wanted to put across his ideas on a metropolitan plane' and this could be done only in English—a predicament that is faced by (post-)colonial writers. Tagore was indeed after an 'international fraternity of ideas and ideals wholly opposed to provincialism or regional interests'.[27]

[22] B. Chakravarty (1998), p. 12.
[23] S. Dasgupta (2013), p. 174.
[24] B. Chakravarty (1998), pp. 1–12.
[25] Das (1994), pp. 20–1.
[26] Das (1994), pp. 10–16.
[27] B. Chakravarty (1998), p. 19.

To this end his manner of translation, widely criticized for diluting the poetic substance of the originals, was motivated less by linguistic considerations than governed by the desire and need to convey ideas and establish rapport on the level of idea(l)s. That this contributed to the decline of his reputation as a poet in 'the West' is now widely accepted and was also understood by Tagore himself.[28]

The complex variety of both style and language were lost in translation, making it hard for non-Bengali speakers, as one critic has noted, 'to recreate the rich, vibrant and tragic background of the deeply religious *Gitanjali*';[29] or appreciate the power of the poetic mind expressing itself through the combined workings of 'verse-form, rhythm, structure, language, feeling, imagery, moral depth, wit', all of which has made Tagore such a great poet in Bengali.[30] But if Tagore is to be blamed for presenting himself to the European audiences in less than adequate English translations of his Bengali originals, particularly in his post-Gitanjali publications, it is also a fact that 'there was no one in the English speaking world competent enough to translate this great poet from the original language.'[31] Indeed, the colonial conditions after Macaulay presented his minutes on education that gave supremacy to the English language over Indian languages were not congenial to creating such individuals.

It should be noted here that the impact of Tagore's translations on his reputation in the English-speaking world, apart from other cultural and political factors, did not necessarily suffer parallel fortunes in some other parts of Europe and the world. In Spanish, French, or Slovenian, for example, Tagore translations, though twice removed from the original, paradoxically functioned better than they did in

[28] Most candidly, in a letter to Edward Thompson, dated 2 February 1921, Tagore wrote: 'In my translations I timidly avoid all difficulties, which has the effect of making them smooth and thin. I know I am misrepresenting myself as a poet to the western readers' (U. Das Gupta 2003, p. 128). For more on Tagore's translations, see Mukherjee (1981); Das (1986).

[29] Dutta-Roy (2001), p. 62.

[30] Radice (2003a). See also Dutt (2001) for a close analysis of how Tagore in his translations left out the sensual imagery from his Bengali songs, rooted in the erotic imagery of Vaishnava poetry, to pander to the perceived Anglo-American sensibilities informed by Christian morality.

[31] Dyson (2003), pp. 34–5.

English, where the adopted forms of 'thou' and 'thee' imbued the poems with an antiquated air that distanced them both from the original Bengali as well as contemporary poetry being written in English. These translations into Spanish, French, and Slovenian were also done by first-rate poets like Jiménez, Gide, and Gradnik respectively.

For all his intentions to be known in the West, it must finally be underlined, Tagore never tried to re-create himself into an English author, even as he adopted the language for foreign addresses and lecture tours, effectively turning himself into a bilingual writer.[32] For the purpose of creative expression, the natural or adequate medium for him remained Bengali. Unlike some of his predecessors, most notably Michael Madhusudan Dutt and Bankimchandra Chatterjee, who started out as writers in English and then switched to Bengali, he was never seduced into the dilemma of linguistic choice that confronts a writer under colonial domination. What he seemed to have been drawn into, however, to some extent at least, was fulfilling the perceived expectations of the metropolitan public, something that Timothy Brennan has generically assigned to the so-called 'Third World Cosmopolitan celebrities'—the elite globetrotters who express doubts over rooted modes of belonging and seek shelter in the suggestive but elusive construct of 'the world' from their privileged positions of 'in-betweenness', often making a virtue of their dual heritage that is but an accident of colonial history.[33] Ketaki Kushari Dyson has put the accent differently: 'There is a game that the West plays with men from the East: first, craving gurus, then criticising them for preaching like gurus.'[34] Any discussion of Tagore's reputation in the West is necessarily complicated by his conscious or subconscious pandering to the metropolitan site which had the power to lend legitimacy and authority to a cultural product. The dubious Western identity Tagore came to acquire in the process was at least partially the outcome

[32] Tagore's English writings tend to be sidelined, or not taken as seriously as his Bengali works, by the Bengali-speaking community, as pointed out by the editor of Tagore's three volumes of English writings, Sisir Kumar Das, who, in contrast, stresses the importance of Tagore's original English writings for understanding his full range and complexity as a writer and thinker; see Das (1994), pp. 26–7.

[33] Brennan (1989), p. 9.

[34] Dyson (2003), p. 30.

of his own eagerness, as Somjit Dutt unsparingly put it, 'to win the favour of a newly appointed headmaster who knows nothing about his students' background and abilities'.[35] Tagore was shrewd enough to understand that he needed validation from the West to make his position stronger at home.

As for the earlier comparison with Brennans's class of cosmopolitan intellectuals, this comparison does not hold beyond the fact that Tagore became 'the first global superstar or celebrity in literature'[36] and, in that sense, their precursor.[37] On the question of both language and domicile, Tagore remained attached to his native background, though the migratory instinct in him made him constantly reach beyond his grassroots selfhood to acquire a fuller identity.[38]

The Nobel Prize and After[39]

It was Tagore's third visit to England in 1912 that paved the way for his receiving the highest honour in the world of letters. The story is well known and documented by now.[40] Very briefly then: when Tagore arrived in England this time, he came with an exercise book

[35] Dutt (2001).

[36] A. Chaudhuri (2001), p. xviii.

[37] Brennan's wholesale critique is aimed at the post-Rushdie generation of writers, most of whom live in the West and write in the erstwhile colonizers' languages.

[38] Sanjukta Dasgupta, for example, refers to a well-known Rabindrasangeet 'ami chonchol hey ami sudurer o piyashi' ('I am restless, I long for the distance') to suggest that Tagore's subjective self was more tipped to the baire (the world/unknown) as opposed to the ghare (home/familiar). That this can be linked to a tension also in self-identity and a duality of Tagore's creative identity—the English Tagore and the Bengali Thakur, the global versus the desi—is part of the larger discussion of whether English still signifies linguistic imperialism and whether, as Dasgupta fruitfully suggests, there can now be a gradual metamorphosis of an English Tagore and a Bengali Thakur into 'an international alloy—brand Tagore'; see (2013), pp. 174–5.

[39] Some of the material featuring in this and the next two sections dealing with Tagore's more specific reception in the East-Central part of Europe (and particularly amongst Slovenes) in view of the orientalist debate have appeared in an shorter, earlier format in Jelnikar (2011).

[40] See, most recently, Radice (2012) and Collins (2012).

filled with his own translations, or rather authorial transcreations, of some of his poems and songs. He showed them to the English painter William Rothenstein, who, impressed by what he read, sent on the manuscript to W. B. Yeats. Before the year was out, a slim volume of one hundred and three poems edited and enthusiastically introduced by the Irish poet was published in England, first by the India Society of London and then by Macmillan in a larger edition.

Entitled *Gitanjali* or *Song Offerings*, the book created a huge sensation and was reprinted as many as thirteen times within a year. For a short time, Tagore became the attraction of the Anglo-American literary elite, including Ezra Pound and Ernest Rhys. In November 1913, through the efforts and orchestration of his supporters, most notably Yeats, Pound, and Sturge Moore, he became the first non-European to receive the Nobel Prize in Literature.[41] What followed was an unprecedented response to any poet in the history of letters. Alex Aronson gives a good idea:

> Wherever he went, he was received with the same unbounded almost delirious enthusiasm. His picture was flashed across continents and oceans. He travelled in the special trains put at his disposal by the Fascist Government of Italy and went to Russia on a special invitation of the Soviet Government; he was the guest of presidents of democratic republics, of kings, both before and after their abdication, of the greatest men of letters and science [among them Romain Rolland, André Gide, George Bernard Shaw, Thomas Mann, Bertrand Russell, Albert Einstein, Werner Heisenberg]. We see him speaking to audiences of many thousands, and to millions through the radio. His portrait has been painted by several hundred artists [including the Slovene painter Božidar Jakac (1899–1989)], his bust could be seen in almost all the exhibitions of the outstanding sculptors of the world. Yet, wherever he went, he wanted to see the children; perhaps he felt, they were the ones who understood him.[42]

Many interrelated factors came into play as various countries, groups, and individuals responded to Tagore, each in their own way, even as

---

[41] For further detail, see B. Chakravarty (1998), Foster (1998), pp. 465ff. For more on Tagore and the Nobel Prize, cf. Radice (2003b).

[42] Aronson (1978 [1943]), p. vii.

they drew on the common stock of perceptions that guided Western imagination as regards 'the East' in the early decades of the twentieth century.[43] Often his reputation could not be sustained, complicated as it was by false and narrow expectations, changing literary trends, and weak translations. Particularly in the Anglo-American world, the tremendous enthusiasm with which the 'mystic from the East' was initially received soon deteriorated into disappointment and rejection. Amit Chaudhuri, for example, finds it 'shocking' that 'respectable people like Yeats and Pound' lost their regard for Tagore's work so quickly, and that as a result Tagore's reputation was seriously damaged in the English-speaking West.[44]

The extraordinary impact Tagore had on the minds of literary men and women as well as the sheer sensationalism surrounding the poet can be partly explained circumstantially (and Aronson's study validates this). Broadly speaking, the West in the early decades of the twentieth century was once again in need of a spiritual injection from the East. The following lines from Srečko Kosovel capture the atmosphere of disillusionment and general spiritual bankruptcy after the events of World War I:

A tired European
stares sadly into a golden evening
even sadder
than his soul.
…
A civilization without heart.
A heart without civilization.

[43] For the complete compendium of Tagore's global reception from every quarter of the world, see Kämpchen (1999). Other relevant works published prior to this about Tagore's reception in various countries include: Hay (1962) for his reception in America; Kämpchen (1991, 2013) for Germany; Bangha (2008) for Central Europe (particularly Hungary); for Tagore's place within the Czech Bengali studies, see Knotková-Čapková (2013). For more on East–West encounter, see Ivbulis (1999).

[44] R. Chaudhuri (2002), p. xviii. For a critical reading of Yeats's 'Introduction' and his role in launching the Orientalist myth of Tagore-the-prophet, which set the tone for the falsified mainstream Western image of the Bengali poet, see Jelnikar (2008).

An exhausting struggle.
An evacuation of souls.[45]

Exhausted from what another European poet would call a 'filthy modern tide',[46] people in the West were ready for 'a book of the soul' in which 'life is the visible expression of the eternal', to quote one enthusiastic reviewer of *Gitanjali*.[47] Branded, predictably, a Wise Man from the East, its author was seen to be representative of Indian civilization itself; his was the quintessentially Indian voice.[48] It must be conceded, with his white beard and long-flowing robes, he fitted the part well. Nirad C. Chaudhuri's tongue-in-cheek remark may well have been right: 'After the decline of [Tagore's] literary reputation his looks remained his greatest asset as a prophet in the West'.[49]

I would agree with Rustom Bharucha, however, that Tagore's self-styled dress had little to do with choreographing for a Western audience. His striking outfit conjoining a Hindu–Muslim dress through the wearing of the *chapkan*, a loose overcoat, on top of a *jubba* (tunic) was an expression of 'a deeply personal introspection, in direct response to the politics of culture at home'. In contrast to Gandhi's politics of khadi to affirm swadeshi politics, Tagore's hybrid style was, 'like his poetry, a distinctive invention' that had no ulterior purpose but to express his 'own sense of personhood'.[50] Neither was it there to represent a quintessentially Indian dress (for which it was misunderstood), nor was it meant as an outfit to be emulated. The lack of understanding of Tagore's personal background and the consequent mismatch between the personal and the public, however, often sent out mixed signals and complicated Tagore's reception in the West.

There was also something of a tension in the format itself of Tagore's post-Nobel travels. On the one hand, the award gave him a long-sought opportunity to establish personal contacts with the different countries

[45] 'Kons' (1925?), translated by Bert Pribac and David Brooks, Kosovel (2008b), p. 100.

[46] 'The Statues', in Yeats (1985), p. 375.

[47] *The Daily News and Leader*, 21 January 1913, in Kundu, Bhattacharya, and Sircar (2000), pp. 18–19.

[48] On this, see also Lago (1972), p. 5.

[49] N. C. Chaudhuri (1987), p. 630.

[50] Bharucha (2006), p. 131.

and many remarkable individuals across the globe, but on the other, the unnatural celebrity outfit obstructed the possibilities of spontaneous exchange and communication for which Tagore craved. For all the privileged treatment the poet received wherever he went, the burden of being a celebrity figure inconvenienced him in no small measure, though he was certainly not above enjoying flattery or impervious to criticism. From Vienna, for example, he wrote to Rolland: 'Every morning I wake up from sleep I find myself in a world where there are men who have no names, who are a moving mass, like clouds, who can only envelop you but cannot offer you company.... Unfortunately for me I have a big reputation and people expect from me a big effect, a sensation in a wholesale quantity. What a waste!'[51] At the other end of the spectrum: 'Is there any other individual today in the world who is so fortunate as I am in gaining the adoration of such a multitude of peoples in spite of the insuperable obstacles against making himself fully known ...?'[52] While appreciating fame 'like a buffalo does the luxury of a mud bath', as he put it in a letter to Thompson in 1921, Tagore understood how much 'unreality there is in a literary reputation'.[53]

The gap between Tagore and his audiences was also widened in cases where his visits were orchestrated and controlled by the political elites, inevitably wrong-footing him with the anti-establishment intellectual circles. Tagore, politically rather naïve in countries of which he lacked politico-historical insight, became 'a useful and innocent tool which they knew how to handle for their own ulterior purposes'.[54] The 1926 episode with Benito Mussolini who had charmed the poet by gifting an almost complete library of Italian classics to Visva-Bharati and then used his visit for Fascist self-aggrandizing propaganda makes for the most objectionable chapter in Tagore's international career.[55] In Aronson's strongly worded formulation:

[51] Tagore, letter dated 13 July 1926, in Dutta and Robinson (2005), p. 329.

[52] Tagore, letter to Leonard Elmhirst, 7 October 1926, Dutta and Robinson (2005), p. 340.

[53] Tagore, letter to Edward Thompson, 20 September 1921, in U. Das Gupta (2003), p. 133.

[54] Aronson (1978 [1943]), p. ix.

[55] Eventually, through the intervention of Rolland, Tagore was made to see the scope of his misjudgement, and reacted by writing an open letter denouncing Fascism. For the open letter, written in Vienna on 20 July 1926,

Only utter political innocence could explain the grotesque spectacle of gentle poet and mad megalomaniac exchanging polite meaningless words over a cup of tea, a scene worthy of a drama of the absurd where the lines dividing the comic and the tragic become blurred and the human condition is shown to be as incomprehensible as it is revolting.[56]

Part of the disaffection with Tagore that some Western readers experienced arose also from their perception that he was somehow not 'Indian' or 'Eastern' enough, despite his looks. He did not sustain their expectations derived from the exotic diet of Omar Khayyam or even Kipling.[57] Prefabricated conceptions of 'East' and 'West' presented a major drawback to a critical appraisal of the writer's literary sensibility. The reception of his works was harmed also by the tendency to judge his writing by European standards. Tagore's short stories, for example, were set against the aesthetic norms of Edgar Allan Poe and were found lacking because they did not have the 'single effect'.[58] Similarly, his drama, believed to be strongly derivative of Maurice Maeterlinck's symbolist technique soon fell into disrepute for treating themes differently from the Belgian playwright.[59] Tagore's novel *Gora* was relentlessly compared with Kipling's *Kim*; and finally, as a poet, he was branded a mystic (indebted strongly, it was believed, to Christian mysticism), so when the devotional poems of *Gitanjali* were followed by the publication of Tagore's early secular love lyrics *The Gardener* (1913), some reviewers saw this 'move away' from spiritualism as a weakness.[60] Tagore

---

see Tagore, *EW* 3, pp. 771–6. For further insight, including the many letters to Andrews and others, see Dutta and Robinson (2005), pp. 328–38; on Rolland's reaction to Tagore's visit in Italy, see Dutta and Robinson (2003), pp. 269–70; for Tagore's relations with Italy, see Flora (2008).

[56] Aronson (1991), p. 32.

[57] For more on this, see Aronson (1978 [1943]), pp. 11–20.

[58] Pandit (1995), pp. 208–9. The 'single effect' theory refers to E. A. Poe's instruction as to what made a good short story. According to him, every work should be written in a way that it aims for a single effect—an intense feeling, a mood or experience in the reader. A good short story would thus achieve its unity by achieving a single emotional effect on the reader.

[59] For a critical engagement with the reception of Tagore's plays in Europe and America, see Lal (2001).

[60] *Pall Mall Gazette*, 14 October 1913, in Kundu, Bhattacharya, and Sircar. (2000), p. 22.

understood the logic at work. In response to one such review, he said: '[T]hey have labelled me a mystic and when I produce something that is not mystical they are offended.'[61]

The problem of the narrowness of such Eurocentric readings also presented itself forcefully to Aronson as he laboured through the vast body of responses to Tagore published in Europe (and the United States) between 1920 and 1940: 'Again and again literary critics refuse to discuss the East in terms of human beings and human experiences.'[62] This attitude has since been theoretically instituted as 'Orientalism' and the Westerners who look at the Orient and 'conceive of humanity either in large collective terms or in abstract generalities', giving little, if any, scope to 'existential human identities' as 'Orientalists'.[63]

True, Saidian cultural critique provides, at least to some degree, a relevant template for analysing the way Tagore was perceived in the West, and how his constructed image served to reinforce the dominant imperialist point of view, but—aside from the reservations one might have against distilling human curiosity about, and desire ·to know, 'the other' exclusively to conscious, or unconscious, motivations of power—Said's analysis proves to be of much more limited use once we move away from Western imperialist nations to the margins of the European world.

Germany is the example most often cited to demonstrate that the association of Orientalism with colonizing power is at best only partly true. The fact that German scholars were foremost translators and commentators of ancient Indian texts at the beginning of the nineteenth century, and that Germany then had virtually no interests in India or China, disproves any necessary direct link between Orientalism and the project of colonial subjugation.[64] This is not to say that there were no continuities between the German view of an idealized East and that of the colonizing European powers. As Imre Bangha notes, German scholars too perceived Asians as 'the other',

[61] Tagore, in a letter to Edward Thompson, recorded in Thompson's private record, 17 November 1913, published as Appendix A in E. P. Thompson (1998), p. 116.

[62] Aronson (1978 [1943]), p. 15.

[63] Said (1995 [1978]), pp. 154–5.

[64] Clarke (1997), p. 27.

but having themselves been 'subjects of a fragmented nation and dominated by nearby foreign powers', their view of Indian culture threatened by European imperialism was often underpinned by sympathy.[65] Their cross-cultural response was framed by their perceived sense of commonality and joint purpose with the Indian poet.[66] Their sympathies often lay with the Indian freedom movement, and they genuinely looked to Tagore (and/or Gandhi) for moral sustenance as well as for alternatives to imperialist ideologies, seeking 'to substitute a more holistic paradigm for old mechanistic and dualistic ways of thinking'.[67]

J. J. Clarke's study of the encounter between Asian and Western thought differentiates the Saidian thesis by foregrounding the counter-cultural and counter-hegemonic dimension to the orientalist discourses themselves. Without disputing the basic premise that when Western thinkers drew on Eastern thought—the religious and philosophical ideas of India, China, and Japan—they did so in line with their own goals and pursuits, Clarke rightly argues that these ideas were 'often in the business not of reinforcing Europe's established role and identity, but rather of undermining it'.[68] They provided a source that would be exploited for a critique and re-evaluation of thought systems indigenous to the West and which was often 'an energiser of radical protest':

> ... one of the pervasive features of orientalism which prevailed right throughout the modern period is the way in which, though perceived as 'other', Eastern ideas have been used in the West as an agency for self-criticism and self-renewal, whether in the political, moral, or religious spheres [for purposes, Clarke acknowledges, good and bad].[69]

The perceived otherness of the Orient is indeed not exclusively one of mutual antipathy, a way of affirming Europe's triumphant superiority; it 'also provides a conceptual framework that allows much fertile cross-referencing, the discovery of similarities, analogies, and

[65] Bangha (2008), p. 14.
[66] Bangha (2008), p. 14.
[67] Clarke (1997), p. 105.
[68] Clarke (1997), p. 27.
[69] Clarke (1997), p. 27.

models'.[70] Clearly, then, we must allow for various motivations and responses, even within the same parameters of othering, when discussing how 'the West' engaged with and related to 'the East'. A more open and reciprocal model of otherness and intercultural (textual) encounters is needed if we are to arrive at a fuller understanding of the European response to Tagore.

That the orientalist image of Tagore as sage and mystic *was* largely a European construct, Tagore's self-orientalizing notwithstanding, need not be disputed in this. How this image was essential to the larger picture of rationalizing colonial domination, when such rationalization was needed, is also a valid point. Merely the fact that Tagore's reputation in England plummeted no sooner than he raised his political voice and spoke against imperialist/nationalist politics, points to a tight discursive control of the subjugated other and its dependence on 'the other' to speak in a prescribed way. Tagore's book *Nationalism* in 1917 was anathema to the English reading public, and his resignation of Knighthood two years later, in 1919, practically destroyed his reputation.[71] On the other hand, it is unfortunate that Tagore, who did not accept the idea of one West (nor a purely negative critique of the Enlightenment), and who spoke so strongly about cross-civilizational and cross-cultural interdependencies, could in his foreign addresses slide into the dominant nineteenth- and early twentieth-century discourse of the 'spiritual East' and 'the materialist West', thus reinforcing the binarism of the imperial imagination, and drawing to himself some of the aura projected by a man of very different orientation, Swami Vivekananda (1863–1902), two decades earlier at the Parliament of the World's Religions held in Chicago in 1893.

And yet, all said, it needs to be recognized that the trope of the mystic and spiritual guru was not invariably in the service of imperial ideology or the motivations behind it. Ideas of spirituality, as argued by Clarke and others, could be, as they indeed were, deployed to articulate an alternative self-definition, providing a means of empowerment

---

[70] Clarke (1997), p. 27.

[71] None of Tagore's Anglo-Saxon literary friends—neither Bridges, Rhys, Yeats, Moore, Trevelyan nor Pound—once mention Tagore's political writings in their letters to the poet. See the fine volume of these letters in B. Chakravarty (1998) and his excellent 'Introduction'. This point is stated on p. 45.

rather than oppression.[72] Orientalism allows for a variety of subject positions, and this in turn is closely linked with the cultural and power politics of the country, group, or individual in question.

Identification Paradigm

Moving further towards the margins of what is often still seen in monolithic terms as the colonizing world, Imre Bangha's research on the links between East-Central Europe (more specifically Hungary) and India provides relevant insights when we come to consider the specifics of Kosovel's appreciation of Tagore from his own East-Central European regional context. Bangha has drawn our attention to how Hungarian readers would often sympathize with the Indian freedom struggle as opposed to sharing the colonizer's viewpoint. Their ideas of the mystic orient were partly indebted to the German romantic attachment to, and view of, the East—what, in fairness, Said also cursorily acknowledges as 'an element in a Romantic redemptive project' within the tradition that looked towards 'the Orient'[73]—and the ideas were partly engendered through a strong sense of identification with 'the East' stemming from an understanding of their own putative Eastern origins:

> Till the present day Hungarians think that speaking a non-Indo-European language they are a lonely oriental people in Europe.... this

[72] In the context of Irish Orientalism, for example, L. Innes has pointed out that feminists, such as Annie Besant, Eva Gore-Booth, Charlotte Despard, and Margaret Cousins drew on Oriental sources—initially through Madame Blavatsky's theosophy, with its stress on the equality of male and female principles and on Isis as a female goddess of wisdom and equality—to voice an alternative tradition to the world of male domination. Their feminist aspirations were in turn often linked with the nationalist cause: Annie Besant, for example, was not only a staunch Home Rule supporter, but when she moved to India, she became one of the founding members of the Indian National Congress. Margaret Noble, another Irishwoman, joined Tagore in the nationalist agitation against the British partition of Bengal in 1905, before she became a disciple of Vivekananda and helped develop a pan-Asian spirituality to oppose the materialist culture of the West; see Innes (2002), pp. 154–5.

[73] Said (1995 [1978]), p. 154.

idea is continuous with the romantic view in as much as it merges the idealised past of a nation into an imagined pristine East.[74]

The Hungarian scholar from Transylvania, Alexander Csoma de Körös (1784–1842), is the most well-known exponent of the romantic drive to establish proof of kinship between the Hungarians and the East combined with a passion for learning. From a small ethnic group, the Széklers, who in his time saw themselves as descendants of the Huns of the fifth century, Csoma set out in search of the origins of the Hungarian language, mastering Tibetan, Sanskrit, and four vernacular Indian languages, including Bengali, along the way. Despite the fact that he found nothing worth publishing on the origins of Hungarians in Asia, his idiosyncratic search resulted in the creation of Tibetology: he authored the first scholarly Tibetan–English dictionary and Tibetan grammar. A Hungarian William Jones of sorts, he spent many years, between 1831 and 1842, in Bengal, working mostly at the Royal Asiatic Society in Calcutta, the institution Jones had founded.

His association with the British—the fact that his research was enabled by and conducted under the regime of the East India Company, the precursor to the rule of the British Crown, and spurred by an intellectual climate where knowledge of the Tibetan language and culture was strategically important to the British—has given rise to, not dissimilar to the postcolonial revisionist readings of Jones' achievements,[75] a Saidian interpretation that has left recent scholarship ambiguous about this man. Bangha, however, discredits such patently reductionist readings that completely overlook the fact that Csoma came from 'the periphery of European cultural circulation', a minority ethnic group, whose memories of the Habsburg imperial oppression formed a strong part of their collective identity. Nor do they give any consideration to Csoma's 'patriotic enthusiasm' that sent him out 'searching for relatives', let alone to the simple curiosity factor that guides explorations of the unknown. Furthermore, in the straightforward aligning of Csoma's point of view with an imperial one, the evidence of the actual, far more nuanced, relationship between Csoma and the British is completely overlooked. Entirely

[74] Bangha (2008), p. 15.
[75] 'To rule and to learn, then to compare Orient with Occident ... these were Jones's goals' (Said 1995 [1978]), pp. 77–9.

missing from the analysis is, for example, the fact that Csoma was ridiculed in colonial circles and kept himself at a certain 'discreet distance', engaging only to the extent required to fulfil his end of the agreement but rejecting all other advances or perks. We are told he rejected lodgings in the house of Major Lloyd, preferring instead a simple Indian hut.[76]

Many individuals and groups from within Europe, it has to be acknowledged, celebrated Indian civilization and Tagore from their own real or imagined position of 'otherness'. We only need to look at the letters Tagore received from an average European reader to appreciate this point. Many of these show that apart from identification along personal lines, there were numerous marginalized groups and organizations who wrote to the poet for endorsement of their cause. Alongside appeals by various women's organizations from across Europe,[77] the letters included, for example, an appeal from a *Hilfskomitee* for German emigrants in what was then Czechoslovakia,[78] or a submission from the editors of a Roma[79] journal describing the plight of the Roma under Tzarist Russia and contrasting it with the more favourable circumstances emerging with the October Revolution.[80] A letter from the Czech 'Union of German societies for the prevention of cruelty to animals' asked Tagore for moral support to set up an anti-vivisection hospital.[81]

---

[76] See Bangha (2008), pp. 41–8.

[77] For example, Tagore received a letter from the 'Hungarian Section of the Women's International League for Peace and Freedom' outlining the scope of their work as a joint fight for woman suffrage, equal rights and peace, asking Tagore to give a talk at their organization as part of his Hungarian trip (Budapest, 6 July 1926, Letters to Rabindranath Tagore in 1926, Rabindra Bhavana Archives, Santiniketan).

[78] Letter, 13 December 1937, Serial no. 74, Czechoslovakia File, Rabindra Bhavana Archives, Santiniketan.

[79] 'Roma' refers to the Romani people, widely known across Europe also as 'gypsies', who originate from the northwestern part of the Indian subcontinent.

[80] Letter, 24 September 1930, Serial no. 333, Russia File, Rabindra Bhavana Archives, Santiniketan.

[81] Letter, 30 January 1935, Serial no. 74, Czechoslovakia File, Rabindra Bhavana Archives, Santiniketan.

I see the value of these letters primarily in showcasing the broad range of concerns that drew people to Tagore, as they intuited shared predicaments and concerns with him in what was a case of *situational identification*.[82] Tagore in turn took these gestures seriously, giving support where he could. In September 1940, to give one last example, he received a letter from a Polish woman by the name of Marya Falk, a lecturer in Slavonic languages at the University of Calcutta and initiator of the newly established Indo-Polish Association there, to which Tagore then accepted the honorary chairmanship.[83] Her letter conveyed sympathy derived from identifying Poland's struggle for independence with India's historical predicament, from which, the author hoped, echoing Tagore's sentiments, the 'call to true humanity might again be heard in the world'. Tagore in turn sent the message: 'I warmly associate myself with the 150th Anniversary of the May Constitution of Poland—may justice and humanity prevail in a peaceful reconstruction of civilization.'[84]

Once again, letters such as these make us appreciate the scope and diversity of responses Tagore occasioned *within* Europe. It is also here that the lines between colonial, nationalist, class, and gender struggles get blurred and merge into a broader emancipatory discourse.[85] Freethinking individuals and groups would often forge transnational links and solidarities, seeking solutions to oppression in international fraternalism.

Elleke Boehmer has written pertinently about the phenomenon of anti-imperialist struggles asserting themselves in dialogue with

---

[82] For this notion see the 'Introduction', pp. 11–12.

[83] See Pobozniak (1961), p. 354.

[84] Letter, 12 April 1941, Serial no. 297, Poland File, Rabindra Bhavana Archives, Santiniketan,

[85] In a different context, Leela Gandhi has drawn our attention to links existing between anti-imperialism and a broad variety of other 'minor' anti-hegemonic discourses. Vegetarian and animal-rights campaigners, anti-vivisectionists, theosophists, homosexuals, all, she argues, articulated their singular programmes as a variation on the theme of anti-imperial politics. Her perspective seeks 'discursive and ethical continuities between the critic of the fox hunt and the critic of the empire' on the grounds that the two are joined in opposition to the binarism of imperial reason that insists on dichotomies between races, cultures, genders, sexualities, and so on (Gandhi 2006, pp. 1–11).

other anti-imperialist struggles, thus swivelling the more conventional centre-versus-periphery axis around to see 'how resistance emerged not so much from the place of otherness as *amongst others*', through cross-cultural and transnational influences and solidarity.[86] The 'anti-colonial hand holding' that she sees in the Irish Sinn Féin (Ourselves) supporting the Bengali Swadeshi movement or in the Irish nationalists supporting the Boer minority in the Anglo-Boer War (1899–1902), even if primarily motivated by self-interest, did emerge from grievances against the 'common enemy'. That such resistance was enabled by the empire itself—the worldwide colonial networks of communication in the form of newspapers, the telegraph, new road, railways, and faster sea links—is of course worth noting.[87]

Personal relationships and networks, realized through travel and correspondence, were indeed crucial for creating worldwide platforms of solidarity. When in 1919 Romain Rolland sent Tagore, along with his first letter to him, a document entitled 'Declaration of Independence of the spirit', it was an explicit attempt to forge closer ties between the East and the West. It sought to enlist Tagore's support for a protest mounted in the name of the ideal of spiritual oneness of humanity that would obliterate the frontiers of nations. Tagore was only too glad to put his name down to a document, a part of which read as follows:

> We serve Truth alone which is free, with no frontiers, with no limits, with no prejudices of race and caste. Of course we shall not dissociate ourselves from the interests of Humanity! We shall work for it, but for it as *a whole*. We do not recognize nations. We recognize the people one and universal—the people who suffer, who struggle, who fall and rise again, and who ever march forward on the rough road, drenched with their sweat and their blood—the people comprising all men, all equally our brothers. And it is in order to make them, like ourselves aware of this fraternity, that we raise above their blind battles the Arch of Alliance, of the Free Spirit, one and manifold, eternal.[88]

Tagore, who had long been looking towards Europe for signs of common purpose, gladly accepted the invitation to 'join the ranks of those

---

[86] Boehmer, emphasis author's, (2002), p. 2.

[87] Boehmer (2002), pp. 29–30, 12.

[88] Cited in Aronson and Kripalani (1945), p. 22.

free souls', as he wrote back to Rolland, encouraged that 'the higher conscience of Europe had been able to assert itself'.[89]

Another more politically ambitious manifesto, The Clarte Manifesto (1919), drawn up in the same year by a group of French intellectuals and activists and spearheaded by Henri Barbusse, was sent to Tagore for signing. This manifesto, richer in social content, spoke 'bluntly against privilege and inheritance, against concentration of power and wealth in the hands of a few, and advocated class-struggle as a means to end war and classes'. Tagore lent his name in support, alongside other writers such as Anatole France, H. G. Wells, and George Bernard Shaw. A copy of it came into the hands of the nationalist Bipin Chandra Pal, who drew on segments of it in a public speech in Calcutta on 12 December 1919.[90] How internationally resonant such documents were is borne out also by the fact that Kosovel translated and published the very same document—Rolland's *Déclaration d'independence de l'esprit*—into Slovenian in 1926, adapting it somewhat to the Slovenian context.

The utopian thrust and revolutionary fervour of such documents certainly found explicit echoes in some of Tagore's grander proclamations (as it did in Kosovel's): 'Our fight is a spiritual fight, it is for Man. We are to emancipate Man from the meshes that he himself has woven round him—these organizations of National Egoism.'[91] While standing in contrast to the poet's more realistic project of building an educational institution in India for the encouragement of hermeneutical dialogue between the East and the West, the proclamation nonetheless reflects Tagore's active involvement in the orientalist enterprise (of Clarke's kind), which the winning of the Nobel Prize had at once promoted and complicated.[92]

---

[89] Cited in Aronson and Kripalani (1945), p. 106.

[90] See Poddar (2004), pp. 149–51.

[91] Tagore, in S. Bhattacharya (2005), p. 55.

[92] Undoubtedly, as argued by any number of cultural critics since Nabaneeta Dev Sen's seminal essay (1996) on the topic of Tagore's 'foreign reincarnation', Tagore took it upon himself to represent Indian culture and philosophy in the West—in the words of Sanjukta Dasgupta—'as alternative ways of thought that could be enlightening and liberating after the horror and tragedy that wars had brought on the collective social psyche of the West' (2013, p. 180). This was visible not only in the manner of his own English translations but also in the choice of texts he himself wrote, translated or had others translate for him into

Cross-border metropolitan contact zones at the turn of the twentieth century were important meeting grounds for the colonial elites, where, alongside new political and religious ideas, modernist and avant-garde cross-pollinations were taking place. It was in this expanded cosmopolitan context that in 1912, Ezra Pound, who secured six of Tagore's poems for publication in the journal *Poetry*, wrote that the personal encounter with the Orient captured in the translated poetry of Rabindranath Tagore would usher in a vital period of 'world-fellowship'.[93] But if Ezra Pound's interest in Tagore seriously dwindled even before Tagore won the Nobel Prize,[94] and Yeats' not long thereafter—Tagore's fame in the Anglo-American world had practically altogether run the length of its course by the end of the second decade of the twentieth century—on the continent, it was positively on the rise. Tagore's 'most astonishing successes' were his European tours of 1921, 1926, and 1930.[95]

It was indeed in the 1920s that Tagore's reception across Central and Eastern Europe reached new heights, and it is to this wave of his popularity that Kosovel's response belongs. As Bangha has also observed in relation to Hungary, Tagore's greatest supporters were to be found among the readers and writers who were born or lived in regions 'lost' after World War I. These writers, he claims, 'had an additional motivation to perceive the irrationality of western thought that led to a war and then to a peace that they considered unjust. Their disillusionment urged them to examine whether Rabindranath would offer an alternative to western thinking'.[96] Something similar can be said of Srečko Kosovel whose hometown had been unjustly 'lost' to Italy following the break-up of the Austro-Hungarian Empire and who indeed looked towards his 'Green India' for consolation and a reaffirmation of life.

Having established the diversity of responses that Tagore elicited within Europe, particularly with respect to the more marginalized individuals and groups, and the various networks of transnational

---

English. These were predominantly philosophical discourses dealing with Indian philosophy, universalism, religion of man, spiritual introspection, and so on.

[93] Cited in Boehmer (2002), pp. 22–3.

[94] For more on Pound and Tagore, see Hurwitz (1964).

[95] Radice (1994a), p. 27.

[96] Bangha (2008), pp. 89–90.

solidarity this gave rise to, it is worth noting that Tagore, in turn, felt himself drawn to the margins of Europe, sensing, as he wrote to Leonard Elmhirst, 'a mysterious feeling of kinship' with the less industrialized part of the continent as opposed to the powerful countries of the West.[97] Recovering from severe exhaustion at the sanatorium at Lake Balaton in Hungary on what was his fifth and longest European tour, he wrote in the same letter:

> Doctors advise me to take the shorter eastern route to India through Yugoslavia, Serbia, Constantinople, Greece and Egypt. The prescription is very much like the French wine ordered for me in Milan; it is tempting. The people [in] this eastern corner of Europe are perfectly charming—their personality unshrouded by the grey monotony of a uniform civilization that has overspread the western world. It is mixed with something primitive and therefore is fresh and vital and warmly human. How naively simple and direct is the expression of their feeling for me. I am the guest of the people here, their one object being to nurse me into health taking real pride in rendering this service.[98]

His return journey to India took him on a whistle-stop tour of the Balkans, and between 13 and 17 November, he stopped for two days in Zagreb (Croatia) and two in Belgrade (Serbia), before heading on to Bulgaria, Romania, Greece, and Egypt to finally return to India.

Travelling in special government-provided coupes and meeting various heads of state on the way, however, Tagore brought criticism upon himself for ignoring the political realities behind his staged receptions. 'Our Great Tagore, after his visit to Mussolini', objected Rolland, 'has once again been ill advised to have himself received and patronised by the criminals who are torturing Bulgaria and Romania.'[99] Tagore's refusal to pay heed to political systems need not really surprise us. He prioritized the individual over any system. In contrast to Rolland, he was also less convinced of the greater righteousness of Western Europe compared to Eastern Europe. 'The big nations' with

[97] Tagore, in a letter to Leonard Elmhirst, 7 November 1926, in Dutta and Robinson (2005), p. 340.

[98] Tagore, in a letter to Leonard Elmhirst, 7 November 1926, in Dutta and Robinson (2005), p. 340.

[99] Romain Rolland, in a letter to Kalidas Nag, 6 December 1926, excerpt cited in Dutta and Robinson (2005), p. 339.

their 'reckless career of political ambition and adventures of greed' had, in his view, forfeited their 'natural privilege ... to stand for the right when any great wrong is done to humanity'.[100] Srečko Kosovel's life was cut short just months before Tagore came to Yugoslavia, so he never had the chance to partake in the Tagoreana surrounding the poet's visit to the Balkans.[101] Before we move on to at last considering Kosovel's own response to what he did know of Tagore's life and work, a word or two about Tagore's more general reception amongst the Slovene reading public seems in order.

Claiming the Indian Laureate

When Tagore's English *Gitanjali: Song Offerings* first came out in 1912, edited and famously introduced by W. B. Yeats, the Irish poet's eulogy to Tagore travelled far beyond the English-speaking world. In the first article to be written on Tagore in Slovenia, Oton Župančič (1878–1949), the leading modernist poet of the pre-war generation, based his piece largely on Yeats's laudatory preface.[102] If Tagore's fame in England was launched through the efforts of the Anglo-American-Irish literary elite, in Slovenia, it was also the enthusiasm of some of the country's foremost writers that introduced Tagore to the general reading public and generated what was in its day an unprecedented response to a literary figure of international stature.[103] Following some of the early translations done by Miran Jarc (1900–1942) and France Bevk (1890–1970), it was the talented poet Alojz Gradnik (1882–1967) who devoted himself wholeheartedly to translating Tagore's works. During the war, he came across a copy of *The Crescent Moon* in a bookshop in Trieste, and taken by what he read he decided to introduce as much of Tagore's poetry as was then available in English to the Slovenian readership. He wrote:

[100] Tagore, in a letter to Leonard Elmhirst, 7 November 1926, in Dutta and Robinson (2005), p. 340.

[101] For more on Tagore's reception in former Yugoslavia in 1926, see Ch. 6, pp. 305–7.

[102] Župančič (1914).

[103] Slovenes, at the time living between a number of provinces of the Austro-Hungarian Empire, were amongst the smaller language communities in Europe to translate Tagore's works into their own language.

How I grew to love this wonderful Indian is evident from the fact that I transposed five of his books into Slovene. All these translations were motivated by my wish that Slovenes too get to know this wonderful poet, philosopher and apostle of peace and brotherhood between nations.[104]

Tagore's first poetry collection to come out in Slovene was not the Nobel-winning *Gitanjali*, but the volume of Gradnik's personal choice: *Rastoči mesec* (*The Crescent Moon*, 1917),[105] to be sold out within months and republished in 1921. One after another the following collections appeared: *Ptice selivke* (*Stray Birds*, 1921), *Vrtnar* (*The Gardener* 1922), *Žetev* (*Fruit-Gathering* 1922), and finally *Gitandžali: Žrtevni spevi* (*Gitanjali: Song Offerings* 1924). If it were not for Gradnik's personal commitment, it remains doubtful whether so much of Tagore's poetry would have been translated into Slovene.[106]

Gradnik's translations closely followed the Macmillan text of Tagore's own English reworkings. They strove to be faithful renditions of Tagore's English rhythmic prose. Although the adopted forms of 'thou' and 'thee' were lost in Slovene, Gradnik's translations were still full of archaisms and inversions, which was in accordance with the dominant biblical style through which Tagore's poetry was domesticated in Europe, and which made the poet seem less a contemporary and more a poet from a bygone era. Gradnik may have realized this when he came to revise his own translations in the late 1950s, dispensing entirely with old-fashioned vocabulary and antiquated inversions. These collections are being reprinted to this day.[107] With many

---

[104] Gradnik, in Rudolf (1958), pp. 83–4.

[105] The edition contains glossary of Indian terms and notes, and four colour reprints of the paintings of Nandalal Bose, Asit Kumar Haldar, and Surendranath Ganguly.

[106] *Rastoči mesec* and *Žetev*, for example, did not make it into Serbian or Croatian until very recently. In 2006, Robert Mandić, another Tagore enthusiast, took the initiative and came out with the selected poems of Tagore entitled *Sakupljanje voča i još poneki plod* (*Fruit-Gathering* and some other fruits; comprising poems from *Stray Birds*, *The Crescent Moon*, and *Fruit-Gathering*), published by Paralele in Split (Croatia).

[107] Both *Vrtnar* and *Gitandžali: Žrtevni spevi* were republished in a new edition in Slovenia in 2009, and were made a feature of a popular weekly programme *Knjiga mene briga* (For books I care) on national TV channel (TVSl 1) on 27 May 2009. *Gitanjali* was taken up by another translator Janko Moder in the late 1970s.

newspaper and journal articles about the poet, as well as translations of his novels (*The Home and the World, The Wreck, Gora*), essayistic writings (*Sadhana*, excerpts from *Nationalism*, and *The Religion of Man*), and the staging of two of his plays, *The Post Office* and *Chitra*, at the Ljubljana City Theatre, Tagore can be said to have found a permanent place in the Slovenian letters.[108]

Tagore's fame with Slovenian readership peaked around the time of these first poetry publications, which laid the ground for a more serious appreciation of the poet's artistic credo. Kosovel's response to Tagore's poetry and philosophy belongs to this particular wave of popularity in the 1920s, during which appreciation of Tagore, the creative writer, was beginning to take precedence over the earlier more politically motivated appraisal. This was also the time in which a number of works dealing with Indian religious and philosophical traditions were published in Slovenia in response to a growing interest in Asian religions across East-Central Europe in general.[109] For example, a man called Josip Suchy (1869–1941), whose diplomatic service took him to Ceylon in 1910, where he got drawn into studying Buddhism, brought out two books in Slovene in 1921 by way of introducing the Slovene readership to the basic tenets of Buddhism.[110] The books received a lot of atten-tion in the press and raised some dust amidst cultural circles, not least because of the overwhelmingly negative Catholic take on Buddhism as essentially nihilistic. If the Catholic response to Suchy's publications was less than commendable, a journal with a strong socialist base called *Kres* (Bonfire) praised, and even recommended, the books explicitly

---

[108] For Tagore's wider reception in former Yugoslavia, see Petrović (1970) and Jelnikar (2014a).

[109] Prior to that, in the latter part of the nineteenth century, first direct translations from Sanskrit were undertaken by the Indologist Karol Glaser (1845–1913). On his translations of Kalidasa and his overall contribution to Slovene Indology, see Pacheiner-Klander (2008).

[110] *Uvod v budizem* (Introduction to Buddhism) and a selection of the most famous Jātaka tales in a book entitled *Staroindijske basni, bajke in pravljice* (Ancient Indian fables, myths and tales). For further details and a comprehensive overview of the Slovenes' encounter with Asian thought sys-tems in the nineteenth and early twentieth centuries, see Šmitek (1986); the discussion related to Suchy is on pp. 166–9. For a digest version in English, see Črnič (2008), pp. 91–4.

to the working classes. Later that year, in the same publication, Suchy himself published an article on Buddha, in which he underlined how the central moral tenets of Buddhism (rejection of castes, social equality, and Buddha's selfless love for all beings) can be dovetailed neatly with the fundamental aspirations of socialism.[111]

Similarly, Ivan Vuk's translation of Vivekananda's lecture 'God and Man' published in 1924—which enabled the Slovene reader to read about the Advaita Vedanta in his own language for the first time—was intended also as an agitprop for the revolutionary idea of social equality and class struggle.[112] It needs to be stressed that acquaintance with Indian philosophy, Vedanta, Buddhist thought, and theosophy was largely mediated through the German sphere of influence and scholarship, for the most part adapted from German literature (and sometimes also from Serbo-Croatian translations). But it was also the Slovene intellectuals studying in Vienna, Graz, and Prague who were instrumental in spreading theosophical ideas amongst the Slovene readership as well as incorporating them into their own work. The poet Oton Župančič (the author of the first article that came out on Tagore in the Slovene press as mentioned earlier), is known to have encountered theosophy in Germany over a decade before the Theosophical Society was established in Ljubljana in 1923.

Arthur Schopenhauer's philosophy, on the other hand, exacted a strong hold on the imagination and poetry of Alojz Gradnik, Tagore's foremost translator in Slovene. Kosovel too mentions Schopenhauer in a number of his letters. In fact, in a letter to his sister Karmela from 1923, he asks her to turn to Schopenhauer once she is done with reading Tagore.[113]

The initial response of the Slovenes to Tagore, though largely dominated by extra-literary factors rather than any real appreciation of the poet's sensibility, marks an important stage in the building of his reputation and needs to be briefly commented on. It bespeaks a sense of shared concerns, for which Slovenes were sympathetically drawn to Tagore and what he stood for from the very start.

In the first substantial article in Slovene on Tagore, 'Last year's rivals for the Nobel Prize' (1914), his winning of the Nobel Prize is juxtaposed

---

[111] Šmitek (1986), p. 168.

[112] Šmitek (1986), p. 172.

[113] Kosovel, letter to Karmela Kosovel, 18 September 1923, *CW* 3, p. 500.

to the defeat of the Austrian poet Peter Rosegger (1843–1918). For the Slavic peoples who were most exposed to the Germanization pressures under the Habsburg rule, Tagore's winning the Nobel Prize became a matter of preference over the Austrian poet. For Slovenes, Rosegger was less a literary name and more a figure resented for his associations with the nationalist organization called Südmark Schulverein, which aided German-language schools in ethnically Slovenian or mixed territories as part of the Germanization policy pursued against Slovenes in southern Carinthia and southern Styria.[114]

Against this background, the author of the article, Janko Lokar, sets 'a spiritual giant of enormous horizons' in opposition to a parochial writer who 'fans the flames of nationalist hatred'. Tagore, perceived as one who 'bleeds from the love of his fettered country' and yet 'firmly acknowledges the rights of the opponents, even stresses them', is celebrated for his love of humanity as opposed to love of nation. His patriotic songs are seen as perfect expressions of 'his universalism'. They are not 'boisterous fighting hymns', the author stresses, but 'soft idealisations of his country, fuelled by unselfishness and firm belief in the day when his enslaved country will rise'.[115]

In spite of the narrow framework in which the discussion of Tagore is positioned by this article, the poet's vision of India's anti-colonial struggle is portrayed with some insight. The poet is hailed as 'a patriot' whose voice is tuned to the deepest harmonies of humanity, refusing to surrender the task of his country's liberation from under foreign rule to a nationalist agenda. Indeed, as argued in previous chapters, Tagore's anti-colonialism rejected nationalism in a bid for a larger search for liberation. It was precisely this high universalist ideal underscored by the article that was to resonate with Kosovel, who strove for a like-minded resolve with respect to Slovenes and their struggle for independence. In fact, from its beginning, Tagore's popularity amongst the Slovenes was connected less with the romantic side of Orientalism that saw in Tagore above all 'the exotic and bearded Oriental prophet',[116]

---

[114] This force in the Germanization of the Slav population in the region was similar to the role of the Italian Lega Nazionale in the Slovenian Littoral, Kosovel's native region. For more on the latter, see Novak (1970), pp. 3–22.

[115] Translation mine, Lokar (1914), p. 246.

[116] Petrović (1970), p. 13.

and more with a sense of identification with the poet and his people, derived from a perceived common goal of cultural and political independence. So strongly did Slovenes identify with Tagore and his historical predicament under the British that they imagined themselves to have played a vital part in his international fortunes.

In an interview in the 1960s, Tagore's poet-translator Alojz Gradnik said that Slovenes were directly responsible for Tagore's wining the Nobel Prize, something, he regretted, not many people were aware of. The interviewer, Vladimir Bartol, somewhat surprised by this stupendous claim, asked him to elaborate. Presenting the already familiar details of Rosegger's nomination for the Nobel Prize in the same year as Tagore's, Gradnik provided the additional connection between the alleged undermining of the Austrian poet's credentials as a Nobel Prize candidate by the Slovenes, and the Swedish Nobel Prize Committee's coming to know of this protest. But how did the Swedish Academy come to learn that Rosegger was an unsuitable candidate, denying Slovenes the right to their language and culture? We are told it was the priest-poet Anton Aškerc (1856–1912), himself an Indophile, who made the vital intervention. With the help of his Swedish friend Alfred Jensen (1859–1921), an influential man of letters and member of the Nobel Committee, the Swedish Academy came to learn of Rosegger's dubious character. The Austrian poet was subsequently dropped from candidacy. Hence Tagore had no rival—or so the logic runs.[117]

It seems hard to believe that Rosegger would have seriously stood a chance against Tagore, as indeed against Thomas Hardy (1840–1928) or Anatole France (1844–1924), two other contenders for the distinction of the highest literary award in 1913, and who, unlike Rosegger, are not given a word of mention in any of the Slovenian articles. Considering also that Aškerc died in June 1912, there is further reason to question the above inferences—but it could be possible that he still had time to convey his grievance to Jensen.

[117] Bartol (1961). According to Lokar, Germans, resenting this turn of events, saw in the Swedish Academy's policy a clear bias for the Slavs. The old Slavic–Germanic animosity came to play a significant part in the shaping of perceptions of Tagore's winning the Nobel Prize on both sides (Lokar 1914, p. 246).

Whatever the case may have been, Gradnik's point had an altogether deeper meaning, to suggest, in his own words, 'that between Indians, Tagore and [Slovenes], there is a certain affinity—for the soft and romantic lyric.'[118] Tagore's lyrics have since been read and cherished by poets, writers, and general readers alike. They were also included in the school curricula.[119] Srečko Kosovel, however, did more than just enjoy Tagore's works. As Gradnik had done before him through the act of translation, Kosovel, through the act of writing, integrated Tagore's verses and ideas into his own poetic and intellectual horizon, thereby making it an indelible part of his own literary tradition. It is as much Tagore the soft lyricist that can be sensed behind some of Kosovel's lines, in poems such as 'Klic po samoti' ('Call for Solitude', Appendix, p. 329), as is Tagore, the fierce critic of nationalism, that transpires through much of Kosovel's thought. In fact, the two strains that inform Tagore's Slovenian, as well as wider Yugoslav, reception in the twenties—the political and the aesthetic—converge in the legacy of Kosovel's work, to which we turn next.

[118] Lokar (1914), p. 246.

[119] The poem 'Authorship' from *The Crescent Moon* (1913) in Gradnik's translation ('Pisateljevanje') was included in the seventh grade Slovene language and literature (cf. *Sedmo Berilo za Osnovne šole* [*Seventh Primer for Primary School*], Ljubljana: Mladinska Knjiga, 198, p. 77). Tagore's works were also on the curricula at the secondary school level as the obvious representative of modern Indian literature, and nowadays his works are studied at university language and literature courses as part of the world and postcolonial literature component.

5 Europe and Its 'Others'

Kosovel Looks 'East'

Hey, green parrot!
Tell us how it is in Europe?
The green parrot replies:
Man is not symmetrical.[1]

In 1913, Rabindranath Tagore became the first non-European to receive the Nobel Prize in Literature. Prior to that he was practically unknown outside India, but when he was awarded the highest honour for literary achievement on the basis of his works that he himself had translated, he became world famous overnight and was further translated into countless languages of the world. Like many individuals from across Europe in the 1920s, Srečko Kosovel too felt strongly drawn to the newly available works of Rabindranath Tagore, and at the same time urged his artistic friends and colleagues to read the Indian poet, convinced that here was someone who would show a new direction out of the crisis Europe in general and the Slovenian people in particular were experiencing in the disillusionment and disorientation of the post-Great War years. Affected by the modernist *angst* of what Robert Musil called 'incoherent ideas spreading outward

---

[1] Kosovel, 'Green Parrot', translated by Bert Pribac and David Brooks.

without a centre',[2] the young poet strove to find a centre that would nevertheless hold. Tagore, in Kosovel's view, was 'the one artist capable of infusing into people such fullness of soul life as needs to express itself in art. According to Kosovel there was, at that time, 'no one greater than him ... on the horizon ...'[3]

Tagore's place among Kosovel's community of admired artists—the ones he felt were conscientious in their creative ambitions, striving to broaden existential and imaginative possibilities of art—is, however, secured not from some robust act of appropriation, but through a strong sense of shared concerns grounded in an anti-imperialist, universalist ethos. Tagore was perceived to be a kindred spirit not because Kosovel was suffering from some kind of a delusional fantasy—what after all could a young, still anonymous poet, barely out of his teens, have in common with a mature world-renowned figure of Tagore's stature?—but because, sensitized by Slovenian circumstances, he was able to identify with him and relate to his historical predicament of colonial subjugation. It is therefore more in the spirit of parity and equality that Kosovel approaches Tagore, as opposed to an Eastern guru at whose feet one should sit, or, following the colonial mindset, an inferior 'Oriental' who deserves to be patronized.

Instead of pointing to the contrasts between these two so very different literary figures and their respective backgrounds, I wish to concentrate on the common ground that brings them together into an unexpected relational framework. It is against their similar positioning within their regions as a subjugated 'Other' that Kosovel's endorsement of Tagore's ideas can be more fully appreciated. Instead of the conventional one-way model of 'influence', I therefore adopt the more dynamic framework of 'situational identification' where solidarities are forged between individuals on the basis of feeling or intuiting that one might share someone else's predicament and is therefore interested in their ideas as well as solutions.[4] The moment of reciprocity, however,

---

[2] Musil (1995 [1930–43]), p. 15.

[3] Kosovel, letter to Dragan Šanda, 26 December 1924, in Kosovel (2006), p. 189. All translations of excerpts from Kosovel's letters, notes, and journal entries are mine.

[4] For more on 'situational identification' see previous chapter, p. 170 and the Introduction chapter, pp. 11–12.

breaks down in this rather asymmetrical 'encounter', since Tagore was certainly completely unaware of Kosovel's existence, nor would he have known much about the plight of the Slovenians. On the other hand, Kosovel too never got to meet Tagore and his knowledge of India or, for that matter, Tagore's own particular context, was necessarily limited by what he had read or heard about it. So, the interesting point here that unites these two disparate individuals who never met across their geographic and cultural distance is, in fact, the broad similarities of an international context that could in turn produce strong convergences in their worldviews, so much so that Kosovel had no trouble identifying with Tagore. The rich intertextuality characterizing Kosovel's work will also reveal joint references that defy any clear unilateral flows of ideas, whether, as in this case, from 'East' to 'West', or vice versa.

Before we go on to consider the points of convergence between the two differently placed contemporaries, we first need to establish the historical grounds for their comparison. As we situate Kosovel against the larger politico-historical forces that powerfully inflected his concerns, it will become clear that it was the political circumstances of the early decades of the twentieth century, when Slovenes were caught in the crossfire of a number of aggressive nationalisms (external and internal), that in large part galvanized the poet to grapple with the problematic of nation, nationalism, and nationhood. Not without irresolvable tensions, but certainly with the creative insight of a poet, Kosovel strove for a definition of 'Slovenianness' that even as it remained sensitive to the perceived needs of his people, espousing their right to self-determination, refused to yield to an inward-looking or separatist stance.

POLITICAL GEOGRAPHIES: THE KARST, TRIESTE, AND THE WIDER WORLD[5]

Srečko Kosovel was born in 1904, in the small town of Sežana, some twenty miles away from the city of Trieste. Both Trieste and

[5] Segments of this chapter related to Kosovel's background and the various aspects of his identification with Tagore have appeared in a shorter earlier version in Jelnikar (2014b).

his hometown region of the Karst—the limestone hinterland to the east of the city, from which it takes its name—were then part of the Austro-Hungarian empire, as was the territory that joined the newly established South-Slavic state after the war and became fully independent as Slovenia over eight decades later. The youngest of five children, he was brought up in a well-established and respected family. His father Anton Kosovel (1860–1933) was a school teacher and headmaster who taught in the Slovene language. He belonged to the generation of teachers who, in keeping with a tradition of defending and cultivating their language against the centuries-old Germanic tutelage and assimilative pressures, still felt their vocation was a 'national' mission. Teaching in the mother tongue for them meant cultivating a vital bond amongst a people who were then dispersed between several Habsburg provinces, living almost entirely in the Austrian half of the dual monarchy.

Until the latter half of the nineteenth century, the Slovenes were largely illiterate peasantry living in Habsburg-ruled territories where the language of administration and education was either German or Italian. But since modern nationalism required widespread literacy—and following the revolutionary wave of 1848, known across East-Central Europe as the 'Springtime of Nations'—the so-called Slovene awakeners made it their primary goal to develop and disseminate a standardized Slovene language and ascertain the right of its public use in schools and administration. The nineteenth century under the Habsburgs was the time in which the modern era with the Enlightenment ideals dawned for the Slovenes. It came in the form of the Napoleonic wars, in which Ljubljana for the short stint between 1809 and 1814 became the capital of the Illyrian Provinces (the French-captured territories of the Austrian Empire) and the Slovene language came into official and educational use. The 'indigenous Enlightenment', on the other hand, was propagated by a number of individuals, most notably by Žiga Zois (1747–1819), a wealthy baron who was a major patron of the arts and learning; philologist Blaž Kumerdej (1738–1805), who was involved in the setting up of primary Slovene education initiated by Empress Maria Theresa; the scholar-poet Valentin Vodnik (1758–1819), whose poem 'Illyria Resurrected' is a paean to Enlightenment ideals; Marko Pohlin and Jernej Kopitar who wrote important grammars at the time. But it was not until a rector of the University of Vienna by the name of Franc Miklošič (1813–1891) published a massive four-volume *Comparative Grammar of the Slavic Languages* in German that Slovene scholarship earned international recognition. In the world of letters, however, and against the backdrop of romantic nationalism, the first half of the nineteenth century was dominated by the man widely acclaimed as the Slovene national poet, France Prešeren (1800–1849). The national anthem of independent Slovenia is based on the seventh stanza of his poem 'Zdravljica' (A toast), a stanza with a clear message of universal brotherhood, granting self determination to all the peoples of the world.[6]

Between the 1860s and 1900, the establishment of reading societies (*čitalnice*) augmented rising national consciousness and increased literacy.[7] By the first decade of the twentieth century Slovenes had achieved almost universal literacy and had, in turn, also become nationally conscious of themselves as Slovenes.[8] Literary creativity flourished and book culture became an important social value. In the words of historian Igor Grdina:

> In prestige, writing as vocation did not lag behind the endeavours in science or professorial jobs; the author's word in public was a-priori deserving of attention.... The rapid disappearance of illiteracy across Central Europe, especially in Germany, but also in the Western part of the Austro-Hungarian Empire, turned the book from an emblem of emancipatory culture—which is what it was in the bourgeoisie era—into something self-evident in an increasingly more complex civilization. The written word was becoming a common referential point of human destiny.[9]

[6] Cox (2009), pp. 7–14.

[7] The first Slovene language newspaper was *Kmetijske in rokodelske novice* (Agricultural and artisan news); established in 1843 by Janez Bleiweis, for the next thirty years it had a seminal role in the Slovene 'national revival' (Cox 2009, p. 18).

[8] Rusinow (2003), pp. 15–16.

[9] Grdina (2013), translation mine, pp. 1151–2. It is interesting to note that the first Slovene novel appeared in 1866, Josip Jurčič's *Deseti brat* (The tenth brother), which is more or less coterminous with the first appearance of this modern-day genre in India. Bankim's *Rajmohan's Wife*, often regarded as the first Indian novel (which also happens to be the first 'Indian English novel'), came out in 1864 to be followed closely by his first Bengali novel, *Durgeshnandini*, a year later.

While the culturo-linguistic movement preceded the political one, rising national consciousness amongst the Slovenes in the second half of the nineteenth century also meant increasing pressures from their political elites on the central government in Vienna to grant them fuller autonomy within the Empire. Until quite late in the day (not much before the end of World War I), in orientation and their goals, the Slovene leading intelligentsia remained decidedly 'Austro-Slav' rather than 'Yugo-slav' ('yug' meaning 'south'). With the exception of the young radical group of pro-Yugoslav and openly anti-Austrian revolutionaries that formed around the journal *Preporod* (Revival) in 1912,[10] Slovenes before the war envisioned the unification of all Habsburg Slav territories into an autonomous entity, but within the Empire.[11]

Given these attitudes, we can begin to appreciate why on the eve of World War I, when the 65th anniversary of Emperor Franz Joseph's rule was being celebrated, Srečko's father Anton, otherwise a staunch defender of 'Slovenianness' (*slovenstvo*), organized a commemoration in their village to mark the event, and Srečko, then aged ten, read a poem entitled *Moja Avstrija* (My Austria).[12] On the other hand, Anton's proud Slovenian stance, which was far from being incompatible with a sense of belonging to an Empire, often got the family into trouble with the Austrian authorities. Soon after Srečko was born, they were made to move to the nearby town of Pliskovica. Two years later, they were forced to move again, this time to Tomaj, where they settled for good, and where Kosovel was to spend the better part of his early childhood.

Tomaj was a village of slightly more than 600 inhabitants, predominantly wine and wheat producers, battling the harsh conditions of the wind-swept, dry landscape of the Karst region. Anton Kosovel was also a musician (a choirmaster and an organ player) with an additional interest in farming. He made sure that his children were

[10] They aimed for Slovenes' unification within an independent South-Slavic state, an orientation that gained currency after the war.

[11] Velikonja (2003), pp. 85–6; For further details, see the chapter by Oto Luthar on the history of Slovenes during the transition period from under the Habsburgs to the Kingdom of Yugoslavia, in Luthar (2008).

[12] Cenčič (2004), p. 4.

given a broad education spanning cultural and economic matters.[13] Part of the regional scheme to ameliorate the Karst region at the time was to introduce the black pine, which would prevent rapid erosion from the violent bora winds and prepare the ground for easier water collection and agriculture. (Both the Karst's northwesterly wind and its pine trees became potent landmarks in Kosovel's poetry.) Anton was at the forefront of these initiatives, and hoped that his youngest son would choose a practical vocation that would help address the region's problems with water and infertile land. Though Kosovel did not follow his father's wishes to become a forester, as a child he dutifully planted pine seeds given to him by his father. Lines such as 'I saw the pines grow' can thus be taken quite literally, as can the far more chilling laments of 'no more water in Europe' in his apocalyptic verse 'The Ecstasy of Death' (both poems will be discussed later).

If Srečko inherited some of Anton's passion for Slovenian matters, he took from his mother, Katarina Stres (1862–1938), a defiant streak and a curiosity about the world. As a young girl with a little formal education, Katarina had rebelled against her own parents, refusing to marry the man that they had chosen for her. She ran away from her native village of Sužid to the city of Trieste—the cosmopolitan hub of old Austria and the seventh largest port in the world. There she had taken up with a Greek noble family, the Scaramagnas, as a nanny for their two daughters.

By the age of seven, the Kosovel children were learning German, French, and Russian. Srečko's literary horizons were certainly not confined to readings of native sources and literature in translation. He is known to have read books and journals in French and German, and to have translated Russian short stories, as he kept abreast with the literary trends of the 1920s. The Kosovel household attracted artists and intellectuals seeking a haven for open discussion in what were politically turbulent times.[14]

Srečko's happy childhood years were interrupted by the outbreak of World War I. A new front opened up along the river Soča (Isonzo),

[13] Anton Kosovel ran classes for adults, taught schoolchildren how to grow vines, tend fruit trees, and championed Karst forestation to improve the soil for agriculture.

[14] For the biographical detail in this section, I draw on Berger (1982), Cenčič (2004), Jelen (2004), Mislej-Božič (2004), and Vrečko (2011).

not even fifteen miles to the west of Tomaj, where some of the fiercest fighting between the Austrians and Italians took place.[15] His parents sent the twelve-year-old boy, together with his sister Anica, to Ljubljana (Laibach, as it was then known, was a provincial town of some fifty thousand inhabitants at the Empire's southern extreme). By then he had already seen the horrors of war from up close, and his childhood innocence soon passed into the knowledge of death. His eldest sister, Antonija, remembered young Srečko witnessing a truckload of wounded soldiers brought to Tomaj, where the village school had been transformed into a makeshift hospital. She described him as transfixed by the blood he saw dripping from the sides of the cart.[16]

For the remaining decade of his short life, Kosovel lived in Ljubljana, returning home only for the summer and during term breaks. During these holidays, he often visited Trieste—'the city sandwiched between Italy and Yugoslavia'[17]—which together with his native Karst, and adopted home of Ljubljana, was one of the three most important locales defining the spatial geography of his life. The importance of Trieste for Kosovel cannot be overstated, and it is not unsurprising, given that Trieste was the closest urban centre to his childhood home. A look at Trieste's turbulent history and the shifting

[15] It is said that 'almost two-thirds of Austria–Hungary's casualties in the war occurred on this front. About 80,000 Slovene civilians were evacuated from the region as well, spending the remainder of the war in other parts of Slovenia or in refugee camps near Vienna' (Cox 2009, p. 27). For a vivid retelling of the history of the Italian front and the vast destruction it brought to all the parties involved in the conflict, see Thompson's book *The White War: Life and Death on the Italian Front 1915–1919* (2008). The famous novel *A Farewell to Arms* (1929) by Ernest Hemingway—who was volunteering as an ambulance driver for the Italians—is set there. The Slovene writer Prežihov Voranc (born Lovro Kuhar, 1893–1950), who himself had fought on this front, gave a vivid description of the mindless savagery of war in his novel *Doberdob* (1941). For an excerpt in English from the novel, see Voranc (2014).

[16] From conversation with Pavle Skrinjar, a former director of the Kosovel museum at *Ljudska univerza* in Sežana and a friend of the late Antonija Kosovel, one of Kosovel's three sisters.

[17] Hametz (2005), p. 144.

political designations of the city and its hinterland—what has been referred to as 'the Adriatic boundary region'[18]—in the pre- and post-World War era is thus in order, since it will not only help us situate Kosovel in relation to Slovenes and Europeans but will also open up the broader logic behind his *identification* with Tagore.

Trieste was brought into the modern world in the eighteenth and nineteenth centuries by the Habsburgs who declared it a free port in 1719, and, not unlike Calcutta, it was transformed from a small fishing village into an imperial city.[19] For generations, political antipathies between subjects and rulers notwithstanding, this contemporary of Calcutta thrived as a commercial and trading port, largely unperturbed by notions of ethnicity, race, or religion. Rapid urbanization, encouraged by its status as a free port, soon turned Trieste into a microcosm of Europe, bringing together Italians, Austrians, Germans, and Slovenes—the largest ethnic Slav minority—alongside Croatians, Serbs, Bosnians, as well as Greeks, Armenians, Hungarians, Jews, English, and others.

In his study of James Joyce's long-standing relationship with the city, John McCourt tells us that the early twentieth-century Trieste was 'the third urban centre in the empire after Vienna and Prague [and] the world's seventh busiest port'.[20] Located at the crossroads of competing cultures, this 'dynamic city characterized by commercial solidity and also notable for its intellectual curiosity and openness', was a melting pot of nationalities, languages, and cultures.[21] The mix of nationalities and cultures that came to participate in the region persistently frustrated attempts at neat classification based on absolutes of national difference, while at the same time invited precisely such clean-cut categorizations. The history of Trieste (Triest for Austrians and Trst for Slovenes and Croats) was vitally bound up with the representation of cultural/ethnic/racial difference of its diverse populace,

---

[18] Sluga (2001), p. 13.

[19] This comparison occurred to me while reading Jan Morris's book on Trieste, where she mentions other 'imperial cities', including Calcutta (Morris 2001, p. 26).

[20] McCourt (2001), p. 29.

[21] McCourt (2001), p. 30.

where models of heterogeneous identity clashed and competed with essentialist models grounded in homogeneity.[22]

In Trieste before the war, the Kosovel children would often watch a play by Strindberg or Ibsen at the popular Teatro Verdi or Teatro Rossetti, as well as performances at the Slovenian Theatre House (founded in 1903 as the first Slovenian theatre).[23] One imagines that the family may have been part of the same audience as James Joyce, or that Kosovel may have strolled along the stretch of coastline from Trieste to one of his favourite places, Duino (Devin), where Rainer Maria Rilke was composing his *Duino Elegies* at the castle just above.

While today the city is predominantly Italian—Slovenes forming a small ethnic minority—the turn-of-the-century Trieste had a larger Slovenian population than did Ljubljana at the time.[24] It was thus an important centre of Slovenian culture, where its institutions were established soon after the revolutionary year of 1848, and the Slovene political party Edinost (Unity) was founded in 1874. At the same time—and importantly so for young Kosovel—it was a rich and vibrant cosmopolitan city.

In the course of the nineteenth and early twentieth century, as different narratives of national identity were being constructed, Trieste and the boundary region were transformed from what was 'imaginatively represented as mixed' into 'an unproblematically "Italian" space'.[25] In the decades leading up to the collapse of the Empire, the city's multiethnic composition, thoroughly shaken through the consequences of war and further unsettled by the revival of old enmities between Italians and Slavs, crumbled into factions vying for their political dues: 'Slavic propagandists championed the rights of the Slovene and Croat populations' and 'Italian nationalists clamoured for the redemption of "Trento and Trieste"', seeking to unite all

---

[22] Sluga (2001), p. 17.

[23] Pahor (1971), p. 25.

[24] According to the 1910 Austrian census 'the city of Trieste was 62 percent Italian, and 25 to 30 percent Slovene' (Sluga 2001, p. 30). Slovene historians have largely adopted these figures, invariably quoting 60,000 as the number for Triestine Slovenes and 52,000 for Ljubljana's Slovene population.

[25] Sluga (2001), pp. 6–7.

Italian populations under the flag of Italy'.[26] Racial bigotry erupted, and with the political barometer decidedly pro-Italian, Slavs became the butt of persecution.

Kosovel referred to the year of 1918 as a 'catastrophic defeat'. He further wrote, 'our destiny was decided by foreigners and not ourselves'.[27] He must have been referring to the Secret Treaty of London (1915), in which Britain had promised Italy, as an incentive to enter the war on the side of the Entente, the possession of large swathes of territory including Trieste, the whole of eastern Adriatic coastal region (excluding the port town of Rijeka/Fiume), the islands off the coast of Istria and Dalmatia, as well as African colonies.[28] After the war, when Slovenes joined the new South-Slavic Kingdom of Serbs, Croats, and Slovenes, the disputed border area was settled—with crucial input from the international mediators—in favour of Italian claims, though not to the extent promised by the London Treaty. When the Rapallo Treaty of November 1920 was signed and the Italo-Yugoslav border established, some 350,000 Slovenes and Croats were inhabiting regions handed over to Italy.[29] The whole of Istria and Primorska (Slovenian Littoral), including the Karst region that centres on the port of Trieste and the Isonzo valley with its main urban centre in Gorica/Gorizia, were ceded to Italy.[30] Together with additional territorial losses in Southern Carinthia along the north frontier with Austria,[31] these border adjustments effectively resulted in one third of the Slovenian

[26] Hametz (2005), p. 14. Italian irredentists (from *irredentismo*, the condition of being unredeemed) were nationalists who, following Garibaldi's motto 'free from the Alps to the Adriatic' saw Trieste as a 'natural'—and unredeemed—part of Italy's unified body politic.

[27] Kosovel, 'Razpad družbe in propad umetnosti' (Social breakdown and the collapse of art) 1925/6, *CW* 3, p. 34.

[28] Sluga (2001), p. 26.

[29] Velikonja (2003), p. 87.

[30] Pirjevec (1993), p. 63. Pro-Yugoslav Slovene and Croatian nationalists from Italy founded an illegal organization TIGR (acronym for Trieste, Istria, Gorizia, Rijeka) in 1924, which fought for the annexation of South Slav populated Italian territories to Yugoslavia.

[31] For more on the 1920 plebiscite in the southern Austrian province of Carinthia (German Kärnten, Slovene Koroška), a region which had a sizeable Slovene population, see Moritsch (1992).

population remaining outside the newly formed state. Kosovel did not mince his words as he reflected on the situation:

> Slovenes are not finding it easy to cope in the midst of this sick European secret diplomacy, which bargains off territories of small peoples, appeasing their dumbfounded looks with the League of Nations, where sit the very people who had sold these territories, the very people who now tyrannize them.[32]

The 'catastrophic defeat' Kosovel refers to was lent force by the aggressive policies of assimilation adopted by Italians towards the Slovene population now living within Italy's borders. In Trieste, 'a straightjacket of Italian officialdom was imposed on the city's multi-ethnic and multi-cultural identity, notably through acts of violence and persecution directed towards the Slovene community'.[33] On 13 July 1920, the seat of Slovene cultural life, the *Narodni Dom* (National House), which housed the oldest Slovene bank, the theatre, library, and leisure associations, was torched by a mob with the consent of the Triestine police and authorities. This signalled the beginning of outright persecution and enforced assimilation, which gained broad legitimacy as Benito Mussolini came to power in 1922. Policies adopted between 1924 and 1927 'transformed five hundred Slovene and Croatian primary schools into Italian-language schools, deported one thousand "Slavic" teachers (personified as "the resistance of a foreign race") to other parts of Italy, and closed around five hundred Slav societies and a slightly smaller number of libraries'.[34]

Kosovel's family did not remain unaffected by these events. Kosovel's father was forced to retire for refusing to abide by the Italian-only language policy, and was replaced by the more pliant Slovene

---

[32] Kosovel, 'Razpad družbe in propad umetnosti' (Disintegration of society and the collapse of art) 1925/6, *CW* 3, p. 40. Kosovel's double critique of the 'Pseudochrist in Geneva', the fake saviour of the League of Nations, on the one hand, and of the incompetence of the Slovene people to take destiny into their own hands on the other, comes across most powerfully in his acutely antagonized and acerbic poem 'Eh, Hey' (cf. Kosovel 2010a, p. 59, Appendix, p. 335).

[33] Pizzi (2001), p. 243.

[34] Sluga (2001), p. 48.

Ivan Kosmina.[35] This brought the family severe financial difficulties. They even lost the roof over their heads, since their accommodation was tied to Anton's teaching post. By 1926 non-Italian names had to be Italianized (Srečko, meaning 'lucky' became Felice; under Austrians he had been Felix), and by 1927, soon after Kosovel's death, the use of Slovene was prohibited in public. Periodicals were banned, Slovenian clergy persecuted, and all political parties except for the Fascist Party dissolved. Many intellectuals and artists went into exile; some crossing the border into Yugoslavia, while others emigrated to Argentina and the United States.[36]

Soon after the war broke out, Srečko, as already mentioned, was sent to Ljubljana, where he was enrolled into the German-medium Realgimnasium. Going home for holidays meant crossing the Italo-Yugoslav border, a passage fraught with the risk of not being allowed to return to his studies in Ljubljana. According to his elder brother Stano (himself a poet, journalist, and editor), Srečko was a 'refugee' in Ljubljana, though, strictly speaking, that was not true.[37] Thousands of people were indeed displaced from the villages alongside the Italo-Austrian front, but the village of Tomaj was never forcefully evacuated. But even if Kosovel was not a refugee, he was, for sure, exiled. His relationship to the new capital of Ljubljana was fraught with ambivalence. In some of his most despondent lines Ljubljana represented spiritual suicide:

> Ljubljana: cemetery of youthful dreams.
> Life doesn't much differ from death.
> Ljubljana makes people average
> or unhappy.
> Resist Ljubljana![38]

[35] In many instances, criteria other than ethnicity such as class or financial status came into play, complicating issues of identity. Many upwardly mobile ethnic Slovenes, for instance, adopted Italian as their first language, setting their class allegiance above their ethnic belonging. See Hametz (2005), p. 6; Moritsch (1992).

[36] Luthar (2008), p. 399.

[37] Stano Kosovel (1971), p. 12.

[38] 'Kons: X', translated by Bert Pribac and David Brooks, in Kosovel (2008b), p. 141.

The small history of his family's dislocations—the dispersal of its members across what became three separate nation-states—made displacement and exile a formative experience of Srečko's youth. The complicated sense of belonging and not belonging that this gave rise to—and which characterized both Kosovel's and Tagore's historical experiences—evolved into a commitment to a world of men and women much larger than any encapsulated by geopolitical boundaries. His displacement hints possibly at a more universal writer's condition, one that the Palestinian poet Mahmoud Darwish described as exile beginning inside one's homeland.[39]

Italian irredentism was the most threatening manifestation of a post-war nationalism that affected Kosovel's immediate environment. The plight of Primorska under Italy provides the most direct backdrop to my analysis seeking to establish Kosovel's sense of identification with Tagore. Still, the prior context of the disintegration of the Austro-Hungarian Empire with its culturo-political sphere of influence, even if only indirectly relevant, deserves a comment. Michaela Wolf has written pertinently on the subject of decolonization, comparing the realities of the collapse of the Austro–Hungarian Empire with the Third World countries' gaining independence from the colonizing powers:

> Decolonization affects both the colonized and the colonizer: both feel fragmented, dismembered, exhausted, inferior and weak. The new situation is marked by ambivalence on both sides. A shared coat, which somehow held together different cultural manifestations, is shed, and both parties must look for a new coat or create a patchwork from the remnants.[40]

We will see how fraught Kosovel's search for a new coat became—quite literally in his poem 'A Small Coat'[41]—as he witnessed the 'empty spaces' being filled with 'nationalism, fundamentalism and essentialism',[42] as new political subjects came of age, and Italians, Austrians,

---

[39] From an interview with the poet in a film portrait of the poet, *Mahmoud Darwish: As the Land Is the Language*, directed by Simon Britton and Elias Sanbar (1998).

[40] Wolf (2000), p. 128.

[41] For the poem, see Ch. 7, p. 320, or Appendix, p. 330.

[42] Wolf (2000), p. 128.

Hungarians, and Slovenes 'awoke' to their exclusive national interests and identities, and began asserting their rights through mobilizing nationalism as the legitimizing force of self-identification.[43] Historians often point out that up until the end of the feudal system and before the formation of the bourgeois and intellectual classes, there was a more or less peaceful coexistence between different ethnic groups in urban centres across Central Europe, social hierarchies and antipathies notwithstanding. And even though the various individual national groups within the Empire did not have equal opportunities, the overall cultural climate was not repressive or entirely unfavourable.

> Under Austrian rule, the various states maintained a large part of their cultural traditions. If literary and artistic productions were censored, overall cultural output was not suppressed or wiped out, as was the case in Latin America and Africa. Consequently, after the disintegration of the Austro-Hungarian Empire, the independent countries found themselves in a culturally weakened … situation.[44]

Towards the second half of World War I, Slovenes shifted their orientation from Austro-Slavism to Yugo-Slavism. It had become more or less clear that the expectations of the democratization of the Empire were unfounded, and any remaining hopes were dashed under the oppressive Habsburg war regime. For reasons of protection against Italy and Austria, as well as guarantees of national and cultural emancipation, the idea of Yugoslav unity, which had in fact been around for almost a century, garnered wide support.[45]

Broadly speaking, there were two strands of Yugoslavism (the Yugoslav idea). The first was the so-called integral or assimilative Yugoslavism, which aimed for a single Yugoslav nation by either denying the separate nationhoods of Slovenes, Croats, and Serbs, or by superseding them through an overarching Yugoslav identity. The other strand was in favour of a multinational state of related peoples

[43] On this see Pirjevec (1993), pp. 63–5. On the new mode of identification which replaced the traditional identifications on the basis of occupation, class, or religion, with the national one in this context, see Wachtel (1998), pp. 19–21.

[44] Wolf (2000), p. 128.

[45] Velikonja (2003), p. 87.

perceived as having shared interests and common aspirations, which sought federal devices to acknowledge separate nationhoods.[46] Slovene pro-Yugoslav attitudes largely (but not entirely) rejected the former, and endorsed the second in accordance with their 'separatist cultural nationalism' based on perceptions of their linguistic and cultural uniqueness vis-à-vis other South Slavs, rather than on notions of a glorious past or lost medieval kingdoms.[47] Accepting the newly-formed state, within which they were indeed able to set up their own educational and cultural institutions—the Ljubljana University in 1919, the National Gallery, the Slovene radio in 1928, and the Slovene Academy of Sciences and Arts (SAZU) in 1938—Slovene intellectuals were at the same time eager to preserve their distinct language and, by implication, culture.[48]

Ivan Cankar (1876–1918), a major Slovene writer of the period and one of the chief representatives of the so-called Slovene *Moderna*,[49] was probably the most influential in voicing the dominant intellectual stance as regards the Slovenes' desired future for themselves within Yugoslavia at the time. In a lecture entitled in translation 'The Slovenes and Yugoslavs', delivered in Ljubljana in 1913, he called for South-Slav unification within a single state, but made it clear that his pro-Yugoslav views were political, rather than cultural. For him 'the

---

[46] Rusinow (2003), p. 26.

[47] Wachtel (2003), p. 246.

[48] Velikonja (2003), p. 89. John Cox, for example, puts it neatly: 'Slovenes understood Yugoslavism, in both its political and cultural variants, as more a matter of solidarity and affinity rather than identity' (2009, p. 31).

[49] This term relates to the Latin word *modernus* as in contemporary (modern) and has come to be an umbrella term for the 'new' literature written between 1899 (the year marking the publication of Cankar's ground-breaking poetry collection *Erotika* (Eroticism) and Oton Župančič's *Časa opojnosti* (Cup of Intoxication) and 1918, spanning a diversity of styles and trends, from symbolism to impressionism and expressionism in Slovene literature. Dragotin Kette, Josip Murn, and Alojz Gradnik, alongside Cankar and Župančič were some of its main representatives. In his letters and notes, Kosovel often mentions Tagore alongside Ivan Cankar and Romain Rolland (1866–1944), whose manifesto, *Déclaration d'independence de l'esprit* (1919), he translated and adapted for the Slovenes in 1926 (cf. Kosovel 'Manifest svobodnim duhovom', *CW* 3, pp. 43–5).

Yugoslav problem' was exclusively a '*political* problem ... some kind of Yugoslav question in the cultural and overall linguistic sense' did not exist for him at all.[50] Typically, Slovenian intellectuals would oppose plans for cultural unification or a linguistic and cultural synthesis on the grounds that this would lead to the disappearance of their language or Serbo-Croatization of their populace. Wachtel even speaks of 'Slovenia's more or less isolationist attitude' within Yugoslavia in the interwar period, as shown in one of the leading cultural periodicals of the day *Ljubljanski zvon* (The Ljubljana Bell),[51] to which Kosovel also contributed. Kosovel, on the other hand, strove to challenge cultural isolationalism, also with respect to the artistic currents coming from Belgrade (especially the avant-garde Zenitist movement).[52] It will do then to consider his particular treatment of the Slovenian national question against the dominant climate in which it seemed vital to keep a separate Slovenian identity in order to withstand assimilation. At a time when the Yugoslav state centralism was gaining the upper hand (to culminate in King Alexander's dictatorship in 1929) Kosovel wrote a short essay 'Separatisti' (Separatists, 1925), which is worth looking at.

Against charges of separatism levelled against Slovene critics of Yugoslav integralism,[53] Kosovel retorted: 'Are a people automatically separatist, if they want to live? If they want to evolve, following their own path, and to crystallize their own body in their own spirit?'[54] If this amounts to a classic espousal of a separatist cultural nationalism, in the very next line Kosovel interrogates the whole notion of 'separatism' as used in political discourse by lodging it in the very human condition: 'Man is by his nature a separatist.' His focus is on the individual rather than a collective:

[50] Cankar, cited in Wachtel (1998), emphasis in the original, translator not stated, p. 86.

[51] Wachtel (2003), p. 87.

[52] To be discussed in more detail in the next chapter, pp. 260, 263.

[53] The term itself, and related charges, regained political currency after World War II at the birth of second Yugoslavia, as Slovene critics of Yugoslav integralism were criticized as 'egoists', 'traitors', 'separatists', 'destroyers of Socialist Yugoslavia'; see Velikonja (2003), p. 94n28.

[54] Kosovel, 'Separatisti' (Separatists), *CW* 3, p. 59.

Walking along the street, you chance upon a friend who wants to say
something to you or simply feel your friendship. But, as it happens, you
are not in the mood. In your state of mind you know your words would
come across as too bitter. So you prefer to go off on your own, sit in a
café, read the paper, and dwell in your own thoughts. You are—what
else—a separatist. Or, say you get invited to a dance. Though you like
watching people enjoy themselves ... you prefer to keep yourself at a
distance. Again, you are a dangerous separatist.[55]

This rather tongue-in-cheek exposition of the individual's right to
'separatism' is finally reconciled in a philosophy that carries an undeniable Tagorean imprint: 'All of us are walking with different faces,
distinct motives; each one of us has our own way, our own goal, but
only seemingly so; in the depth of our souls we all strive for one
thing: harmony.... Let us be one in spirit and love, but maintain our
own faces'.[56]

The progression from the individual through the (inter)national to
the universal is representative of Kosovel's reasoning and is perhaps
best encapsulated in these striking words of self-identification: 'My
life is mine, *Slovenian, contemporary, European*, and eternal'.[57]

Although this trajectory reveals him assuming a 'Slovenian' cultural
identity aligned with contemporary 'Europeanness', we will see how
he comes to question the naturalness of both.

Any reference to a 'Yugoslav' cultural identity, for reasons discussed,
is conspicuously missing from the above formulation. As a political
option, however, when Kosovel was presented with the choice of having an Italian passport or a Yugoslav one, he, along with many other
Slovenes, opted for the latter. This enabled him to apply for a scholarship as a student of Romance languages, the Slovene language, and
philosophy at the Faculty of Arts in Ljubljana University. When his
application was unsuccessful, he lashed out at the 'egocentric centralism' of the new state, deriding both 'the Greater-Serbian hand' that
had reached as far as the university and the Slovene political parties
that had failed to 'defend the university as an a-political institution'.

[55] Kosovel, 'Separatisti', *CW* 3, p. 59.

[56] Kosovel, 'Separatisti', *CW* 3, p. 59.

[57] Kosovel, emphasis author's, letter to Šanda, 26 December 1924, *CW*
3, p. 321.

Knowing for sure that hegemony can have a foreign as well as a domestic face, Kosovel despairingly castigated Slovene political elites for being unsuccessful in protecting the interests of their own people. The task of educational institutions was, he further admonished, to 'lay the foundations for the development of humankind, and not one party or one class'.[58] Left to his own resources, Srečko would henceforth struggle on the money he earned from coaching students.

It is at a time such as this, one imagines, that he composed a prose poem[59] entitled 'Bread' (Appendix, p. 330). Set in the Academic Collegiate of Ljubljana, where he lodged for a while as a student, the poem describes five students: besides the poet himself, there is 'a young, dark Bosnian' reading Tagore, transfixed by the content and looking out towards another, presumably better, life; two others, dubbed as 'technicians' and 'Slovenes', who are bent over a technical drawing, and someone else, studying. Receiving light from a single lamp, all of them seem completely engrossed in what they are doing, until, suddenly, they get distracted by a feeling of hunger.

> One thought, one dissonance: Bread.
> 'I'm hungry.'
> All the worlds crushed. Faces crumpled. Straight lines gone crooked and mathematical proofs mere riddles. Tagore hushed, spring stopped. A new mystery appeared: Bread.[60]

The poem can be seen to initially operate with various markers of identity, from the blatantly racial 'dark Bosnian' (literarily 'black') to national and ethnic designations, but at the end dissolves them with a mysterious reference to 'človek (man/human being; in Slovenian gender is unmarked) and 'the pilgrim'. It is almost as though the

[58] Kosovel, 'Na tiho' (Stealthily), *CW 3*, pp. 75–6.

[59] Though Kosovel's scholars have designated a body of Kosovel's writings as being prose poetry, there is, I would say, still a question mark over the designation, since Kosovel never referred to these poems as such and it is virtually impossible to ascertain whether they had been intended as prose poetry or were simply short prose pieces, or even just notes. Certainly, they are interesting enough to merit analysis.

[60] 'Bread', translated by Ana Jelnikar and Barbara Siegel Carlson, in Kosovel (2010a), p. 109.

poem sets forth the identity repertoire only to displace it with a grand universalist gesture. The juxtapositioning of a 'technician' and 'Slovenian' aligns nationality with cold mechanisms, a constant theme in Kosovel's work, and the repetition of the word 'one' ('one light', 'one human being') is in permanent tension with the evident plurality of the world (and this poem is packed with numbers), signalling beyond distinctions to a oneness of humanity. The reference to Tagore is thus laden with significance. The forgetting of the pilgrim in the very final line, however, casts a gloomy portent over the future.

With this we have more or less sketched the historical backdrop to Kosovel's short life. World War I and its aftermath presented a major turning point not just in Kosovel's life but also for Slovenes in general. As a result of the war, the Austro-Hungarian Empire would disappear from the face of Europe, and the Slovenes, who were largely loyal to the government in Vienna during the war, found themselves negotiating a new future for themselves in a South Slavic state of closely related peoples. The war in itself was traumatic, claiming a great number of lives. The Slovenes lost tens of thousands of their soldiers, 'reportedly the highest percentage of any nationality in the army'.[61] With the participation in the war, however, there came also 'a sense of empowerment through military action', which spilled across into demands for popular sovereignty in line with the contemporary mood of nationalism. This was true, as Cox rightly notes, of 'all the countries that participated in it, including the colonies of the British and French'.[62] Indeed, in India the British had enlisted over a million soldiers and labourers to the Allied war effort in Europe and the Middle East, where tens of thousands of Indian soldiers lost their lives, so the expectations of fulfilment of promises of self-rule in return for the Indian support were running high there too after the war.[63] With the British going back on their promises and resuming repressive policies introduced during the war, which culminated in the Amritsar massacre of some 400 peaceful demonstrators on 13 April 1919 by the British troops, all hopes of imminent independence

[61] Cox (2009), p. 25.
[62] Cox (2009), p. 24.
[63] See Mishra (2012), p. 192.

were dashed and Britain lost its already depleted moral ground in the eyes of a number of Asian intellectuals, including Tagore and Gandhi. Further, with 'the Wilsonian moment'[64] promising self-determination to all peoples of the world after the war, exposed as nothing more than empty rhetoric, anti-imperialist and anti-Western feelings were palpably on the rise.[65] Kosovel's caustic comments asserting that the League of Nations was a big lie safeguarding the interests of the imperialist Western powers is of a piece with the disillusionment experienced by many intellectuals from across Asia at around the same time.[66]

In the immediate aftermath of the war, Slovenes also found themselves in dire straits, politically, with many co-nationals in minority positions on Italian and Austrian territories, facing pressures to give up their self-identity as Slovenes. The shifting political geography of the Adriatic region made the whole question of a 'national identity' an acute issue for Kosovel, at once corroborating and undermining it. The multiple names Kosovel was obliged to adopt as governments changed hands certainly reflect the political and cultural pressures he was under. Similarly, adoption of three passports in so short a life must have seriously thrown into question the notion of nationality and citizenship as something 'natural' or organic to one's identity. It is against these forces that we see Kosovel striving to redefine Slovenianness along broadly universalist and humanist lines.

Mental Geographies

Having looked at the political geography of Kosovel's short life, it remains for us to consider the significant ideological undercurrents—the mental geography, as it were—that powerfully influenced the course of historic events in the Adriatic border region. This mental geography—and the focus is once again on Kosovel's native region of Primorska—lent legitimacy to the often violent repression of cultural and linguistic difference in the region by drawing on historical

[64] See Manela (2007)

[65] Mishra (2012), p. 203. For further discussion, see chs 4 and 5, pp. 186–241.

[66] How the Bolshevik Revolution presented a source of inspiration for a world of greater justice and equality will be addressed later.

perceptions of the antithetical notions of 'East' and 'West' within Europe and representations thereof. In this representational framework, different nationalities were accorded a separate racial status in a hierarchical set-up: 'Germans and Italians were regarded as cultural equals: bourgeois, modern, nationally evolved, and essentially Western', and 'Slavs were backward peasants, lacking national consciousness, and Eastern'.[67] What helped justify and consolidate the Italian claim to authority over the disputed area was their alleged racial, cultural, and linguistic superiority. According to an Italian irredentist Virgino Gayda (1885–1944), for example, whose pre-war writings were published in English and circulated internationally, Slovenes did not have a language, but a dialect. The fact that most Slovene Triestines were bilingual was seen as proof of their cultural backwardness. It pointed to a lack of national consciousness, their meekness, and suggested an essentially assimilatory character that could easily be subsumed into the superior *italianità*.[68]

Such valorizations of Italian culture, however, were no irredentist or Fascist novelty but were grounded in a tradition of representation going back to the Enlightenment.[69] A host of Western literary and academic writing has over the centuries explicitly generated this bipolar view of Europe, in which 'Eastern Europe' or 'the Balkan East' is imagined as the Western half's lesser other. These perceptions influenced political decisions on a number of levels. In relation to the Adriatic question, for example, British diplomats, harbouring notions of the Slav's 'doubtful capacity for self-government', readily assented to Italian claims to the territory on grounds of their 'cultural and political precedence'.[70]

Apart from the fact that in the days of its maritime glory, the city of Trieste was commonly referred to as *la porta d'oriente*—the

[67] Sluga (2001), p. 2.
[68] Sluga (2001), p. 27.
[69] For the seminal study, see Wolff (1994).
[70] Sluga (2001), pp. 37, 35. Robert William Seton-Watson, the founder of the University of London's School of Slavonic and East European Studies, a one-time advisor to the British Foreign Office, and editor of the review *The New Europe*, wrote in one of his articles dealing with the Adriatic question that the region was 'a centre of Italian culture and sentiment', and should be assigned to Italy 'on moral and spiritual grounds' (Sluga 2001, p. 31).

gateway to the East—for its real contact with the Orient,[71] the category of the 'East' as popularly understood by Italian Triestines, or Western Europeans more generally, resonated with associations of territories and peoples within much closer proximity than the far-off world the city traded with. Often 'the East' would be no further away than the rocky escarpment extending above the city known as Kras (Carso in Italian, and Karst in German). The identification of Eastern and/or Balkan Slavs with a backward rural folk as opposed to the modern and urbanized Italians was lent force by the physical geography in which Trieste stood apart from the Slav-populated villages atop the barren limestone plateau overlooking the city. In the wake of political conflicts pre- and post- both World Wars, it gave rise to popular anxieties of Slavic invasion from the 'barbarous East'—their descent from the mountains, as it were—so much so that Trieste came to be seen as the 'last bulwark of the West in the face of cultural and psychological anarchies perceived as predominant in an aggressive East'.[72]

The novelist Jan Morris, for example, lends her voice to these perceptions of the region: 'The permanent element of dissent in Trieste … its immovable reminder of an alternative world of strangeness, harsh challenge, mystery and unconvention … the city's real zone of disorder is the Karst'.[73] Savage, dangerous, and set beyond the pale of civilization, the landscape invited associations with places much further removed in geography, but which lent themselves to a similar kind of romanticization or demonization. For example, Elizabeth Burton, the wife and biographer of the British explorer, writer, and linguist Sir Richard Burton, saw 'the wild Karst' as 'stony Syria'.[74] Today

---

[71] Cf. McCourt (2000), p. 143. Also, 'Trieste became Europe's chief point of contact with the Orient, especially after the cutting of the Suez Canal: even the British, when they wanted to reach their Indian empire in a hurry, sent their mail and couriers across the continent by rail to Trieste, to pick up a Lloyd Adriatico packet to the east' (Morris 2001, p. 175).

[72] Pizzi (2001), p. 157.

[73] Morris (2001), p. 145–6.

[74] Cited in McCourt (2000), p. 30. Richard Burton was the British consul in Trieste between 1872 and his death in 1890. His most celebrated book, the translation of *The Arabian Nights* (1885), was completed in his study in the Opicina/Opčine on the Karstic rim just above the city.

little known, but at the turn of the twentieth century, a highly influential Jewish writer and journalist in Trieste, Haydée (Ida Finzi; 1867–1946) would make African colonies and the Karst into interchangeable settings for her novel *Allieve di Quarta: Il Cuore delle bambine* (Fourth-grade pupils: Hearts of young girls, 1922).[75]

Such conflation of categories and settings is commonplace in imperialist attitudes towards their colonies. Certainly, the more entrenched the essentialized perceptions of difference between 'Italians' and 'Slavs' became, the more divisive was the mental border separating them.[76] The bipolar imaginary of 'us' and 'them', coupled with a blanket treatment of the 'other', presented one of the most formidable challenges to what both Tagore and Kosovel felt was the mission of their age.

Against this background, informed jointly by concrete historical events and representational practice thereof, broad discursive similarities between Tagore's and Kosovel's respective positions can be discerned. Namely, they were both projected as members of an inferior and governable race, Indian and (Balkan) Slav respectively. Both were at the receiving end of what Raymond F. Betts has termed 'the peculiar geography of imperialism', whereby Western Europe was the centre of the world, 'radiat[ing] outward' from its core 'those attributes we describe today as "modern"'.[77] They were both, in other words, perceived as occupants of 'the East', and their respective identities were rehearsed through the common stock of racial platitudes (irrational, infantile, incapable of self-rule, lacking national consciousness, backward, barbaric, and so on) employed to validate the hegemonic mission on the one hand while bolstering the ruler's sense of superior self on the other.[78] Not wanting to oversimplify what is a complex topic, the point I am trying to make is simply that it is from the

[75] For further detail see Pizzi (2001), pp. 141–7.

[76] For the history of the extended contact between the Slovenes and Italians in Trieste and the forging of mythologies of 'Italian' Trieste and 'Slovene' Trieste, see Cattaruzza (1992) and Verginella (2005) respectively.

[77] Betts (1998), p. 7.

[78] In Tagore's case this was somewhat different. Being an Indian 'aristocrat' belonging to an ancient civilization made Tagore acceptable to the British colonizers. He was knighted by the British and awarded the Nobel Prize through their support. But if he refused to toe the line, he was demoted to an Indian 'babu'. See Jelnikar (2008).

particular historical juncture when Slovenes under Italian occupation were culturally and politically oppressed (and ideologically othered) that Kosovel saw himself as occupying the same space vis-à-vis the imperial West as Tagore. This is the logic underlying his sympathetic reaching-out to him in what Elleke Boehmer has aptly called 'anti-colonial hand-holding'—resistance that emerges between 'others'.[79]

Tagore often referred to the 'question of race pride', regretting the obstacle it presented to mutual cultural exchange. 'Can the West fully acknowledge the East? If mutual acceptance is not possible, then I shall be very sorry for that country which rejects another's culture'—he said in an interview with H. G. Wells.[80] Against racial, cultural, and class divides that shaped perceptions of how people saw each other, Tagore and Kosovel both defended the possibility of genuine human contact.

Michael Collins is right in saying that Tagore saw the British rule in India as essentially 'a failure of imagination and intellect'.[81] He also rightly suggests that Tagore's interaction with a number of individuals from the anglophone world was part of his commendable transnational 'politics of friendship'.[82] Burdened with notions of class, race, and religion, these attachments were never uncomplicated, but they do present us with a human face to the often overlooked realities of the empire.

With respect to Kosovel and his 'transnational' or 'cross-colonial' friendships, his encounter with the Italian philosopher, journalist, and political scientist, Carlo Curcio (1889–1971) deserves mention. Originally from Naples, Curcio was posted as a lieutenant in Dutovlje in 1918, and first met Kosovel's sisters, Karmela and Anica, when they came to his garrison to obtain a border-pass. As related by Anica nearly forty years later in an interview with the Triestine Slovene writer Boris Pahor (b. 1913), the students had come home to visit their parents during the term-break from Ljubljana, but the Italian occupation forces would not issue the passes, thus making it impossible for them to return to their studies. This made the father very angry; not with the authorities, but with the children for having

[79] Boehmer (2002), p. 30.

[80] Tagore (2002l [1936]), p. 909.

[81] Collins (2012), p. 13.

[82] On Tagore's anglophone friendships with William Rothenstein, W. B. Yeats, C. F. Andrews, Edward Thompson, and others, see Collins (2012), chs 4 and 5, pp. 101–43.

come home in the first place. Anica and Karmela tried to save the day and went to the nearest garrison:

> We knocked. The Lieutenant was in the room. A young man. And so we began by saying how our father was angry, and that in any case we were students … And he said: '*Gli studenti son il fiore della nazione*' (Students are the flowers of the nation). Indeed, we said, and while a brother and one of the sisters are studying in Ljubljana, another sister is visiting the music college Tartini in Trieste [that was Karmela]. So not all '*fiori della nazione*' (flowers of the nation) are lost. He promised to speak to the General. As we left the garrison, laughing, we heard footsteps. *Tenente* (the Lieutenant) came after us, wanting to know where we lived. So Karmela and I began talking about Michelangelo and Raphael, and his eyes lit up with astonishment as to what these Karstic people knew. The next day he brought us the permits and Karmela played for him a piece by Beethoven.[83]

The sisters then also intervened on behalf of other students, and soon Curcio became a personal friend of the family, often coming to their house for visits, until his service came to an end a year later. Their conversations revolved mostly around literature, and as a farewell present, Curcio gifted the family the two volumes of Francesco De Sanctis's famous *History of Italian Literature* (1871). He would return to visit them on a number of occasions; he stayed in touch with the family, exchanging many letters and postcards until his death in 1971.

It was in October in 1922 that Kosovel and Curcio met in Ljubljana, where for three days Kosovel became his 'tour guide', taking him around the Slovenian capital, introducing him to some of the leading artists and intellectuals of the day, including the impressionist painter Rihard Jakopič, art historian Izidor Cankar, essayist and literary critic Josip Vidmar, and others. In their subsequent correspondence—they wrote to each other in French, since Kosovel was better versed in French, which he was studying, than in Italian—they exchanged their views on the future of Europe, their allegiance to the idealistic strain of philosophy (Kant, Hegel, Rolland, and Tagore), and Kosovel critically engaged with Curcio's writings (as for example with his essay *L'Ideale della vitta* [The ideal of life]). In assessing their relationship, Miran Košuta believes this exchange to have been crucial in Curcio's

---

[83] Cited in Pahor (1971), translation mine, p. 34.

overcoming his earlier racist attitudes towards 'the Slavs' and his support for Mussolini, and eventually coming to defend the cause of the Slovenes, upholding every people's right to self-determination.[84]

Kosovel retained links with Trieste even after the war (unlike Joyce, who left the city once it succumbed to bigotry). He was particularly drawn to the important current of international socialism there, mediated to him by his Triestine Slovene friend Vladimir Martelanc, a young communist who supplied him with Marxist literature.[85] Seeing the city regress into crude nationalism and race hatred, he deplored both Italian irredentism and Slavic nationalisms. 'The heart-Trieste is ill', he would come to write in the lyric 'Almost Midnight' (Appendix, p. 331), and the city's setting became the locale for his apocalyptic vision expressed in the nine-sequence poem 'Tragedy on the Ocean'.[86]

In another lesser-known poem, ironically entitled 'Italian Culture', Kosovel lays out his concerns as regards the 'national' question in an almost programmatic fashion. This poem is also unique for its reference to Gandhi,[87] and once again shows Kosovel searching for

---

[84] For further details on their relationship, see Košuta (2004), pp. 176–83; see also Rojc (2008), pp. 276–81, who too observes in her illuminating contextualization of Kosovel's work and thought amongst his Italian contemporaries, that it is 'probably the striving for universality, which is the main force behind Kosovel's friendship with Carlo Curcio' (translation mine, Košuta 2004, p. 277). Letters Curcio wrote to Kosovel are touching for the depth of love and friendship he felt towards Srečko—'But I would always be thinking of you, my comrade in ideals, my tour guide in Ljubljana, in one word: my friend, a friend beyond compare', in a letter dated 5 May 1923, in Kosovel (2008a), p. 121.

[85] Vladimir Martelanc (b. in Trieste, 1905–44) joined the communist movement formed around the editorship of the newspaper *Delo* (in Trieste) in 1923. After leaving for Vienna in the same year, he co-edited the journal *La Fédérationa Balkanique*, an influential international and multilingual review, championing the rights of national minorities in the Balkans, for which it earned the support of notable European intellectuals such as Romain Rolland, Henri Barbusse as well as Albert Einstein. The journal was disseminated across the Slovenian Littoral by the Slovene wing of the Communist Party of Italy and Kosovel is known to have read it (cf. Kodrič 2011, p. 103).

[86] Kosovel (2010a), pp. 155–67.

[87] Strictly speaking, Gandhi gets another mention in Kosovel's poetry, in reference to the six-year sentence that was passed against him in 1922 after the Chauri Chaura incident. See the poem 'Cons XY', Appendix, p. 338.

alternative cultural models; as Slovenian cultural institutions were under attack in Trieste, Gandhi was launching his Non-cooperation Movement in the subcontinent in the attempt to oust the British.

> The Slovenian National House in Trieste, 1920.
> The Workers House in Trieste, 1920.
> Wheat fields in Istria on fire.
> Fascist threat during the elections.
> The heart is becoming as tough as a rock.
> Shall Slovenian workers' homes
> continue to burn?
> The old woman is dying at her prayers.
> Slovenism is a Progressive Factor.
> Humanism is a Progressive Factor.
> A humanistic Slovenism: synthesis of development.
> Gandhi, Gandhi, Gandhi!
> *Edinost** is burning, burning,
> our nation, choking, choking.[88]

> **Edinost* ('Unity'): a Slovenian political association, a printing press, and the name of the main Slovene daily newspaper, published in Trieste, the premises of which were attacked several times by Italian Fascists in the 1920s, and finally torched in 1925.

Lacking verbs, the first two lines give the poem a slow and tortured start. The brutal alignment of bare facts, dates, and their repetition, acquires agency only with the mention of 'Fascist threat' in the fourth line. Henceforth the poem gathers in speed, as it oscillates between despair and hope, investing trust in the evolution of the human spirit symbolized in the figure of Gandhi,[89] only to sink back into the depressing state of the present.

[88] 'Italian Culture', translated by Bert Pribac and David Brooks, in Kosovel (2008b), p. 137.

[89] It is fair to assume that Kosovel was more attracted to Gandhi as a champion of non-violence than the leader of Non-cooperation. The political goings-on in India, especially surrounding Gandhi's Non-cooperation Movement, were summarily reported in Slovene daily newspapers of the time, under the rubric of international news. See, for example, a piece entitled in translation 'Dissolution in Gandhi's Party', *Jutro*, year VI, no. 54, 4 March 1925, p. 2; or 'Mahatma Gandhi' in *Slovenski republikanec*, year V., no. 8, 27

What makes this poem significant is that the crisis it evokes between 'us' and 'them' in the first stanza is telescoped inwards in the second one; Slovenism, or the idea of Slovenianness (slovenstvo), if it is to progress in evolution, must hold on to humanist ideals, themselves subject to evolution. The noun of Fascism points to a verb of human intervention so that 'national' identity, cast in a changing and progressive mould, is salvaged from anti-humanist practices. Slovenes, whatever they do, must not jeopardize basic human values. Or, as Kosovel would write elsewhere: 'A nation only becomes a nation when it becomes aware of its humanity.'[90] Both Kosovel and Tagore believed in the perfectibility of human beings.

This poem can also be read in terms of the larger debate on whether 'slovenstvo provides a bulwark against assimilation and homogenization, or whether it is a hurdle Slovenes need to clear to become a cosmopolitan, integrated society'.[91] For Kosovel, the question of Italian dominance (or 'culture') was by no means a straightforward issue. In the same way that Tagore, despite the violence and humiliation of foreign rule, refused to succumb to an outright dismissal of everything British or, in turn, an uncritical valorization of everything Bengali/Indian, Kosovel too made it a point to discriminate between imperialist forces that deserved reprobation and forces that he felt were (for the) good, even if coming from the wrong quarters. Both writers strove to override politics in an open acceptance of what they felt was commendable in any given culture, laying themselves open to charges of collaboration with imperialists or to denationalized surrender.

For all the catastrophic talk that we have noted earlier in Kosovel, he is in fact remarkably free of resentment towards the Italian oppressors,

---

February 1925, p. 2. A more substantial article on Gandhi was published in 1921 in the major Catholic newspaper *Slovenec*, cf. Terseglav (1921). Kosovel may also have read Romain Rolland's book, *Mahatma Gandhi* (1924), which was available in the German translation by Emil Roniger and was published in Zürich by Rotapfel-Verlag in 1924. His notes reveal that he was planning a lecture on 'Tagore and Gandhi: Two Solutions to the Question of Nationhood', in *CW* 3, p. 746, as part of the activities of the Literarni in dramski klub IC (Literature and theatre club Ivan Cankar), which he co-founded and ran as a student.

[90] Kosovel, letter to Dragan Šanda, 15 September 1925, *CW* 3, pp. 323–4.
[91] Cox (2009), p. 38.

and he certainly disavows the path of victimhood.[92] While he perceived the 'defeat' of 1918 as a 'hard blow', in his eyes it was 'deserved'—a sobering-up of sorts that would jolt Slovenes out of lethargy and lead to desired emancipation.[93] It is hard to imagine that Kosovel would have, in any degree, accepted the terms of Italy's conquest as a mission to 'civilize' and bring order to the 'barbaric East', but at the same time his response does reveal the degree to which persistent cultural denigration is internalized by the oppressed, even as it is—and in his case adamantly so—challenged. The trauma of imperialist hegemony transpires precisely through his relentless protest against slavish conformism (underpinned by the centuries-long history of foreign rule) that he identifies as an inherent trait in his countrymen. 'We prefer to remain servile and dream,' he admonishes them, 'rather than live and rule ourselves.'[94] Clearly, the notion of servility and alleged incapacity for self-rule (the vocabulary used by imperialists to justify their claim over foreign territories), is here subverted into a compulsion for liberation, but evidently it is also impossible for him to go beyond the master–slave dichotomy:

> At a time when we are being lashed by European imperialisms, we are down on our knees, praying to God to grant us our rights and give us righteous masters. And these masters let us have our God but take away all the rights God has given to man.[95]

To lodge his call for resistance and liberation, Kosovel builds on the notion of inalienable human rights. A scion of the Enlightenment, he evokes the rights of man as man in the secular sense, which is also an

---

[92] I entirely agree with Peter Scherber that 'it is at first sight astonishing to see [Kosovel] primarily in opposition to his own Slovene compatriots and the Yugoslav politicians, and hardly ever as a critic of the Italian occupiers of his own home territory, the Karst, and the Slovene coastal region' (1991, p. 157).

[93] Kosovel, 'Razpad družbe', *CW* 3, pp. 34–5.

[94] Kosovel, 'Razpad družbe', *CW* 3, pp. 34–5. This is a familiar argument also in the Bengali/Indian context. The idea that there is something inherent in the character of Indians themselves that invites foreign rule was voiced, for example, by Bankimchandra Chatterjee, as mentioned on p. 53 of Ch. 2.

[95] Kosovel, 'Razpad družbe', *CW* 3, pp. 34–5.

important moment for Tagore's universalism.[96] His artistic temperament in the final instance celebrates the meeting of 'East' and 'West'
and extends the notion of 'East' to encompass Asia:

> We happen to be living at the crossroads of Western and Eastern Europe,
> on the battlefront of Eastern culture with Western, in an age which is
> the most exciting and the most interesting in its multiplicity of idioms
> and movements in politics, economy and art, because our age carries
> within itself all the idioms of the cultural and political past of Europe
> and possibly the future of Asia.[97]

The reference to Asia is no doubt a direct allusion to Tagore's own
understanding of Asia's future relationship with the world, which
Kosovel was familiar with from reading Tagore's book *Nationalism*
(1917). And the fact that Kosovel saw his own position defined in
terms of an 'East–West' juncture—at once a point of division and
contact—enabled him to relate to Tagore's own project of exploiting
the divide for a creative encounter: the forging of a new emancipated
individual who would somehow be free of these divisions.

Towards a Comparative Framework: Theoretical Precedence

Before going on to explore further the close association Kosovel surmised between himself and Tagore in his quest for (self-)liberation,
we need to address briefly the stretching of the parameters of colonialism and imperialism so as to encompass geographical spaces within
Europe. In postcolonial studies, Bhabha and Spivak have frequently
been singled out as the two theoreticians who have contributed most
to extending the explanatory notion of 'colonialisation' to cover 'all
situations of structural domination'.[98] My approach does in part rest

[96] The disputed legacy of the Enlightenment thought has been discussed
in Ch. 1. To avoid the bipolar for-or-against paradigm, it is important to see
the Enlightenment's legacy as split between both colonial and anti-colonial
agendas: 'There are certainly elements of Enlightenment thought in colonial
ideology. However, Enlightenment principles also form the basis for a great
deal of anticolonial thought and action' (Hogan 2000, p. 27).

[97] Kosovel, 'Igo Gruden', 1926, *CW* 3, p. 178.

[98] McLeod (2000), p. 244.

on such stretching of the vocabulary, whereby Tagore and Kosovel are seen to occupy structurally similar spaces within their respective and distinct historical settings and 'colonial' experiences. Both were exposed to forces of cultural domination, whereby one culture was privileged to the exclusion of another (differences are a question of degree but not of principle), and in both cases these forces ultimately failed, as Bengali and Slovenian literatures continued to grow, even flourish, as was the case in the 'Bengal Renaissance'.[99]

With respect to Kosovel it can be argued that the measures employed in de-nationalizing Slovene (and Croatian) communities within Italian borders were more violent than the policies adopted by the British in India to maintain their cultural supremacy. The latter were possibly more subtle and perfidious, perhaps also more effective. The old saying, however, that the empire is won and maintained by the sword is probably true of all rulers wanting to hold on to their power (the Amritsar massacre of 1919 is just one example in the context of Tagore's life).

As much as my analysis rests on the assumption of structural (and discursive) similarities that connect Kosovel with Tagore, this is not in any way to suggest that their experiences of Italian and British rule, respectively, were identical or that they had affected their cultures in the same way. Differences are many and obvious. Italian control over the specified territory and not the entire region of what is today Slovenia lasted a few decades, whereas the British rule over India (both of the East India Company and the direct rule after the Sepoy Rebellion) extended over a much longer period, although, strictly speaking, the British never ruled over all of India.[100] Then, at least part of the territory subjected to Italianization was mixed and disputed. With the mandate of Italianization, however, Slavs lost their settler status and were perceived mainly as usurpers and invaders. Often they were rationalized as being a foreign element introduced by the Austrians for their own political gains vis-à-vis the Italians. Hence, they had no

---

[99] In terms of artistic creativity, the period before and after the Great War, as one historian has put it, 'probably represents the golden age of Slovene high culture' (Cox 2009, p. 21).

[100] The Austro-Hungarian Empire is a separate issue, and one I have briefly addressed above.

territorial rights and could be expelled at a whim. At best they were seen as 'guests'.[101] Istrians and the Karstic people, on the other hand, lived in largely Slovene- (or Croatian-) populated territories. The implementation of the Rapallo border brought these lands under Italian control.

Both the duration and nature of colonization as it affected these regions would also help explain why the rich literary crossover that is so much a part of Indian cultural history and the legacy of colonialism never became a significant part of Slovenian experience. The contact zone from which Kosovel came seems to have been pervaded by so harsh a political conflict that the possibility of an unaffected cultural exchange—of which he, like Tagore, was a powerful advocate—was grossly diminished. Literary historian Franc Zadravec has shown that of all romance-language literatures (Italian, French, and Spanish), Slovenes have responded least heartily to the Italian body of literature in spite of Slovenia's closest geographic proximity to Italy. His conclusion, which confines itself to an analysis of translated foreign literary works and their evaluation in the Slovene press between 1918 and 1948, leaves little doubt as to the reasons behind this cultural impasse:

> The cause for what is undoubtedly a cold reception of Italian literature [in Slovenia] was not just its recession in the time of Fascism, but above all Italian colonial de-nationalizing policy over a significant portion of occupied Slovenian territory. [I]t was marked by a revolt against the haughty pose of the Roman she-wolf who was gifting the 'barbarians' her culture, while stifling their own, as she was stifling their language.[102]

The tone of this particular passage, in what is elsewhere a sober and detached scholarly analysis, is proof enough of the continuing

---

[101] 'Although Slavs were historically resident in the area, there was a widespread tendency to perceive the Slovene community as foreign and intrusive: in the dialectic insiders versus outsiders, Slav populations were frequently and literally represented as a *disease* attacking the healthy body of *italianità*' (Pizzi 2001, p. 186). On this see also Sluga (2001), pp. 27–33.

[102] Zadravec (1974), translation mine, p. 82.

troubling impact of this episode of Slovenian history on the Slovenian psyche.[103]

Applying the postcolonial theoretical tools to political and literary spaces within Europe itself is hardly a novel proposition and has come to figure prominently over the last decades in the fields of Central, East European, and Balkan studies, though as far as postcolonial studies go, Eastern Europe, alongside East Asia, Latin America, and the Middle East, is still a neglected area of enquiry. The Balkan strain, in particular, has been most directly indebted to the premises outlined in Said's book *Orientalism* (1978). Vesna Goldsworthy, for example, imports the Saidian critique practically wholesale as she analyses literary constructions of the Balkans in British fiction in her study entitled *Inventing Ruritania: The Imperialism of the Imagination* (1998). Others, most notably Maria Todorova, are more cautious in adopting the Orientalist model for this particular region. While acknowledging the underlying pertinence of Said's theoretical vocabulary for the Balkans, her study *Imagining the Balkans* (1997) proposes a new discursive category, 'Balkanism', so as to foreground the geographical, cultural, and political specificities of the region.

While Goldsworthy has made a convincing case for the view that 'the Balkans' have been imaginatively functionalized as the 'Orient' of Europe,[104] perhaps her too exclusive a reliance on Said prevents her from taking into account the Balkans' liminal status. Geographically located within Europe, a status often only grudgingly accorded to them by economically superior Western-European powers, makes the Balkans an *internal* 'Other'. Marked thus by a duplicity of status as simultaneously an insider and an outsider, the Balkans, itself a shifting category, is subject to a split self-referentiality that is different to 'conventional' colonization. Nonetheless, I agree with one commentator

---

[103] One is, of course, made to wonder, whether this could be a blind spot on the part of Slovenian scholarship, similar to the implicit or explicit denial of the impact of the Soviet centre on the postcolonial cultures of Central and East Europe that Steven Tötösy de Zepetnek has observed in the intellectuals of the region, who, on the other hand, accept the influence of a Western centre such as Germany as an unproblematic given. See Tötösy de Zepetnek (2002), p. 11.

[104] Goldsworthy speaks of 'imaginative textual colonization' in relation to the Balkans, acknowledging the absence of a 'fully-fledged conventional imperialism' (1998, p. 211).

who says that '[t]o view the relationship between Western Europe and the Balkans as homologous to colonialism is an approach that, if used with reason (and if historicized), has validity and can be fruitful.'[105]

If geographically the tradition of representation that is interrogated by the Balkan studies relates primarily to the region that was historically under the Ottoman rule, then its relevance to our area of enquiry is arguably only indirect or itself liminal. Nonetheless, the perpetuated symbolic geography of 'eastern inferiority' can be seen to have affected—differently and at different times—both spaces, and the liminal status where 'eastern' is employed antithetically to the noun 'Europe' has also had bearings on the Italian-ruled interwar region of Primorska. It must be noted too that the orientalist discourses have played a prominent part in Slovenian political and intellectual life in the more recent history to demarcate their own 'superiority' or 'Europeanness' vis-à-vis the rest of 'the Balkans'.[106] Though this is a matter for a different, if not irrelevant, discussion, it alerts us powerfully to the shifting line of exclusion and inclusion that underlies the symbolic map of Europe. We cannot ignore the existence of a hierarchical axis in the European symbolic geography 'declining in relative value from the north-west (highest value) to the south-east (lowest value)'. Bakic-Hayden and Hayden speak of a 'system of "nesting" orientalisms', in which, 'in terms of distinguishing disvalued Others ... there exists a tendency for each region to view cultures and religions to the south and east of it as more conservative or primitive'.[107] Slovenes, in this scheme, have been no exception.

A differentiated map (of the perceptions and constructions) of Europe is therefore essential here. The theoretician of Central and Eastern European cultures, Steven Tötösy de Zepetnek, has been a proponent of the applicability of the postcolonial studies model for parts of Europe,[108] but he has fine-tuned the centre–periphery and

[105] Fleming (2000), p. 1221.

[106] See Bakic-Hayden and Hayden (1992) for further discussion of the exceptionalist, orientalist discourse of Slovene politicians and intellectuals to justify their split from Yugoslavia in the 1990s.

[107] Bakic-Hayden and Hayden (1992), p. 4.

[108] What lends his postcolonial approach 'factual' credence is the four-decade-long condition of 'Soviet colonialism' exercised over a large part of Central and Eastern Europe. Although former Yugoslavia was never part of

centre–margin notions with respect to the existing internal economic, political, and cultural hierarchies:

> In reality, there are several centers, France, Germany, and there are 'near centers' such as Italy, the Benelux, the Nordic countries, etc., and these centers reflect economic and political power. And then there are several peripheries such as Southern and East Europe, Portugal, the Baltic countries, etc. In this differentiated view of Europe, Central and East Europe comprises the successor states of the Austrian empire and beyond, with their Austro-German and German economic, cultural, political, etc., spheres of influence. In general social discourse as well as in scholarship, Central and East European cultures, owing to their situation of peripherality, need to proclaim within Europe that they are Europeans and that they belong to Europe while the sliding scale of cultural hierarchies based on economic realities from West to Central and to East Europe remains an established practice although more implicit than explicit, yet practiced rather than admitted and discussed.[109]

In historicizing the region with respect to its many political, economic, and cultural centres, Tötösy extends the vocabulary of centre/margin through the category of 'in-betweenness'. The sliding scale of cultural hierarchies along the West–Central–East geographical and economic axis positions these cultures in between their own 'self-referential national culture' (that in reality is never as homogenous as proclaimed) and the various other centres or sources of influence.[110] It is precisely this liminal status of 'the peripheral subject'—a subject that is yet to claim its 'European' status from the margin position of an 'inside other'—that has endowed Kosovel with the double perspective of questioning while asserting, or rather asserting *through* questioning, his own Slovenian and European culture and identity. The situation of India vis-à-vis Europe is of course different in this respect and has affected Kosovel and Tagore differently. This becomes evident when

---

the Soviet Empire, what validates Tötösy's approach as regards Kosovel is the fact of Italian occupation combined with the region's peripheral status perceived as the divide between Europe's eastern and western halves.

[109] Tötösy de Zepetnek (2002), pp. 8–9.
[110] Tötösy de Zepetnek (2002), p. 12.

a little later in this volume we compare and analyse their respective 'tirades' against Europe or the West in two of their poems.

Making Connections

Let me recapitulate the main points made in relation to Kosovel's background from which he derived a sense of shared concerns with Tagore. I have dwelt on the embattled history of the Adriatic Region and Trieste, for the reason that it was Trieste, in many ways a city the poet felt more at home in than in Ljubljana, that sensitized young Srečko to models of subjective identification that could either accommodate difference (the city before the war was a place where diverse nationalities and groups were able to share the same territory without conflict) or violently repress it (as was the case once the city and its environs were designated as exclusively Italian and assimilation became the order of the day).[111]

The post-war situation (aggravated also by centralizing tendencies of the new state and Germanization pressures from the north) alerted Kosovel in a most powerful way to the pathology of nationalism and the raising of barriers along ethnic lines, where being Italian, Austrian, Slovene, or of any other nationality, overrode notions of a shared human identity or precluded the possibility of hybrid or multiple identities. His task became twofold: to show that nationalism was 'a lie' and an imposition[112]—in this he was as passionate as Tagore—and to salvage the concept of *narod* (a people) from being hijacked by nationalism. 'A *narod* for us can only ever mean a nation which has freed itself from nationalism.'[113] There is obvious tension here between a people and a nation, and a possible resolution to the intransigent problematic of '*narod*' and 'nationalism' lay in an appeal to a *new* humanism.

---

[111] James Joyce may have been thinking about the pre-war Trieste when he made Leopold in *Ulysses* utter this brilliant sentence: 'A nation is the same people living in the same place.'

[112] Kosovel, letter to Ciril Debevec, 10 September 1925: 'Now they are dissolving our societies and founding "Lega nazionale".... At least now I know that nationalism is a lie' (Kosovel 2006, p. 245); incidentally, on the next page of the same letter he mentions publishing his book *Zlati čoln*. 'Nationalism is a lie' is also a line in his poem 'Spherical Mirror', cited in full in the next chapter, pp. 310–11.

[113] Kosovel, emphasis author's, Notes VI, 1925, *CW* 3, p. 642.

Located at the cusp of Europe where the European 'East' and 'West' faced, and drew from, each other, burdened with the antithetical notions on the one hand, and animated through diverse social and cultural forms on the other, Kosovel could understand both the violence of the colonial encounter based on the binaries of imperial imagination, and the opportunities that came with cross-cultural contact. That he was able to see and feel even beyond the geographic confines of his immediate environment is borne out not just through his reading and appreciation of Tagore, but through his explicit reaching out to the colonized and the suppressed the world over. 'Injustice is injustice, whether suffered by one, thousands or millions.'[114] In his writing, he aligned the plight of Primorska he came to align in his writing with the 'unnatural act' he saw in the 'colonisation of non-European lands'.[115] If the suffering of his own people was a symptom of global social forces—those of capitalist Europe with its imperial onslaught on Asia and Africa and a world outlook promoting sharp distinctions between races and civilizations—then the solution too had to be sought across the world in a new social order:

> No one will help us, if we do not help *ourselves*, but helping *ourselves* is not enough. It is only in a mighty phalanx of all who are suppressed that our salvation lies. Only those who are suppressed can feel and create new justice, a new world built for Man.[116]

[114] Kosovel, 'Refleksije ob Koroškem dnevu, 11. Oktobra 1925' (Reflections on the day of the Carniolan plebiscite, 11 October 1925), *CW* 3, p. 48.

[115] Kosovel, 'Refleksije', *CW* 3, pp. 65–6. Also: 'Millions of people are suffering in colonies, in occupied territories, there are millions belonging to national minorities who are groaning under the steel heel of European capitalism ... They are our brothers, even though we don't know them, even though they might be Italians or Hungarians or Slovenes or Germans or Serbs' (Kosovel, 'Samomori' [Suicides], *CW* 3, p. 71).

[116] Kosovel, emphasis author's, 'Refleksije', *CW* 3, p. 49. It is in Kosovel's reaching out to the rest of the world that I see in him an ideational precursor of the Non-aligned Movement. Tagore's ideas too have been seen to foreshadow the Non-aligned Movement and post-Independence India which united the subcontinent and Yugoslavia in the same global political stand. The whole movement was the brainchild of Jawaharlal Nehru, the Egyptian President Nasser, and Tito of Yugoslavia (supported by Sukarno of Indonesia and Nkrumah of Ghana). The first NAM summit was held in Belgrade in 1961.

As we read this, we are reminded of the more famous postulation made by Frantz Fanon in the wake of African decolonization of the 1960s, namely, that humanity, somehow, belongs to the oppressed. 'When I search for Man in the technique and style of Europe, I see only a succession of negations of man, and an avalanche of murders,' wrote Fanon towards the end of *Les damnés de la terre*, 1961 (*The Wretched of the Earth*, 1968). The idea was to 'try to create the whole man, whom Europe has been incapable of bringing to triumphant birth'.[117] But ultimately, what this Martinique-born psychiatrist, who joined the Algerian war of liberation, wanted, was to transcend the polarities between 'us' and 'them', 'the colonizer' and 'the colonized', and do away with, to reiterate, 'the absurd drama others' had 'staged' round him' and 'reach out for the universal ... through one human being'.[118] It is impossible here not to think of Kosovel's own evocation of 'one human being' in a manifesto he wrote in 1925 (but never published). Entitled *Mehanikom* (To the mechanics), this is perhaps the most cogent expression of his universalist aspirations. Here is an excerpt:

> Dawn is breaking! Can you feel the shimmer? There are no more peoples, no nations, no humanity. There is one Man standing in the centre of the world [...] One Man, and everyone around him are his different faces. (Whether he is a miner, a tanner, a docker, a peasant, a functionary, a writer, an intellectual or a beggar, I cannot make out. Whether he is a Slovene, a German, a Russian or a Frenchman, I do not know, all I know is that I am awfully fond of this Man, whoever s/he is, whatever s/he is.[119]

Kosovel's 'one Man' could very well be the Fanonian 'whole man', healed of the Manichean split produced by racial imagination (imperialist or anti-imperialist). Perhaps an interpretational stretch, but once Kosovel's sentiments are aligned with other thinkers and poets of decolonization, the final two lines of the poem 'Black Walls', 'Man emerges/from the heart of darkness' (Appendix B, p. 331), resonate with a meaning that can only be described as truly 'postcolonial', by which I mean going

[117] Fanon (1963 [1961]), p. 252. On Fanon as a proponent of 'a new humanism', see Chapter 1, pp. 30–2.

[118] Fanon (1986 [1952]), p. 197.

[119] Kosovel, 'Mehanikom! (Mehaniki in Šoferji!)' (To the mechanics! [Mechanics and chauffeurs!]), *CW* 3, p. 114.

beyond the division of the self and the other. If 'the heart of darkness' is a trope for Africa, assuming, of course, that Kosovel was referring to Joseph Conrad's novel published in 1902, and by extension to all the wretched of the earth (outside and within Europe and the West), then it is the task of the downtrodden to give birth to the 'whole man' and surpass, or improve on, the claims of Western civilization.

Kosovel certainly saw himself as writing in solidarity with those 'intellectuals, famous artists and scientists' within and outside of Europe, who, he felt, had taken up 'a relentless fight against injustice and violence'.[120] Though Rabindranath Tagore is the only non-European he mentions alongside Henri Barbusse, Romain Rolland, Selma Lagerlöf, and Ernst Toller, the signatories of the *Déclaration d'independence de l'esprit* (1919), Kosovel's perspective on Europe bears similarities with ideas of liberation shared by many individuals across the colonized world. Often this is not a question of influence or borrowing, or even situational identification, but a question of a parallel voicing of ideas against the backdrop of similar hegemonic dialectics.

I have stressed the links and associations which extend Kosovel's vision beyond the borders of Europe to suggest that Kosovel's poetry is part of a more complex global configuration of anti-imperial politics and ethics.[121] Seeing Kosovel as someone who on the back of his historical predicament addressed themes and problems of global relevance, allows us to appreciate his work in a new light. New accents and even concerns begin to emerge if we read Kosovel alongside some major poets of resistance and decolonization, or poets of liberation. Focusing on issues such as language, representation, resistance, migrancy, modernity, and nationalism—all central to postcolonial literatures—points to ways in which his poetry can be interpreted afresh. My line of questioning, while acknowledging the pertinence of all these overlapping perspectives, focuses primarily on the subject of nationalism and national identities, more precisely on the point at which a nationalist discourse gives way to a post-nationalist—universalist—perspective.

[120] Kosovel, 'Umetnost in proletarec' (Art and the proletariat), *CW* 3, p. 27.
[121] This politics is itself a prehistory of postcolonial academic discipline. Cf. Gandhi (2007).

To clarify and expand on the latter, I want to bring in the concept of 'antitheticality' that Hazard Adams developed with respect to W. B. Yeats's notoriously elusive nationalist position, and which has relevance for both Kosovel's and Tagore's post-nationalist orientations. Adams says that the Irish poet's nationalism was 'from beginning to end *antithetical* in the sense of critical opposition to forms of nationalism that tended toward superficiality and suppression'.[122] It was essential for Yeats and his conception of art that the poet 'remain *in opposition*'.[123] If there are two obvious sides that engage a given culture's passions, of which one is privileged over the other (English over Irish, body over soul, West over East, centre over margin), to be in opposition in the antithetical sense does not mean to reverse the dyad and oppose just one side of the contrariety, but to stand against the opposition itself. At the same time, however, an antithetical stance proper must not triumph over the opposition, for this would merely create a new suppression. The point is to maintain 'continual active tension with the negations current in the culture'.[124]

For Tagore as well as for Kosovel there were always three sides to every argument. In his poem 'Italian culture', Kosovel does not commit the negation of one side of the opposition between Italians and Slovenes, but aims to go beyond the opposition itself. The contrariety, however, is maintained, as passions and differences cannot be ignored or levelled out, but the possibility of a third position is held forth by what Kosovel refers to in the poem as a 'progressive factor' in an ongoing personal and collective 'development'.

Both Tagore and Kosovel (like Fanon) were aware of the danger of simply reversing existing dichotomies and therefore looked to antithetically oppose them through understanding the complex nature of cultural identities and their interdependencies. In this, both thinkers sought to transform anti-colonial dissent into a creative project of liberation, with emphasis on creativity rather than ('national') authenticity. Instead of espousing an uncritical return to the 'pre-colonial' past, they adopted a rhetoric of futurity which allowed them to imagine, as Tagore would put it, the 'dawn of a new era, when man shall

---

[122] Adams (1991), emphasis mine, p. 165.

[123] Adams (1991), emphasis author's, p. 169.

[124] Adams (1991), p. 164.

discover his soul in the spiritual unity of all human beings'.[125] That this utopian perspective informed Tagore's very practical answers has been discussed in detail, and that the same can be said of Kosovel will be seen once we come to look at his practical activities as well.

Turning 'East'

In an elegy for W. B. Yeats, W. H. Auden wrote 'mad Ireland hurt you into poetry'.[126] Had he written an elegy to Kosovel, who died at the age of twenty-two, he would have said 'mad Europe hurt you into poetry'. Kosovel's Europe, 'the madhouse of rational spirits', 'the madhouse of civilization and hyper-intellectualism', was in deep crisis, and her crisis, the anguished poet cried from the rooftops, was 'a crisis in humanity'.[127] This is neither a surprising nor a unique response from a poet writing against the climate of World War I, the shock of which administered a severe blow to the already crumbling edifice of the old world, reinterpreted through thinkers like Karl Marx, Sigmund Freud, and Friedrich Nietzsche. Artists and poets were responding to a whole set of complex forces, as they obsessed over what felt like 'the end of a phase of human experience'.[128] Theirs was a reality profoundly unsettled through scientific discoveries, technological change, industrial revolution, changing global relations, volatile cosmopolitanism—a general upheaval going back to the nineteenth century, underpinned by imperialisms' first and subsequent global crises. The scale of human destruction wrought by the war only exacerbated a compounding sense of doom, and the myth of civilization and progress, upon which the age of imperialist expansion rested, became harder to uphold once the European peoples had turned also against each other. The historian John Lukacs writes:

> By the end of the nineteenth century and the beginning of the twentieth, the number of thinkers who, directly or indirectly, began to question this kind of progressive optimism increased. They had their forerunners such as the Neapolitan Vico two centuries earlier; but now there were different writers, such as Nietzsche or Valery or Spengler, who, in their

---

[125] Tagore (2001a [1917]), p. 455.

[126] 'In Memory of W. B. Yeats', Auden (1991), p. 248.

[127] Kosovel, *CW* 3, p. 27

[128] Hough (1991), p. 317.

different ways, tried to remind their readers of the symptoms of decline and of the ultimate fallibility of Western civilization.[129]

Lukacs correlates this new climate of the West's self-questioning with the gradual coming to an end of what he dubs as 'the European Age'. His geopolitical sketch of the rise and fall of the era accompanied by the rise and fall in Europe's confidence is instructive for understanding the artistic proclamations of the death of Europe (and the demise of the West) of the same period. It is significant that the word 'European' (in the sense of defining the inhabitant of a continent) came into currency coextensively with colonial expansion. The beginnings of 'the European Age' are therefore located in the year 1492 with the 'discovery' of the Americas. Over the next five hundred years, European powers put up their posts and established colonies across the world, so that by 1914 the entire continent of Africa, discounting Liberia and Abyssinia, belonged to or was ruled by a European colonial empire. Eighty years onwards, and following the two World Wars, Europeans were forced to give up their colonies and leave their erstwhile 'African and Asian homelands'. While European institutions, Christian churches, industries, and forms of art and expression survived 'the reflux of whites', the European Age was by then pretty much over. For sure it was finished by 1945—if not, as Lukacs contends, already by 1917—as the United States and Russia became the two world superpowers facing each other across the 'the middle of conquered Europe'.[130]

If the shattering of the myth of 'Western civilization' rests on the global historical transformation climaxing in two events: the outbreak of World War I, and the Russian Revolution of October 1917, it is not surprising that the turn of the twentieth century and the decades following comprise a period in which a number of writers worldwide can be seen to proclaim a crisis or the death of Europe. While in the late 1920s, Tagore would still hold that 'Europe today is the predominant factor in the human world', though regretting that 'she has come to the East, not with an ideal, but with an object that primarily concerns her own self-interest',[131] his most uncompromising

---

[129] Lukacs (2002), p. 8.

[130] Lukacs (2002), pp. 10–11.

[131] Tagore, letter to N. Zwager, 16 September 1927, in Dutta and Robinson (2005), p. 352.

attack on 'Western civilization' and prognostication of its demise was penned decades earlier, precisely on the last evening of the nineteenth century (the poem will be discussed shortly).

It is indeed the case that 'poetry can be a bellwether, a signifier of change, long before the change has registered its presence in political or economic spheres',[132] as it is also true that poetic language can capture the mood of a historical moment better than any other discourse. To read W. B. Yeats's poem 'The Second Coming' (1919) written just after the Russian Revolution and before the Irish Civil War, or Georg Trakl's *Abendland* (translated as 'Occident' and referring to Western European nations) written in the last months before the poet committed suicide in 1914, is to get a profound sense of an end to a civilization, portended by an approaching rough beast in the former and the descending night in the latter.

This elemental dialectic between death and regeneration seems to have guided the imagination of many poets of the pre- and post-World War I era. We should not assume any kind of uniformity in their responses, even as we identify certain common traits, motivations, or themes (such as Europe's death). Nor should we commit the Eurocentric mistake and confine 'the sense of an ending', to borrow Frank Kermode's phrase, as something belonging exclusively to Western literary modernism, in itself a phenomenon with a pronounced international base and orientation, indebted to worldwide cultural and aesthetic influences.[133] For indeed, the conventional art-historical narratives that trace the '"poetics" of internationalism' to the trenches of World War I and then equate it with twentieth-century European avant-gardes, overlook the fact, as pointed out by Neil Larsen, that pre-imperialist, not to mention pre-capitalist, societies had all spawned their own cosmopolitan and international aesthetic cultures. They also forget to ask: 'Are Picasso and Breton the redeemers of art after 1914 rather than, say, Diego Rivera and Tagore?'[134]

Bringing Tagore and Kosovel back into the picture from their respective global 'margins' (Kosovel's writing from the periphery of Western Europe and Tagore's from the overseas colonial empire) will

---

[132] Mehta (2004), p. 9.

[133] On this, see Boehmer (2002) pp. 123–4.

[134] Larsen (2000), p. 31.

lead us to explore what Timothy Brennan too has observed was until quite recently an under-acknowledged link between the interwar avant-gardes, the colonies, and anti-imperialist consciousness.[135] It is here that the year 1917—the watershed date for the end of 'the European Age'—enters as a crucial marker of 'a broader culture of anti-imperialism'.[136] If one event needed singling out as *the* event in eliciting a response from intellectuals across the political spectrum, left or right, apart from World War I, it would be the October Revolution of 1917.[137] Deeply responsive to the social and political forces of the age, the avant-gardes, broadly defined by one theorist as 'an intellectual movement' or 'the action of the intelligentsia',[138] played a prominent part.

In that sense, Lukacs' 'European Age' and the demise thereof can be seen as an emerging postcolonial space in which the age of imperialism came into direct confrontation with the age of the proletariat. Certainly for those writers who resisted the civilizational crisis in anti-bourgeois and anti-capitalist terms, the Bolshevik revolution offered a realistic hope (however short-lasting) for the ideal of a new classless society. Moreover, it unleashed what Timothy Brennan has argued was 'a full-blown *culture* of anti-imperialism for the first time'.[139]

In wanting to reinstitute interwar Marxism with the recognition it deserves as a precursor to postcolonial studies—for the parents to reclaim their orphaned child, as it were—Brennan submits that 'the Russian Revolution ... was an anticolonial revolution'. He comes to this conclusion from 'its sponsorship of anticolonial rhetoric' which 'thrived in the art columns of left newspapers, cabarets or the political underground, mainstream radio, the cultural groups of the Popular Front, Bolshevik theatre troupes', meeting with responses and contributions from the various avant-garde arts.[140] Referring to the more

---

[135] Brennan (2002), pp. 185–203; see also Clarke (1997), p. 101. Since Brennan's observation, the vacuum has been filled by, amongst others, Taoua (2002) and Puchner (2005).

[136] Brennan (2002), p. 196.

[137] Brennan (2002), p. 192; see also Williams (1989), p. 60.

[138] Szabolcsi (1971), p. 57.

[139] Brennan (2002), emphasis author's, p. 191.

[140] Brennan (2002), p. 192.

dissident wings of European thought, Brennan gives ample evidence
to counter the claim that anti-imperialist theory arose only after World
War II. Even activist writers such as Frantz Fanon and Amilcar Cabral,
the most formidable anti-imperialist voices of the 1950s and 1960s,
belong to the lineage that is, the author maintains, a 'direct product
of interwar Marxism'. But it was

> especially (and significantly) the Marxism of the Eastern periphery
> of Europe that played the largest role in nudging intellectuals into a
> liberatory view of non-Western societies between 1905 and 1939.... It
> was not the Frankfurt school but cultural Bolshevism and the larger
> networks of fellow travellers it spawned that made possible the early
> twentieth-century sensitivities towards colonial oppression.[141]

Locating the epicentre of anti-colonial sentiment in the Russian
Revolution, the aftershocks of which were felt throughout the
world,[142] Brennan cannot overstate the implications of the revolution for the 'the idea of the West'. It 'delivered Europe', he says, 'into
a radical non-Western curiosity and sympathy that had not existed
in quite this way before'. It 'altered European agendas and tastes by
situating the European in a global relationship that was previously
unimaginable'.[143]

If we now think back to Kosovel's sympathetic gesturing towards
the non-Western world and recall his staunch anti-imperialist stance
(corroborated, no doubt, by his direct experience of hegemony by a
Western imperial power), his fascination with Tagore assumes a logic
and relevance that is part of a more general moment in history when
'a distant, instinctive reaction to the colonies'[144] was inscribed into
the very logic of the social, political, and artistic forces fuelling that
moment. What, more precisely, is the logic that connects the proletarian

[141] Brennan (2002), p. 190.

[142] For this point, see Hobsbawm (1994), pp. 65–6. For the context of India
and how in the 1920s, various movements, groups, and people drew inspiration from the Bolshevik Revolution rather than from Wilsonian internationalism, contributing to an 'Asian anti-imperialist movement held together by
anti-colonial and working-class solidarity', see Stolte (2014), p. 57ff.

[143] Brennan (2002), pp. 192–3.

[144] Brennan (2002), p. 195.

revolution with the anti-imperialist energies, the outcome of which was a radical 'decentring' of Europe, must be considered next.

While historians have pointed out that the imperial enterprise of the interwar years seemed for the most part quite secure, and for most people of Western imperialist nations 'it was just there' either as 'a source of national pride ... a source of entertainment [or] a source of tales of daring', there was now 'a small but vocal number of individuals' who profoundly questioned the world order, challenged the conceits associated with the alleged civilizing mission of the colonizers, and cast in doubt the civilization that made it possible.[145] In this respect the Russian Revolution, communism, and the Third International or Comintern (1919) became a vital source from which the historical lesson in self-liberation was to flow.[146] And the idea of social revolution was now combined with anti-imperialist thought. This was because an analogy was being made between the capitalist's exploitation of the worker and imperialist's exploitation of the colonized:

> Imperialism, in this global scheme of things, was rapacious capitalism expanded overseas in a desperate search for new markets and resources to command, other people to oppress, all motivated by the desire for investment opportunities and subsequent profit.[147]

Within such a framework, anti-colonial or anti-imperialist protest is but an extrapolation of the Marxist critique of capitalism, the twin logic of which was compellingly elucidated by Vladimir Lenin in his book *Imperialism, the Highest Stage of Capitalism* (1916).[148] Indeed,

[145] Betts (1998), pp. 10–17.

[146] See Stolte (2014).

[147] Stolte (2014), p. 13.

[148] The significance of this pamphlet (when it was first published in 1917) for Asian thinkers is underlined by Mishra, who calls it 'the *ur*-text of many anti-colonial activists and thinkers', amongst whom the idea that European fighting for the spoils of Africa had led to the Great War was common. Lenin had also exposed the secret agreement between France, Britain, and Tsarist Russia to divide amongst themselves the Middle East, and Bolsheviks exposed a number of treaties that outlined how Britain, France, Italy, and Japan would share whole empires after the war. Soon after the October Revolution, Lenin and Stalin sent out the message to the peoples of the East to topple the imperialist 'robbers and enslavers', see Mishra (2012), pp. 194–5, 198.

in this treatise, 'Lenin assumes the social standpoint of those whom modern capitalism as a world system most exploits and oppresses, even when they are not "proletarian" in a conventional sense'.[149]

When Kosovel pondered the irony of the situation in which Slovenes had achieved a historically unprecedented measure of political autonomy (within the newly established Kingdom), only for a substantial segment of their population to come under a new threat from their neighbours, he was distraught to think that his people 'might die in the final hours of capitalist imperialism'.[150] It is evident from this formulation that he subscribed to a Leninist view of imperialism.[151] Furthermore, in his essay titled *Kriza* ('Crisis', 1925) he motivated the new developments in the arts with the new consciousness arising out of the realization of the horrors of imperialist wars:

> Amidst the expectations of war, new art was born. Amidst the eerie silence already betraying bloodshed, it was born. Amidst the eerie silence which was all along a mercantile war. Amidst malicious calculations that went after profit and not people.[152]

Profit over people, to use the Chomskian phrase,[153] was for Kosovel at the root of Europe's spiritual and moral crisis, which had forsaken human values in its greed for riches and power. If the Great War was its disastrous outcome, leading to 'chaos, anarchy, nihilism' and overall 'moral depression',[154] then the only way forward was to reclaim our lost humanity and clamber out of what the poet elsewhere referred to as a 'negative total' (Appendix, p. 332). It also put 'man' at the heart

[149] Larsen (2000), p. 29. Larsen too, like Brennan, argues here that the genealogical centrality of Lenin's treatise must be recognized for postcolonial studies.

[150] Kosovel, 'Razpad družbe', *CW* 3, p. 39.

[151] See the groundbreaking essay on Kosovel and Lenin by Komelj (2014), in which the author magisterially interprets two sonnets written by Kosovel on the occasion of Lenin's death in January 1924 that have escaped criticism as well as publication in the latest edition of Kosovel's collected poems that claims for itself on being a comprehensive publication.

[152] Kosovel, 'Kriza', *CW* 3, p. 12.

[153] Reference to Noam Chomsky (1999).

[154] Kosovel, 'Razpad družbe', *CW* 3, p. 39.

of his evocations in poetry and confronted art with a new set of questions, which effectively meant breaking with tradition and traditional representation in art. In a similarly titled piece 'Crisis in Civilization' (1941), penned over a decade later, as the world was collapsing into another world war, Tagore too, writing against a like climate of disillusionment and depression, spoke of 'the new dawn [coming] from the East' when 'unvanquished Man will retrace his path of conquest, despite all barriers, to win back his lost human heritage'.[155]

When Kosovel turned towards the 'East' for inspiration, it was with the same kind of idealistic fervour that he anticipated a 'new morning', but his 'new morning' would come 'in a red mantle', hence its irradiating core was the Soviet Union and not, in the primary instance, 'the East' or 'the Orient' of Tagore.[156] And yet, of course, the two were closely related. Having taken a lesson from Brennan's recovery of anti-imperial intellectual history of the interwar years and its close links with the Russian revolution (its promise of a new, non-exploitative social order), and having shown anti-imperialism to have been conflated with anti-capitalism, it becomes possible to make sense of the close convergence between what motivated Kosovel's artistic expression, his 'revolutionary' (but non-Party) poetic and social(ist) avant-gardism, and his immediate and direct response to Tagore—the writer he pressed his colleagues to read as a guiding light in those tumultuous times.[157] Indeed, Kosovel perceived in Tagore a spiritual and intellectual kin, hence he co-opted him into the ranks of those 'intellectuals, famous artists and scientists' who

[155] Tagore (1961m [1941]), p. 359.

[156] Kosovel, 'Kriza v slovenski umetnosti' (Crisis in Slovene art), *CW* 3, p. 93. The full sentence gives a sense of its caustic tone: 'Because, gentlemen, a new morning is at hand, from the East it comes into the cold winter atmosphere, it comes in a red mantle, and if Ljubljana's art, or rather Slovene art, is asleep, this is but a sign of her complete decrepitude. Let it sleep, let it rest in peace! Amen.'

[157] How Kosovel came to associate his own objections to any regime (party, church, or other) can be seen from his inspired rewriting of the first poem from Tagore's collection *The Gardener* into a parody entitled 'Pesnik in stranka' (Poet and the party), in which he mocks the poet for making himself indispensable to party politics (*CW* 3, pp. 54–5). For Tagore's poem, see Tagore (2002), pp. 1–3.

had 'joined the proletarian movement'.[158] Under the broad concept of 'a "revolutionary" world *aesthetic*—as opposed to a tradition, canon or culture', posited by Larsen as a corrective to the more parochial and regionally bounded conceptions of the avant-gardes, the new (anti)imperialist internationalism subsumed 'both proletarian and all-purpose liberal-humanist forms'.[159]

Indeed, for all of Kosovel's close association with the thought of revolutionary Marxists (through his friend Ivo Grahor,[160] Vladimir Martelanc, and Fanica Obidova-Mirjam), his conceptualization of the proletariat—as well as art and creativity—was *not* Marxist in the strict sense. It was not 'historicist', that is to say based on a dialectically materialist reading of history, in which the 'proletariat' is confined to the context of the industrial age and capitalism, rather it was generic or 'typological'—an umbrella term covering the suppressed, the exploited, and the disenfranchised of all eras and the world over.[161]

At some non-literalist level too, in co-opting Tagore into the ranks of the 'proletariat', Kosovel was not entirely off the mark, for the way that he himself took inspiration from the Soviet Union—sceptical of the emerging 'political dictatorship of the Bolsheviks', but full of praise for its vast and consistent efforts to bring education and culture to the Soviet people[162]—was not at all dissimilar to Tagore's response to Russia in 1930, when he visited the country, coming away impressed with the Soviet education system and the alleged self-respect it brought to the peasant and the worker, but doubtful about the political direction it was taking.[163]

---

[158] Kosovel, 'Umetnost in proletarec', *CW* 3, p. 27.

[159] Larsen (2000), emphasis author's, p. 31.

[160] Ivo Grahor (1902–44) was a writer and political activist who became Kosovel's 'authentic informer' on post-revolution Russia, where he spent some time in 1924.

[161] Grdina (2013), pp. 1166–8. In the closing paragraph of his essay/lecture 'Art and the Proletariat', Kosovel writes of the need of the proletariat to become aware of what 's/he had lost in the course of the dark millennia …' (Kosovel, 'Umetnost in proletarec', *CW* 3, p. 30).

[162] Grdina (2013), p. 27.

[163] See Tagore's notes of the conversations he had in Russia on his trip there in 1930, published in *EW* 3, pp. 916–39.

Perhaps the principal importance of Tagore for Kosovel lay in the fact that here was a voice from outside Europe, grappling with similar issues but articulating an alternative viewpoint, and offering what the historian of Chinese science Joseph Needham, years later, formulated into a rationale:

> It is necessary to see Europe from the outside, to see European history, and European failure no less than European achievement, through the eyes of that larger part of humanity, the peoples of Asia (and indeed also of Africa).[164]

To show the relevance of the foregoing for Kosovel's creative work, I now turn to his critique of Europe as expressed in his poem 'Ecstasy of Death' (1925), considered to date one of the finest specimens of expressionist lyrics written in the Slovene language, and one of the few poems that Kosovel published during his lifetime.[165]

'Europe' Interrogated

The poem 'Ecstasy of Death' (Appendix, p. 332) can be seen to belong to a series of Kosovel poems that take up the theme of Europe's death and rebirth,[166] a theme that runs almost refrain-like through his essayistic writings as well. This particular poem, however, has been unanimously greeted as Kosovel's most successful treatment of the subject, executed in a predominantly expressionist vein; it was particularly the more abstract revolutionary and messianic strain of expressionism that registered the sense of disenchantment with Western/modern civilization in stark apocalyptic terms. While Kosovel critics have analysed the poem in detail within the European sphere of influence, none have so far taken it beyond its immediate and more obvious context.[167] And yet, as I have tried to show, at least

[164] Needham (1956), cited in Clarke (1997), p. 107.

[165] Published in 1925 in *Ljubljanski zvon*, and republished in 1946 in the first volume of the *Collected Works*, pp. 307–8.

[166] Some others include 'Our Eyes', 'Europe is Dying', in Kosovel (2008b), pp. 104 and 105; and 'Heartless People', 'Destructions', in Kosovel (1998), pp. 114 and 115.

[167] To date, Kosovel's poetry has been considered in the context of European avant-gardes (Pokorn 1998; Vrečko 2005, 2011) and, more precisely, German expressionism (Legiša 1969; Kralj 1986), Italian futurism (Troha 1988,

three interrelated observations call for such an analysis: first, the fact that Kosovel was writing under pressures (and dilemmas) pertaining to a culture dominated by another and therefore shared some of the intellectual and artistic concerns characteristic of the 'colonized' world; second, his liminal status within Europe gave him a predilection, if not a privilege, to see 'Europe' from both within and without; and third, Kosovel wrote in the post–World War I and post–Russian Revolution atmosphere, which in itself was charged with a much broader and more critical inquiry into Europe's imperialist politics than seems to be conventionally recognized. These separate threads intertwine in concrete intertextual evidence as Kosovel's poem is seen to correspond, almost directly in parts, with Tagore's own writings and critique of Western politics of domination. 'Ecstasy of Death', I want to say, is an anti-imperialist, indeed, a liberational, poem *par excellence*. It resonates powerfully with other anti-imperialist writings of Asia and Africa that both precede and follow it. By reading it alongside Tagore's poem 'The Sunset of the Century' (1899), his collection of essays *Nationalism* (1917) and, for example, Aimé Césaire's indictment of Europe in his *Discourse on Colonialism* (1955), I hope to reinstitute it to its wider historical context from which it has arguably emerged, and with which it resonates.

In a mixture of grotesque imagery and romantic flight, set to the harrowing beat of the refrain, 'Everything is ecstasy, the ecstasy of death', this poem pronounces a death sentence upon a civilization that is already seen to be in rapid decline. A Spenglerian vision unfolds, as 'glittering bastions of the West' and the 'white domes' of civilization topple over and drown in 'the burning red sea' of the setting sun. This last metaphor intriguingly echoes the 'blood-red clouds of the West' in Tagore's poem 'The Sunset of the Century', itself a chilling sentence pronounced upon the West that had made 'the world its food' and was then engulfed in the flames the 'funeral pyre' of its own destruction—'dead under its own excess'. Similar overlap in imagery between the two poems can be detected in the next line in which Kosovel's European is seen to be intoxicated in the 'bath of the falling sun' and

---

1993), Balkan Zenitism, and Russian constructivism (Zadravec 1966b; Pogačnik 1984; Flaker 1984; Bajt 1985, 1986; Vrečko 1986, 2011; Ocvirk 2003 [1967]), and in relation to the Polish avant-gardes (Tokarz 2004, 2013).

Tagore's West caught up in a 'drunken delirium of greed'. The frenzied language of consummation, intoxication, and fiery disarray is inherent in both poems, with clear thematic and stylistic echoes, though the two poems also significantly depart from each other. But let us deal with 'Ecstasy' first.[168]

The sun is about to set on the continent, and Europe, 'a luxurious queen in gold', is ready to close her golden eyes, as everything either turns into blood or is coloured by it. Blood, the speaker of the poem says, 'fills his spent heart'. Clouds rain blood. Europe has no more water, so people drink blood. No one, it seems, is unaffected by, or exempt from, this terrible blood-bath:

> Hardly born, already you burn in the evening fire.
> All the seas are red, all the seas and lakes
> full of blood, there's no water,
> no water to wash the guilt away,
> for this human to wash his heart,
> no water to quench this thirst
> for the quiet green nature of morning.
> Everything is evening, and there will be
> no morning till we all die, we who bear
> the guilt of dying, until the last of us
> dies...

The sense of guilt looms large as blood and water come to represent (inherited or inherent?) guilt and redemption, and evening and morning, death and regeneration. The pronouncement is harsh: 'Europe', to borrow from Césaire, 'is indefensible', for colonization, let it be clear, is not civilization, but 'the principal lie' from which all others stem.[169] Europe (the poem's 'we') is guilty of inflicting death, and now she stands to be judged, the murderess, herself engulfed by

---

[168] Tagore's poem was published in Slovenian translation (by Karel Ozvald) in the journal *Socialna misel* (Social thought) in 1922, as 'Solnčni zahod stoletja', p. 41.

[169] Kosovel revises meanings of 'culture', 'civilization', 'humanism' throughout his opus. A good example of his questioning the notion of 'culture' in the manner of Césaire is found in the short prose piece 'Pismo' (Letter): 'How can I believe in the meaning of culture and in its great powers? Cultured nations, they murder, subjugate, kill. Is that cultural ethics?' (Kosovel 1991, p. 74).

her own 'reddened waters', the boomerang effect of what Césaire in his *Discourse* develops into the notion of 'Hitler', a synecdoche for colonialism, which Europe tolerated, vindicated and failed to see as barbaric for as long as it was directed against 'the Arabs of Algeria, the coolies of India and the blacks of Africa'.[170] The thirst 'for the quiet, green morning land' in the world as Kosovel perceives it can no longer be quenched, or as Yeats would have it in his apocalyptic verse—'the ceremony of innocence is drowned'.[171] Indeed, the one glimmer of hope held by the image of green nature—a reference to the poet's native region, itself a victim of imperialism, which one would think would exempt it from the collective European guilt—dissolves into an incredulous cry:

O, will you, evening sun,
send your blazing rays
into this land, this green
dewy land? This land too?

The collective ordeal by fire and water—with their allusions to purgation and flood—is total:

The sea overflows the green plains,
the scorched blood-sea of evening
and there's no salvation, none
till you and I fall,
till all of us fall,
till we die under the weight of blood.
Then the sun's golden rays will shine
on us, European corpses.[172]

Clearly, Europe, in some absolute sense, has failed or outlived itself and must die. To think of the young poet giving a debut reading of 'Ecstasy' on the evening of 23 February in 1926 to an audience of miners in the industrial town of Zagorje, is to get a precise sense of the thrust of the poem's critique. In the lecture Kosovel wrote for the

[170] Césaire (1972), pp. 9–15.
[171] 'The Second Coming', Yeats (1985), p. 210.
[172] 'Ecstasy of Death', translated by Ana Jelnikar and Barbara Siegel Carlson in Kosovel (2010a), pp. 151–3.

occasion and titled *Umetnost in proletarec* (Art and the proletariat), he explained the death motif as signifying the end of the liberal-bourgeois capitalist system, acknowledging his debt to Oswald Spengler's epochal book *The Decline of the West* (*Der Untergang des Abendlandes*, vol. I, 1918 and vol. II, 1922–3)—incidentally also a book that commanded huge respect among the Negritudinists, including Césaire and Senghor, offering, as one scholar noted, 'the hope of a reversal of current European dominance of the African world'.[173] If capitalist Europe has proven incapable of establishing rights for all men and women, creating rather insuperable distances among them through relations of domination and subjugation, then Kosovel looked towards a new social order that promised to do away with all this. With hopes embodied in the Russian Revolution, he thought the days of capitalism were numbered. But socialism, to reiterate, was for Kosovel essentially 'a new humanism' (as it was for many writers and poets of liberation). His critique of capitalism was also never absolute or wholesale. Capitalism, he would argue, produced 'a strong spiritual culture' and art, deserving of respect; the problem was that it made it subject to class privilege, rather than making it available to and appropriable by everyone (including the 'proletariat'). 'The task of the proletariat', Kosovel wrote, 'is not to despise this culture, but for everyone to enrich oneself with it', and then create a new 'humane culture' that would not be implicated in the 'blood of slaves'.[174] The flaw of capitalism lay in its logic to hoard and acquire on the back of someone else's toil, and then limit the distribution of its wares—therein lay its exclusivism, anti-humanism, and injustice—but the culture that emerged under its aegis, or previously under feudalism, was not in itself inimical to 'the proletariat', it was merely not available to them, worse still, it was taken away from them as a right.[175] 'Only an educated person can know what their work-earned rights are.'[176] In the same way that

---

[173] Arnold (1983), p. 112. Césaire began to compose his long 'surrealist' poem *Cahier d'un retour au pays natal* (1939), which explores the concept of Négritude, on a trip he made to Yugoslavia when he visited an island in the Adriatic Sea with his friend, the latter-day professor of French at the University of Zagreb, Petar Guberina. Cf. Césaire chronology in Césaire (2001), p. 65.

[174] Kosovel, 'Umetnost in proletarec', *CW* 3, p. 29.

[175] On this, see Grdina (2013), p. 1163.

[176] Kosovel, 'Umetnost in proletarec', *CW* 3, p. 26.

Kosovel's typological notion of the 'proletariat' as coextensive with the downtrodden and the suppressed across time and geography transcends the categories of a historically determinist Marxist reading, his understanding of art and culture too defies any determinist logic. Grdina captures Kosovel's outlook precisely: 'Culture, in some measure, is marked by relations and conditions in which it has emerged, but this in itself cannot destroy what makes it an essential premise of life.'[177] As a social phenomenon it was fundamentally linked with a universal human trait and aptitude for creativity.

Tagore's critique of the—imperialist, capitalist—West, as expressed in his poem 'The Sunset of the Century', to come back to poetry, is even harsher than Kosovel's 'Ecstasy', at least in its English, and further Slovenian, reincarnations. Originally written in Bengali on the last day of the nineteenth century, the poem was translated by Tagore himself almost two decades later and included as an appendix to his essays on *Nationalism* (1917), presumably as a poetic corollary to the book. It voices a stark, almost grotesque, protest against the power-mongering Western civilization, and Tagore's lambasting of 'the West' shares some of the frenzy seen in Kosovel's expressionistic shriek (I visualize 'Ecstasy' as Munch's agonized figure hollering against the blood-red skyline in his painting *The Scream*, 1893).

> The hungry self of the Nation shall burst in a violence of fury from its own shameless feeding.
> For it has made the world its food,
> And licking it, crunching it, and swallowing it in big morsels,
>   It swells and swells
> Till in the midst of its unholy feast descends the sudden shaft of heaven piercing its heart of grossness.

The West for Tagore is identified with the abstract dehumanizing machine of 'the Nation' that has come to feed on India in the form of imperialism. In the same way that Kosovel's poem anticipates an end to capitalist–imperialist Europe, Tagore too prophesies an end to this abnormal feast that must die 'under its own excess'. Both their visions contain a promise of hope and renewal. For Kosovel this hope

[177] Grdina (2013), p. 1162.

is embodied by the 'green, dewy landscape' of his native Primorska, and Tagore too projects his hopes into his India. But the dichotomy thus emerging between an essentially aggressive (and masculine) West and an innocent, uncorrupted 'Motherland' is sharper in Tagore's poem, as India, associated with the new dawn coming from the East, stands in direct opposition to the West:

> Keep watch, India.
> Bring your offerings of worship for that sacred sunrise.
> Let the first hymn of its welcome sound in your voice and sing.[178]

As she awaits the new dawn, Tagore turns to her poverty and simplicity as a source of strength and endurance:

> Be not ashamed, my brothers, to stand before the proud and the powerful
>   With your white robe of simpleness.
> Let your crown be of humility, your freedom the freedom of the soul.
> Build God's throne daily upon the ample bareness of your poverty
> And know that what is huge is not great and pride is not everlasting.[179]

Both the critique and solace in this particular poem come unequivocally from outside the imperial West. This gives the speaker a certain distance as well as assuredness that he can fall back on something uncontaminated by what he is resisting. Kosovel's speaker on the other hand is in a far more ambivalent position. Both an outsider and insider in Europe, Kosovel's resolute call to Europe's destruction is not without an undertone of lament. If Tagore's West is portrayed in scarcely human terms, more as a gluttonous monster, Kosovel's Europe is imagined—no less hyperbolically—as a beautiful queen. While the target for their critique is the same, Kosovel, himself a European, is up against a moral dilemma Tagore does not have to

---

[178] It must be noted here that his poem was written against the background of the Second Boer War (1899–1902), and Tagore was, in that period, 'burning with indignation against abuses of European imperialism … aggressively defying Western racism, militarism, and economic exploitation' (Kopf 1988, p. 294).

[179] 'The Sunset of the Century' in Tagore (2001a [1917]), translated by the author, p. 466.

face. As in a number of works of the European poets from Baudelaire, Rimbaud to the surrealists, there is an undercurrent of bitterness and self-hatred that runs through Kosovel's poetry, a tone which Tagore does not visibly share. As a writer Tagore seems to have a confidence Kosovel does not, and indeed cannot have. India might be colonized, but unlike Europe, she is not 'sick'. Even as Tagore addressed many of India's social ills, he had a huge cultural reservoir at hand from which he could draw a cure.

It will do to recall in this respect another of Tagore's anti-imperialist poems. The following lines from his late poem 'Africa' assume a poignant relevance if we imagine Kosovel to be the addressee:

> Come, poet of the end of the age,
> Stand in the dying light of advancing nightfall
> At the door of despoiled Africa
> And say, 'Forgive, forgive—'
> > In the midst of murderous insanity,
> May these be your civilization's last, virtuous words.[180]

This is a direct appeal to the conscience of any European poet, insofar as he or she is ready to assume European colonization of Africa as their own historical freight. A poet like Marinetti would perhaps be the more obvious addressee here, but 'Ecstasy of Death' too plumbs the question of European guilt in no comforting terms. As its subject progressively shifts from 'them' ('the West' of the first stanza) to 'us' ('we people' in the middle of the poem) and finally assumes an individual perspective in the 'I' at the end, demanding death without exception, the poem collapses the line between 'good' and 'evil', 'us' and 'them', bringing the divide, far more disturbingly, into the heart of every civilization, culture and, crucially, individual. As Césaire would chillingly have it, it acknowledges that there is a Hitler inside every European. 'The green dewy landscape' is a myth, and is thus sacrificed in the catastrophic ordeal. At the end of the age, Kosovel does not exactly say 'forgive', but he sets out to reconstruct the remains of a fallen civilization by addressing the failure of Christian, bourgeois humanism. He frames the task of 'new humanism' as coming into

---

[180] 'Africa', 1936, translated by William Radice, in Tagore (1994), p. 103.

touch with another human being, but 'not', as he says at the end of his essay 'Crisis', 'beyond good and evil, justice and injustice, not with a superhuman lie: but as people ... in the midst of the very good and evil, justice and injustice'.[181]

The shift to the poetic 'I' in this poem is crucial and should not be muted by general statements, which have dominated the readings of 'Ecstasy', and which detect in this sample of Kosovel's activist expressionist lyrics a conscious giving up of individualism for the perspective of the collective 'we' of universal brotherhood.[182] Kosovel may be taking on the perspective of the future of all mankind, but his universalist goal is projected emphatically as a task for the individual. The New Age will not be brought about through violent revolution, but by an inner transformation of each and every person: 'I am convinced that the only way Europe will be cured is if every individual remains in touch with his or her inner life'.[183]

The 'I' of Kosovel's 'ecstatic' vision is the split European subject of an age in crisis, a subject at once subjected to the dominant imperialist logic and having agency to challenge and resist it. Kosovel's 'new man' embodies this overcoming of an imperialist mindset, to—antithetically—think and feel outside the hegemonic binaries and false dichotomies of his culture. The much older meaning of ecstasy as derived from the Greek *ekstasis*—from *ek* 'out' and *histanai* 'to place/cause to stand'—implies precisely that. In 'Ecstasy', Kosovel already *is* the 'new man' of his poetic evocations, but not in any politically doctrinaire sense, but as a poet and artist:

> Only the artist who has stepped out [*izstopil*, in Slovenian; ek-stasis] of the marshes of contemporary society and entered a new society, which he felt within himself, only such an artist is the new priest of truth, justice, humanity and goodness. The rest will die along with the old world.[184]

---

[181] Kosovel, 'Kriza', *CW* 3, p. 20.

[182] See, for example, Kralj (1986), p. 183; see also Vrečko (2011), pp. 72–6.

[183] Kosovel, letter to Karmela, 13 July 1923, *CW* 3, p. 497.

[184] Kosovel, 'Sodobno evropsko življenje in umetnost' (Contemporary European life and art), *CW* 3, p. 650. The association between the 'new man' and 'new artist' will be explored in the following chapter.

For all its seeming abstractness, the poem 'Ecstasy of Death' is nested in layers of concrete references and meanings. One can imagine that the poem grew out of Kosovel's first-hand witnessing, as Stano had written of his brother, of 'hordes of soldiers going off to battle never to return';[185] of seeing blood drip from a cart of wounded men, as related by his sister Antonija; of seeing poverty and misery from up close in the Karst villages during and after the war and experiencing it himself as an impoverished student in Ljubljana. His engaged encounters with the lives of workers and his friendships with leftist intellectuals, in particular Ivo Grahor and Vladimir Martelanc,[186] are also part of the personal background to the poem. Knowing also that there was a dearth of water in the Karst in Kosovel's lifetime, to the extent that, during the war years, water sources had to be put under military guard,[187] gives the lines 'O, no more water in Europe/We people drink blood' an acuteness and urgency that works simultaneously on the concrete and metaphoric levels.

It can indeed be said of Kosovel that in the manner of best 'regional' poets, he gave a particular landscape and geography an expression that made the Karst and its fate communicable across time and space. He universalized the historic experience of Primorska in images of pine trees and landscape threatened by extinction:

> I saw the pines grow
> into the sky. Calm stoics
> through the flaring sun.
> I saw a fire once
> that would burn them up.[188]

And as he, at other times, turned to Primorska for solace and source of renewal, away from the greys of Ljubljana, imbuing the landscape

[185] Stano Kosovel (1971), p. 16.

[186] For Grahor, see footnote 161, on p. 231. Vladimir Martelanc (b. in Trieste, 1905–1944) joined the communist movement formed around the editorship of the newspaper *Delo* (in Trieste) in 1923, and supplied Kosovel with Marxist literature.

[187] Stano Kosovel (1971), p. 14.

[188] 'I Saw the Pines Grow', translated by Ana Jelnikar and Barbara Siegel Carlson, in Kosovel (2010a), p. 45. For the full poem, see Appendix, p. 333.

with brighter colours—the autumnal greens and golds of his favourite season—he would also embed in his lines a call to resistance. This is perhaps most subtly expressed in one of his best-known poems 'Pines'. A poem that resists translation into other languages because of its strong sound orchestration once again identifies the Karst landscape and its upright (resilient) people with its—ironically non-indigenous— pine trees.[189] The haunting repetition of *bori* can simply mean 'pines' (which is how this line has always been understood), but if read as a verbal construction and not a noun phrase, 'bori' resonates with the meaning 'to fight'![190]

> Pines, pines in silent horror,
> pines, pines in mute horror,
> pines, pines, pines![191]

Substitute 'pines' for 'fight', since '*bori!*' can evoke both—an equally expressive double meaning presents itself in English—and these 'sentinels' and 'mute witnesses' of the next stanza are summoned to fight and resist the horrors perpetuated under Fascism in Primorska. Is 'bori' a code word for struggle?

In Kosovel, as in many other poets of resistance, poetry and poetic language become in themselves a form of resistance. As Barbara Harlow writes on the subject of resistance literature:

> Poetic language is not envisaged here as a rarefied or transcendent means of expression, detached from the political reality of struggle, but

---

[189] For its exceptional melodiousness conveyed through the repetition of the broad [ô] sound in the original, the poem has been set to music by various composers (B. Šček, A. Srebotnjak).

[190] Strictly speaking the verb 'to fight' in Slovenian is a reflexive verb (*boriti se*), but the stem 'bori' is fully present in the plural noun form of 'a pine tree' (*bor, bori*). In a letter to Debevec, Kosovel actually uses the stem of the word to mean 'fight', when he urges his colleagues that they *stopiti v* '*bor*' (the singular noun form for the pine tree) *z vso slovensko javnostjo, ki je gnila do korenik* (enter into 'a fight' with the entire Slovenian public sphere, which is rotten to the core), 9 July 1925, in Kosovel (2006), p. 209.

[191] 'Pines', translated by Ana Jelnikar and Barbara Siegel Carlson, in Kosovel (2010a), p. 19; the full poem is given in the Appendix, p. 334.

rather it is considered an integral part of the ideological foundations of the new social order, personal as well as public, the language of decrees no less than of love letters. The new language, the language made from the combined forces of resistance and poetry [embodied in *bori*], is still to be forged.[192]

Indeed, the revolution Kosovel defended and called for meant primarily an *aesthetic* revolution of poetic expression in direct response to the political and personal struggles of life. 'Artistic form,' he noted, 'is but the artist's personal relationship with life.'[193] And the courage to live out life's contradictions and give them shape in art was a mark of true existence.

Modernity for Kosovel, on the other hand, was a mandate for change and cultural growth, and thus an important intervention into the traditional and the local:

> Our art has become local and not Slovenian in an absolute sense. Our art has become imitative and not modern in the global sense of the term. Our artists have not learnt from European artists, but they have imitated them blindly.[194]

Kosovel urged Slovenian artists to engage with European art, making a point to differentiate between learning and imitation, but, like Tagore, he also warned against the danger of surrendering one's selfhood in a-priori acceptance of the cultural hegemony of the 'centre'. The Europe Kosovel is referring to in the citation is, of course, the Europe of the powerful centres, such as Germany, France, Britain, and Italy. With his inherited otherness as a Slav and writing from the margins of the 'European/modern' fold, the poet can be seen to half-accept and half-reject this hierarchization of cultures:

> We have been modelling ourselves too much on Europe and too little on ourselves. We did not see ourselves as members of Europe who must go abreast with European movements and yet go their own way; we saw ourselves only as a small people, who must surrender to European ideas, lest we should be destroyed by them.[195]

---

192 Harlow (1987), p. 60.
193 Kosovel, 'Journal VII', *CW* 3, p. 657.
194 Kosovel, 'Razpad družbe', *CW* 3, p. 41.
195 Kosovel, 'Razpad družbe', *CW* 3, p. 40.

Time and again, Kosovel wrote of the need to pursue freedom of individual cultural expression, and yield neither to slavish conformism nor to patriotic self-centredness, or 'egocentric self-love', as he put it.[196] The 'patriot' in Kosovel's books is as short-sighted as the 'underling', and the two representatives of what he perceived as the dominant tendencies existing within Slovenian culture came under constant attack in his writing. 'A higher incarnation of the Slovenian underling is the patriot.'[197] The Slovenian people needed to progress beyond the stage of merely defending a people and instead needed to rise up to the pressing task of liberating them.[198] Moreover, as he wrote in a letter to his colleague Vinko Košak: 'When our relationship towards ourselves, the world and people is deep, lucid and great, then our art will be great too.'[199] And this, he stressed, required the assertion of an independent and critical relationship with Europe, lodged in a high ethical ideal: 'Our ideal is the European man, separate in his many faces, but one in his tremendous striving: to love all people and work in that love.'[200]

Kosovel's commitment to resistance was not only reflected in his numerous stylistic metamorphoses as a poet, in which he successfully combined new means of expression with traditional themes and local concerns (the subject of the next chapter), but also in the way he reflected upon this commitment, seeing in it, as it were, a historical imperative. At the root of his cultural eclecticism was his critique of nationalism. It is here that his thinking is most directly indebted to Tagore, as seen from an essay he wrote in 1923 and entitled 'Narodnost in vzgoja' (Nationhood and education),[201] drawing largely on Tagore's book *Nationalism* (1917) alongside Romain Rolland's biography of Tolstoy, while addressing Slovenian concerns.

---

[196] Kosovel, 'Napake slovenstva' (Flaws in Slovenianness), *CW* 3, p. 60.

[197] Kosovel, 'Kriza', *CW* 3, p. 14; see also his essay 'Razpad Družbe', *CW* 3, p. 41; 'Napake slovenstva', *CW* 3, p. 61; notes X, *CW* 3, p. 701.

[198] Kosovel, 'Napake slovenstva', *CW* 3, p. 60.

[199] Letter to Vinko Košak, 2 August 1925, Kosovel (2006), p. 226.

[200] Kosovel, 'Separatisti', *CW* 3, p. 59.

[201] 'Narodnost in vzgoja' was published in *Učiteljski list* (Pedagogical Gazette), a journal of the Association of Slavic Pedagogical Societies in Trieste, which gathered around it a group of socially committed Slovenian writers and publicists, with whom Kosovel collaborated. An article on Tagore's book *Nationalismus* had already appeared in 1922 in the gazette, no. 29, year III.

Based on Tagore's definition of the Nation as organized power, Kosovel sets this negative 'materialist' notion against what he sees as a positive spiritual category of *narodnost* (nationhood), which he defines as 'a sum total of all the elements of a people's spirituality'.[202] Narodnost seems to correspond most closely to Tagore's definition of 'society' as 'the expression of those moral and spiritual aspirations of man which belong to his higher nature'.[203] Kosovel takes directly from Tagore where the abstraction of Nation comes under attack on the grounds that it dissolves 'personal humanity' and that 'when [society] allows itself to be turned into a perfect organization of power ... there are few crimes it is unable to perpetrate'. He then applies Tagore's distinction between the nation-state and society (a people) to distinguish between what he calls 'ethical socialism' and 'materialist socialism'. While the former, according to Kosovel, remains bound to the high ethical ideal of '*equality of all people* and *nations*' (emphasis author's), the latter has surrendered human ideals to the principles of power and organization. He already sees the ideology of socialism as having sailed 'the materialist waters' by failing to distinguish between the nation-state and nationhood and by sacrificing the individual and his spiritual needs to a soulless organization. 'Materialist socialism' is deemed as undesirable as are nationalism and militarism, since they all cater to—as Tagore would have it and Kosovel agreed—'the man of a limited purpose'.[204]

Following Tagore's argument against nationalism closely, citing substantial sections from the book, Kosovel is fully in consonance with Tagore on the idea of having to find a basis of unity, which is not political.[205] His notion of 'nationhood' as a spiritual principle, while it can bind a particular people in unity, rests on the assumption that cannot be delimited by geopolitical boundaries:

> 'Nationhood' is a part of the human soul, and it is the basis from which culture emerges. But culture does not encompass the soul life of only one people; it extends towards infinity ... it is the outcome of man's striving to attain as closely as he can that spiritual beauty, goodness, that

---

[202] Kosovel, 'Narodnost', *CW* 3, p. 66.
[203] Tagore (2001a [1917]), p. 421.
[204] Kosovel, 'Narodnost', pp. 63–5.
[205] Kosovel, 'Narodnost', pp. 66–7.

perfection which he intuits and knows exists. That goal is something which defines human culture in general...[206]

Because this goal is generic of human culture as such, all peoples and individuals are 'on their way towards perfection'. Impossible as it may be to define what perfection is—it can only be intuited—our contemplating it, in whatever shape or form, will safeguard us against selfishness and egotism. 'Perhaps the whole point of eternity', Kosovel suggests, 'is in that it is there for us to tend toward'.[207] Driving a wedge between nationhood and nationalism meant for Kosovel demarcating the important sense of national selfhood from a self-indulgent celebration of one's own identity. The two, he understood, could easily converge. Nationhood thus requires a measure of selflessness, lest it should lead down 'the wide road of national egoism'.[208] Therefore, it remains vital to cultivate the perspective of 'the soul'. The acknowledgement of spiritual or soul reality, upon which Kosovel's conceptions of culture and nationhood rest, was for him a prerequisite, a kind of a regulative mechanism for both individuals and collectives. 'Altruism stems from a higher recognition that our physical existence needs to be in harmony with our spiritual one'.[209] This for Kosovel could have simply meant to think with one's heart, for the soul, like the heart, is the centre of emotions, and thus a much-needed antidote to what he elsewhere dubbed 'the heartless, hyper-intellectual civilization' of the West.[210]

Adopting such a spiritual view of nationhood and rebutting nationalism which uses nationhood to rally support for its essentially aggressive and expansionist goals, Kosovel finally addressed the important question of cultural and civilizational difference. Though he defined nationhood as the foundation from which culture emerges, Kosovel came to the conclusion that 'civilization is inherently international' because culture can never be exhausted by the soul-life of one people. While different nationhoods are akin to different faces, in their essence, they are, he contended, 'the same, even if it is often barely possible to say that they are similar'.[211] This was Kosovel's

[206] Kosovel, 'Narodnost', p. 68.
[207] Kosovel, 'Narodnost', CW 3, p. 68.
[208] Kosovel, 'Narodnost', CW 3, p. 67.
[209] Kosovel, 'Narodnost', CW 3, p. 67.
[210] Kosovel, 'Umetnost', CW 3, p. 27.
[211] Kosovel, 'Narodnost', CW 3, p. 68.

rephrasing of Tagore's concept of unity in diversity. Differences, as Kosovel and Tagore both understood, never operate simply between different individuals and cultures, but are constitutive of one and the same individual or culture. For Kosovel, a human being is inherently 'cosmopolitan,'[212] and Tagore's inclusive creed of 'the larger "We"' we have already discussed.[213]

Like Tagore, Kosovel rejected nationalism and propagated a kind of rooted universal humanism, insisting time and again that '*narod* must see itself in the mirror of humanity'.[214] At the same time he was no advocate of passionless participation or abstract individualism. He saw identities as being vitally shaped by whatever relationships and attachments entered into them. 'Man,' Kosovel stressed, 'is embedded in his surroundings, in relationship with his people, landscape, and animals.'[215] Art, too, must be anchored in concrete experience and express its relationship with the world; it ought to, he said, 'reflect our life struggles and our aspirations [and] grow out of our own self-perfection'.[216] Tagore, thinking of the poet Yeats, wrote to the same effect in 1912:

> Certain individuals are born with a need for direct experience, and they do not permit any barrier to come between that experience and its inner realisation. With absolute self-confidence and sincerity, they express the essence of the natural and human worlds in their own idiom. They have the courage to break all the conventions of contemporary poetry.[217]

Because of real (and imagined) imperial to Slovenian existence, Kosovel was up against a climate in which traditionalism and domesticity—the known and the norm—were the prescribed modes. Guarding and affirming cultural separateness was seen as essential.[218] In contrast, Kosovel's quest for 'Slovenianness', at times feverish,

---

[212] Kosovel, 'Journal IV', *CW* 3, p. 627.

[213] See Ch. 2, p. 91.

[214] Kosovel, 'Journal VIII', *CW* 3, p. 683.

[215] Kosovel, 'Kaj je kulturno gibanje?' (What is a cultural movement?), *CW* 3, p. 57.

[216] Kosovel, 'Kriza', *CW* 3, p. 20.

[217] Tagore, 'Kabi Yeats' [Poet Yeats], 1912, translation by Krishna Dutta and Andrew Robinson, in Dutta and Robinson (2005), pp. 94–5.

[218] On this, see Poniž (2004).

especially towards the end of his prematurely cut-off life, refused to succumb to narratives of cultural identity that harp on ideas of origin, race, or some other allegedly 'natural' essence. Instead, he projected a new type of human being—a 'new man'—who would resist assimilation into coercive identity politics and institute a future world of harmony and solidarity. No doubt utopian in their thrust, his ideas nevertheless posed a challenge to fixed mono-cultural roots prevalent in the nationalist thinking of his day. For certainly, by the standards of the more jingoist quarters, where preserving 'authentic' national values was the priority, and were mainly employed in the 'struggle against the corrupting influence of the West', such a launching of aspirations for cosmopolitan Slovenianness was seen as suspect at best, and treacherous at worst.[219]

With respect to formal and linguistic innovations in Slovene literature, traditionalism too held the upper hand. This was because, historically, smaller Slavic cultures had forged a very close link between language, literature, and politics, so that literature was seen as the sacred shrine of national values, and language *a national value* itself. Some Slavic theorists of the avant-garde have even dubbed them 'philological nations ... constituted through their national language'.[220] Given the sacred role literature and literary language were thereby entrusted with, any violation of traditionally sanctioned forms was seen as a direct attack on the national body itself.[221]

The next chapter will take up Kosovel as a poet, and how, more concretely, his protest against nationalism manifested itself in his use of language as he pushed against the boundaries of acceptable literary expression.

> Destroy, destroy, destroy!
> Millions are dying,
> but Europe lies.
> Destroy, destroy, destroy![222]

---

[219] Djurić (2003), p. 80.

[220] See Bošnjak (n.d), pp. 157–8, cited in Djurić (2003), p. 80.

[221] Djurić (2003), p. 66.

[222] 'Destruction', translated by Ana Jelnikar and Barbara Siegel Carlson, in Kosovel (2010a), p. 117. For the full poem, see Appendix, pp. 334.

6 Avant-Gardist with a Difference ·

> An age that has no constant models is a progressive, dynamic age; it moves in the name of a spirited, unacknowledged creative ideal.
>
> —Kosovel, 1925, journal entry

Kosovel responded to the challenge of a rapidly globalizing world by simultaneously turning to his own heritage and endorsing what came to him from other parts of the world. In spite of the historical pressures his fellow Slovenians were under to protect and preserve their 'national' identity, he did not go by the narrow focus of cultural 'authenticity', and adopted instead an increasingly active stance to promulgate cross-cultural interactions and foster internationalization in art. This led him to negotiate the concept of 'Slovenianness' not only within the wider European framework but also, as I have argued, in alignment with non-European resistance to the global forces that had brought the overwhelming part of the non-Western world under colonial domination.

Starting out as a poet in a more or less traditional vein, rooted in the literary culture of his origin, Kosovel seized the 'internationalist moment' towards radical reform of poetic expression and became Slovenia's foremost modernist and avant-garde voice of the interwar years. The shift in his style has been understood entirely as the outcome of the poet's engagement with the European literary avant-gardes (German, Italian, Russian, French, and Yugoslav). This chapter, however, explores the impact Tagore's works had on Kosovel's

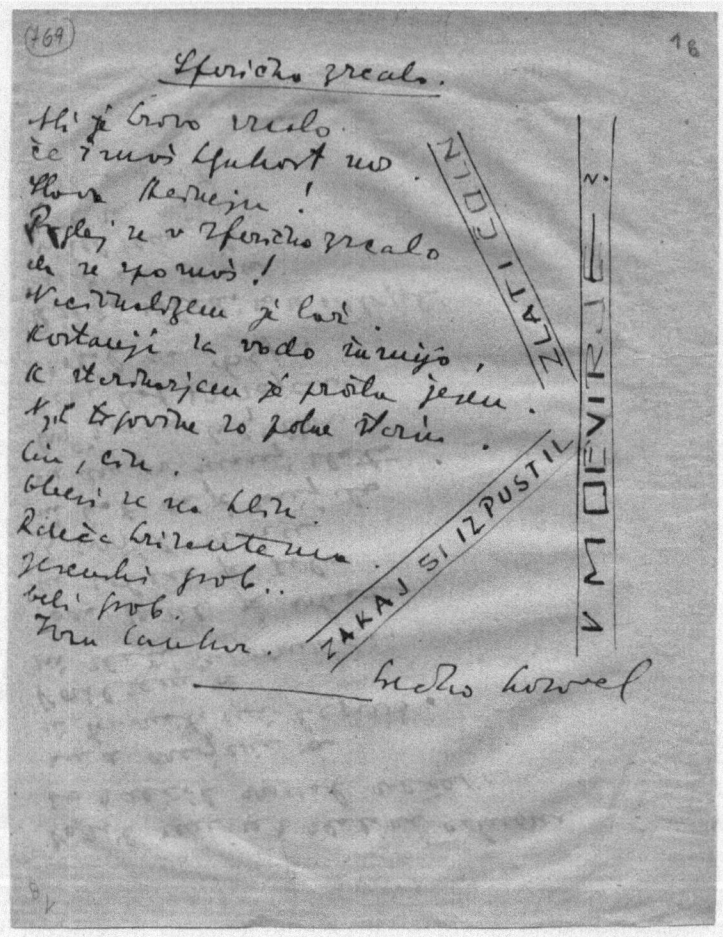

Figure 6.1 Scanned original of manuscript of Kosovel's poem 'Spherical Mirror', reproduced here by courtesy of the National University Library (NUK) in Ljubljana.

thinking and poetics with respect to his writing in general and to his personal avant-gardism in particular, arguing in the process for a less regimented approach to the so-called peripheral modernisms and avant-gardisms. The common Western perceptions of the Indian poet as a 'mystic' and a 'romantic' have set up a framework within which the avant-gardes and the Indian 'seer' are seen as mutually exclusive, but Kosovel's intellectual engagement with Tagore tells a different story.

Its significance is inscribed in the very title Kosovel chose for the book of poems he wanted to publish in the last year of his life. He called it *Zlati čoln* (*The Golden Boat*), in direct allusion to Tagore's *Sonar tari*. Moreover, in the preface to the collection, the only surviving part of the manuscript, Kosovel announced his intentions as a poet to move away from the 'velvety lyrics', the badge of a 'sentimental youth', and endorse a style better suited to the harsh realities of the rapidly changing modern world.[1] His reading of the Indian poet and his modernist shift are, I believe, intimately linked. Before we go on to explore this link, however, a brief analysis of Kosovel's publishing history, and some related issues, is in order.

FROM *ZLATI ČOLN* TO *INTEGRALI*

In his short life Kosovel managed to publish no more than a few dozen poems, a small number of articles, and a few short prose pieces. Soon after his death, he was marked out as one of the most important voices of his generation, and his work also began to be presented in independent publications. Kosovel's output, both voluminous and diverse, was 'processed' and 'packaged' in stages; it took over half a century for the various sides of his artistic personality to be fully revealed.[2] The first book of his poems, bearing the title *Pesmi* (Poems), was brought out by his immediate circle of friends in 1927, a year after his death. It contained sixty of what today pass as his 'traditional' lyrics. Four years later this collection was supplemented by *Izbrane pesmi* (Selected poems, 1931),[3] a slightly larger but no more 'adventurous' a sampling of his poetry, this time edited by Anton Ocvirk, Kosovel's younger contemporary and latter-day founder of

---

[1] Kosovel, *CW* 1, p. 413.

[2] By 1977, once the final book of Kosovel's *Collected Works* was published, it was thought that most, if not all, of Kosovel's literary estate (including his letters, journals, and notes) was available to the public. It turned out this was not the case, and the process of discovering and presenting Kosovel to the general readership has been going on ever since. See Kosovel (2008a, 2008b, 2010b, 2013).

[3] Cf. bibliography for full entries. Both publications, however, are unreliable, since they uncritically reproduced the poems that previously appeared in journals in bowdlerized form.

comparative literature in Slovenia.[4] At this point, Ocvirk had already become the chief holder and editor of the poet's literary estate, taking it upon himself to present Kosovel to scholars and lay readers alike.

Between 1946 and 1977, Ocvirk edited four large volumes of the prestigious *Zbrana dela slovenskih pesnikov in pisateljev* (Collected works of Slovenian poets and writers), bringing together over a thousand pages of poetry and several hundred of prose, consisting of vignettes, polemical essays, literary criticism, journals, notes, and a large body of letters—all of which he richly annotated. This was a commendable job by any standard, but compromised by the kind of monopolization that is the outcome when, in the absence of the author, one person becomes, as Ocvirk did for several decades, the sole arbiter in organizing, disseminating and, to a large extent, also interpreting a poet's legacy.[5]

---

[4] For more on Ocvirk's seminal study *Teorija primerjalne literarne zgodovine* (Theory of comparative literary history, 1936, cf. Juvan 2008, p. 31), as well as for his role as a mediator of Indian literatures after establishing the Department of Comparative Literature at the Faculty of Arts in Ljubljana, see Pacheiner-Klander (2008).

[5] The fact that Kosovel's papers were transferred to the archival holdings of the National University Library (NUK) in Ljubljana in 1962, but were not accessible to researchers apart from Anton Ocvirk, prompted Kosovel's close friend and associate Alfonz Gspan, the editor of the first book of his poems, to bring out what he personally possessed with respect to the poet—mainly some letters and notes. His book (cf. Gspan 1974), apart from filling one of the many gaps still existing in presenting Kosovel's works to the public, marks also the beginning of a fierce polemic surrounding Kosovel's long-drawn-out canonization that has affected much of subsequent Slovenian scholarship. Now that Kosovel's papers are openly available to researchers and the process of editing is understood as a sequence of arbitrary choices, it is possible to move beyond this polemic, which is essentially extraneous to Kosovel's writing, and engage afresh with the texts themselves, most of which are now available to (cautious) readers also in an unadulterated form. The facsimile publication of a corpus of his writings published in 2004 with transcriptions underneath (where the writing is undecipherable, different possibilities are stated, or even gaps are left) is a clear invitation to the reader to establish a direct relationship with the texts, unmediated through editorial intervention (cf. Kosovel 2004b). The process of presenting *all* of his poetry to the reader has now been supposedly completed by the publication of the

Variously referred to as 'co-author of Kosovel'[6] or as his 'literary executor',[7] Anton Ocvirk, it must be said, faced neither an easy nor a straightforward task. The majority of Kosovel's poems, left in at times barely legible manuscript form—writings fragmented and hastily thrown on loose scraps of paper, invoices, napkins, and the like— were by and large undated. In the disordered heap of paper that he took over, there was in fact nothing by way of guidelines that would prescribe the manner in which Kosovel's work ought to be organized. The compilation of it became of necessity an act of construction on the part of the editor.[8]

The collection *Zlati čoln*, which Kosovel had ready for publication in October 1925, but which he failed to publish, is a case in point. When eventually, in 1954, a book *Zlati čoln* did appear, clearly to honour the poet's intended publication, the composition of it—the selection, number, and order of the poems—was Ocvirk's. The manuscript itself had been lost and no definitive list of contents were found or satisfactorily reconstructed. The only surviving 'item' of the original manuscript was the preface, but this too was only remarked upon in the editorial introduction, rather than fully reproduced, since the publication was not—and could not be, as Ocvirk alleges—Kosovel's original book. In just under ninety poems, twice as many as Kosovel had intended,[9] *Zlati čoln*, however, supposedly compiled 'the most representative creations from the *entirety* of Kosovel's literary heritage'.[10] Soon it turned out this was not the case. Indeed, what is today generally considered to be the most exciting section of the poet's opus (now perhaps somewhat one-sidedly as regards his more traditional body of work), his avant-garde writings, was not part of the collection (neither would it have been in Kosovel's intended publication). When the editor realized—prompted no doubt by the new wave of the avant-gardes and the

volume edited by Neža Zajc (cf. Kosovel 2013). However, missing poems have already been identified, for instance, Kosovel's two poems written after the death of Lenin (Komelj 2014).

[6] Dović (2005), p. 207.

[7] Juvan (2005), p. 192.

[8] Dović (2005), pp. 209–10.

[9] Cf. letter to Fanica Obidova, 1 September 1925, in Kosovel (2006), p. 241.

[10] Ocvirk (1973), emphasis mine, p. 119.

emergence of concrete and visual poetry in the 1960s[11]—that what he had previously thought of as 'by and large rough and unfinished notes' and 'mere experimentation' were in fact fully fledged poems, he made amends for his error of judgement by bringing out an independent collection of Kosovel's as yet unseen modernist texts—some 155 poems—giving it the title *Integrali '26* (Integrals '26).[12] The book, when it was released in 1967, made for one of the most 'outrageous' events in Slovenian literary publishing history, sending shock waves of surprise and indignation across the literary establishment: where had these poems been until now?

Kosovel, the poet of predominantly traditional lyrics, by then already considered a Slovenian 'national' classic, became a radical modernist overnight. At once he was claimed by the modernist poets of the 1960s as their direct forerunner, a long-suppressed contemporary, and the establishment found in him a missing piece in Slovenian literary history, according him in retrospect the central place in the so-called historical avant-garde.[13] Translated into numerous European languages since, *Integrali '26* has acquired somewhat of an iconic status, and not unlike Tagore's English *Gitanjali* (1912), though, of course, on an incomparably smaller scale, brought Kosovel international

---

[11] See Djurić (2003), pp. 79–80.

[12] Ocvirk (1974), p. 563. To be precise, a dozen poems from *Integrali* were in fact published already in the first volume of *Collected Works* in 1946, mostly between pp. 238–43, but were then excluded from the revised edition of 1964, because they were perceived collectively as part of Kosovel's last 'constructivist' phase, and so made part of the new collection, which is where Ocvirk felt they ultimately belonged.

[13] The theoretization of Yugoslav avant-gardes is a relatively recent phenomenon in literary studies. The contention of the British scholar and translator John Willet (1917–2002), put forth in his study *Art and Politics in the Weimar Period: The New Sobriety, 1917–1933* (1978), that there were no avant-gardes south of the line running from Vienna to Budapest—the West–East divide again holding sway over scholarly imagination—was conclusively invalidated in the mid-1980s (cf. Vrečko 2005, p. 177), as serious research was undertaken to theorize the avant-gardes of the 1920s, collectively labelled as the historical avant-garde. Cf. Flaker (1982); Kos (1986); Vrečko (1986); Djurić and Šuvaković (2003).

exposure.[14] Interestingly, it was in French rather than in the Slovene original that sixteen of these poems first saw the light of day.[15]

This elaborately designed collection was no 'innocent belated publication' but once again, for better or worse, a construct.[16] Again, Ocvirk took the title from Kosovel to name what is essentially his own editorial selection from the poet's more radical writings, arguing that this corpus of poems marked the last stage of Kosovel's creative evolution, his so-called 'constructivist' poetry—hence the '26' appended to the title.[17] Discounting some of the errors that arose from inaccurately transcribing the manuscript versions, there is also the question of the suitability of the book's design. Kosovel's experimental lyrics which incorporated pictorial and typographical elements were 'translated' from handwritten manuscripts on to a typed page in a way that was more attuned to the avant-gardes of the 1960s than those of the 1920s, thus linking Kosovel to a different time framework (though its attempt to foreground the very important visual aspect of his poetry deserves credit). But what presented the most controversial aspect of this book and has fuelled much scholarly debate since is the title, particularly since scholars have tried, against all odds, to pin down a corpus of poems to fit it.

Janez Vrečko, for example, has delimited 'integrals' from Kosovel's Kons poems (the word *kons* being an abbreviation for what translates into English as 'construction', 'constructive' and 'constructor', and

---

[14] Cf. bibliography for translations.

[15] The French poet Marc Alyn came to Slovenia in the 1960s with the intention of putting together a book of selected poems of Kosovel for the Parisian publisher Pierre Seghers and their eminent *Poètes d'aujourd'hui* series. With the assistance of Viktor Jesenik, who provided French literals (including some poems from the *Integrali* manuscript awaiting publication), Alyn completed the translation project, complementing it also with a substantial introduction (Alyn 1965). For further details, see Ocvirk (1974), pp. 565–6. The French publication, entitled *Srečko Kosovel* (1965), which predated the publication of *Integrali* by two years, put Kosovel on the map of the twentieth-century European poetry.

[16] Dović (2005), p. 210.

[17] Ocvirk (1974), pp. 560–9. For a critical analysis of the publication, see Gspan (1974), pp. 99–111.

which appears in the title of some twenty poems),[18] linking the former with Kosovel's 'social-revolutionary' lyrics and arguing that they were written in the aftermath of his so-called constructivist phase, a genealogy that is in itself questionable.[19] Bożena Tokarz has put forth a different understanding of 'integrals', speculating originally on the notion behind the term, while acknowledging that 'the integrals are merely an expression of an artistic idea, which Kosovel did not manage to realize' and that it is impossible to ascertain which poems Kosovel had in mind with this term.[20] Alfonz Gspan's older analysis, however, is the most convincing in my view, as it stems from a close reading of Kosovel's usage of the word itself in his two journal entries and a letter, and can help us avoid some unnecessary confusion.

In the summer of 1925, as it appears from his journal entries, Kosovel was toying with the idea of setting up his own publishing house called Strelci (archers), the name taken from one of Oton Župančič's poems, which in turn would publish a series of books called 'Integrali' (Integrals), each of which would be accompanied by a foreword or an introduction.[21] Devoted to publishing individual works of the club members who wrote in different literary genres but were united in their openness to new ideas, the book series, Gspan logically concludes, would in itself enact a meaning of 'Integrali'—'a bringing together of different parts into a larger whole'.[22] It is indeed very likely that Kosovel would have included his own poetry collection, *The Golden Boat*, as part of the series, were he not depending on the honorarium he was promised by his publisher. Two pages later in the journal, Kosovel mentions 'Integrali' as a title of a book, alongside some other book titles,[23] possibly shifting from the more ambitious goal of a book-series and settling for a more realizable one.[24] And, finally two months later, in a letter to Fanica Obidova (incidentally the same letter in which he mentions publishing *Zlati čoln*) he speaks

---

[18] These will be discussed further on in the chapter.
[19] See Vrečko (1985).
[20] Tokarz (2005), p. 167.
[21] Kosovel, 'Journal IX', 1925, *CW* 3, p. 698.
[22] Gspan (1974), p. 101.
[23] Kosovel, 'Journal XI', 1925, *CW* 3, p. 699.
[24] Gspan (1974), p. 100.

of having embarked on 'an extreme path in poetry', and that his latest 'cycle of poems'—'Integrals'—has 'entirely its own, idiosyncratic character'.[25] It is this particular formulation that has, understandably, sent scholars in search of the Integrals and made Ocvirk adopt the word as a book-title, but while the Kons poems can be identified in what has survived of Kosovel's poetry, since they are titled so, the Integrals simply cannot be. It is certainly the case that Kosovel's extant corpus offers many examples of such 'extreme', avant-garde poetry, but only one poem so titled (Appendix, p. 335). We cannot be sure that he ever finished the 'cycle', or even if he had, whether the cycle had survived. Therefore to avoid confusion in terminology which has dogged writing about Kosovel's avant-garde poetry for so long (as scholars and lay readers persistently refer to Kosovel's 'kons' *and* 'integrals' as though it was clear what the latter was or consisted of), I will use the word *integrals* only if referring to the actual poem, or in reference to Ocvirk's 1967 publication, which has, for all its problems, assumed an important life of its own.

If such a debate seems quite extraneous to the existing body of texts that we can engage with as readers and critics, regardless of whether they were meant as *integrals* or not, what is of course pertinent to consider, and bear in mind, is the suggestiveness of the word *integral* itself—clearly a very important one to Kosovel, as he held on to the word, while progressively scaling down his ambitions to an ever-smaller realizable goal. Both its verbal meaning, 'to integrate' (to bring together or incorporate parts into a whole), from the Latin *integrare*, which originally meant to renew and restore, and its mathematical sense, to perform the operation of integration, are worth bearing in mind when we come to analyse Kosovel's poetry.

If the history of Kosovel's reception and canonization 'must be read as a history of editorial appropriations and adaptations',[26] a further complication underlying it rests also in the positivist literary historical foundations that pursue a linear trajectory according to which an author evolves through a set of artistic stages. Without a fixed chronology to go by, Ocvirk, in organizing Kosovel's heritage, resorted to the

[25] Kosovel, letter to Fanica Obidova, emphasis author's, 1 September 1925, in Kosovel (2006), p. 241.

[26] Dović (2005), p. 210.

principle of stylistic and thematic clustering.[27] Organizing the texts into four distinct but interdependent 'stylistically and thematically rounded-off units', as he calls them, with 'impressionist poems' in the first, 'sonnets' in the second, 'social-revolutionary poems' in the third, and 'intimate-confessional lyrics' in the last, with each section further subdivided into a progression of motifs from the Karst poems to poems dealing with death, the editor expressly aimed to 'create an internally cohesive whole'.[28]

It is this forging of the impression of inner unity in Kosovel's body of work, tied to a linear progression of styles from impressionism, via expressionism to constructivism, that has shaped the way 'Kosovel' has been constructed and overdetermined by neat, but ultimately reductive, categories. In turn he has been projected as it befitted the ideologico-historical occasion: a melancholy bard of the Karst turned expressionist visionary, turned avant-gardist, turned socialist revolutionary and, finally, an engaged social realist. Even as it became clear that the poet wrote in a diversity of styles at one and the same time and scholars acknowledged the simultaneity of his different poetics, recognizing that his growth was not linear or progressive in any predetermined way, there was still remarkable persistence in Kosovel scholarship to establish some kind of a linear logic to his evolution, neatly partitioning it into separate stages, recording clean-cut transitions between them.[29]

---

[27] Some poems can be dated through their alignment with correspondence, journal entries, and notes, where often the same phrases or words appear. This method has proven consequential for establishing that Kosovel did in fact write in a variety of styles simultaneously.

[28] Ocvirk (1964), pp. 414–15.

[29] For example, Janez Vrečko states: 'Kosovel's poetic opus, which, due to his untimely death, he completed at the age of 22, encompasses impressionist lyrics, followed by, after the poet experienced "an inner revolution", a resolve for constructivism, which, in line with numerous European avant-gardists, petered out into revolutionary lyrics'. Thus laying out the stages of Kosovel's poetic development, the author continues: 'And yet, it is interesting to note that Kosovel was working with all three "trends" simultaneously, that in the time of his avant-gardism and political activity [sic], he did not give up his impressionist—"velvety" lyrics' (Vrečko 2002, p. 13). The idea is that Kosovel moved on from his early poetry, but at the same time did not quite move

Regarding a poet who died so young, whose writing 'career' spanned no more than five to six years, who had no chance to organize his output or exercise any influence over the construction of his poetic self, and who left so many plans unrealized, this 'ultimate' search for a totalizing narrative of artistic evolution seems, frankly speaking, absurd. Although perhaps at odds with the project of cultural nationalism that has underpinned much of literary historiography in Slovenia—a country that achieved its full-fledged political independence only in 1991 and in which literature, particularly poetry, has been the historical mainstay of its national identity[30]—it would be more useful to approach Kosovel's extant opus as *unrealized potential*, for all that there is clearly realized and ahead of its time.

Poetic Synergy

Musil's line from his epochal novel *The Man without Qualities*—'Time was making a fresh start just then (it does so all the time), and a new

---

on. This in itself is not a problematic conclusion, what is problematic is that despite the recognition of simultaneous existence of various styles and an on-going search for new ones, there is remarkable insistence to delimit precisely and with finality the point at which Kosovel stopped writing in one style and moved on to the next one. As for Kosovel's so-called political activity, beyond editorial work, engaged readings, founding of a literary club, it is doubtful whether Kosovel became 'politically active' in the narrow sense of joining a political party, as is implied here and stated elsewhere, and as has been passed into 'common' knowledge (cf. Jovanovski 2005, p. 96). From my conversations with Dragica Sosič (b. 1936; her uncle was married to one of Kosovel's sisters and until recently few years ago, she looked after the Kosovel house in Tomaj) in September 2007, I was told that, to her knowledge, Kosovel had never joined the communist party.

[30] For a critical stance on the shortcomings of Slovene comparative literature, which has, despite its 'cosmopolitan' efforts, continued to pursue the model of cultural nationalism, perceiving 'national literature' as the basic conceptual unit that delimits the space of cross-cultural comparisons, see Juvan (2008), pp. 25–38. One of the demands of cultural nationalism in relation to Kosovel is also the need to 'prove' that he was 'on-a-par' with 'European' trends and movements.

time needs a new style'[31]—captures the very logic of the young poet's search for a form that would reflect and engage with the reality of the fast-changing modern world. This search reveals a tremendous readiness not just to respond to experience but to seek out experience and avail himself of whatever literary models came his way. In the 1920s, keeping his finger on the pulse of the present, Kosovel was engaging with a great many of the major '-isms' of the day: from post-impressionism and symbolism to German expressionism, Italian futurism, Russian constructivism, and French Dadaism and surrealism, much of which was mediated to him through the new, eclectic Balkan Zenitist movement.[32] Hence it is not surprising that many of his poems resonate with a range of poetic styles, relaying their allegiance to the 'foreign' and 'indigenous' in a dialectical interplay that frankly incapacitates any clear-cut distinction between the two. Indeed, once cultures and traditions are recognized as inherently plural, internally heterogeneous, and in a perpetual state of flux, the dichotomy between foreign and indigenous becomes artificial and hard to uphold.

Another look at Kosovel's 'Ecstasy of Death' evinces correspondences with a host of literary contemporaries across a wide stylistic spectrum. From German expressionist tradition, to which this poem has been assigned foremost indebtedness, Jakob van Hoddis, Ernst Toller, and especially Georg Trakl and Franz Werfel are singled out

---

[31] Musil (1995), p. 15.

[32] This movement formed around the review *Zenit* (Zenith), a leading journal for the dissemination of new art and culture in the Kingdom of Serbs, Croats, and Slovenes. With a strong international orientation, publishing articles in the original languages (French, German, Russian, Flemish, Hungarian, Italian, Esperanto even), it became a lively platform for introducing and debating the most contemporary trends in the art world. It was also amongst the foremost European avant-garde journals of the 1920s, alongside *Der Sturm, L'Esprit Nouveau, 7 Arts, De Stijl, Vesc/Gegenstand/Object* etc. First launched in 1921 in Zagreb (Croatia) by the controversial figure of Ljubomir Micić, then transferred to Belgrade in 1923, the journal produced 43 issues before it was banned by the authorities in 1926 on the grounds of alleged Bolshevik propaganda. (The digital version of the review is available online through Narodna Biblioteka Srbska at http://www.digital.nbs.bg.ac.yu/novine/zenit/swf.php?lang=scr).

by scholars as formative influences.[33] The impact of futurism in this particular case has not received as much attention as it deserves because of the general tendency to see this segment of Kosovel's writing as exclusively expressionist, a point noted by Zbigniew Folejewski in his comparative study and anthology of global futurist trends.[34] Since both trends were reported in Slovene periodicals and their theories and manifestos hotly debated within the literary circles, there is no reason to presume they would not have been both absorbed and incorporated, with considerable overlap, into artistic expression as well.[35] The role of Yugoslav Zenitism with specific contributions from Ljubomir Micić, Ivan Goll, and others has also been related to Kosovel's poem,[36] not to mention the fact that by the time Kosovel came to write 'Ecstasy', Slovene writers such as Anton Vodnik, Miran Jarc, and most radically Anton Podbevšek had already lent their individual voices to apocalyptic pronouncements on bourgeois mores and Western civilization, no doubt in affinity with some of the same sources.[37] As to Kosovel's social(ist) sensibility, one cannot go past the

[33] See Zadravec (1966c), pp. 102–10. Van Hoddis's poem 'The End of the World', 1911, is the opening poem of Kurt Pinthus's famous anthology of expressionist poetry, *Menschheitsdämerung* (in English the title is rendered either as Twilight of Humanity or Dawn of Humanity), 1919, which Kosovel is known to have read in German. Many Slovene poets and writers studied in Graz, Prague, Vienna, or Münich, among them were Kosovel's sister Karmela, his artist-friend Avgust Černigoj, and literary colleague Ciril Debevec. Kosovel drew on all these connections to inquire about the latest developments in art and have books sent to him. He would also have been familiar with the then leading expressionist journals *Der Sturm* and *Die Aktion*.

[34] Folejewski (1980), p. 106. This unique study devotes a section to Slovenian futurist poetry, alongside Polish, Czech, Portuguese, and Brazilian futuristic trends, as well as those of Italy, Russia, and Ukraine. Together with a brief introduction and commentary, it samples poems of Anton Podbevšek, Vladmir Premru, and Srečko Kosovel in both the original and English translation.

[35] For more on futurism in relation to Kosovel's poetry, see Troha (1988; 1993, pp. 107–9).

[36] See, amongst others, Kralj (1986), p. 133; Ocvirk (1977), p. 982.

[37] For samples of their work, see the anthology of Slovene futurist and expressionist lyrics, Zadravec (1966a).

influence of Ivan Cankar, the foremost symbolist/modernist writer of the older generation.[38] And, last but not least, there is the notable intertextual 'presence' of Tagore, inscribed directly into the poem, as I have shown in the previous chapter. The stylistic composition of 'Ecstasy of Death' is likewise inherently dialogic and polyphonic, bringing together traditionalist idiom with expressionist tropes, hyperbolic and grotesque in turn, as well as distinct futurist echoes.

Thus, when we say that Kosovel's poetry demonstrates command of a multiplicity of styles, this is not only to say that he has poems which are characteristically 'traditional' and 'romantic' in form and sensibility (if by that we understand an adherence to a classical form, rhyme scheme, and a particular mode of lyricism) at one end of the spectrum and poems that are decidedly avant-garde at the other, but also that a mixture of poetic styles is often inscribed into one and the same text. Once Kosovel, energized by a host of idioms, set out to reinvent literary language—his poetic intentions were reflected on not only in his meta-poetic writings such as his preface to *Zlati čoln*, but also in a number of poems about poetry—he came to combine traditionalist expression with modernist styles, the 'classical' with the 'avant-garde', in ways uniquely his own. Of course this meant going deeper than simply adopting a few formal innovations. Artistic originality in Kosovel's case combined a wide range of contemporary styles—exercising substantial freedom in cross-linking them from his own experiential angle (social, cultural, psychological)—in reconciliation with traditional antecedents.

It is instructive to refer here, once again, to Marko Juvan's contribution to Kosovel scholarship, particularly with respect to the poet's hybrid modernism. Juvan neatly jettisons the prevalent method of unpacking Kosovel along the lines of separate, internally homogenous, literary trends and artistic stages by pointing to the inherent hybrid and international nature of modernism itself.[39] Referring to the work of Steven Tötösy, he rightly argues that searching for 'Kosovel's primordial and decisive avant-garde ideal' is a misguided endeavour, given the specific features of the Central European 'literary zone of "in-between peripherality"' (though the phrase 'in-between peripherality' does

[38] On this, see Legiša (1969), pp. 222–35.

[39] Juvan (2005), p. 196.

seem unnecessarily obscure), where the avant-gardes were themselves creating 'unusual mixtures'. Thus, rather than forcing Kosovel's individual texts into 'constructivist', 'zenitist', 'futurist', 'surrealist', or other moulds, he simply opts to call them 'avant-garde texts', a strategy I agree with and intend to follow.[40]

The fact that Kosovel would adopt free verse and keep writing sonnets, or abandon normative poetic conventions in his radical avant-garde Kons poems but, at the same time, write 'I love them, the simple words/of our Karst people', or, as Gspan tells us, compose an 'impressionist' poem on one side of a sheet of paper and a poem in 'the constructivist' technique on the other[41]—in short, his simultaneous usage of a plurality of poetic discourses, often, as it turns out, in one and the same text—need not surprise us, as he was someone who, along with many other modernists, 'persisted in th[e] inter-space, *in between* various literary discourses of the 1920s.'[42] Pablo Picasso's ability to carry out highly divergent projects simultaneously and go back and forth effortlessly between idioms, his cubist and classical representation switching hands or coalescing in one and the same work of art, is one obvious example that Juvan alludes to in this respect, while, in poetry, he recalls Fernando Pessoa as the most dramatic example of multiple poetic identities.

It is worth noting here that Kosovel was familiar with Picasso's work, though to what extent it is difficult to establish. The fact that his poem sequence called 'Prisoners' concludes with an allusion to 'Picasso's portraits' calling them 'a book of new faces', seeing in them the artist's genius of shedding 'new light' on the prison-house of old ways, and allowing 'new truths' we carry inside us to be born[43]—suggests he took inspiration from the cubist master, fashioning his sense of 'the new artist' from such new perspectives. The revolution Picasso produced in the visual arts, summed up succinctly by Guillaume Apollinaire (one of the first people to champion Picasso's art) as 'the world is as he newly represents it', applied also to literature,

---

[40] Juvan (2005), p. 193.
[41] Gspan (1974), p. 107.
[42] Juvan (2005), emphasis author's, p. 196.
[43] Kosovel (1998), p. 159.

and Kosovel's aspirations in literature proceeded from that very same grappling with the question of representation.

The combination of brutality and graciousness that Apollinaire detects in Picasso's paintings stems from the artist's 'technique' of singling out the various elements that make up an object (a face) and rearranging them into a dynamic composition of planes in such a way as to utterly disassemble it and yet not dispense with the semblance of nature, so that its effect on us, despite the strangeness of the new object, is still 'as intimate as that of nature itself'.[44] This combination, as will be shown, characterizes Kosovel's most radical avant-garde experiments, his Kons poems. The following famous short poem enacts the transition from the 'traditional' to 'avant-garde', but on the level of the content rather than form, and can be read as homage to one of Picasso's rearranged objects:

> My poem's an explosion,
> savage rending. Dissonance.
> My poem won't reach you,
> who by God's will and providence
> are dead aesthetes, museum moths.
> My poem is my face.[45]

How a 'lyrical painter' like Picasso—the term is Apollinaire's[46]—featured in Kosovel's newly derived, artistic worldview can be gleaned from a journal entry in which his name appears in parenthesis next to the following statement: 'Modern art searches for a synthesis'. This notion Kosovel elaborates as 'a bringing together of all our quests under the horizon of perfection'.[47] If this is the artistic goal of modernity as Kosovel perceived it, then we can assume that the word 'integral'—a synthesized or synergic whole—was for him a conceptualization of this goal.

---

[44] Apollinaire (2001a [1913]), p. 280.

[45] 'My poem', translated by Ana Jelnikar and Barbara Siegel Carlson, Kosovel (2010a), p. 51.

[46] Apollinaire (2001b [1918]), p. 458.

[47] Kosovel, 'Journal XV', *CW* 3, p. 763.

Before going on to consider the drama of his artistic search in relation to Tagore, one final comment on Kosovel's openness to new styles and energies. Kosovel's own geographic 'in-betweeness', in which his 'Slovenianness' as well as his 'Europeanness' were not unproblematic givens but historically contested, afforded him a sensitiveness towards difference, even as he never stopped 'pining' (reaching out in the manner of his pines) for a meaningful—*integral*—whole. In graphic terms, this receptiveness towards 'an age' that he saw as 'most exciting and most interesting in its multiplicity of idioms and trends in politics, economy and art',[48] could be described as both horizontal and vertical: horizontal in the sense that it practised unabashed eclecticism, taking from across the board of new trends in poetry, incorporating principles also from the visual arts and music, and vertical in its spiritual insistence upon internalizing these influences, vitalizing them through lived experience so as to give them individual expression. 'To widen the circle of one's understanding, not just by chance, but to seek new realizations, with [one's] ... soul, to live them,'[49] he wrote in his journal in what is an expression of his universalist credo *par excellence*. It certainly comes as no surprise to have him refer to Tagore's poetry collection *Vrtnar* (*The Gardener*) in the very next line of the entry. Ketaki Kushari Dyson has noted of Tagore that 'it is his capacity for growth that marks him out as a modern'.[50] The same could be said of Kosovel, as it would be to claim what Michael Hamburger has written with regard to Rainer Maria Rilke, namely that it was the poet's 'diverse experiments' that 'made him a decidedly modernist poet, far in advance of his near-coevals'.[51]

Going Naked or Disrobing the World?

In October 1925, seven months before his death, Kosovel wrote:

> Whoever chances on this book and reads it, let him not dismay too much
> over the velvety lyrics that were composed by the young man I have now

[48] Kosovel, 'Igo Gruden', *CW* 3, p. 178.

[49] Kosovel, Journal XII, *CW* 3, p. 730. See also his letter to Maksa Samsa, 7 September 1925, *CW* 3, p. 561.

[50] Dyson (1996), p. 16.

[51] Hamburger (1996), p. 98.

parted with. They are indeed velvety lyrics! Golden stars all bedewed
with spring rain, graves bedecked with white flowers ... Our poets and
non-poets did not send their books into the world with prefaces. At least
not prefaces written by themselves ... But this age of ours is such that
one has to apologize for the soft word shed by a fresh, young heart ...
for in an age when infernal machines are put on the altar of this global
god [i.e. world capital], it is indeed odd for a young man to dare speak
simply, plainly, softly because he happened to get lost on a balmy spring
night and is wandering across the dream-filled landscape under the stars.[52]

This was to be the opening paragraph of Kosovel's short preface to his
first book of poems, *Zlati čoln*. It resounds with all the ambivalence
of a farewell from the 'sentimental youth'. Partly humoured and partly
ironized, the young man is sent packing, but not without a deep sense
of loss. The realization that he 'has been run over and crushed by the
wheels of time' and that his poems no longer possess the power to ring
true nor rise above the clamour of the chaotic age is not a comforting
one. It comes, moreover, with the imperative to assume new responsibilities towards the world and stop indulging in dream fantasies: 'His
hand still trembles in mine, still trying to pull away, evade the clutches
of the world, but it cannot.' Although Kosovel accepts the inevitability
of their parting, he remains hopeful that a day may return when this
young man can be resurrected. The concluding sentence suggests all
the trauma of farewell: 'Only now that I am saying goodbye to you,
can I feel how I am your brother ...'[53]

Indeed, even as Kosovel came to wrestle with the question of
which direction his poetry should take in this age of upheaval and
scientific discovery, and embarked on what he called 'an extreme
path'[54] in poetry, he neither disowned his 'velvety lyrics' nor lost a

[52] Kosovel, *CW* 1, p. 413.
[53] Kosovel, *CW* 1, p. 414.
[54] Here I am in disagreement with Vrečko's to my mind over-tendentious
and politicized interpretation of this word as meaning 'socialist' and 'revolutionary' (Vrečko 2004, p. 55). In the larger context of Kosovel's usage of the word I
see it as referring to the latest, most modern developments in literature and art
(rather than politics), though Kosovel, no doubt, was a 'Leftist' by conviction. For
instance, when discussing the plan for the literary club, he wrote to a colleague:
'In the literary part we will get to know all the modern and extreme strivings

penchant for them.[55] In all its various guises, even the most daringly experimental ones, his poetry, as critics have unanimously pointed out, has persistently drawn on a core set of romantic concepts, amongst which 'soul', 'heart', 'anguish', 'beauty', 'dreams', 'solitude', and 'eternity', to name but some recurring ones, proved to be unshakable constants, even if often ironized.[56] Kosovel's resolute endorsement of the 'soft word' throughout his writings perhaps need not be seen as a paradox, as suggested by some commentators, an anomaly undermining his modernist experiment, if one allows for a version of modernism that resists Mallarmé's notorious ban on the word 'heart' in poetry.[57]

Kosovel's 'romantic avant-gardism'[58] strikes me more as a self-conscious gesture, underpinned by the poet's critical stance and refusal to buy wholesale into novel creeds, even as he availed himself of new poetic devices and ideologies, becoming, as he put it in a poem, 'an active spirit' who 'collects impressions'.[59] Kosovel was indeed wholly

---

and some great writers, poets and playwrights'; see letter to Vinko Košak, 2 August 1925, in Kosovel (2006), p. 224. Or: 'With regards to poetry, I am now developing towards the most modern. Many perspectives are opening out to me'; see his letter to Fanica Obidova, 27 July 1925, in Kosovel (2006), p. 223.

[55] In the few letters where he mentions the book, he says how genuinely pleased he is with the collection, even as he has now moved on to new style(s). Cf. the letter to Obidova cited in the footnote above, and letter to Ivo Grahor, 15 August 25, in Kosovel (2006), p. 227.

[56] For the same point, see also, for example, Kos (2004), p. 164; Paternu (1985), p. 252.

[57] For an interesting distinction made between 'naked' poetry and 'pure' poetry, in which the former is understood as striving for wholeness and oneness with nature (Yeats, Jiménez), whereas a 'pure' poet such as Mallarmé, sees an irrevocable dichotomy between the mind and the body, and is preoccupied with form, formal experimentation etc., see Wilcox (1983), pp. 116–18.

[58] The term is Flaker's. See Flaker (1982), pp. 47–55.

[59] Kosovel, 'Why Get Upset?', in Kosovel (1998), p. 67. This can be demonstrated with Kosovel's endorsement of futurist principles, but not the ideology, or his guarded response to Zenitism, whose evocations of the Barbarogenious (a Balkan adaptation of Nietzsche's Übermensch) was invented as the Balkan's antidote to spiritually depleted Europe (cf. Djurić 2003, pp. 68–79), and which did not appeal to him. For more on this dynamics, see Ocvirk (1974), pp. 704–5.

committed to the here and now in the categories of the new—a real 'follower of fashion', to put it crudely—but, even at twenty he was neither as categorically opposed to the past nor as injunctive as was the official avant-garde line. When he pronounced death upon the old, which he did time and again, he warned that this death must be 'justified': it must do away with 'what is stereotypical, chauvinist', but that which is 'good', he was convinced, 'never dies'.[60] There is ample evidence throughout his writings, not least in his poetry, that his position was a fiercely embattled one, but ultimately, no matter how adverse the circumstances, he upheld the belief which Tagore, in response to a charge that his poetry lacks realism, brilliantly defended in 1915 as the poet's prerogative—'The poet's verse will endlessly repeat the mantra: "Truth is beauty, beauty truth!"'[61] By the same token—and like Tagore—Kosovel did not permit himself to be robbed of his faith in humanity. The closing lines in one of his many letters to his beloved feminist 'confidante' Fanica Obidova sums it up:

> When the world robs you of your illusions and you 'sober up', you become the saddest person in the world. As cold as autumn. They've taken everything away from me except my belief: belief in humanity. Humanity to me is a sacred word.[62]

The letter is postscripted: 'I have just received a summons to the army tribunal in Trieste. As you can see, we live highly romantically!'[63]

Part of Tagore's astute defence of poetry that celebrates 'jiva-lila, the play of living creation' and names it lila (play) rather than 'the struggle of life',[64] consists of his meditation on the linked phenomenon of joy and pain. Drawing on the Upanishads, Tagore wrote:

---

[60] Kosovel, letter to Vinko Košak, 2 August 1925, in Kosovel (2006), p. 224.

[61] Translated by Swapan Chakravorty, Tagore (2001g [1915]), p. 279.

[62] Kosovel, letter to Fanica Obidova, 1 September1925, in Kosovel (2006), p. 242. Almost to the exact wording, these ideas are found in Kosovel's poem 'Autumn Landscape' (Appendix, p. 340).

[63] Kosovel, letter to Fanica Obidova, 1 September1925, in Kosovel (2006), p. 242.

[64] Translated by Swapan Chakravorty, Tagore (2001g [1915]), p. 276.

it is only because joy is the final truth that the world can endure pain and strife. Not just that, pain is the measure of joy. We know love to be true in proportion to the suffering it is able to bear. Thus suffering undoubtedly exists, but it exists because of the joy beyond it—or else there would be nothing, not even hatred and violence. When you acknowledge pain, you exclude joy; but by admitting joy, you do not rule out pain.[65]

Kosovel pained and anguished extensively in his writing and was, for the most part, quite literalist about it. Tagore, who had misgivings about such rawness in poetic expression would most probably not have identified with this mode. Still, bearing in mind Tagore's perspective on life's suffering through a vital acknowledgement of joy, an admission which is not intended to diminish or obfuscate the reality of strife, but encourages one to see beyond the sense of discord and friction as the ultimate reality, we can see a side to Kosovel that seems to be underappreciated. What can be made of the concluding lines from the poem 'Why Get Upset?' if not that Kosovel too refused 'pain' or 'suffering' to be the last word. The allusion to Tagore is telling:

In the golden boat I sail.
Ladle from suffering everything
that I need.[66]

Kosovel's perception of suffering as a vitalizing force; his 'obstinacy' in remaining enchanted with the world ('Facts drive art away'— another line from the same poem); his refusal to see power struggle as primary reality—all bring him close to Tagore in sensibility, if clearly not in style. 'Is beauty not impoverished if we cast aside the veil that reveals rather than obscures the beauty of creation?' Tagore put forth in his essay 'Modern Poetry' (1932) when asked to present his ideas on the modern-versus-Victorian controversy then current among the literary circles. His response reveals a guarded view of literary modernism, one that is not keen on 'publicly disrobing the world', particularly if such disrobing is no more than an expression

---

[65] Translated by Swapan Chakravorty, Tagore (2001g [1915]), p. 276.

[66] 'Why Get Upset?', translated by Ana Jelnikar and Barbara Siegel Carlson, Kosovel (2010a), p. 175. For the full poem, see Appendix, p. 336.

of 'a mannered poeticism in an inverted way', a fad rather than a fresh way of seeing.[67]

This, however, is not to say that Tagore's theory of modernism did not accommodate a search for a greater audacity and terseness of language characteristic of modern poets. On the contrary, the 'bright and pure' seeing of 'undeluded vision' that Tagore submits as the mark of modern consciousness beyond confines of time or geography, went hand in hand with his own poetic inclination towards a poetry of greater verbal economy.[68] This direction is famously expressed in his poem no. 7 of the English *Gitanjali* (1912), a poem which has been shown to have infatuated Jiménez and Yeats, two of Tagore's European admirers, ringing true as it did to their own poetic reorientations towards a poetry shorn of extraneous trappings. Here is Tagore's poem, in his own transcreation:

> My song has put off her adornments. She has no pride of dress and decoration. Ornaments would mar our union; they would come between thee and me; their jingling would drown thy whispers.
>
> My poet's vanity dies in shame before thy sight. O master poet, I have sat down at thy feet. Only let me make my life simple and straight, like a flute of reed for thee to fill with music.[69]

Robert Johnson seems to be the first Western critic who discussed the striking resemblance between this poem (as also the poem No. 8 from *Gitanjali*) and Yeats's poem 'A Coat'. Though published in 1914, 'A Coat' was written in 1912, in the year Yeats met Tagore and collaborated with him on editing and introducing *Gitanjali*.[70] In what reads like a terser version of the Tagore poem, Yeats portends an aesthetic transformation with which he 'abdicates the throne of the twilight',[71] a gesture comparable to Kosovel's symbolic parting with the sentimental youth.

---

[67] Translated by Swapan Chakravorty, Tagore (2001h [1932]), pp. 282–3.

[68] Translated by Swapan Chakravorty, Tagore (2001h [1932]), p. 288. For a magisterial 'defence' of Tagore's modernism see Ayyub (1995), as also Bhabatosh Chatterjee (1996) for an in-depth analysis of Tagore's 'serious attempt to come to terms with the modernist mode', p. 10.

[69] Tagore, Gitanjali, poem no. 7, in *EW* 1, pp. 44–5.

[70] Johnson (1965), p. 541.

[71] MacNeice (1967), p. 108.

I made my song a coat
Covered with embroideries
Out of old mythologies
From heel to throat;
But the fools caught it,
Wore it in the world's eyes
As though they'd wrought it.
Song, let them take it,
For there's more enterprise
In walking naked.[72]

Partly the outcome of Yeats's own self-critical reappraisal of his early poetry, seen as deficient, if for nothing else, because it was so easily imitable, Yeats's resolution to endorse a new 'naked' style is no doubt also closely connected to the poet's shedding of illusions, both political and personal in nature.[73] It had little to do, as critics have pointed out, with experimental bravado or recklessness, for Yeats never experimented for the sake of experimentation. Doctrines of art for art's sake excluded 'nationality' from literature, which was for the Irish poet (as also for Kosovel) ultimately unacceptable.[74]

The closeness of the two poems on the level of metaphoric language and idea—even as Yeats's poem is more defiant in tone, has no reference to God and is terser in expression—is so striking that one would think this cannot be mere poetic coincidence. It seems fair to suggest that Tagore's poem, at least its first stanza, was a direct source of inspiration for Yeats, who then handled the image in his own way and developed the idea of 'nakedness' more explicitly. The concept of 'naked poetry' brings to mind Juan Ramón Jiménez's famous exposition of La Poesía Desnuda in another paradigmatic poem that enacts and celebrates the simplicity and directness of poetic expression. The parallel, again, seems more than a happenstance and has also been commented on by various critics.[75] Beginning with the famous Vino, primero, pura,/vestida de inocencia (She came, at first, pure/dressed in innocence), this poem is often taken to be a self-conscious elaboration

---

[72] 'A Coat' in Yeats (1985), p. 221.
[73] Ellman (1973), p. 84.
[74] Jeffares (1961), p. 28.
[75] Johnson (1965); Mirza (1977), pp. 10–15; and Wilcox (1983).

of the entire evolution of Jiménez as a poet, from child-like innocence through the various stages of acquired sophistication of *no sé qué ropajes* (I know not what clothing) to a re-attainment of total naked-ness (*desnuda total*).[76] The theme of casting off a false disguise as an essential next step for poetry to take is once again handled with the metaphor of disrobing.

Since Jiménez, as Johnson informs us, 'became interested in Yeats at about the same time that he began to translate Tagore', the echoes detected between the three poems offer enticing material for specula-tion on the impact of Tagore's poem on the poems of both Yeats and Jiménez. Scholars have been led to different conclusions. Johnson, for example, feels that 'Jiménez is closer to Tagore than Yeats',[77] whereas Wilcox detects no more than superficial resemblances in the texture of Jiménez's and Tagore's poems, but on the other hand a '"deep" structural resemblance between Jiménez and Yeats'.[78] Both, however, and rightly so, refrain from drawing any easy conclusions as to the 'influence' or direction in which the motif of 'naked poetry' necessarily passed. What is, however, indisputable in this fascinating triangle of cross-literary correspondence and intertextuality is that something did come to pass between these three poets and left an indelible imprint on the poems of both Yeats and Jiménez. Since Tagore's poem was chronologically the first, and both Yeats and Jiménez became, for a time, intensely involved with his work rather than vice versa, it is only fair to assume that his was 'the centre' from which the flame spread. And yet, had there been no sense of common ground, the spark would not have caught fire. The fact that within a striking temporal proximity of each other, these four poets—for it is time to bring Kosovel and his *Golden Boat* preface into the picture again—each from his own specific background and angle of poetic vision, spanning 'East' and 'West', were not only experiencing a critical juncture in their own artistic trajectories, but had also framed it in such similar paradigmatic terms, bespeaks rather a shared outlook made possible by 'global' or 'cosmopolitan' modernity, which all of them were negotiating from their respective 'peripheries' in the largely pre-industrial societies of India, Ireland, Spain, and Slovenia.

[76] Florit (1957), p. xxi.
[77] Johnson (1965), p. 544.
[78] Wilcox (1983), p. 512.

With respect to cosmopolitan modernity, it will do here to evoke again Partha Mitter's concept of the 'virtual cosmopolis' to denote the shared terrain of modern ideas with which the elites of 'the centre' and 'the periphery' were critically engaging 'on the level of the intellect and creativity'. Borrowing from Benedict Anderson the idea of 'imagined community' based on print culture, Mitter's 'virtual cosmopolis' helps explain how the members of this global community 'may never have known one another personally, and yet shared a corpus of ideas on modernity'. For example, artists and intellectuals worldwide may have found themselves united in a front against urban industrial capitalism, or in a 'quest for an alternative to materialism'. It is mostly through virtual cosmopolitanism that Indian artists could discern clear parallels between their own resistance to Western imperialism and Western avant-garde critics of European civilization, or, as importantly, the other way round.[79]

Was it not then this same internationalist space of ideas and forms that enabled Kosovel, who travelled little but read widely, to so readily respond to Tagore, as he felt himself to be on a similar quest for an alternative to 'materialism'? The outcomes of these quests were of course far from uniform, as were the reasons underlying them or the goals they were put to. 'Global primitivism' in painting, for example, was one critical form of modernity shared across the globe, but the main object of criticism for Western primitivists was the predicament of urban modernity, whereas in India, the mode was primarily deployed as a critique of colonial culture. In fact the 'cosmopolitan' and heterogeneous character of the avant-garde needs to be properly recognized, in the same way that global modernity must be understood more in terms of a 'two-way dialogic transaction' between the West and non-West with 'multilateral and multi-axial origins'.[80] The kind of intellectual or 'soul' community surmised between Tagore, Yeats, Jiménez, and Kosovel, and inscribed into their poetic variations of the same trope clearly defies any simplistic view of cultural influence as a one-way flow of ideas from the West to other cultures. If anything, in this particular case, it is rather the

[79] Mitter (2007), pp. 11–12.

[80] Mitter (2007), p. 13. For a discussion of the impact of primitivism and expressionism on Tagore's art, see Dyson and Adhikary (1997).

reverse story of 'the modern European enchantment with Eastern thought and art'.[81]

Kosovel's enchantment with Tagore was in some ways typical of the dominant Western perceptions of an Eastern sage or guru, and drew on aspects of the same language commonly used to refer to Tagore throughout Europe. Some of the qualities Kosovel perceived in Tagore, notions such as 'simplicity', 'naturalness', 'child-likeness', as also his comparing the power of Tagore's language to that of the Gospels[82]—were all part and parcel of the stock attributes that guided the imagination of Europeans when they turned towards 'the East' in the first decades of the twentieth century, and which have since been rightly criticized for their orientalizing thrust.[83] Like Goethe and a number of other intellectuals from Europe and America, Kosovel too was drawn to the idea of reincarnation as a source of solace and hope, and seeing it as central to Eastern religions.[84] His most explicit tribute to Tagore in his creative writing, the already-mentioned poem called

---

[81] Johnson (1965), p. 540.

[82] See Kosovel *CW* 3, letter to Karmela, 20 December 1924: 'Again, I want to understand Tagore who is full of simple greatness, who is a child and a human being' (p. 509). Or, in his letter to Maksa Samsa, 19 August 1925: 'Read Tagore's poems and study them! There you will learn about the mighty simplicity of the word such as you may find in the Gospels. There you will intuit the depth of the tiniest phenomenon in man and nature which are one', p. 558. Or in a letter to the same friend a few weeks later, on 7 September 1925: 'I am glad you are reading Tagore's "Gardener". In those seemingly so simple lines there is all of life's greatness. That is what it means to be simply great. That is what it means to plunge into the depth of meaning; into truth. That is what it means to be simple, but not banal ...', p. 561.

[83] See Introduction and the previous chapter for the various dimensions to 'Orientalism'.

[84] Goethe famously wrote in a letter to I. Folk: 'I am certain I have been here as I am now a thousand times before, and I hope to return a thousand times.' W. B. Yeats would say in his Irish orientalist fashion in his poem 'Under Ben Bulben': 'Many times man lives and dies/Between his two eternities,/That of race and that of soul/And ancient Ireland knew it all' (in Yeats 1985, p. 398); Closer to Kosovel's home, poet Simon Gregorčič (1844–1906) simply exclaimed in one of his most famous poems, 'And—there's no death!'

'In Green India', which imagines the Indian poet dwelling 'among silent trees' in a symbolist meditation on timelessness and life caught 'like eternity ... in a tree', is replete with such quintessentially 'Eastern' ideas. For where Tagore lives, in 'green India',

> Time there is spellbound, a cerulean circle,
> the clock tells neither month nor year
> but ripples in silence
> as if from invisible springs
> over ridges of temples and hills of trees—

And the final couplet:

> There nobody's dying, nobody's saying
> goodbye—life is like eternity, caught in a tree ...[85]

But to stop here would be to stop short of appreciating why Tagore was so important to Kosovel or how those concepts might have actually contributed to the project of self-emancipation both poets shared. The 'green' of Kosovel's India, I dare say, goes beyond the romantic and exotic associations derived from reading Rudyard Kipling,[86] or a sense of India as a distant land of plenty, a notion that has its roots in century-old South Slavic folksongs, tales, and sayings, surviving to this day in the still popular phrase 'India Koromandia' ('Koromandia' referring to the Coromandel Coast where St Thomas preached Christianity).[87] It bears closer affinity with what Gandhi felt about reincarnation and stated in his weekly English journal *Young India* many years after Kosovel's death:

> I cannot think of permanent enmity between man and man, believing as I do in the theory of rebirth, I shall live in the hope that if not in

---

[85] 'In Green India', translated by Ana Jelnikar and Barbara Siegel Carlson, in Kosovel (2010a), p. 97.

[86] Rudyard Kipling got the Nobel Prize in Literature in 1907 and the first work to be translated into Slovene was *The Jungle Book* (1894), in Slovene *Džungla* (Ljubljana: L. Schwentner) and published in 1908.

[87] See Šmitek (2011).

this birth, in some other birth I shall be able to hug all humanity in friendly embrace.[88]

Like pain, for Kosovel, death too cannot be the final word, and 'green' for him is ultimately a colour of hope and renewal.[89] For all the enthusiasm that Kosovel felt towards his older Indian contemporary, there was also nothing of blind veneration in the way he perceived him. Rather he studied his poetry and his philosophical writings seriously, taking 'lessons' when they struck a chord, and urging others to do the same. Tellingly, when works were not yet available in the Slovenian translation, as was the case with *Nationalism*, *Sadhana*, and *Personality*, he got hold of them in other European languages, primarily German.[90] From the exchange of letters between him, his family, friends, and associates, many of whom were at the time living abroad (in Munich, Paris, Prague, and Trieste), it becomes clear that there was in fact a whole group of young Slovenian writers, musicians, and artists who responded to Tagore from a deeply felt, creative need that went beyond mere fashion.

[88] Gandhi, *Young India*, 2 April 1931, p. 94.

[89] Amit Chaudhuri spoke about this particular poem in detail at a literary event in Calcutta, 'Creative Encounters: Slovenia and India; Evening of poetry and song in Slovene, English and Bengali', conceptualized by myself and hosted by the Embassy of the Republic of Slovenia, New Delhi, and the Consulate of the Republic of Slovenia, Kolkata, on 7 March 2013. Comparing it to Jorge Luis Borges's poem 'The Other Tiger', he identified a moment of self-reflexivity in the poem through the use of language that is central to Kosovel's more overtly avant-garde poetic practice. Indeed, the poem, with its imagery and use of colour, at once lyrical and telegrammatic, a code language, as it were, self-consciously constructs an idea of Tagore; this idea, according to Chaudhuri, also happens to correspond to Tagore's own secular vision of 'green India' or Nature. The forebear of Tagore in this is the Sanskrit poet Kalidasa; see Chaudhuri (2013), pp. 61–116 (98ff.).

[90] From his letters and journals it can be established that he read *Sadhana* in German, as also *Personality* (*Personlichkeit*, CW 3, p. 683), but *Nationalism* was available to him in German or Croatian (translated by Antun Barac), both published in 1922. Tagore's poetry, however, he read in Gradnik's Slovenian translations. For the bibliographical detail of Slovenian translations of *Stray Birds*, *The Gardener*, *Fruit-Gathering*, and *Gitanjali*, see Bibliography.

For Kosovel, reading Tagore meant encountering a voice that shared some of the age's deepest cultural and intellectual concerns, spanning nationalism, scientific and technological revolutions, environmentalism and feminism alike, and that helped him articulate both a critique of Europe and portend a solution to it. Coming from a poet rather than a social scientist, as well as from a mind in its youth, his critique carries a good deal more emotional than theoretical weight. It is indeed a poem such as 'Ecstasy of Death' that marks its fuller realization than any essay Kosovel wrote on the subject. And the relationship between freedom and language—particularly in the context of political oppression—becomes the space in which new identities can be imagined and the pursuit of justice envisioned (as for example in Kosovel's poem 'Italian Culture' or Tagore's poem 'Africa').

It is the crossing of formal boundaries in language that opens a way to freedom of thought and self-expression, forming an integral part of the continual re-creation of cultural meanings through which individuals and societies effectively bring about change.[91] At times of social upheaval and rapid modernization, the 'crisis' of language is felt with particular urgency. Questions as to which road poetry should take and what its destination should be were for Kosovel of paramount concern in an age which he perceived as dangerously dominated by the machine and devoid of basic humanity.[92] A war that started on horseback and ended with tanks threw this into sharp relief.[93] The artistic junction Kosovel reflected upon in the preface to *Zlati čoln* meant having to discard received meanings and forms (his 'velvety lyrics') so as to create new ones. This raises the question as to what

[91] On this, see Williams (1961), pp. 19–56.

[92] See his manifesto 'To the Mechanics', discussed in the previous chapter on p. 220. Tagore, wrote that the main reason why the 'East' and 'West' fail to show signs of true meeting is because of 'red tape' and 'machinery', as opposed to 'humanity', so that he gave Kipling's famous lines a twist: 'Man is man, machine is machine/And never the twain shall wed', in Tagore (2002d [1922]), p. 115.

[93] It is worth also noting that the first time an aeroplane dropped a bomb in history was in 1911 when the Italians seized Libya. As Pankaj Mishra observes: 'The experience of this new form of warfare, along with that of more conventional Italian brutalities, shocked many Muslims' (2012, p. 190).

extent Kosovel was prepared to jettison meaning, break with tradition and 'go naked'.

Quest for Meaning

In the fall of 1925, roughly at the same time during which he wrote his preface to the *Golden Boat*, Kosovel jotted down these thoughts in his journal: 'Do you write with your heart?/No, with a pen. But what comes not from the soul will not reach the soul.'[94] This short exchange reveals the poet's intention to offer means of communication free of sentimental trappings while retaining the power of description born out of lived—'soul'—experience. In Aristotelian terms, the *techné* or the craft of writing is an essential but insufficient condition for *poïesis*. Poetry detached from life as it is lived, Kosovel suggests, will not move; it will not bring forth what he argued all good art should—'a living realization'.[95] From this it follows that, if a poem (or art in general) is to succeed, much depends on the artist's ability to transmit his experience in a way that enables that experience to be actively re-lived in those to whom it is offered. That in turn will depend on the artist's own ability to live the experience in the first place: 'The secret of new forms,' writes Kosovel, 'lies in living the experience.'[96]

There can be in that sense no separation between 'content' and 'form' but rather, as the poet argues, it is the content that creates its own form.[97] Without a personal verification, or without what Kandinsky often wrote and spoke about as the 'inner necessity' that drives every artist to create,[98] the artist is likely to lapse into superficial imitation and the work of art to fall short of its function to communicate, which is to say, at another level, to fall short of its intention

[94] Kosovel, 'Journal XII', *CW* 3, p. 735.

[95] Kosovel, 'Pismo' (Letter), *CW* 3, p. 96.

[96] Kosovel, 'Pismo' (Letter), *CW* 3, p. 96. I find Raymond Williams' discussion of the communicative function of art useful here. 'By living the experience we mean that, whether or not it has been previously recorded, the artist has literally made it part of himself, so deeply that his whole energy is available to describe it and transmit it to others' (Williams 1961, p. 50).

[97] Kosovel, 'O "umetnosti"' (On 'art'), *CW* 3, p. 104.

[98] Kandinsky, cited in Whitford (1991), p. 98.

to transform the existing world of relationships.[99] We should not go to 'new art' for its novelty in form, Kosovel asserted, but for what it can tell us about 'man'.[100]

Not always easy to grasp, Kosovel's ideas, his basic understanding of the role of a creative mind vis-à-vis society, appears straightforward enough. The individual and his environment, Kosovel says, are locked into a relationship whereby they interactively transform each other. The artist takes from the environment, creates his form which in turn recreates him and his environment.[101] It is the compulsion, moreover, to retain a 'vital' relationship with one's surroundings—in that sense Kosovel was a real 'vitalist'—that I see as underlying his extraordinary literary metamorphoses as a poet. It also explains his pre-eminent concern with the present and its host of new literary idioms. The latter liberated creative expression, and in doing so not only bridged the gap between 'life' and 'art' but also freed real potential for changing the world. Kosovel of course was not alone in his optimism about the possibilities of art as a vehicle for social change, or in projecting a vision of a world based on what he evoked as 'the high ethical ideal of *equality between all people and nations*'.[102] Such and other similar utopian proclamations were part of the moral reorientation of the young generation that survived the war and refused to be shattered by it:

> 'I no longer know what beauty is!' cries modern man. He knows the history and understands the nature of beauty as being relative throughout

---

[99] In the same essay Kosovel writes: 'New art is on its way—it marches in most varied uniforms—and now we are faced with a vital question: Where? Today after this slogan, tomorrow after that one? ... If we follow ourselves and not fashion, we will always have the vital base for the emerging art....' Kosovel disapproved of some young poets in Slovenia who in his view were trying simply to imitate Tagore's style, for example, Gaspari in his collection *Cvetoča pisma* (Blossoming letters), letter to Samsa, 7 September 1925, *CW* 3, p. 561.

[100] Kosovel, 'O "umetnosti"', *CW* 3, p. 105

[101] Kosovel, 'O "umetnosti"', *CW* 3, p. 100. See also his essay, 'Kaj je kulturno gibanje?' [What is a cultural movement?], *CW* 3, pp. 56–7.

[102] Kosovel, 'Narodnost in vzgoja' (Nationality and education), emphasis author's, *CW* 3, p. 65.

the different ages. But beyond this relativism there must be something, something absolute.[103]

It was only against an ideal that the crumbled world could somehow be pieced together again. The tension between this fundamental intuition of an absolute reality and the relativism of the manifest world—what Kosovel elsewhere described as the gap between 'I' capitalized and 'i' in small letters, or between what 'Is' and what 'is'[104]—runs through most of his creative work and is played out, as in this poem, with broader social implications.

> I speak with you, yet I am far from you.
> A shadow grew to a thousand shadows.
> I can't tell myself apart, or know myself.
> How then can I know where?

The sense of the speaker's disorientation looms large in a universe robbed of God's presence, in a dominion ruled by shadows and death.

> Cold ashes lie with the shadows.
> Nerves exhausted
> from my own vague shape.
> God. I don't know his face.

But a sense of new-found direction (the answer to the question 'Where?') emerges in the next stanza, with stirrings of social consciousness:

> One thing burns: a thirst for Justice and Liberation.
> One thing sacred: the Simple, True.

The juxtaposition and complementariness of these two lines—the first one referring to social reality and the second to the world of art where simplicity and truthfulness are extolled as supreme virtues—are significant for a poet for whom artistic and political revolutions were one and the same. For the social critic clamouring for change, the

---

[103] Kosovel, 'Umetnik in publikum' (Artist and the public), *CW* 3, p. 99.
[104] Kosovel, letter to Karmela, 1 January 1924, *CW* 3, p. 503.

poem's projected ideal is painfully at odds with the reality lacking in rigour and imagination:

> But above us
> the melancholy greys of pavement
> like corpses that cannot die.

The poem ends on what could be read as a complete disdain or utter defiance:

> P. S. I know, you cannot understand.[105]

The poem 'Ecce Homo' enacts what Kosovel described in one of his most frequently cited letters as *a shift, a turn around*, from 'absolute negation, nihilism ... to the positive side'.[106] When the mood of the first two stanzas changes from despondency into an active liberation-ist stance; when the metaphysical perspective, as it were, is displaced by a critical social gaze, then creative work—the striving for 'truth' and 'simplicity'—becomes a surrogate for the distant God. Truth, as Kosovel writes in the same letter, becomes two-dimensional as opposed to one, and life enters the logic of a paradox:[107] the simplic-ity Kosovel exalts in art is not any straightforward simplicity but a Tagorean simplicity attained only on the back of complexity. This adopted 'paradoxical' stance is a celebration of relativity[108]—'*Relativity*

---

[105] 'Ecce Homo', translated by Ana Jelnikar and Barbara Siegel Carlson, in Kosovel (2010a), p. 43.

[106] Kosovel, letter to Obidova, 27 July 1925, in Kosovel (2006), p. 222.

[107] 'Be paradoxical! That is to say, show the patriotic bourgeois man that in the place of one truth there are now two truths' (Kosovel 2006, p. 222). The term 'paradox' in Kosovel's usage can be linked to the then current Zenitist terminology and understood as agility and flexibility of the mind and as such a vital component of true existence rather than an absurdity (cf. Vrečko 2005, p. 175).

[108] The term 'relativity' here relates explicitly to Einstein's theory of rela-tivity that was objected to by Catholic theologians on the grounds of being godless. Kosovel in his poem 'Kons: 4' (cf. Kosovel 2008b, p. 89). On the other hand, objects most strongly to the Church's collaboration with politics and its silence on the crimes committed by the Catholic colonial superpowers of France and Spain in Morocco, see Kodrič (2011), pp. 108–9.

makes the world beautiful and human endeavour great.[109] It does not dispense with 'the absolute' but translates its absence into a generator of self-overcoming and self-perfection through creative work.[110] For Kosovel, this meant stepping into the vanguard of a *literary* revolution,[111] the goal of which was to capture the demise of one world and the birth of another. '*How and why,*' he wrote, '*is the task for every individual.*'[112]

The subject of this transition is taken up in another poem that can in itself be seen as a transitional poem, framed within the traditional rhymed and scanned poetics but declaring an ideational shift from the past into the present. Correspondingly, it evokes the archetypal figure of a boatman—'the golden boatman'—and we can begin to appreciate the relevance and potency this metaphor held for Kosovel. The boatman takes out his golden boat for a leisurely ride 'across the red waters of evening'. As he is coasting along the 'grassy shore', all of

[109] Kosovel, letter to Obidova, 27 July 1925, emphasis author's, in Kosovel (2006), p. 222.

[110] Telling in this respect is the follow-up to Kosovel's meditation on the difference between ideal and lived life (between 'I' and 'i') in the same letter: 'For me [this gap] is precisely the cause for my work, I want to bridge it, so I am building the bridge ...' Kosovel was also fond of technical/technological metaphors for creativity—cons/construction/constructivist—derived from his friend Avgust Černigoj and the Bauhaus (to be discussed shortly). It would be wrong to assume that Kosovel dispensed with the idea of the 'Absolute' or 'God', even as he derided institutionalized religion as crooked ideology; rather he secularizede it, transposing it into the realm of human creativity, of creating from within oneself what is indestructible. On this see also Grdina (2013), p. 1165.

[111] Kosovel, letter to Obidova, 27 July 1925, emphasis mine, in Kosovel (2006), p, 223. I emphasize the word 'literary' here, since interpreters have persistently taken several sentences out of this letter to substantiate Kosovel's alleged 'turn' into 'active' politics, conveniently ignoring statements such as: 'We must of course understand what is going on in politics, but my work is in literature!' (Kosovel 2006, pp. 223–4, emphasis author's). See Osojnik (2012) for a probing analysis of the political in relation to Kosovel's avant-garde poetry, where the author brings in Jacques Rancière on the politics of literature to differentiate between 'political' in the narrow (ideological) sense and the 'political' as the 'truth' of poetic enunciation.

[112] Kosovel (2006), p. 224.

a sudden a storm strikes. The sun is made to fall 'from its height' and the world, rather than sinking into darkness (elsewhere a common Kosovel trope), comes more sharply into its own:

> as though everything else,
> less golden, shone forth
> more clearly, more alive.

Relativeness is presented as positively invigorating and the poet as boatman—having survived the tempest and having himself fallen from his own Parnassus heights—is able to step ashore with a renewed sense of worldly purpose:

> Red clouds tore
> from my heart.
> I saw them,
> followed them
> across the world.[113]

Kosovel's new sense of direction, both as outcome of personal growth and as product of historical inevitability, could be interpreted as a new work ethic.[114] His position is made clear in a letter to Grahor: 'I work. Life is tragic only in one instance: if it is ignorant and sheltered.'[115] Kosovel's raison d'être of human beings is clear: 'I live, therefore I can create.' The model of authenticity is dropped in favour of a model of creativity. 'History', according to the poet, 'does not repeat itself, but it creates itself', so rather than nostalgically turning to the past for 'our model', we should create it 'in the living present we feel inside us'.[116] Kosovel's relationship to the past (like Tagore's),

---

[113] 'I Went for a Ride', translated by Ana Jelnikar and Barbara Siegel Carlson, Kosovel (2010a), p. 85.

[114] 'Work—that is our ethics and art our religion: religion of the greatest beauty mankind has created./My perspective is the perspective of the soul' (Kosovel, 'Journal XI', 1925, CW 3, p. 698).

[115] Kosovel, letter to Ivo Grahor, 31 August 1925, in Kosovel (2006), p. 23.

[116] Kosovoel, 'Umetnik in publikum', CW 3, p. 100.

however, is not one of negation (or suppression or eradication), but one of critical distance.[117]

We have come full circle in pointing to some of the main ideas that preoccupied Kosovel and which, if not directly entering his poetry, certainly motivated his artistic search. It was in the sphere of the relationship between the artist and his medium that Kosovel's striving for 'new man' and 'new artist' began to be played out. This struggle, if genuine, is more often than not a painful one. Creative agony, as Raymond Williams asserts, should be taken quite literally and not merely as a romantic hyperbole. Neurologists, he says, have shown that the process of internal organization of new sensory experience and the effort this process entails is tantamount to what we understand by 'physical pain'.[118] Robbed of language as he knew it, Kosovel faced the painful task of reinventing himself as a poet:

> But look, I have nothing left,
> my heart's an altar cracked in half,
> my words are all wounds.
> Each one of them bleeds.[119]

A sense of one's limitations, as seen from the following lines of another poem, makes the task at hand a daunting prospect:

> It's not you who will tame the world
> and sink in silence, one with time.
> Scorched with pain, you will long
> with a voice cracked raw.[120]

Clearly, the separation of 'the pen' from 'the heart' spelt out a crisis in which a language needed to be lost in order to be regained. How gravely Kosovel felt this is evident from the sheer number of poems

---

[117] For the same observation of Kosovel's attitude towards the past, see Grdina (2013), p. 1155.

[118] See Williams (1961), pp. 43–3.

[119] 'One Word', translated by Ana Jelnikar and Barbara Siegel Carlson, Kosovel (2010a), p. 21. For the full poem see Appendix, p. 340.

[120] 'It's Not You', translated by Ana Jelnikar and Barbara Siegel Carlson, Kosovel (2010a), p. 23. For the full poem, see Appendix, p. 341.

he wrote dealing with the subject of poetry, often with the same kind of directness and resolve we note in the Tagore–Yeats–Jimenez trio complex. The following lines from the aptly titled poem 'If You Can't Speak' give an idea:

> You have to wade through a sea
> of words to come
> to yourself. Then alone,
> forgetting all speech,
> go back to the world.

In poem no. 12 of the *Gitanjali*, an almost identical insight is offered by Tagore:

> The traveller has to knock on every alien door to come to his own, and one has to wander through all the outer worlds to reach the innermost shrine at the end.

Kosovel, in the same poem says:

> He finds a new word;
> Today, it's not clear
> what your word is.

And Tagore again:

> It is the most distant course that comes nearest to thyself, and that training is the most intricate which leads to the utter simplicity of a tune.[121]

Kosovel says:

> Speak as the solitude speaks, with unutterable mystery.[122]

Putting these two poems in dialogue with each other serves two purposes. The first is extrinsic to the poems themselves and can be treated

---

[121] Tagore, poem no. 12, in Tagore (2004a), p. 25.

[122] Translated by Ana Jelnikar and Barbara Siegel Carlson, in Kosovel (2010a), p. 66.

as an aside on the formal direction of Kosovel's writing in relation to Tagore's *Gitanjali* and other translated works. The second and more interesting of the two, however, turns on the deeper unities that link these two poems and poets together, even though their style of writing is clearly worlds apart.

One of the formal innovations Kosovel came to adopt in a substantial body of his poetry was free verse. The constraints of rhyme and metre seem to have been the first casualties in a process of cutting down on poetic embellishments that eventually led Kosovel to a radical democratization of poetic discourses whereby mathematical and chemical signs, political slogans, journalism, and everyday speech were seamlessly interwoven into the loosened fabric of the poem.[123] It also led him to the 'prose poem', that hybrid genre where, as Tagore put it, 'prose is touched by the essence of verse and verse by the seriousness of prose'.[124] We must note here that Tagore's English *Gitanjali* (fully published in Slovenian in 1924) alongside his other translated poetry collections came to Kosovel as an instance of this new genre, for Tagore, as is well known, translated his own formally intricate verse into a kind of prose-poetry long before he had himself begun writing prose poems in Bengali. Looking back on this, Tagore sees one possible reason for the popularity of his English *Gitanjali* precisely in the fact of their prose incarnation. At a time of growing popularity of the prose-poem in Europe, the English poets, he writes, were ready to accept his translations 'as part of their own literature'.[125] With respect to Kosovel, it is possible to show that alongside the more evident literary antecedents such as Charles Baudelaire,[126] Tagore's 'influence' can be traced, both

---

[123] See the poem 'Rhyme', another manifesto type of poem to record this shift (Appendix, p. 338). There is, however, no clear-cut logic to Kosovel's use of rhyme. In the poem 'Cons XY' (Appendix, p. 338), for example, new diction and traditional rhyme are exploited to maximum effect, and Kosovel availed himself of 'traditional' poetic techniques to the end. For more on Kosovel's deployment of scansion, see Novak (2004).

[124] Translated by Swapan Chakravorty, Tagore (2001i [1938]), p. 334.

[125] Translated by Swapan Chakravorty, Tagore (2001i [1938]), p. 333.

[126] Pavel Karlin's translation of Baudelaire's *Le Spleen de Paris* came out in 1923 under the title *Charles Baudelaire: Pesmi v prozi* (Poems in prose). For other connections and related issues, see Ocvirk, *CW* 2, pp. 659–65.

in content and form, in a number of Kosovel's lyrical works now designated as 'prose poems'.[127]

The other observation that can be derived from the interleaved reading of Kosovel's 'If You Can't Speak' and Tagore's poem no. 12 from the *Gitanjali* relates to what I regard as one the more fundamental beliefs of both poets: the belief that as human beings we are endowed with the faculty of self-perfection and that this self-perfection of individuals (and societies at large) must be pursued through cultural transmission (knocking on every alien door in Tagore's poem, wading a sea of words in Kosovel's). But the long convoluted journey thus undertaken is as much an inward one as it is an outward one, as much vertical as it is horizontal. Both poems articulate a direction in which reaching 'an innermost chamber' (Tagore) or 'a self' (Kosovel) is seen as the ultimate goal. It constitutes a personal quest for truth, a striving to penetrate some essential quality behind manifest phenomena (a theme recurrent in Tagore's *Gitanjali* and elsewhere) where language is tested at its very limits: on the border of ineffability ('unutterable mystery' in Kosovel; 'utter simplicity' in Tagore).

Kosovel came to rephrase for himself the whole enterprise of modern art in explicitly teleological terms, conceiving it as the 'religion of modern life'.[128] In contrast to the scientific—'objective' and partial—view of the world, he saw art endowed with the 'religious' task of elucidating 'wholeness', evoking a sense of man's essential communion with nature and cosmos. More often than not, this communion was not harmonious, and art should testify to both 'creation and destruction'. In Kosovel's view, 'disharmony' was a constituent part of 'the rhythm of cosmos' and he welcomed 'the conflict between various life's forces and forms' as a stimulus for 'movement

---

[127] The designation of a body of Kosovel's poems as 'prose poems' is questionable from the perspective of literary history (refer to footnote 2) and is yet to be addressed fully by scholarship. Nonetheless, the texts designated as 'prose poems' such as 'Novemu življenju naproti' (Towards new life, pp. 99–100), 'Metulj na oknu' (Butterfly on a window, p. 40), 'Kozmično življenje' (Cosmic life, p. 60), 'Umetnik' (Artist, p. 68), 'Daleč' (Far, p. 114), all carry something of a Tagorean air about them. The page numbers refer to the collection of prose poems in original Slovene, Kosovel (1991). The poems, barring a few, are yet to be translated into English.

[128] Kosovel, 'Pismo', *CW* 3, p. 96.

and growth'.[129] When obstacles got in the way of physical life, he noted elsewhere—attributing this to something he had read of Tagore's—'a means to a new, higher form of spiritual life' presented itself.[130]

Kosovel's religious 'doctrine' of art was vitalist and individualist, not only in opposition to all forms of dogmatization or institutionalization—'All art must be a-confessional and a-political'[131]—but also based on the necessary coalition between everyday life and the activity of thought and expression. It is the dignity that a spiritual lens accorded the everyday and the mundane that so attracted Kosovel to Tagore's poetry and perhaps contrary to the expectations of those who might see in this no more than an infatuation with an otherworldly allure, the effect Tagore's poetry had on Kosovel, totally in step with the Indian poet's own affirmative stance on life, is that it set him more resolutely on the path of this-worldly affairs. The one colour that crops up regularly in Kosovel's poetry and holds associative links with Kosovel's idea of Tagore, beside the obvious gold, is, as already noted, the colour green—and green for Kosovel was the colour of life, joy, action, regeneration, and the promise of a new world.

The following excerpt from a letter Kosovel wrote to a young aspiring woman poet of his generation, Maksa Samsa, who sought him out after finishing high school as a 'mentor' for her first attempts at writing poetry,[132] is perhaps the most perspicuous instance to be found in Kosovel's opus conveying the kind of hope Tagore held out for him:

---

[129] Kosovel, 'Pismo', *CW* 3, p. 97.

[130] Kosovel, 'Journal VII', 1925, *CW* 3, p. 651. It may have been this passage from Tagore's book *Nationalism*:

> For man the easiest path is not his truest path. If his nature were not as complex as it is, if it were simple as that of a pack of hungry wolves, then, by this time, those hordes of marauders would have overrun the whole earth. But man, when confronted with difficulties, has to acknowledge, that he has responsibilities to the higher faculties of his nature, by ignoring which he may achieve success that is immediate, perhaps, but that will become a death trap for him. For what are obstacles to the lower creatures are opportunities for the higher life of man. (Tagore 2001a [1917], p. 419.)

[131] Kosovel, 'Pismo', *CW* 3, p. 95.

[132] Kosovel and Samsa exchanged a number of letters from November 1924 up until Kosovel's death in May 1926. Most of them mention Tagore, see *CW* 3, pp. 552–64.

Read Tagore's poems and study them! ... There you will encounter the cosmic perspective of our lives. There you will learn what a person can experience if they truly live and not live merely on borrowed time. There you will understand that there is no need to avoid the mundane and the everyday; we just need to get through it, understand it. There is really just one thing to understand: even the most seemingly isolated little village is a part of the cosmos. I too am a spiritual centre of my own living cosmos vibrating in the soul revealed to me through snatches of experience. There are no miracles in this world, because everything there is, is a miracle and miraculous. But enough of this.[133]

This conception of everyday existence as being in some sense a part of a much larger and meaningful whole—in other words, this perception of a universal dimension to our individual lives—is no doubt one key 'message' that Kosovel imbibed and reaffirmed through his reading of the Indian poet. It is an insight that helped him face personal trials and life's privations (cf. 'Bread'), as it also lent expression to his democratic aspirations and led him to assertions of individual dignity beyond the terms of class, ethnicity, or other social divisions: 'in our innermost being, there are no classes or nations.'[134] 'Whatever life it may be, the main thing is for me to live it.' It is on this affirmative stance towards—and respect for—people's lives in general that Kosovel derived inspiration from Tagore: 'Every person's life is important, and Tagore is right in saying that human existence is justified by the mere fact that we live it.'[135]

While this deeply humanist orientation made him extend his sympathies to the peasant and the worker, it also led him to perceive artistic labour as fundamentally linked to ordinary social activities and recognize in it a powerful force that directs people's lives as much as do politics and economy.[136] Art in that sense cannot be viewed in isolation, as a separate domain of aesthetics, but needs to be regarded in coexistence with, in Kosovel's words, 'other cultural sectors of the great cultural circle: economy, politics, religion [and] science',[137]

---

[133] Kosovel, letter to Samsa, 19 August 1925, *CW* 3, pp. 558–9.
[134] Kosovel, 'Umetnik in publikum' (Artist and the public), *CW* 3, p. 102.
[135] Kosovel, 'Pismo', *CW* 3, p. 87.
[136] Kosovel, 'Pismo', *CW* 3, p. 86.
[137] Kosovel, 'Kaj je kulturno gibanje?' (What is a cultural movement?), *CW* 3, p. 57.

in turn becoming, as he put it in his journal notes, 'an aesthetic, ethical, social, religious, revolutionary problem, in other words, a problem of life'.[138] Culture is no longer perceived as the prerogative of 'cultural workers' but is the domain for the 'participation of *everyone*'.[139] Its terms are what Williams put forth as 'a whole way of life' in which art and politics, science and religion, economy and family life are wedded together in 'a whole world of active and interacting relationships' where institutionalized meanings are constantly being tested, subverted, and displaced by creative thought and interpretation.[140] With this we can finally approach Kosovel's avant-garde creativity.

Between Destruction and Construction

When Kosovel worked to translate into practice his poetic vision that valued what was 'human' and humane beyond everything else, he aimed for what he called 'contemporary unadorned art'[141] that would not only penetrate the real face of things, but reflect man in his nakedness. This 'naked man', as he put it in another essay, would be disrobed of 'lies', 'romantic ecstasies [and] empty phrases'. In the context of Kosovel's criticism of European civilization and the violence it perpetrated against its others both outside and within Europe, this meant breaking the mould of the old 'romantically sentimental *humanism*' to strive for new humanism where 'the elemental face of man' would replace this mask of 'civilization'.[142] This elementary face Kosovel predictably—and romantically—linked with the peasant and

---

[138] Kosovel, 'Journal VII', *CW* 3, p. 650.

[139] Kosovel, 'Kaj je kulturno gibanje', emphasis author's, *CW* 3, p. 56.

[140] Williams (1961), pp. 55–6.

[141] Kosovel, 'Umetnik in publikum', *CW* 3, p. 101.

[142] Kosovel, 'O "umetnosti"', emphasis author's, *CW* 3, p. 104. Kosovel's personal quest for what he called 'contemporary unadorned art' that would reveal 'the elemental face of man', or the 'naked man' stripped of lies and hypocrisy, can once again be linked to the Tagorean notion (acted on by a number of other modern European poets as we have seen in the earlier section) of having to get behind manifest phenomena, to some essential quality, or larger—soul—purpose.

the worker, who in his view stood for the aspiring traits of strength, resilience, and a healthy moral direction.[143]

The German philosopher Nietzsche, whom Kosovel read and may have had in mind while conceiving his poem 'Ecce Homo', argued in a similar manner that truth had to 'cast off the trumpery garments of supposed reality of civilized man'.[144] Stripping away all mannerisms was thus for Kosovel the logical step in undermining the humanist rhetoric that supported the edifice of the liberal-bourgeois society, a step that had both political and ethical implications. Characteristically for Kosovel, this task rested with every individual:

> Each one of us must get through [our] ... own inner revolution, to be revitalized, to have [our] ... coat of hypocrisy torn off, so that [we] ... are finally able to take in with every pore of [our] ... body the sharp but healthy air of truth, openness. That is the condition and foundation of [the] *new* man, and only [the] *new* man will be able to create *new* art.[145]

With this end in view, the artist could avail himself of any available means, express himself pictorially or linguistically, as long as he was tuned into the goal of, in Kosovel's vocabulary, 'seeking the soul' and lending his ear to the words of 'this downtrodden man, this humiliated and desecrated man [within us]'.[146] The outer perspective needed to be replaced by an inner vision, a static view of the world by a dynamic conception, and a fixed perspective by a shifting point-of-view in a process, the prime object of which, Kosovel argued, was no longer the creation of beauty in the traditional romantic sense (something exalted and removed from life) but to provoke in us a sense of 'the real' and 'the true' in what we experience. 'Aesthetics,' he wrote, 'is no longer a discipline about objects that are in themselves

---

[143] See his short essay 'Napake slovenstva' (Errors of Slovenianness), in which he pits 'Slovene philistines' against 'peasants, workers and those intellectuals who are still robust, resistant and strong in their striving, and who will carry forward on their backs the destiny of the Slovene nation' (*CW* 3, p. 60).

[144] Nietzsche, cited in Wilcox (1983), p. 517. For more on the place of Nietzsche and Kosovel's thought, cf. Kos (2003).

[145] Kosovel, 'Umetnik in publikum', emphasis author's, *CW* 3, pp. 98–9.

[146] Kosovel, 'O "umetnosti"', *CW* 3, p. 105.

lovely or unlovely, but one on the intensity of the connection we feel with these objects.'[147]

In other words, meaning and significance are constructed rather than discovered as existing objectively out there. They are relational—and this shift in outlook and artistic practice has in theory been described as a shift from an art whose representational practice is mimetic to an art that is 'ontologically constructivist' in that it enacts, or rather performs, what it represents.[148]

Before we go on to consider an example of the poetry that Kosovel wrote in line with his own understanding of 'constructivism' where the content and form are inseparably wed, one reinforcing the other,[149] it must be underlined that the aesthetic ideal of truth as beauty mentioned earlier is also a Tagorean maxim (in the letter from which the excerpt above is taken, Tagore is one of the key references). At first sight entirely an outgrowth of Romantic ideology, this Keatsian concept was, however, emphasized differently by Tagore. As Tagore grew critical of Western aestheticism, believing it to be 'a sort of sectarianism', separating out values as though they were detached from the whole of life, he would always refer to 'Beauty is truth' from the opposite end as 'Truth is beauty'. This shift in emphasis signals a significant shift in perspective: it places what is true and real above the aspiration to create the beautiful in art.[150] Put in another way, what is true may not be beautiful in the conventional sense of the term but it is nevertheless beautiful because it is true. In a late poem Tagore wrote, 'Truth is hard,/and I loved the hard:/it never deceives'.[151] He also said, 'In blood's alphabet/I saw my countenance'—a line that could very well be Kosovel's. Indeed, 'art is not a pleasure trip, it is a battle [and] a way of self-discovery'.[152]

---

[147] Kosovel, letter to Karmela, 1 December 1924, in Kosovel (2006), pp. 146–7.

[148] Pogačnik (1984), p. 167.

[149] See Kosovel, 'Kriza', *CW* 3, p. 13. 'The difference between content and form in art disappears once and for all into the museums of aesthetes; the content wants to express itself in a vibrant, free organic form; it wants to be both content and form at the same time, hence constructivism.'

[150] On this, see Roy (2002), p. 69.

[151] Translated by Ketaki Kushari Dyson, Tagore (2010a [2003]), p. 245.

[152] Roy (2002), p. 69.

It is above all, as both poets insisted, an emotional journey. If poetry was to be a most direct expression of reality (social, physical, and spiritual), and grip a person's heart *and* mind, as Kosovel hoped it would, then genuine communication depended on curbing the referential meaning of words, allowing them to speak afresh.[153] Tagore, it seems, began to feel this problem with greater urgency towards the end of his creative life, when he not only took up painting to express himself in an alternative non-verbal medium (a function in part already fulfilled in his vast body of songs) but also wrote a number of books of nonsense verse, alongside some of the best poetry of his last years.[154] Kosovel, on the other hand, in a manner visibly indebted to the poetic techniques of the European avant-gardes with which he intensely engaged, but in a spirit and intention very much in consonance with Tagore, came to negotiate the question of meaning in poetry in a way that was uniquely his own. Let us consider one example from the body of his avant-garde writings:

> Our windows are netted.
> White barricades.
> The Indians[155]
> don't know a thing
> about gravity.
> But the dynamite explodes also
> in Novaya Zemlja.[156]

---

[153] On an indirect comment to this, see Kosovel's poem 'Rhyme' in Appendix, p. 338. Tagore, meanwhile, would also state: 'That words have meanings is just the difficulty. That is why poets have to turn and twist them in metre and rhyme, so that meaning may be held somewhat in check and feeling allowed to express itself' (translated by Surendranath Tagore, 2003b [1917], p. 271).

[154] See, for example, his late poem 'On My Birthday—20', in which the poet imagines languages to have broken free of constraint and 'words shot of their meaning/Hordes of them running amuck all day', translated by William Radice, in Tagore (1994a), p. 124. See also Radice's commentary to the poem on pp. 176–8.

[155] The reference here is to American Indians.

[156] Novaya Zemlja means 'the New World' in Russian but is also the name of an island in the Arctic Sea.

A gentleman with an astrakhan cap!
There is no arithmetic centre
between the old and new worlds.
A person can be young or old.
A golden boat on the horizon.
Natural law $\equiv$ Ethics ???
You can understand the universe
even without physics.

The hanged men
Swing from the telegraph poles.[157]
Admission: one dinar.[158]
It rains.
You talk with the universe.
A barn in front of the window.[159]

This poem radically contradicts the composition principle that presupposes a logical progression of a particular motif and a perspective that is largely fixed, identifiable, and homogeneous. In this poem it is not clear who, or where, the speaker is; the lyrical subject is decentred and deterritorialized,[160] defying expectations raised by the romantic title with its promise of a dialogue or conversation. Instead the text is made up of snatches of more or less autonomous and unrelated information in what is a radically open, even unfinished, composition. This random

[157] As a motif, hangings crop up in several of Kosovel's avant-garde poems and are related to political events in Bulgaria when in May 1925 several men, held responsible for the assault on the cathedral of St Nedelya in Sophia, were publicly hanged, an event reported in Slovenian newspapers. In another article, Kosovel could also have read that seventeen people were awaiting death by hanging in the city of Osijek (in present-day Croatia); see Ocvirk (1974), pp. 586–7.

[158] In mid-June 1925, Ljubljana saw the arrival of the Russian Kludsky Circus. The entry fee was one dinar. Kosovel glued the original ticket as part of the title of the poem he wrote following the occasion, 'Kludsky Circus, Seat 461' (Appendix, p. 339), an original meditation on nature versus culture, man versus machine, man versus animal (cf. also Kons XY, Appendix, p. 338).

[159] 'Conversation at Twilight', translated by Bert Pribac and David Brooks, Kosovel (2008b), p. 88.

[160] See also Juvan (2005), pp. 198–9.

sequencing of images suggests a world lacking in connection, where man is at the disposal of things—the products of the industrial age (barricades, dynamites, telegraphy)—where connections and relations are yet to be forged. Correspondingly, the style is heavily nominalized, telegrammatic, pared down, drawing on code systems outside traditional poetic language, traversing the vocabulary of science ('arithmetic mean'), journalism (reference to people being hanged), public notices ('Entrance: one dinar') as well as pure lyricism (the title and final line). There is no apparent hierarchy between these various idioms legitimized by the poet's (dis)ordering consciousness, which throws them up as baffling snippets of lived/observed/read/imagined reality that oscillate between intimate, public, planetary, and cosmic spaces. It is worth noting here that Kosovel's frequent reference to foreign places and peoples throughout his avant-garde verse (Morocco, China, India, France, etc.) as also very often to personal names, some closer to home than others (Einstein, Stravinsky, Tagore, Gandhi, etc.), not to mention to the political vocabulary (slogans, paroles, personalities, and events), not only at times draws his poetry very close to reportage but is also in itself a product of mass media and print culture.

In an important respect, the 'real life' that Kosovel draws upon in his writing is mediated to him through newspapers, journals, books, and cinema: it is, in that sense, both textual and virtual. New technological developments (the coming of electricity, automobile, telephone, etc.) enter his poetry as signifiers of contemporary civilization and open it up to reflections on the wider world. In subject matter and formal treatment, Kosovel moves outside the tradition of Slovenian poetry, even as in an important sense, he also continues it.

For all the jumbled nature of textual construction, to come back to the poem 'Conversation at Twilight', Kosovel neither dispenses with the meaning of individual words in the manner of, for example, the Russian futurist poet Velimir Khlebnikov and his 'заум/zaum' poetic experimentations,[161] nor does he forgo the meaning of the poem as a whole. Rather, he makes it simultaneously operative on two levels, where the semantic gap between the referential meaning of disjointed fragments and the hidden meaning of a derived—integrated—whole

[161] Translated into English as 'transreason', but literally made up of the prefix за = 'behind' and ум = 'the mind'.

needs to be bridged by the active participation/imagination of the reader. The aesthetic distance between the text and the reader thus annulled, the undermining of meaning (through decontextualization and fragmentation) serves the purpose of its reassembling: destruction and construction, disintegration and integration are two sides of the same coin. Since a completed whole can never be derived from the various fragments that have been taken out of their original contexts, what can emerge is a dynamic whole, subject to perpetual change.[162] The transition from the old world to the new suggested by the word 'twilight' and further underlined in lines eight and nine, lies in widening out the interpretative possibilities of the world through the struggle for meaning and the forging of relations ('conversations'). A poem becomes an instrument of emancipation.[163]

Kosovel's most radical writing: his leap into unbounded poetry that included also experimentation with typography and 'pictorial poetry', marks an attempt to materialize, in his words, 'the idea of constructive affirmation of life' in the aftermath of 'nihilistic negation' experienced by his generation.[164] For indeed, the death of Europe and demise of the European man is not the final stop for Kosovel, because, as Grdina has succinctly observed, '[t]he New Man, for whom art is essential—and not mere decoration—has more scope and more depth than the old one; in everything that is already created, s/he will find material for constructiveness'.[165]

The 'constructive' mode that has thus come to define Kosovel's approach to life and poetry is, no doubt, formally indebted to the European avant-garde trends Kosovel was familiar with and studied

[162] On this see also Tokarz (2005), pp. 169–70.

[163] Peter Bürger's classical account of the avant-garde points out the contradictions inherent in the historical avant-garde movements' negation of the autonomy of art and its corresponding dream of the integration of art into the praxis of life. If the distance between the two is done away with—that is, praxis is aesthetic and art is practical—then art's purpose can no longer be discovered; the distance, he suggests, is a prerequisite for 'that free space within which alternatives to what exists become conceivable' (1992, pp. 57–63). An extreme example of 'practical' art would be art as commodity, the purpose of which is to enslave rather than emancipate.

[164] Kosovel, 'Journal VII', CW 3, p. 650.

[165] Translation mine, Grdina (2013), p. 1158.

(from futurism to constructivism)—connections which have been widely explored by critics[166]—but much of the conceptual and spiritual rigour behind Kosovel's experiments, I want to suggest, point to Tagore, to whom Kosovel turned as a vital source of inspiration.

> I seek meaning everywhere, in every step, in every thought, in every word that expresses my life, every heart-beat, every breath. Again I want to understand Tagore, who is so full of that simple greatness, who is a child and a human being ... I am after entirely new ways, perhaps I will find them.[167]

Significantly, from Kosovel's correspondence it can be derived that the summer and autumn of 1925, which has been established as the period that gave birth to some of Kosovel's most radical avant-garde verse, is the time in which Tagore's name appears with the greatest frequency in the surviving letters. Acknowledging this does not in any way suggest a direct correspondence between Tagore's and Kosovel's respective poetic practices. The kind of avant-gardism Kosovel launched into when seeking 'entirely new ways' is worlds apart from Tagore's own poetic practice, and in fact much closer to the successive post-Tagore generations (the *Kallol* circle of writers, Jibanananda Das) who brought this kind of more overtly self-conscious modernism to Bengali poetry. Tagore, born in 1861, was indeed Kosovel's *elder* contemporary.

The 'entirely new ways' the young poet sought he most dramatically realized in a body of poems he called 'Kons', the title also being an abbreviated form for the constructivist journal *Konstruktor* (Constructor), which he was planning to launch in 1924 with the artist friend, Avgust Černigoj. Although many of his most radical poems are to be found in this group of nineteen poems linked by the title Kons in its various permutations ('Kons: ABC', 'Kons: Cat', 'KONS KONS KONS' 'Kons: 4', etc.), Kosovel's avant-gardism is neither confined to this group nor in fact intrinsic to it. Some, such as the poem entitled simply 'Kons', are executed in a traditional lyrical vein, and many are a combination of old formal properties (rhyme, stanzaic structure, fixed lyrical subject) and

---

[166] See previous chapter, note 167. On the nature of the destructive–constructive principle, see further Brazzoduro (1984); Grdina (2013); Pogačnik (1984), pp. 163–9.

[167] Kosovel, letter to Karmela, 20 December 1924, *CW* 3, p. 509.

new moods and subjects in what seems to be a striving for a deliberate effect of discrepancy between the old and the new. Contrast, Kosovel felt, was a prerequisite for perception and meaning, for nothing can be seen or understood in isolation, independent from something else of a different quality: 'I paint black alongside white, since this provokes contrast and since this contrast signifies something, I paint brown, because I can differentiate it from green.'[168]

This heterogeneous body of Kons poems brought under a joint title demonstrates that Kosovel did not feel himself to be constrained by any one single school of thought, or discipline, be it constructivist, futurist or Zenitist, but sought a synthesis that was—and had to be— entirely his own. By the same token, he opened up his literary creativity to directions derived from music and the visual arts—the contrast 'doctrine' and the above quote almost certainly owe something to the then revolutionary teachings of the Bauhaus[169]—aspiring to unite 'the sensibilities of a painter and musician, poet and philosopher'.[170]

The kind of self-conscious formalism, economy of expression, and slide into abstraction allied simultaneously with a timeless lyricism, that defines Kosovel's avant-garde poetic practice comes perhaps—if one risks a cross-generic comparison—closer to the modernist spirit of some of Tagore's paintings than his poetry. Although it would be reductive to think of Tagore's paintings as entirely separate from—or doing something entirely new to—his novels, plays, or poetry, which also perpetually cross the boundaries of convention, the ostensibly 'darker' side that critics have noted with respect to Tagore's visual art, where grotesque imagery, irony, and free play stand to repudiate the 'conventional' language of beauty,[171] is a novelty in Tagore's artistic

[168] Kosovel, 'Journal X', 1925, *CW* 3, p. 705.

[169] The famous Bauhaus preliminary course (Vorkurs), set up by the painter (and great colourist) Johannes Itten (1888–1967) under the directorship of Walter Gropius and subsequently enriched by the theoretical teachings of the Swiss artist Paul Klee (1879–1940) and the Russian painter Wassily Kandinsky (1866–1944) revolutionized elementary visual language based on colour and form. Students were often asked to make collages from contrasting materials, textures, forms, and colours with the aim of deriving the artwork's meaning from its underlying structure (cf. Whitford 1984).

[170] Translated by Ana Jelnikar, Tokarz (2005), p. 94.

[171] Mitter (2007), pp. 76–7.

expression,[172] and can be linked to the 'anti-poetic' thrust of Kosovel's avant-garde verse.

For example, the function of the face as a mask that crops up repeatedly, almost obsessively, in Tagore's paintings has conceptual overlaps with Kosovel's avant-gardism. On the one hand, the image of the face as mask is Tagore's personal expression of the phenomenon of global primitivism—that critical form of modernity that forged its language through exposure to Native American, Oceanic, and African ritual masks to articulate its dissent from materialist culture[173]— but on the other, it is a trope for the veil obscuring authentic existence and the artist's role to get behind this outer reality. In both senses, but more in the latter, the objective is shared by Kosovel-the-avant-gardist who clamoured for a world stripped of lies, putting himself in the centre of his personal quest: 'My poem is my face.'

It was as a painter that Tagore, who took up the genre in his late sixties, came to be seen as one of India's foremost modernists and avant-gardists.[174] His paintings have baffled critics in India, Europe, and America concerned with locating the artist. Is he more of Europe or of India? The striking formal affinities between his works and the works of various European modernists, such as Klee, Picasso, Munch, Nolde, and others have led some critics to question their 'Indianness'. Tagore's lack of formal training and his almost self-conscious endorsement of an amateur style may have contributed to this questioning, but to reject something on the basis of a lack of precedence within the existing tradition is, of course, to take a very orthodox view of tradition. It is especially ironic in the light of an artist whose works are so intimately bound up with his personal experiences of the local people and landscape in Bengal,[175] and whose bulk of artistic work emerged after he was done with travelling in the West and had, as it were, permanently settled in Santiniketan.[176]

---

[172] Although the 'darker' side also has a factual grounding in Tagore's actual colour vision, and needs to be taken into account (cf. Dyson 2001).

[173] See Mitter (2007), pp. 12, 71. In Tagore's case, primitivism chiefly fulfils the function of an anti-colonial tool, forming also an important aspect to his educational experiment in Santiniketan (cf. Mitter 2007, pp. 78–9).

[174] Mitter (2007), p. 66.

[175] On this, see Kumar (1999), p. 17.

[176] See Robinson (1989), p. 52.

Tagore defined the purpose of art as self-expression: as the expression of personality.[177] Kumar's explanation of Tagore's concept of personality as 'knowing the world as a "personal fact"' or, said differently, as 'the intimate and mutually transforming encounter between individual man and the world', helps us locate the pronounced internationalist dimension of his art in the bringing together of 'cross-cultural contact' and 'experiential rootedness'.[178] It is true that through his many European tours in the 1920s, Tagore came to experience more of Western art first hand than any of his contemporaries, but it is also true that he deliberately sought out contemporary trends in Europe in line with his internationalist convictions. 'There is nothing so good for an awakening of consciousness as a good jolt from the outside,' Tagore wrote to his two artist nephews, Abanindranath and Gaganendranath, from Japan in 1916, encouraging them to travel and experience more of the world.[179]

In 1922, a number of years before Tagore himself took up painting, he visited Germany, and most probably the school of design and architecture in Weimar, the Bauhaus.[180] This particular trip, according to some critics, proved momentous for the meeting of like minds and an artistic consolidation between 'East' and 'West'. Tagore would have sensed the similarities of pedagogical intentions between his own Santiniketan experiment, with its ideal of 'integrated life', and the Bauhaus' attempt to establish an ideal community in miniature where the creative potential of each and every student would be liberated and students would not just acquire technical skills but develop their personalities as well.[181] The desire to reform society through art education lay at the root of both these projects and it is not difficult to see how the mystically minded Itten, an enthusiast for Eastern philosophy, would have delighted in Tagore's visit. Tagore, in turn, would

[177] See his writings on art and aesthetics, Tagore (2005b), pp. 10–28.

[178] Kumar (1999), p. 17.

[179] Tagore, cited in Robinson (1989), p. 51.

[180] Partha Mitter gives this as an established fact, in Mitter (2007, pp. 16–17), but Dyson and Adhikary (1997) have found the evidence inconclusive. See p. 154 of Chapter 3.

[181] Mitter (2007), pp. 26, 78–81. For more on Bauhaus itself, see Whitford (1991, p. 46).

have also taken to Itten, as also presumably to Kandinsky's spiritual conception of art. Though the monk's habit of Itten and the mystical bent of the institution were eventually displaced by the worker's overalls of the Hungarian László Moholy-Nagy (1895–1946) and his predilection for the machine, Tagore did not, it seems, miss this opportunity to bring the achievements of the Bauhaus closer to his compatriots. Through his request, some 250 Bauhaus exhibits, including the works of Klee and Kandinsky, were shown in Calcutta in 1922, at the 14th annual exhibition of the Indian Society of Oriental Art. According to Mitter, the impact of the exhibition 'sounded the death knell not only for academic art in India but also for orientalism, and its engagements with the past'.[182]

The artistic innovations of the Bauhaus came to Slovenia also via the intervention of one individual—that of the Trieste-born Slovene artist and painter Avgust Černigoj (1898–1985), who also felt, perhaps more radically and certainly with more justification than Tagore, that its capital Ljubljana needed a good jolt from the outside.[183] Born as one of many children in a dockworker's family in the days of the Austro-Hungarian Empire, Černigoj is said to have developed an interest in colour and painting from an early age. His formal art education began at the Secondary School of Arts and Crafts in Trieste, and following a short stint as an art teacher in Postojna and Bologna after service in the war, he decided to continue his education at the Academy of Fine Arts in Munich. For a time, Munich seemed to have satisfied Černigoj's thirst for learning about the latest trends, as it also brought him into a circle of artists who were 'intensely debating the question of modernism, especially the problem of how to settle accounts with the old artistic directions and bring a new art into force'.[184] One day he chanced upon an exhibition of Kandinsky in a bookshop and learnt from one of the books on display that the Russian painter was teaching at the Bauhaus. Having been expelled from the Academy for wanting to do collages that were considered by his professors

[182] Mitter (2007), pp. 17–18.

[183] According to art historian Peter Krečič (1999), Černigoj visited Ljubljana primarily with the intention of 'bringing about an artistic revolution in what he felt was a socially and culturally backward environment' (2004, p. 25).

[184] Krečič (1989), p. 41.

to be 'non-art', he left for the Bauhaus, determined to explore wider artistic interests (including sculpture, architecture, ballet), and craving theoretical knowledge.[185] The theory he received from the Russian artist himself, while the *Formlehre* came from László Moholy-Nagy, whose constructivist direction would lend an entirely new dimension to his work, particularly as regards his collages and sculptures. If previously he was concerned with 'creating new forms according to new techniques', now it was 'a question of realizing these on a higher plane of awareness as regards the basic elements and structures of an abstract composition that is defined through the dimensions of time and space.'[186] With crucial inputs also from other notable professors (Walter Gropius, Oscar Schlemmer, and Klee) as well as with indirect exposure to Russian constructivism through journals and intermediaries (Tatlin, Rodchenko, El Lissitzky, Malevich, and others) and a good insight into the theatre scene (Tairov, Mayerhold, Eisenstein), Černigoj came away from his short stay at the Bauhaus sufficiently equipped to fashion his own brand of constructivism. He did this in two stages, first in Ljubljana (1924–5) and then in Trieste (1925–9).

For all his good intentions to broaden the understanding of art in the Slovenian capital, Ljubljana turned out to be a huge disappointment. His first constructivist exhibition of 1924, showcasing items as diverse as three-dimensional reliefs, architectural models, sculptures, parts of a machine, a motorcycle, an American worker's overalls and accompanied by slogans such as 'Artist must become an engineer, an engineer artist', or 'Capital is theft'—all intended to subvert the 'bourgeois' hedonistic conception of art and good taste—met largely with derision and complete lack of understanding. When in 1925 he decided to drop the provocative approach for a more academic one, and staged another exhibition in which constructivism was contextualized historically as a logical break with impressionism and expressionism, he again met with an outright rejection from his critics, and began to realize he was fighting a losing battle. The nineteenth-century conceptions of art were so entrenched and closely guarded that any deviation from the norm was automatically deemed suspect, in Černigoj's case to the point of being considered a dangerous

---

[185] See Černigoj, memoir, cited in Krečič (1982), pp. 215–18.
[186] See Černigoj, memoir, cited in Krečič (1982), p. 43.

veneer for communism and revolution. On the pretext of possessing a communist paper, Černigoj was reported to the police and obliged to leave Ljubljana within twenty-four hours. He moved back to Trieste, gathered a movement and realized his ambition of creating a constructivist environment based on his experience at the Bauhaus.

It was in Munich that Černigoj met Karmela Kosovel, Srečko's sister, who was then studying music at the *Akademie der Tonkust* under the professorship of the pianist, composer, and teacher Joseph Pembauer,[187] a celebrated artist whose portrait was drawn by Gustav Klimt in 1890. The friendship and romance that developed between Černigoj and Karmela soon drew Srečko into the circle, in which ideas linking visual arts, poetry, and music were fruitfully exchanged.[188] Later the two artists met in person in Ljubljana and Černigoj spent a month in Tomaj during the summer of 1924. The one surviving letter of their correspondence gives some idea of the intensity and contents of their exchange. These snatches of writing already anticipate the collage technique that was to vitalize both the artists' modernist experimentations, while they also sound the new parameters of art in which aesthetic novelty and formal innovation were to be married to a spiritualist understanding of art:

> Every emotion, every sensation is a fragment of the whole of life … Every poem emerges out of an entire chaos of parallelisms, images, thoughts; in the same way that every painting should consist of lines and tones, which may all converge in one idea, but where each of them, in their own right, constitutes one plastic object infusing the painting with life … Of course, this requires mastering the elements of expression first, before using them to construct the painting.
>
> Today all art is in a process of movement, dynamism, music. Its only goal is to endure, to show what is eternal in man, to show the soul at ease; it must show a world in which man is yet to become completely free … so each of his gestures becomes an echo of spirituality.…
>
> To create is to show up spirituality in matter … to spiritualize matter.[189]

---

[187] Rojc (2008), p. 292.

[188] Kosovel wanted to organize 'a week of "young people"' in Gorica/Gorizia, where Černigoj would display his paintings, Karmela would play music, and he himself would lecture on 'building New Europe', in a letter to Karmela, 13 June 1923, *CW* 3, p. 498.

[189] Kosovel, letter to Černigoj, 7 January 1924, *CW* 3, pp. 534–5.

The idea that the spirit of the whole energizes the particular gestures of life and that through art we realize the spiritual unity of life and matter, or, put differently, give matter a new meaning, are very much Tagorean notions, so it comes as no surprise to see that Černigoj, Karmela, and Kosovel were all drawn to Tagore's ideas.[190] In one of the letters Karmela sent her brother in March 1923 from Munich, she states how together with Černigoj and another Slovenian painter, they were 'studying' Tagore's *Sadhana* in the German translation (*Der Weg zur Vollendung*). 'When I get to the end of the part I am reading,' she writes, 'I'll tell you what I think. We would love to have you here with us. I keep talking about you, all of you, so everyone wants to meet you.'[191] In a letter to her sister Anica, written in the same month, the commitment of this knowledge-thirsty, post-war generation becomes clearer still:

> We work a lot, study, take stock of our achievements on a daily basis, and feel satisfied when we are exhausted from work. It is very sweet to rest on the back of knowing that the day has not been unproductive. We encourage each other to work, 'chatting' in the evening in the student's canteen where we go and have dinner, in the evening we then also drink tea and read: Cankar, Župančič, and we have now started on Tagore as well...[192]

Certainly, Tagore's philosophy found fertile ground in the open and seeking minds of these young artists. It would be interesting to pursue the connection also with regard to Černigoj's work (a connection that has had no mention so far) and his development as a constructivist artist. Given that Kosovel and it seems also Černigoj, who were to become the foremost avant-garde artists in their respective fields and

---

[190] For more on Tagore's thinking on art and aesthetics, see the edited selection of his lectures, essays, and letters on the topic in Tagore (2005b); for a critical appreciation of Tagore's philosophy of art and creativity, see Agarwala (1996) and Nandi (1999).

[191] Karmela Kosovel, in a letter to Srečko Kosovel, 19 March 1923, in Kosovel (2008a), p. 105.

[192] Karmela Kosovel, in a letter to Anica Kosovel, March 1923 (precise date unstated), excerpt from letter cited in the afterword to Kosovel (2008a), p. 292. Unfortunately, the cited excerpt ends at this point.

generation,[193] felt so strong an affinity with Tagore's ideas, and that Tagore himself was drawn to the Bauhaus and vice versa, one can at the very least be confident that in terms of resistance to institutionalized art, capitalism, and the ideology of instrumental reason, as well as in terms of a search for spiritual truth, there was a convergence between Tagore's outlook and the European avant-gardes.[194]

The subject would no doubt require a broader study than anything I could have anticipated in these pages. Nonetheless, Tagore's visible impact on Kosovel's art and thinking that has emerged from this study is intended as a contribution towards the larger project of decentring modernism, so as to appreciate more the enriching role of 'the peripheries' as well as adequately acknowledge the 'cosmopolitan' character of the avant-gardes.[195]

There is, of course, no straightforward link between the European avant-gardes and the Indian poet, for not all modernist or avant-garde artists were sympathetically drawn towards Tagore or felt they could learn something from him. Yeats and Pound lost their interest precisely because Tagore was not seen to be modernist enough and too much into God. Whereas closer to Kosovel's own cultural milieu, the Belgrade avant-garde circle spearheaded by the controversial figure

[193] Černigoj's recognition as an avant-garde painter came even later than Kosovel's. In 1978, after much painstaking research to try and trace and reconstruct lost artefacts, a retrospective exhibition of the constructivist era with Černigoj at its centre was staged in Idrija (Slovenia).

[194] By the time Černigoj came to the Weimar Bauhaus and became a pupil of Moholy-Nagy, the atmosphere had changed radically from the days of Itten. 'All the metaphysics, meditation, breathing exercises, intuition, emotional apprehension of forms and colours, were blown out of the window' and supplanted by the form-follows-function doctrine; see Whitford (1984), p. 128. Černigoj steered between the ideological rift between Moholy, whose attitude to the machine bordered on fetishization, and the 'transcendentalist' Kandinsky, who 'wanted nothing to do with it'. Although he veered towards Moholy, who 'topped', as he put it, 'all his other experiences', he nonetheless held that in 'combining materials into constructions, into things never seen before ... [w]hat [they] were doing was not meant to serve anything, except the spirit' (Černigoj, in Krečič 1982, translation mine, p. 217).

[195] On this, see Mitter (2007), p. 13.

of Ljubomir Micić (1895–1971), the founder of Zenitism, forcefully objected to the Indian poet when he came to Yugoslavia in November 1926 on the grounds that he was a fake portender of a new civilization. Let me briefly describe the incident.

For the most part, Tagore's two-day visit in Belgrade was a success, but not everyone was impressed with the poet speaking against the crude materialism and greed of the Western civilization and the stiff entry-fees charged for his lectures. The group around Micić made their sentiments known on the first of Tagore's lectures at the University of Belgrade on 15 November. No sooner did Tagore appear on the stage to the jubilation of a packed hall—with the tickets being sold out, many people thronged the steps leading up to the entrance, just to catch a glimpse of the Indian poet—than was his presence denigrated by shouts of 'Down with Tagore! Long live Gandhi!' and pamphlets were sent flying into the air, carrying an address to the 'Gentle father of Bengal and false prophet' in the Serbian original and English translation. Signed by poets Ljubomir Micić and Branko ve Poljanski, the address protested against Tagore's perceived pro-Western and bourgeois stance in India's independence struggle, as opposed to the grassroots Gandhian approach. The dichotomous view probably owed something to Rolland's book on Mahatma Gandhi.[196] Couched in a discourse of conceit and self-pity, the open letter was vitriolic:

> Your verses are lemonade, your philosophy dung, your mysticism, like all mysticism is—mystification.... We speak truth and only in the name of truth declare ourselves publicly against you today ... the best sons of this country of the Balkans are strangers in their own land ... bow down to your great contemporary Mahatma Gandhi.[197]

That Tagore was seen as a fake trader of 'empty phrases' in the eyes of these self-proclaimed 'barbarians' whose allusions to 'the race vigour

[196] The book was mentioned in the journal *Zenit*. Cf. Rolland (2002), pp. 100–27.

[197] Micić and ve Poljanski (1926), pp. 17–20. The open letter is available online at http://digital.nb.rs/scr/browse.php?collection=no-zenit. It is ironic that Tagore should be seen as Gandhi's opponent, when in an interview published on his visit in the newspaper Vreme, when asked what lessons one could take from contemporary India, Tagore's answer was: 'India today sends forth a new light to the world, and that is Gandhi', in Vinaver (1926).

of the Balkans' could barely mask inverted racism—as rightly pointed out by Petrović[198]—had something to do with the unfortunate circumstances of Tagore's 1926 European tour. The Mussolini affair was still fresh in people's minds and was reported again in the media on the eve of Tagore's arrival.[199] The fact that some of his tour was orchestrated by dictatorial regimes made his political leanings suspect, and the commerciality surrounding his visit with high entry fees jarred with the content of his addresses. Finally, his foreign addresses were not always above 'a train of commonplaces that could have been subscribed to by anybody even in those early times of double talk and double think.'[200] One newspaper condemned the outburst as a 'scandal', and the disruption was apparently swiftly brought under control, so that Tagore, visibly disturbed, was able to begin his lecture.[201]

Kosovel's life was cut short five months before Tagore came to Yugoslavia, so he never had the chance to participate in the Tagoreana.[202] His response, I would like to think, would have belonged to those whom Aronson refers to as 'the lonely and the outcast' who could and indeed 'did adequately respond to what, as far as the mass-media were concerned, was merely one sensation out of many'.[203] The mass outfit of Tagore's foreign lectures and addresses apart, his appeal was, to be sure, intended for the individual.

Thinking back to Kosovel, Černigoj, and Tagore, however, and their achievements with respect to their personal modernisms, we can conclude that all of them significantly widened the creative borders of their respective regions, as they adopted and adapted a host of artistic and intellectual currents without necessarily negating

---

[198] Petrović (1970), p. 15.

[199] See Ilijić (1926).

[200] Petrović (1970), p. 15.

[201] Pejčić (1988), p. 67. How, more precisely, this incident affected Tagore, I have not been able to establish. The one letter existing in the Tagore archives at Rabindra Bhavana in Santiniketan that was sent from Belgrade makes no mention of the incident, and Prasanta Kumar Pal in his biography of Tagore, which covers the year 1926 makes no mention of the incident, or of Tagore's trip to Yugoslavia.

[202] For further detail on Tagore's overall reception in the former Yugoslavia, see Jelnikar (2014a).

[203] Aronson (1978 [1943]), p. xv.

local and regional traits. They all faced resistance from their wider communities, which, to a lesser or greater extent, for a period of shorter or longer duration and for various reasons, perceived unacceptable discontinuities between their 'individual offerings',[204] to borrow the term from Williams, and received traditions. Černigoj was disqualified completely and forced into political exile; Kosovel, no doubt learning from Černigoj's example as well as from the case of Podbevšek, the avant-garde poet of the older generation,[205] kept his Kons poems in the drawer, away from prying eyes, where they were effectively to remain for the next forty years; and Tagore, who in his paintings had least pretensions to be 'recognisably "Indian"' could foresee the antipathy towards his new medium in India, before he put them on display in 1931, a year after he did so in Europe.[206] These innovators were well aware that they were pushing the limits of acceptable expression, but they also knew that without addressing—and transgressing—a system of formal rules there cannot be any creative act of self-perfection. Without destruction, there can be no construction.

Temperamentally, they were of course all artists of a different order. It is hard to imagine that Tagore's 'theory of modernism', which he posited to be 'a theory of the impersonal' in the sense of 'a simple acceptance of the real with a quiet, dispassionate heart',[207] could have very much in common with Černigoj's overtly confrontational, even agitational, stance. Possibly Kosovel was closer to Tagore in this. For all his endorsement of constructivism as he came to understand it, or his initial sympathies towards Zenitism, he invariably refused to identify wholesale with any of the artistic programmes of the post–Russian Revolution upheaval. He warned against the coercive nature

---

[204] Williams (1961), p. 49.

[205] Anton Podbevšek (1898–1981) was Kosovel's forerunner, the central and most radical figure of the first wave of the historical avant-garde in Slovenia, whose collection *Človek z bombami* (Man with bombs, 1925) met with such devastating critique that Podbevešek effectively gave up writing. For more on the poet, see Šalamun-Biedrzycka (1972).

[206] Robinson (1989), p. 53.

[207] Translated by Swapan Chakravorty, Tagore (2001h [1932]), p. 282.

of ideologies per se and their tendency to enslave people's minds: like Tagore, he was after 'sound reasoning' from people, not 'blind faith'.[208] At the same time, he shared Tagore's 'fear of abstraction, that destructive force', to state once again, 'which has no relation to human truth, and therefore can be easily brutal and mechanical'. Without denying the importance of technology in improving people's everyday lives, and with genuine respect for science, Kosovel, like Tagore, could not fully accept 'the teleological certainty of modernity'.[209] Both poets' attitudes towards the urban civilization were ambivalent, to say the least. This rather quirky note Kosovel jotted on the pages of his journal once again suggests the important place Tagore occupied in Kosovel's artistic universe:

> Tagore is someone who has shown an escape route from the cities of Europe across the grey rooftops [a recurring metaphor Kosovel deploys to denote a civilization in decline], a path for the soul to eternity.[210]

With respect to Kosovel's avant-gardism, critics have unanimously noted his peculiar synthesis of poetic formalism with (romantic) emotionalism, rooted in ethical humanism.[211] What I have tried to demonstrate in this chapter is the pivotal role Tagore played with respect to this tension that has kept many of Kosovel's poems alive

---

[208] Kosovel, letter to Grahor, 15 August 1925, in Kosovel (2006), p. 227.

[209] Mitter (2007), p. 12. For Kosovel's characteristic views on the importance of technology for improving people's lives, see a short entry in his journal on bridges, electricity, and automobiles ('Journal X', 1925, *CW* 3, pp. 705–6), and for further discussion on the topic and the contrast between technology and nature, see also Vrečko (2005), pp. 177–8.

[210] Kosovel, 'Journal VII', 1925, *CW* 3, p. 657.

[211] For example, Poniž writes: 'Futurism and Dadaism taught the coldest, most sober and insensitive view of the poetic process, glorifying and focusing on the very means, process, and method of assembly. Instead, constructivism as Srečko Kosovel developed it was put on a different, human ethical basis,' cited in Djurić (2003), p. 79. Or: 'I remain persuaded that the more profoundly Modernist and most valuable significance of Kosovel's constructivism lies in his humanist, pacifist and ethically Socialist conviction: a social revolution must remain constructive rather than destructive' (Pizzi 2005, pp. 245–6).

to the present day. It is intriguing to think that in the following lines there may in fact be something of a Tagorean spirit:

> Dung is gold
> and gold is dung.
> Both = 0.
> $0 = \infty$
> $\infty = 0$
> A B<
> 1, 2, 3.
> Whoever has no soul
> doesn't need gold.
> Whoever has a soul
> doesn't need dung.
> EE—AW.[212]

If, however, 'Kons. 5' only tenuously embodies the connection between Kosovel's and Tagore's ideational worlds, the following poem draws it out explicitly, as it builds the allusion to Tagore's writings into the very logic of the avant-garde text—formally and thematically—in what can only be a symptomatic place.

The Spherical Mirror

> Is it the mirror's fault
> you've got a hooked nose?
> Glory be to Heine!
> Look into the spherical mirror
> to recognize yourself.
> Nationalism is a lie.
> Chestnuts rustle beside the water,
> autumn has come to the secondhand dealers.
> The shops are full of antiques.
> *Cin, cin.*
> Give up on yourself.

THE GOLDEN BOAT

WHY DID YOU LET

INTO THE MARSHES?

---

[212] 'Kons. 5', translated by Bert Pribac and David Brooks, Kosovel (2008b), p. 76. 'EE–AW' refers to the sound for ass's braying. Within the context of this poem, this appears to be a defiant gesture that flies in the face of established poetic convention.

A red chrysanthemum.[213]
An autumn tomb …
a white tomb.
Ivan Cankar.

This text (see also Figure 6.1, p. 250) is another of Kosovel's poems that enacts an uneasy transition between the old and the new worlds. The old is captured in allusions to autumn and shops overflowing with antiquities; it is ironized in references to the German romantic poet Heinrich Heine (1797–1856) and more so in the Romantic image of the rustling chestnuts. But as always with Kosovel, the irony is gently subverted as the old is expected to reincarnate itself in a novel form, and we can never be quite sure of the extent of his irony. The red chrysanthemum must become white (the transition signalled by three dots), as Romanticism must come to terms with modernity. The reference to Ivan Cankar (1876–1918), himself a borderline figure in this transition, is apt indeed, as is the poet's embedded reference to Tagore—the reference to the golden boat—in the pictorial image of the spherical or concave mirror. Significantly, the mirror is also the letter 'K' reversed—another marker of self-identification with the Indian poet and his vision of liberation. But if 'K' is a reference to Kosovel himself, it is also an expression of his faith in the validity of individual conscience: 'Look into the spherical mirror to recognize [literally 'know'] yourself'. And as Kosovel struggled to reinvent himself artistically, he created his 'K'ons poems. To have the allusion to Tagore lodged in the very symbol of the transition from the 'traditional' to the avant-garde is to indicate, in no uncertain terms, that the Indian poet and what he stood for was at the fulcrum of Kosovel's poetic evolution.

The line, 'Nationalism is a lie', rings true with all the conviction of Tagore's statement, 'nationalism is a menace', and requires no further comment. But 'letting the Golden Boat into the marshes' is a more ambiguous statement. Most concretely, the image could simply be

[213] One of Ivan Cankar's works is entitled *Bela krizantema* (The white chrysanthemum), where the flower is a symbolic representation of modern art. Red chrysanthemums on the other hand are flowers associated with death in Slovenia, for they are commonly brought to graveyards on All Saints' Day (1 November).

a reference to Kosovel's first collection of poems *Zlati čoln*, and his coming to regret his decision to publish it, as it became clear that the publisher lacked funding. At the same time his elder brother's patronizing response to the manuscript from a position of an established poet would also have aggravated Kosovel's already strong sense that the Slovenian literary and cultural scene was unbearably stifling, that is to say marshy or swampy. So, the rhetorical question could be a statement of self-reprobation: 'Why did you let *your* Golden Boat into the marshes?'

On the other hand, if the question is considered in the light of Kosovel's wider social and literary preoccupations outlined in this chapter, the image can be read as a potent symbol of the project of liberation that Kosovel shared with Tagore and struggled against the odds to realize through his emancipated and ideal-bound avant-garde poetics:

> Only the artist who has stepped out of the *marshes* of contemporary society and entered a new society, a society he felt within himself, only such an artist is the new priest of truth, justice, humanity and goodness.[214]

The desperate summoning forth of 'a new mode of human being'[215] that Kosovel envisaged went hand in hand not only with the figure of the new artist but with the evocation of a new age, the parameters of which were set as follows: 'An age that has no constant models is a progressive, dynamic age; it moves in the name of a spirited, unacknowledged creative ideal.'[216] Is not this, in the final analysis, a possible meaning of the 'Golden Boat' for both Kosovel *and* Tagore?

Cultural 'Politics'

As early as 1923, Kosovel wrote to Karmela in Munich: 'I intend to go to Paris. Don't laugh at my daring modesty. I set my goals high so I can rise high.'[217] It is of course impossible to know whether

---

[214] Kosovel, 'Journal VII', 1925, emphasis mine, *CW* 3, p. 650.

[215] Brooks (2008), p. 9.

[216] Kosovel, 'Journal XVI', December 1925, *CW* 3, p. 763.

[217] Kosovel, letter to Karmela, 14 May 1923, *CW* 3, p. 494.

Kosovel would have made it to the city of Dada and surrealism after he completed his studies. As things turned out, he did not even make it to Munich. Confined to Ljubljana for most of his short adult life, he often dreamt of escape and when escape proved difficult, tried to realize some of his dreams in his adopted city. In the same letter, he wrote:

> I dream so expansively that nothing can come in the way, not even Ljubljana with its philistine walls. I love her like a child loves its crib; I love her because she is but the only centre of our, Slovenian, spirituality.[218]

In fact, Kosovel became feverishly active in trying to set up an alternative cultural space, one in which 'Slovenian spirituality' would not be an enclosed system but sensitive and responsive to the wider world. His clarion call was high-sounding indeed:

> We need to raise our country to the heights of the countries of the world, to the breadth of human rights, to the depths of ethical problems. That for us is the cultural mission of Slovenianness.[219]

Driven by this mission, Kosovel came to participate fully in the intellectual life of the city. Even while in school he became involved in various extracurricular activities that led to the founding of his own journal *Lepa Vida* (The fair Vida),[220] and as a student of Romance and Slavic languages and literatures at the newly established University of Ljubljana (auditing also lectures in philosophy, pedagogy, and

---

[218] Kosovel, letter to Karmela, 14 May 1923, *CW* 3, p. 491.

[219] Kosovel, 'Napake slovenstva', *CW* 3, p. 60.

[220] Before Kosovel started his own journal in 1922, he had already worked with *Jadran* (Adriatic), *Preporod* (Revival), and *Mlado Jutro* (Young morning). The name of the journal *Lepa Vida* alludes to the popular folk story, in which a young, beautiful woman, Vida, desiring a new life, leaves her husband and child and sets out for the wider world, only to find herself regretting her decision, lured as she was by false promises of happiness. Originally a folk ballad, the motif of beautiful Vida became a potent symbol of unfulfilled yearning, treated by every subsequent generation of writers and linked to frustrated national aspirations, most famously by France Prešeren and Ivan Cankar. Kosovel brought out six issues of the journal, before financial difficulties suspended its publication.

history of art), he became active as a writer, editor, founder of journals and 'clubs', as well as a public speaker. As with Tagore, there was a strong public side to Kosovel's personality. His friend Ivo Grahor wrote of him as a charismatic figure:

> Srečko's typical traits were great loyalty in friendship and seriousness. I always had a feeling that he was mulling over something and that whatever his goal was he would pursue it from all possible sides. Being around him, I finally realized that the reason why Srečko liked to disregard all differences between people was because he wanted to reach the human core in every person; the core was what mattered to him, the rest was disposable. That is how he made friends. His power over people—if that is even the right word—was true and natural. He would never take more than was his due, not even later at the university when he effectively became the leader of an artistic circle.[221]

Like Tagore, Kosovel wanted to extend his vision as a poet into the practical sphere of life through work and education. He argued that everyone is entitled to education so that they know their inalienable human rights.[222] His activities in Ljubljana were clearly meant as a gesture in that direction. After the failed attempt to set up a forum called 'Klub mladih' (Club of the young), the aim of which was to unite the younger generation across the divides of class, religion, and political conviction, he did manage in the autumn of 1925, with the help of his friend Ciril Debevec, who had just returned from theatre studies in Prague, to launch the Literarni in dramski klub IC (Literature and theatre club IC). For a short time, the activities of this group became a recognizable force in the cultural life of Ljubljana. Here, Kosovel's aspirations as regards cosmopolitan education were finally given a platform upon which he could exercise his idea(l)s. His leadership qualities, too, came to the fore, as he relentlessly urged his circle to work and commit to bring about a 'new cultural movement'.[223] It was at this time that some of

---

[221] Grahor (2004 [1931]), pp. 320–1.

[222] Kosovel, 'Umetnost in proletarec', CW 3, p. 26.

[223] Kosovel, letters to Debevec between 9 August 1925 and 10 September 1925, CW 3, pp. 568–5.

his essayistic writings addressing issues of art, politics, nationalism, and education were published in *Mladina* (Youth), a journal he took over from the Independent Farmer's Party in autumn 1925 and was able to take in his own direction.[224]

An ambitious ten-year programme of lectures, discussions, readings, and artistic performances shows him designating tasks to himself and his circle of colleagues across a wide range of fields and interests. The idea was that everyone would work together towards a common goal, but without impinging on each other's individuality. An important segment of the programme is therefore accorded to self-education. This required members to research trends in contemporary art and literature in Slovenia and abroad, evaluating them in the light of contemporary philosophical, social, and political thought, as well as from the perspective of the contribution of 'great personalities', both past and present. Tagore, needless to say, was one such 'great personality'.[225]

As mentioned already, Kosovel felt strongly that education and culture should not be class-bound, but be there for all people to benefit from. Following this persuasion, the club not only organized a series of public lectures with readings in Ljubljana, but took their message to the miners and workers of Zagorje. He envisaged such public events

---

[224] These important essays, from which I have been citing in this chapter, 'Umetnost in proletarec' (Art and the proletariat), 'Razpad družbe in propad umetnosti' (Disintegration of society and demise of art), 'Kaj je kulturno gibanje?' (What is a cultural movement?), 'Manifest svobodnim duhovom' (A manifesto for free spirits'; based on Rolland's *Declaration*), 'Kriza človečanstva' (Crisis in humanity) came out in separate issues of *Mladina* between 1925 and 1926.

[225] Ciril Debevec was assigned to lecture on 'Drama in the light of Slovenian identity from the perspective of contemporary, modern conceptualisation of nationhood (Tagore)'. Kosovel himself, as already mentioned, was to present a paper entitled 'Tagore and Gandhi: two solutions to the question of nationhood'. Another member was assigned to research and give a seminar on the following topics, stated in this order: futurism, modern German artists, Tagore, and, finally Anton Podbevšek ('the Man with bombs'). The fact that Tagore 'sandwiched' thus between supremely avant-garde topics only underlines the centrality of his ideas to Kosovel's modernist 'turn'. Tagore is noted on the programme once more, alongside a lecture on Heine and young Germany, as well as on Serbian Modern Art ('Notes XIV', *CW* 3, pp. 746–9).

316 / Universalist Hopes in India and Europe

to be part of a larger ongoing programme across Slovenia, connecting town and country. The authorities, however, suspicious of the poet's political leanings, intervened and cancelled his second reading in Ljubljana. By then, the poem 'Ecstasy of Death', which he had read at Zagorje in February, had already sounded a chilling foreboding of his own untimely death. The reading had animated a heated debate that led Srečko to miss the last train home. He had to spend the night on a freezing platform, and caught a severe chill. Following further complications, Srečko Kosovel died on 27 May 1926, not even twenty-three years of age.

7 Towards the Symbol of a Missing Fullness

'Human hearts are small and cages are big.'

—Kosovel, 'Kons XY'

When in 2008, two poetry collections came out in English translation with the same title, *The Golden Boat*, this was, of course, entirely coincidental. And yet, in what can only be described as a timely stroke of serendipity, Srečko Kosovel and Rabindranath Tagore were brought out as relevant poetic voices of our time. What is it that connected them in their day and why might they still be relevant? This was essentially the question that guided the comparative study of this rather asymmetrical 'encounter' that in many ways asks us to lay aside preconceptions about what can or cannot be compared. For to compare an almost completely unknown poet, who had a very short life, almost no publications to his name, and barely any public standing, to one of India's most well-established and renowned poets and thinkers, whose remarkable life spanned a much longer period, is to compare a mountain to a mole hill. And if we add to that the substantially different cultural contexts, we are indeed comparing two rather dissimilar sets. And yet, the many and obvious differences apart, what emerges from this study is a concordance in these two poets' concerns and stances, at the core of which lies a dynamic, creative ideal of universalism rather than the omnipresent nationalism, which they saw—and experienced—as hegemonic and exclusivist, and therefore rejected.

At the same time, both were 'true' universalists in the sense of feeling empathy with the less fortunate, shouldering the pain of others and standing up for their rights when they could. From the perspective of the heart, if you wish, the question of stature and standing is extraneous and expendable. When many years ago—in fact, at the time of writing my MA thesis on Tagore and Yeats—I went for a walk one morning in the surrounding hills of Ljubljana to clear my head, as it were, I chanced upon a signpost, which halted my step (see Figure 7.1): *Travnata bilka je vredna velikega sveta, na katerem raste.* In Tagore's own English translation it would read: 'The grass blade is worthy of the great world where it grows.'

I knew then that I was on the right path. Now, of course, I can discern that this Whitmanesque aphorism is a universalist statement par excellence, but then I remember wondering about the intentions of whoever had put it there. Was it meant to alert the passers-by to the beauty of 'the great world' above Polhov Gradec? Or was it there

Figure 7.1 Tagore's name is written in the bottom-right corner. Photograph taken by the author.

to raise awareness about the natural environment, urging us to respect, not destroy what may be small and seemingly insignificant? Was it an expression of small-minded patriotism or an invitation to rise above it?

Tagore's thinking clearly had a place in all this. The question I eventually wanted to explore was, more precisely, the place of the Indian champion of world humanity in the searching heart and mind of young Kosovel. Of course, the unified *Weltanschauung* I have discerned between the two writers' meaningful search for a universalist idiom is substantially underpinned by Kosovel's reading and taking inspiration from Tagore's works. At the same time, however, it also had a deeper—structural—logic to it. It stemmed from similar political and cultural dynamics affecting their respective 'peripheries' vis-à-vis imperialist Western powers. The fact that Kosovel was inspired by Tagore's writings was already a consequence, rather than a precondition, of what I have dubbed 'situational identification'.

For indeed, in the post–Great War, anxiety-ridden but hopeful Europe, Kosovel's response to Tagore was grounded primarily in a strong sense of identification with the Indian poet. Tagore became an inspirational model to the young writer who saw his native region affected by Western European imperialist forces he perceived as similar to those that subjugated India. Though arising primarily out of the specific circumstances of the Slovenian Littoral after the Great War, Kosovel's affective situational identification also rode the internationalist moment unleashed by the Russian Revolution, where sympathies for the exploited worker were logically extended to the colonized in Asia and Africa. In one aspect of his identification, therefore, the anti-capitalist/imperialist and anti-colonial struggles converged, so the 'East' became as much the promise of a new world order associated with the October Revolution as it was evocative of the old romantic 'Orient' that would help heal the deep spiritual 'crisis' of the post-War European generation.

To go beyond the superficial response of 'here is yet another writer attracted to the exotic allure of an Eastern sage', it has been crucial to situate Kosovel in this wider historical framework of interwar Europe and the global anti-capitalist and pro-socialist idiom. But even here, we should not miss important nuances or departures from the more general picture. Tagore may have been co-opted as a champion of the 'proletariat' in Kosovel's worldview, but Kosovel himself was no blind admirer of the Soviet experiment. Like Tagore, he was suspicious of any political or ideological system dominating the individual or the collective. Moreover, his understanding and usage of the term 'proletariat' was much looser than any Marxist doctrine would allow for; it was more or less interchangeable with—in Kosovel's parlance—the 'downtrodden' or 'humiliated man', suggesting a more universal human condition stretching across historic eras and continents. And for all his othering of the Indian poet along the predictable romantic and orientalist lines, his reading of Tagore ultimately frustrates the Saidian critique not only in that the power-nexus was conspicuously missing from the equation but also—and more importantly—that Tagore for Kosovel was not essentially a long-lost voice of ancient India needing recovery in a project of romantic redemption, but rather a relevant contemporary.

So what, more precisely, did Kosovel find in Tagore? At the most personal and existential level, the young man, up against real life's privations, found a source of life-affirming outlook in Tagore's poetry and philosophy, quite contrary to the associations commonly held with the Indian poet. He found in his writings a voice of both reason and imagination as well as generosity of spirit, which confronted him with the ultimate questions of what it means to be free as an individual in a society and live life fully. Freedom was not in the ability to hoard and amass, but in the small invisible things in life and the ability to think and feel beyond social compulsions and dictates:

> I would like to walk around
> in a small coat of
> words—

wrote Kosovel on a modest but hopeful note:

> But hidden underneath should be
> a warm, bright world.
> What is wealth?
> What is luxury?
> For me it is this:
> a small coat I have,
> and this coat is like no other.[1]

---

[1] 'A Small Coat', translated by Ana Jelnikar and Barbara Siegel Carlson.

As a poet abiding by the enduring connection between individuality, language, and freedom, he read Tagore when he himself was in the throes of searching for a new mode of expression that would better suit the new age following the devastations of the war. Kosovel indeed felt himself to be living in a tragic age, and he, like D. H. Lawrence, refused to take it tragically. That Kosovel's personal avant-gardism reveals a strong indebtedness to Tagore's own universalist hopes, grounded in both his intellectual and aesthetic concerns, makes perhaps for the most unexpected and interesting conclusion of this study. It is also a conclusion that importantly challenges Eurocentric perceptions of the avant-gardes and Tagore's place in them.

If this presents one side of the 'encounter', which establishes the importance of Tagore's place for Kosovel's artistic and intellectual preoccupations, the other involved asking about correlations, or 'deeper' unities, between the two writers. It has to be acknowledged, of course, that Kosovel's understanding of India's realities was of necessity limited. We know of what he had read of Tagore, we can speculate about what he knew of Gandhi and India's anti-colonial struggle, and furthermore about his knowledge of Buddhism, Vedanta, and other Eastern religions mediated to him through the German Romantic traditions and philosophy. Tagore, on the other hand, knew nothing of Kosovel, or the particular realities of the Slovenes in the aftermath of the Great War. The understanding Tagore had of the wider history and the problems of Central and South-Eastern Europe was, as critics have commented, tainted by political naiveté and lack of information, despite the fact that he travelled through that part of the world. Kosovel died just months before the Mussolini affair flared up again in the newspapers in former Yugoslavia, just prior to Tagore's visits to Zagreb and Belgrade, and one cannot help but wonder how he, himself a victim of Fascism, would have reacted to Tagore's dubious associations with *Il Duce*. Historic ironies apart, we can be sure that Tagore, had he known of Kosovel's attitudes towards nationalism, would have been heartened to find another European on a similar, honest quest for a universalist idiom, emboldened by his own writings. Therefore, what they shared in terms of their attitudes and emotional attachments is not, for the most part, predicated on any factual or accurate knowledge they may have had about each other's realities, but rather on perceptions and reactions formed against a new era of globalising capital and imperialism, as well as a host of political and artistic idioms emerging in the wake of pre- and post-war upheaval and available internationally through the printed medium. A new literary order was in the making and both Tagore *and* Kosovel were—it must be acknowledged—its rightful heirs and contributors. At the same time, as far as Kosovel's reading of Tagore is concerned, it is important not to stop at the limits of postcolonial discursive analysis that would most probably disqualify Kosovel—with one look at his poem 'In Green India'—as another hegemonic instance of Western appropriation of 'the East'. Perhaps we need to think harder about the many ways in which artists respond to the ideas they form of exceptional individuals from contexts that are relatively unknown to them.[2]

With the benefit of hindsight and comparative study—and despite the fact that they were writers of a different order and standing—let us now look at the more 'structural' similarities between them. Both Kosovel and Tagore wrote from a distinct position of geographic and cultural 'in-betweeness'. The very inception of the Bengali middle class arose from extended contact with the British, and Tagore's family stood at the fulcrum of the many ways in which Western influences were being filtered into Indian society. The various liminalities of Kosovel's personal geography have a backdrop in the geopolitical realities of the post-war era, with the break-up of a multi-national Empire and the emergence of a new South-Slavic state. A move to Ljubljana from his native region, the Italianization of Trieste and Primorska, the dispersal of his family members between three nation states all importantly contributed to his short personal history of dislocations that gave Kosovel what is today more fashionably referred to as 'the double vision'—a perspective of both the insider and the outsider. Always and already exposed to diverse cultural models and trends, both poets found narrow reification of identities along national lines unacceptable. While enriching the traditions they inherited, they were not limited by them.

Both were exposed to the ideological constructs of 'East' and 'West' within their respective geographies and regions, and decried the

---

[2] William Radice and Amit Chaudhuri both read the poem in this non-strategic, non-postcolonial way, recognizing elements in it other than those typically associated with postcolonial criticism.

racism and violence inherent in these essentialist projections. These and other divisive ideological categories they tried to overcome by first questioning them and then emphasizing what connected people across divisions as opposed to what separated them. They both appealed powerfully to common human ground, whether between Muslims and Hindus, Indians and the British, or Italians and Slovenes.

Even as Tagore himself would sometimes construct his arguments in large and problematic notions of 'East' and 'West', and Kosovel endorsed a dualistic view of the world between the suppressors and the suppressed, or 'us' and 'them', neither permitted themselves the luxury of thinking that the solution to the 'world problem' lay in a simple reversal of these dichotomies and the power structures they entailed. Kosovel's poem 'Ecstasy of Death' reveals a mind painfully aware that the fault lines between the *self* and the *other* run deep in the strata of every culture, society, and ultimately the individual, shifting the emphasis from class struggle to the humanist ideal of self-cultivation and self-overcoming. Tagore likewise telescoped the 'self–other' logic of the colonial encounter into an opportunity for a 'self–self' encounter, replacing the clash-of-civilizations concept by evocations of harmony created through a society's growing in critical introspection. In line with his notion of the individual enmeshed in multiple relationships and his understanding of freedom as interdependence, this for him meant forging cooperative ties with societies elsewhere and working towards a non-violent solution. There was almost a certain stubbornness in both their beliefs that gaps between human beings can be bridged and that harmony in social matters is within reach.

The hybridity of their backgrounds was therefore the pool from which they tapped their ideologies of resistance and envisioned a new world. This signals an important shift in perspective, where resistance emerges in the space in-between cultures, which in themselves are never unitary or dualistic in the relation self–other or outside–inside. This could be seen as a version of Homi Bhabha's 'Third Space', a space that cannot be reduced to any one side of the above dichotomies.[3] It could also be seen as 'the internationalist moment' of the interwar years in which both Tagore and Kosovel from their respective 'margins'

[3] Bhabha (1994), p. 36.

participated, and which created solidarities on the basis of wider and more universal principles.[4]

Both Tagore and Kosovel thought *antithetically*, or, indeed, as *universalists*, continuously opposing the dominant oppositions generated within their cultures rather than simply one side of the opposition. Their criticism of inherited traditions made them suspect in the eyes of the countrymen who saw in this a betrayal of national consciousness. Their 'national' consciousness—if we insist on the word 'national'—was engaged rather in a double dynamics of critical introspection of the self (and of the past) while consciously reaching out to the 'other' (and the future) in an ongoing process of self-correction and fulfilment. Openness and inclusiveness were its trademarks.[5]

Of course, they were both merely human, and were not always immune to idealizations of, or bias towards, the home-grown. Kosovel could certainly romanticize his native region, which he had to leave as a young boy, and Tagore, for a period, succumbed to Hindu revivalism only to then emerge—perhaps also by way of self-atonement—as its severe critic. Tagore's example is furthermore interesting in that his commitment to India's freedom brought him, at one point, into the vanguard of anti-colonial nationalist politics, but no sooner had he seen the violent aspects of the Swadeshi movement (1905–8) than he withdrew from active politics. At that moment we see him becoming adamant that attention needed to be shifted from collective and national rights to individual rights and from political to social problems. His lasting contribution to the critique of anti-colonial nationalism was in recognizing the futility and hypocrisy of instituting boundaries between 'the colonizer' and 'the colonized' in a hierarchical society that was itself dependent on exploitative practices of those it deemed inferior. In Tagore's analysis, nationalism was also an inadequate answer in a world not only unified by modern science and technology, but also whose future depended on recognizing and coordinating the great many ways of being within and across societies.

In line with some of the most imaginative anti-colonial or anti-imperialist responses across the world, Tagore's and Kosovel's

---

[4] Zachariah (2011), p. 57.

[5] But the question we need to ask ourselves here is indeed whether nationalism can be inclusive and still remain nationalism; see Zachariah (2011).

liberational stances commanded a pull away from separatist nationalism towards a more integrative view of human community. An individual must undergo a transformation of social consciousness to be able to transcend national consciousness (Fanon) and embrace a more generous pluralistic vision of the world (Ngũgĩ). What they sought was much more than the simple departure of the colonizers: they sought a complex transformation of the colonized, lest alien hegemony merely be replaced by a home-grown one.[6]

Were Kosovel and Tagore then nationalists? Unapologetically, let me say no, they were not, with full awareness how difficult a case this is to argue, then as well as now. Nationalism's legitimizing force in liberation struggles across the globe in the twentieth century, and its naturalization thereafter in its residual form, makes it a resilient category to contend. 'Those who argue that nation-state may be undesirable or waning are seen as not just wrong, but wrongheaded, or worse,' wrote Arjun Appadurai in 2013 in an intensely personal reflection on the irrational sentiments that nations inspire in people.[7] No one is prepared to kill in the name of a global association of mathematicians, but people run at each other's throats to defend their 'nations' and 'national interests'.[8] Once the oppressor and oppressed get identified by nationality, an assumed solidarity with one's 'nation' is taken for granted.[9] Today, when having 'the right to a nationality' is enshrined in Article 15 of the Universal Declaration of Human Rights as one of the basic human rights, and when having a nationality, a circumscribed identity, is a prerequisite for securing civil rights, it is indeed hard to imagine an alternative scenario. For the sake of historic accuracy, we should, however, remind ourselves that 'the "national principle" was not universally acknowledged publicly before the First World War, and its implications were not even fully grasped at the end of the Second World War'.[10]

---

[6] For the above references, see the theoretical discussion on universalism in Ch. 1, pp. 29–30, 38–40.

[7] Appadurai (2013), p. 101.

[8] Appadurai (2013), p. 101.

[9] Zachariah (2011), p. xvi.

[10] Zachariah (2011), p. 84.

What unites these two thinkers across their respective 'colonized' margins is precisely that from within a context in which the only way it seemed possible to claim a legitimate status to equality and independence was through aligning oneself with a nation state, Tagore and Kosovel sounded a warning signal against the hegemony of this principle. Put differently, in an age of compulsory nationalisms, they refused to—drawing on Zachariah's provocative title—*play the nation game*. Tagore did so quite literally when he pulled out of the Swadeshi movement in 1905, and Kosovel by repeating time and again that nationalism was a lie. They were not sore losers, intent on spoiling the game, but wanted to subvert an ideology they considered dangerous and misguided.

Tagore also rebutted one of the cornerstones of Western liberal modernity, and rejected the nation-state altogether as an inadequate organizing principle for human societies in general and Indian civilization in particular. Kosovel, on the other hand, drew a distinction between the nation-state and nationhood, struggling to salvage the latter from narrow usurpations. Certainly, Tagore and Kosovel's compelling critiques of nationalism should not be diminished, not least because they are as relevant today for both Europe and India as they were in their own time.

Time and again Tagore stressed the existence of an always already connected world that transcended the geographies generated by both colonialism and nationalism, and Kosovel would re-imagine 'Slovenianness' along self-consciously international lines. They strongly opposed a politics of identity that divides people socially on the basis of nation, religion, caste, ethnicity, race or other, just as in the domain of ideas they pursued a radical stance of cultural entitlement that likewise transgressed frontiers between 'tradition' and 'modernity', blurring the lines between 'home' and the 'world' or what is 'indigenous' and what 'foreign'.

It is therefore not surprising to find that they also had an active social dimension to their lives and work. Tagore was an educator, who set up an alternative education system that was largely conceived to fight parochialism and avoid the pitfalls of nationalism, while Kosovel too became a founder of a literary club, the objective of which was to cultivate individuals to think and feel beyond their local environment. They were both 'committed' poets, but not in the sense in which the word is generally understood. Their commitment was not driven by any one particular ideology—they were too individualist for that. If anything, they created their own 'ideology', the characteristic of which was precisely that it lacked any political means to actualize itself and could only become a utopian dream.

The 'universal' or 'new man' of their utopian projections who would institute a future world of peace and solidarity was no doubt a product of the age they lived in. Still we might ask, is a utopian mentality entirely out of place in the context of our present-day globalized world? As Leela Gandhi has argued: '[A]t this time of world politics, when our solidarities simply cannot be fixed in advance … a utopian mentality shows the way forward to a genuine cosmopolitanism; always open to the risky arrival of those not quite, not yet, covered by the privileges which secure our identity and keep us safe.'[11]

Certainly, the utopian idea(l)s helped Tagore and Kosovel identify their practical goals and directions, grounding their universalisms in the here-and-now of their immediate environments. Their universalist voice has also enriched the important and on going resistance to national chauvinism and imperialism and can by no means be considered irrelevant today. Moreover, Tagore and Kosovel can help us shift the terms of the theoretical debate on universalism away from the typical discussion of nationality and universality or nationalism and universalism, by making us see a closer link between individuality and universality. For they were both champions of individuality, however, not in the sense of an isolated detached individual domineering over his or her environment, but an individual locked into a mutually enriching relationship with his or her surroundings, both natural and social. Neither could accept isolationism as a viable stance, not even as a short-term strategy to fight colonial injustices and humiliation. Closing in on oneself was but a direct route to cultural and spiritual suicide. The importance of lifeblood coming from a wide network of capillaries lay at the heart of each of their cultural 'politics' as well as their own creative work.

Therefore, the universal that Tagore and Kosovel upheld was decidedly open-ended and not something definitive or purportedly already

[11] Gandhi (2007), p. 31.

out there. But if it was not a fixed entity, neither was it a lack, rather a category perpetually in the making. As a horizon concept or an ideal, it was indispensable to those concrete moments of becoming indifferent to difference through acts of love which allow individuals and societies to grow.[12] Tagore and Kosovel saw themselves and their countries as part of the developing whole, so the universal they upheld was the 'new' universal of Ernesto Laclau's exposition: 'the symbol of a missing fullness'[13]—their *Golden Boat*.

In the final instance, this underlay their creativity as poets, as they continued to grow and experiment with new forms, never stopping, knowing full well there was no end to this discovery. Their own distinct versions of 'universality' came about not by writing *back* to the 'centre', but rather by writing *through* the myriad contesting influences that came to bear on their respective lives, and which gave expression to what within their own traditions and beyond were exceptional feats of literary and poetic imagination.

[12] Badiou (2003), p. 110.
[13] Laclau (1992), p. 89.

Appendix

Selection of Kosovel's Poems

All poems, apart from 'Autumn Landscape' have been published in *Look Back, Look Ahead: The Selected poems of Srečko Kosovel* (translated by Ana Jelnikar and Barbara Siegel Carlson, New York: Ugly Duckling Presse, 2010). The poem 'Autumn Landscape' comes from the book *The Golden Boat: Selected Poems of Srečko Kosovel* (translated by Bert Pribac and David Brooks, Cambridge: Salt, 2008), and I thank the translators for their permission to reproduce it here.

Call for Solitude

That I could come to the midnight landscape
of blue darkness spilling across the field,
that I could escape those streets where
everyone screams, shoves, scrambles and crushes –

That I could come to the midnight landscape
in such solitude for my soul to meet God.
Look, I'm hurt from these ways,
from people's ways my heart hurts.

That I could come to the midnight landscape
where only stars burn and lakes breathe,
where only a shadow spills into eyes,
tree shadows kissing my open eyes,
as I, in my heart, in my sick heart
long for His kiss.

A Small Coat

I would like to walk around
in a small coat of
words.

But hidden underneath should be
a warm, bright world.

What is wealth?
What is luxury?
For me it is this:
a small coat I have,
and this coat is like
no other.

Bread

Room 24. In the room five beds, five white beds. In the windows darkness.
Outside a lone lamp shines on the deserted street. For whom? Why?

Perhaps a wayfarer will turn and remember: Where, how?

But why tell you this. Five of us in the room. Five students. A young, dark
Bosnian—his eyes gazing beyond—reading Tagore. Two Slovenians bent over
mechanical drawings on the table, their hair falling across tense, driven faces.

Five lives, and all drawing light from the same lamp bent low over the
table, a lamp with a green shade.

Quiet. Only the scratching of pens and the rustle of paper.

It's eleven o'clock. Eleven for me looking at Hodler's 'Spring', eleven for the
young Bosnian reading Tagore, then looking away as though he were sitting
by the white shores of the Ganges. Eleven for him studying, and eleven for
the two of them drawing.

One thought, one dissonance: Bread.

'I'm hungry.'

All the worlds crushed. Faces crumpled. Straight lines gone crooked and mathematical proofs mere riddles. Tagore hushed, spring stopped.

A new mystery appeared: Bread.

'Bread.'

I turned to the desolate street where the light burned like a thought trembling in the winter cold.

Then I saw a man walking down that desolate street. He put out the light, for it was now past eleven. A keeper and an extinguisher of light. He forgot the pilgrim.

Almost Midnight

Almost midnight.
Flies are dying in a cup.
The fire's extinguished.
Lepa Vida, bitterness
lives in your memory.
Stravinsky in a car.
The roaring sea.
Oh, to be 5 minutes alone.
Heart-Trieste is sick.
That's why Trieste is beautiful.
Pain flowers into beauty.

Black Walls

Black walls crumble
above my soul.
People fall, extinguished
like street lights.
A one-eyed fish
swims in the dark,
black-eyed.

Man emerges
from the heart of darkness.

Negative Total

This life of ours is a path,
cut off, narrow, with little give,
a longing stabbed through the heart,
the sum total—negative.

The Ecstasy of Death

Everything is ecstasy, the ecstasy of death!
Glittering bastions of the West.
White domes—(everything ecstasy!)—
everything sinking into the burning red sea;
intoxicated in the bath of the falling sun,
the European, a thousand times dead.
—Everything is ecstasy, the ecstasy of death.—

Exquisite, so exquisite will be Europe's death:
a luxurious queen in gold,
she will lie in the coffin of dark centuries,
silently she will die like an old queen
closing her golden eyes.
—Everything is ecstasy, the ecstasy of death.—

O, from an evening cloud (the last
messenger still lighting Europe),
blood fills my spent heart.
O, no more water in Europe.
We people drink blood,
blood from the sweet evening clouds.
—Everything is ecstasy, the ecstasy of death.—

Hardly born, already you burn in the evening fire.
All the seas are red, all the seas and lakes
full of blood, there's no water,
no water to wash the guilt away,
for this human to wash his heart,
no water to quench this thirst
for the quiet green nature of morning.

Everything is evening, and there will be
no morning till we die, we who bear
the guilt of dying, until the last of us
dies ...

O, will you, evening sun,
send your blazing rays
into this land, this green
dewy land? This land too?

The sea overflows the green plains,
the scorched blood-sea of evening
and there's no salvation, none
till you and I fall,
till all of us fall,
till we die under the weight of blood.
Then the sun's gleaming rays will shine
on us, European corpses.

I Saw the Pines Grow

I saw the pines grow
into the sky. Peaceful stoics
through the flaming sun.
I could see the fire
that would consume them.

On a white pillow
old man-mountains have laid their heads
and gone quiet.
The pines rustle.
(Who are they talking to?)

I saw the blazing pillars
go on a pilgrimage—into the sky . . .

My body crumpled to ashes.

Pines

Pines, pines in silent horror,
pines, pines in mute horror,
pines, pines, pines, pines!

Pines, pines, dark pines
like sentries of the mountain
swaying over the rocky woods
in heavy, exhausted whispers.

When a sick soul stoops
on a clear mountain night,
I hear the muffled sounds
and can't go back to sleep.

'Pines exhausted in dreams,
are my brothers dying,
is my mother dying,
is my father calling me?'

No answer,
only the swish
of dead dreams,
as though my mother were dying,
as though my father were calling,
as though my brothers were sick.

Destruction

O lies, lies, European lies!
Only destruction can kill you!
Only destruction.
And cathedrals and parliaments:
lies, lies, European lies.
And the League of Nations a lie.
Lies, European lies.

Destroy, destroy!
All of the pharaohs' museums,

all the thrones of art.
Lies, lies, lies.
O Hagia Sofia, o cathedral.
O you cadavers that will save Europe.
O white cadavers
that guard Europe.
O lies, lies, lies.

Destroy, destroy, destroy!
Millions are dying,
but Europe lies.
Destroy. Destroy. Destroy!

Eh, Hey

Eh, hey: it's raining on the gray houses of Ljubljana,
shrouding them in a gray curtain against the sun.
In Trieste they are burning down our Edinost.
Christ has come into the League of Nations.
No, not the good, beautiful Christ
glowing in a halo of love.
A pseudochrist is in Geneva.
What, is it raining in Geneva too?
Christ has come with the brown rebels
and stands there on the gray street
chasing away the scribes and pharisees.
He shoots and kills.
He shoots and kills.
O, you sheepish, white nation—
Now can you see what you really are?

Integrals

Rotating evening.
Trees by green water.
Rotation of spirit.
My spirit is red.

I love my sorrow.
I work from sorrow.
Even more, even more
from innermost feeling.

From innermost feeling
that all is in vain.
Profiteers
dance the cancan.

Simple Words

I love them, the simple words
of our Karst people,
I love them, love them more
than you, bourgeois poets.

As though I can see the bright land
above the silent green valley,
as though I can see all the rocks
and pines watching over the valley.

I love them, their sharp silence,
like a rough hand
that beckons once more
this lost child...

Why Get Upset?

Why get upset?
That the clock's broken?
The sun's setting.
The spirit collects impressions.
I look for moving images.

Facts drive art away.
Have courage, boys, courage!
What you need

you receive in suffering.
With cat music
we chase off nationalism.
An eye looks for itself in the water.
This calms my spirit.

Soft, soothingly
green is your love
like the water's reflection.
H P.

In a golden boat I sail
past shady trees.
I'm like an electric spark
leaping.
Laissez-faire.
Why get upset,
that the sun goes down?
Let the whole world go to hell!
Nationalism's a lie.
The League of Nations a lie.

At times when I feel hopeless,
I think of you, gentle girl.
All my impressions are green.
So soothing green
and sweet is your love
like water's green reflection.
The spirit collects impressions.
Dead observation is lethargy . . .
The active spirit collects images.
Look back, look ahead!
Facts drive art away.
Have courage, boys, courage.

I have the courage of three.
In the golden boat I sail.
Ladle from suffering everything
that I need.

Rhyme

Rhyme's lost its meaning.
Rhyme won't convince.
Can you hear the friction of wheels?
Poem, be the friction of grief.

What to do with empty words, dear sir?
Shut them up in a museum.
Your words need friction
to seize the human heart.

Everything's meaningless now.
The white sea of a spring night
spills across the orchards and fields.
A hint of the future slips by.

Cons XY

An elephant treads through my heart.
Kludsky Circus—entry 5 dinars.
Don't cry anguish from the rooftops . . .
She smiles: ka-ching, ka-ching.

Human hearts are small and cages are big.
I want to walk through people's hearts.
Are you of this or that clique?
A thousand dinars or 7 days in jail.

The flowers in my heart never cry.
Who wants to be young and dejected.
What if a gendarme comes through the door.
It's a war tribunal—you'll go to jail.

Flowers, stay through these heavy days.
Your eyes, officer, glint like a bayonet,
dumb and mean. (Flowers, don't look!)
Gandhi was locked up for six long years.

Kludsky Circus, Seat No. 461

Circus.
Gallery.
Seat No. . . .
Colombine
undresses, undresses.
Everyone watches.
No one sees
how she's hauled up
by her teeth.
Already at the top.
Spicy remarks.
Shameful laughter.
Now she drops the last veil.
They watch her,
devouring her tender body
with their eyes.
They applaud.
She has beautiful thighs.
Undulating breasts.
They applaud
mocking her pain,
shaming her.
You see: the animal
applauds the human.
The human is animal.
The animal is human.
The latch snaps.
The lions rage.

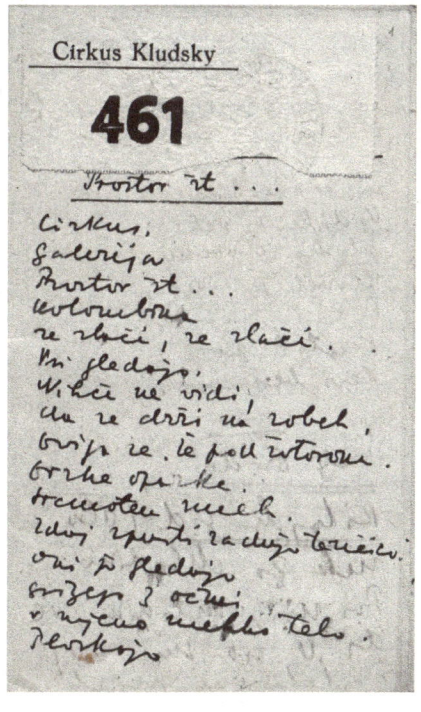

Figure A.1 Scanned original manuscript of Kosovel's poem 'Kludsky Circus, Seat No. 461', reproduced here courtesy of the National University Library (NUK) in Ljubljana.

Autumn Landscape

The sun is autumnally calm
as if it were mourning
behind the slender cypresses
behind the white cemetery wall.
The grass is all red in the sunshine.
Do you wear dogmatic shoes?
A bicycle alone on the autumn road.
You ride through a dying landscape.
A sober person walks over a field,
as cold as autumn
as sad as autumn.
Belief in humankind.
That is a sacred thought to me.
A speechless silence is like sadness.
I am not sad,
because I don't dwell on myself anymore.

> —Translated by Bert Pribac and David Brooks

One Word

I wish I could say one word
just like the spring wind
softly enters your heart.
I wish I could say one word.

But look, I have nothing else,
my heart is an altar cracked in half.
My words are like wounds,
each one of them bleeds.

Dreams don't vault into this dark,
only black walls' rough edges
rise like memories of old times
into the deserted terror of night.

But still there is, there is still
one word—one word at least!
Come, you night-wounded man,
so I can kiss your heart.

It's Not You

It's not you who will tame the world
and sink in silence, one with time.
Scorched with pain, you will long
with a voice cracked raw.

Like the Karst when the wind still hot
kindles the pines, burns through
dark ground—you walk in vain
seeking peace in the dusk.

It's not you who will hold her
when the darkness falls.
You will dream and yearn,
and death will kidnap your dream.

Bibliography

A. PRIMARY SOURCES

I. Rabindranath Tagore:

Collected English Writings and Other Edited Volumes

EW 1   *The English Writings of Rabindranath Tagore: Volume One, Poems,* edited by Sisir Kumar Das. New Delhi: Sahitya Akademi, 1994.

EW 2   *The English Writings of Rabindranath Tagore: Volume Two, Plays, Stories, Essays,* edited by Sisir Kumar Das. New Delhi: Sahitya Akademi, 2001.

EW 3   *The English Writings of Rabindranath Tagore: Volume Three, Miscellany,* edited by Sisir Kumar Das. New Delhi: Sahitya Akademi, 2002 (2nd reprint).

TUM   *Towards Universal Man: Rabindranath Tagore,* edited by Bhabani Bhattacharya (appointed by the Indian Society as the Editor-cum-Chief Translator of the Volume). London: Asia Publishing House, 1961.

SWLL   *Rabindranath Tagore: Selected Writings on Literature and Language,* edited by Sisir Kumar Das and Sukanta Chaudhuri. New Delhi: Oxford University Press, 2001.

Andrews, C. F. (ed.). 2002. *Letters to a Friend: Rabindranath Tagore's Letters to C. F. Andrews.* New Delhi: Rupa & Co.

Das Gupta, Uma (ed.). 2003. *A Difficult Friendship: Letters of Edward Thompson and Rabindranath Tagore 1913–1940.* New Delhi: Oxford University Press.

———. 2006. *Rabindranath Tagore: My Life in My Words.* New Delhi: Penguin Viking.

Dutta, Krishna, and Andrew Robinson (eds). 2005. *Selected Letters of Rabindranath Tagore*. Cambridge: Cambridge University Press.

Lago, M. Mary (ed.). 1972. *Imperfect Encounter: Letters of William Rothenstein and Rabindranath Tagore 1911–1941*. Cambridge: Harvard University Press.

Tagore's Writings

Tagore, Rabindranath. 1961a [1892]. 'The Vicissitudes of Education'. In *TUM*, pp. 39–48.

———. 1961b [1904]. 'Society and State'. In *TUM*, pp. 49–66.

———. 1961c [1908]. 'Presidential Address'. In *TUM*, pp. 101–28.

———. 1961d [1908]. 'East and West'. In *TUM*, pp. 129–40.

———. 1961e [1911]. 'Hindu University'. In *TUM*, pp. 141–57.

———. 1961f [1912]. 'On the Eve of Departure'. In *TUM*, pp. 158–74.

———. 1961g [1917]. 'The Master's Will Be Done'. In *TUM*, pp. 175–201.

———. 1961h [1919]. 'The Centre of Indian Culture'. In *TUM*, pp. 202–30.

———. 1961i [1921]. 'The Unity of Education'. In *TUM*, pp. 231–51.

———. 1961j [1921]. 'The Call of Truth'. In *TUM*, pp. 252–74.

———. 1961k [1926]. 'A Poet's School'. In *TUM*, pp. 285–301.

———. 1961l [1933]. 'The Changing Age'. In *TUM*, pp. 341–52.

———. 1961m [1941]. 'Crisis in Civilization'. In *TUM*, pp. 353–9.

———. 1962. *The Diary of a Westward Voyage*, translated from Bengali by Indu Dutt. London: Asia Publishing House.

———. 1994a. *Selected Poems*, translated from Bengali by William Radice. London: Penguin Books.

———. 1994b. *Selected Short Stories*, translated from Bengali by William Radice. London: Penguin Books.

———. 2000 [1912]. *Song Offerings (Gitanjali)*, translated from Bengali by Joe Winter. London: Anvil Press Poetry.

———. 2001a [1917]. *Nationalism*. In *EW 2*, pp. 417–66.

———. 2001b [1917]. *Personality*. In *EW 2*, pp. 349–403.

———. 2001c [1919]. *The Centre of Indian Culture*. In *EW 2*, pp. 467–91.

———. 2001d. *Particles, Jottings, Sparks: The Collected Brief Poems*, translated from Bengali by William Radice. London: Angel Books.

———. 2001e [1894]. 'Children's Rhyme', translated from Bengali by Sukanta Chaudhuri. In *SWLL*, pp. 101–27.

———. 2001f [1895]. 'Bengali National Literature', translated from Bengali by Swapan Chakravorty. In *SWLL*, pp. 179–93.

———. 2001g [1915]. 'The Poet's Defence', translated from Bengali by Swapan Chakravorty. In *SWLL*, pp. 274–9.

Tagore, Rabindranath. 2001h [1932]. 'Modern Poetry', translated from Bengali by Swapan Chakravorty. In *SWLL*, pp. 280–92.

———. 2001i [1938]. 'The Prose Poem', translated from Bengali by Swapan Chakravorty. In *SWLL*, pp. 331–4.

———. 2001j [1924]. 'Red Oleander (Rakta-karavī)', (translated from Bengali by Ananda Lal). In *Three Plays*, pp. 127–86. New Delhi: Oxford University Press.

———. 2002a [1912]. *A Vision of India's History*. Kolkata: Visva-Bharati.

———. 2002b [1913]. *Sadhana*. New Delhi: Rupa & Co.

———. 2002c [1921. 'Thoughts from Tagore'. In *EW 3*, pp. 29–82.

———. 2002d [1922]. *Creative Unity*. New Delhi: Rupa & Co.

———. 2002e [1925]. *Talks in China; Lectures Delivered in April and May 1924*. New Delhi: Rupa & Co.

———. 2002f [1925]. 'The Indian Ideal of Marriage'. In *EW 3*, pp. 524–37.

———. 2002g [1930]. 'Wealth and Welfare'. In *EW 3*, pp. 623–5.

———. 2002h [1931] *The Religion of Man*. New Delhi: Rupa & Co.

———. 2002i [1932] 'Asia's Response to the Call of the New Age'. In *EW 3*, pp. 658–64.

———. 2002j [1933]. 'Rammohun Roy'. In *EW 3*, pp. 667–9.

———. 2002k [1934]. *Four Chapters*. New Delhi: Rupa & Co.

———. 2002l [1936]. 'H. G. Wells and Tagore'. In *EW 3*, pp. 908–11.

———. 2003a. *Journey to Persia and Iraq: 1932*, translated by Surendranath Tagore (chapters 1 and 3) and Sukhendu Ray (chapters 4–11). Santiniketan: Visva-Bharati

———. 2003b [1917]. *My Reminiscences*, translated by Surendranath Tagore. New Delhi: Rupa & Co.

———. 2004a [1912]. *Gitanjali: Song Offerings*, translated by the author. New Delhi: UBSP.

———. 2004b. *Selected Poems*, edited by Sukanta Chaudhuri. New Delhi: Oxford University Press.

———. 2005a. *Home and the World/Ghare Baire*, translated by Sreejata Guha. New Delhi: Penguin Books.

———. 2005b [1961]. *On Art and Aesthetics: A Selection of Lectures, Essays & Letters*, edited by Prithwish Neogy. Kolkata: Subarnarekha.

———. 2006a. *Of Myself (Ātmaparichay)*, translated by Devadatta Joardar and Joe Winter. Kolkata: Visva-Bharati.

———. 2006b. *Selected Short Stories*, edited by Sukanta Chaudhuri. New Delhi: Oxford University Press.

———. 2008a. *The Golden Boat: Selected Poems*. London: Anvil Press Poetry.

———. 2008b. *Letters from a Sojourner in Europe*, translated by Manjari Chakravarty. Kolkata: Visva-Bharati.

Tagore, Rabindranath. 2009. *Gora*, translated by Radha Chakravarty. New Delhi: Penguin Books.

———. 2010a [2003]. *I Won't Let You Go: Selected Poems*. Expanded edition. Tarset: Bloodaxe Books.

———. 2010b. *Letters from Java: Rabindranath Tagore's Tour of South-East Asia 1927*, translated by Manjari Chakravarty. Kumkum Bhattacharya, Visva-Bharati Publishing Department.

———. 2012. *Gitanjali: Song Offerings*, translated by William Radice. New Delhi: Penguin Books.

Manuscripts

Rabindra Bhavana Archives, Santiniketan:
- Letters to Rabindranath Tagore, 1926.
- Letters from Rabindranath Tagore to others, 1926–9.
- Letters from Persons from Yugoslavia to Rabindranath Tagore between 1929 and 1937.
- Austria File.
- Czechoslovakia File.
- Poland File.
- Romania File.
- Russia File.

Main Tagore Translations into Slovene Published in Kosovel's Time

Rabindranath Tagore. 1917 and 1921. *Rastoči mesec* (*The Crescent Moon*), translated by Alojz Gradnik. Ljubljana: Omladina.

———. 1921. *Ptice selivke* (*Stray Birds*), translated by Alojz Gradnik. Ljubljana: Kleinmazer & Bamberg.

———. 1920. *Povestice* (*Tales*), translated by France Bev. Ljubljana: Jugoslovanska knjigarna.

———. 1922. *Vrtnar* (*The Gardener*), translated by Alojz Gradnik. Ljubljana: Zvezna tiskarna.

———. 1922. *Žetev* (*The Harvest*), translated by Alojz Gradnik. Ljubljana: L. Schwentner.

———. 1924. *Žrtveni spevi* (*Song Offerings*), translated by Alojz Gradnik. Ljubljana: Učiteljska tiskarna.

[For a complete bibliography that includes journal publications and writings about Tagore in Slovene newspapers up until 1978, see Munda (1978)]

II. Srečko Kosovel

Collected Works

CW 1   *Zbrano delo 1 (Collected Works)*. 2nd edn, edited by Anton Ocvirk. Ljubljana: Državna založba Slovenije (DZS), 1964.

CW 2   *Zbrano Delo 2*, edited by Anton Ocvirk. Ljubljana: DZS, 1974.

CW 3   *Zbrano Delo 3*, prvi del (part one), edited by Anton Ocvirk, Ljubljana: DZS, 1977.

CW 3/1 *Zbrano Delo 3/1*, drugi del (part two), edited by Anton Ocvirk, Ljubljana: DZS, 1977.

Other Works

Kosovel, Srečko. 1927. *Pesmi* (Poems), edited by Alfonz Gspan in collaboration with Ciril Debevec and Vinko Košak. Ljubljana: Odbor za izdajo pesmi.

———. 1931. *Izbrane pesmi* (Selected Poems), edited by Anton Ocvirk. Ljubljana: Tiskovna zadruga.

———. 1973 [1954]. *Zlati čoln* (The Golden Boat). Ljubljana, Trst: Državna založba Slovenije, Založništvo tržaškega tiska.

Kosovel, Srečko. 1991. *Pesmi v prozi* (Prose Poems). Maribor: Založba Obzorja.

———. 1998. *Integrals*, translated by Nike Kocijančič Pokorn, Katarina Jerin, and Philip Burt. Ljubljana: Slovene Writer's Association.

———. 2003 [1967]. *Integrali '26*. 2nd edn. Ljubljana: Cankarjeva založba.

———. 2004a. *Izbrane pesmi* (Selected Poems), edited by Matevž Kos. Ljubljana: Mladinska knjiga.

———. 2004b. *Ikarjev Sen; Dokumenti/Rokopisi/Pričevanja* (Srečko Kosovel: Icarus' Dream; Documents/Manuscripts/Testimonies), edited by Aleš Berger and Ludwig Hartinger. Ljubljana: Mladinska knjiga.

———. 2006. *Izbrana pisma* (Selected Letters), edited by Ludwig Hartinger. Ljubljana: Mladinska knjiga.

———. 2008a. *Mon Cher Ami: Dragi Srečko … Neobjavljena pisma Srečku Kosovelu* (Mon Cher Ami: Dear Srečko … Unpublished Letters to Srečko Kosovel), edited by Tatjana Rojc. Gorica: Goriška Mohorjeva Družba.

———. 2008b. *The Golden Boat*, translated by Bert Pribac and David Brooks, assisted by Teja Brooks Pribac. Cambridge: Salt Publishing.

———. 2008c. *Izbrana proza* (Selected Prose), edited by Ludwig Hartinger. Ljubljana: Mladinska knjiga.

———. 2010a. *Look Back, Look Ahead: The Selected Poems of Srečko Kosovel*. New York: Ugly Duckling Presse.

———. 2010b. *Iz zapuščine; pesmi neobjavljene v zbranem delu* (From the literary estate; poems unpublished in the *Collected Works*), edited by Marjan

Dolgan. Ljubljana: Znanstvenoraziskovalni center Slovenske akademije znanosti in umetnosti (ZRC SAZU).

———. 2013. *Zbrane pesmi* (Collected Poems), edited by Neža Zajc. Ljubljana: Študentska založba.

Main Kosovel Translations into Languages Other than English

French
Kosovel, Srečko (translated by Marc Alyn) 1965. *Srečko Kosovel*. Paris: Editions Pierre Seghers.

Italian
Kosovel, Srečko. 1972. *Poesie e integrali*, translated by Jolka Milič. Trieste: L'Asterisco.

———. 2002a. *Kons*, translated by Jolka Milič. Trst/Trieste: Tržaška knjigarna/Libreria Triestina.

———. 2002b. *Il mio canto/Moja pesem*, translated by Jolka Milič. Trst/Trieste: Tržaška knjigarna/Libreria Triestina.

German
Kosovel, Srečko. 1976. *Integrale*, translated by Wilhelm Heiliger. München: Dr. Rudolf Trofenik Verlag.

———. 1994. *Mein Gedicht ist Karst*, translated by Ludwig Hartinger. Klagenfurt-Celovec: Wieser Verlag.

———. 1996. *Gedichte Integrale*. Klagenfurt: Carinthia.

Catalan
Kosovel, Srečko. 2005. *Integrales*, translated by Santiago Martín. Bassarai: Zaragoza.

Slovak
Kosovel, Srečko. 2012a. Zelený papagáj/Zeleni papagaj, edited by Stanislava Repar. Bratislava: Drewo a srd : Vlna ; Ljubljana : KUD Apokalipsa.

Polish
Kosovel, Srečko. 2012b. *Kalejdoskop: izbrane pesmi/wiersze wybrane*, translated by Karolina Bucka Kustec. Kulturno-umetniško društvo Police Dubove. Mikołów: Instytut Mikołowski.

B. SECONDARY SOURCES

Achebe, Chinua. 1995. 'Colonialist Criticism'. In *The Post-Colonial Studies Reader*, edited by Bill Ashcroft, Gareth Griffiths, and Helen Tiffin, pp. 57–61. London: Routledge.

Adams, Hazard. 1991. 'Yeats and Antithetical Nationalism'. In *Literature and Nationalism*, edited by Vincent Newey and Ann Thompson, pp. 163–81. Liverpool: Liverpool University Press.

Agarwala, R. S. 1996. *Aesthetic Consciousness of Tagore*. Calcutta: Abishek Agarwal.

Ahmad, Aijaz. 2006. *In Theory: Classes, Nations, Literatures*. New Delhi: Oxford University Press.

Alyn, Marc. 1965. 'Srečko Kosovel'. In *Srečko Kosovel*, translated by Marc Alyn, pp. 7–96. Paris: Editions Pierre Seghers.

Amin, Samir. 1989. *Eurocentrism*, translated by Russell Moore. London: Zed Books.

Anand, Mulk Raj. 1988. 'Tagore's Religion of Man: An Essay on Rabindranath Tagore's Humanism'. In *Rabindranath Tagore and the Challenges of Today*, edited by Bhudeb Chaudhuri, pp. 83–92. Simla: Indian Institute of Advanced Study.

Anderson, Amanda. 1998. 'Cosmopolitanism, Universalism, and the Divided Legacies'. In *Cosmopolitics: Thinking and Feeling beyond the Nation*, edited by Pheng Cheah and Bruce Robbins, pp. 265–89. Minneapolis: University of Minnesota Press.

Anderson, Benedict. 1991. *Imagined Communities: Reflections of the Origin and Spread of Nationalism*, revised ed. London: Verso.

Apollinaire, Guillaume. 2001a [1913]. 'Pablo Picasso'. In *Apollinaire on Art*, edited by LeRoy C. Breunig, pp. 279–81. Boston: MFA Publications.

———. 2001b [1918]. 'Picasso'. In *Apollinaire on Art*, edited by LeRoy C. Breunig, p. 458. Boston: MFA Publications.

Appadurai, Arjun. 2013. 'In My Father's Nation: Reflections on Biography, Memory, Family'. In *The Future as Cultural Fact: Essays on Global Condition*, pp. 101–11. London, New York: Verso.

Appiah, Kwame Anthony. 1992. *In My Father's House: Africa and the Philosophy of Culture*. New York: Oxford University Press.

———. 1998. 'Cosmopolitan Patriots'. In *Cosmopolitics; Thinking and Feeling beyond the Nation*, edited by Pheng Cheah and Bruce Robbins, pp. 91–115. Minneapolis: University of Minnesota Press.

———. 2005. *The Ethics of Identity*. Princeton: Princeton University Press.

———. 2007. *Cosmopolitanism: Ethics in a World of Strangers*. New York: W. W. Norton.

Arnold, James, A. 1983. 'Césaire at Seventy'. *Callaloo*, 17: 111–9.

Aronson, Alex. 1978 [1943]. *Rabindranath Tagore through Western Eyes*. Calcutta: Rddhi.

———. 1991. 'Brief Chronicles of the Time: Recollections of Shantiniketan 1937–1941'. In *Purabi: A Miscellany in Memory of Rabindranath Tagore 1941–1991*, edited by Krishna Dutta and Andrew Robinson, pp. 20–38. London: The Tagore Centre UK.

Aronson, Alex, and Krishna Kripalani (eds). 1945. *Rolland and Tagore*. Kolkata: Visva-Bharati.

Ashcroft, Bill. 2001. *Post-Colonial Transformation*. London: Routledge.

Ashcroft, Bill, Gareth Griffiths, and Helen Tiffin (eds). 1989. *The Empire Writes Back: Theory and Practice in Post-Colonial Literatures*. London: Routledge.

——— (eds). 1995. *The Post-Colonial Studies Reader*. London: Routledge.

——— (eds). 2002. *Post-Colonial Studies: The Key Concepts*. London: Routledge.

Auden, Wystan Hugh. 1991. *Collected Poems*, edited by Edward Mendelson. London: Faber and Faber.

Ayyub, Abu Sayeed. 1995. *Modernism and Tagore*, translated from Bengali by Amitava Ray. New Delhi: Sahitya Akademi.

Badiou, Alain. 2003. *Saint Paul: The Foundation of Universalism*, translated from French by Ray Brassier. Stanford: Stanford University Press.

———. 2005. 'An interview with Alain Badiou: "Universal Truths and the Question of Religion"', by Adam S. Miller. *Journal of Philosophy and Scripture*, 3(1): 38–42.

Badiou, Alain, and Nicholas Truong. 2012. *In Praise of Love*, translated from French by Peter Bush. London: Serpent's Tail.

Bajt, Drago. 1985. *Ruski literarni avantgardizem: futurizem, konstruktivizem, absurdizem* (Russian Literary Avant-Gardism: Futurism, Constructivism, Absurdism). Literarni leksikon, študije 27, Ljubljana: DZS.

———. 1986. 'Russian Constructivism, the Slovenes and Srečko Kosovel'. In *Slowenische historische Avantgarde/Slovene Historical Avant-Garde*, edited by Aleš Erjavec, pp. 7–17. Ljubljana: Aesthetic Society/Gessellschaft für Ästhetik.

Bakic-Hayden, Milica, and Robert M. Hayden. 1992. 'Orientalist Variations on the Theme "Balkans": Symbolic Geography in Recent Yugoslav Cultural Politics'. *Slavic Review*, 51(1): 1–15.

Balibar, Etienne. 1995. 'Ambiguous Universality'. *Differences: A Journal of Feminist Cultural Studies*, 7(1): 48–75.

Bangha, Imre. 2008. *Hungry Tiger: Encounters between Hungarian and Bengali Literary Cultures*. New Delhi: Sahitya Akademi.

———. 2013. 'Tagore's Reception and His Translations in Hungary'. In *Tagore: At Home in the World*, edited by Sanjukta Dasgupta and Chinmoy Guha, pp. 25–37. New Delhi: Sage Publications.

Bates, Crispin. 2007. *Subalterns and Raj: South Asia since 1600*. London and New York: Routledge.

Bayly, C. A. *Indian Society and the Making of the British Empire*. Cambridge: Cambridge University Press, 1988.

Beck, Ulrich. 2004. 'The Truth of Others: A Cosmopolitan Approach'. *Common Knowledge*, 10(3): 430–49.

Benhabib, Seyla. 2002. *The Claims of Culture: Equality and Diversity in the Global Era*. Princeton: Princeton University Press.

Berger, Aleš. 1982. *Srečko Kosovel*. Ljubljana: Zbirka Obrazi.

Berlin, Isaiah. 1997. 'Rabindranath Tagore and the Consciousness of Nationality'. In *The Sense of Reality: Studies in Ideas and Their History*, edited by Henry Hardy, pp. 249–66. New York: Farrar, Straus and Giroux.

Betts, F. Raymond. 1998. *Decolonization*. New York: Routledge.

Bhabha, Homi K. 1990. 'Introduction: Narrating the Nation'. In *Nation and Narration*, edited by Homi K. Bhabha, pp. 1–7. London and New York: Routledge.

———. 1994. *Location of Culture*. London and New York: Routledge.

Bharucha, Rustom. 2006. *Another Asia: Rabindranath Tagore & Okakura Tenshin*. New Delhi: Oxford University Press.

Bhatt, Chetan. 2001. *Hindu Nationalism: Origins, Ideologies and Modern Myths*. Oxford: Berg.

Bhattacharya, Debraj. 2008a. 'Introduction: Six Notes on a Partly Understood Phenomenon'. In *Of Matters Modern: The Experience of Modernity in Colonial and Post-Colonial South Asia*, edited by Debraj Bhattacharya, pp. 1–17. Kolkata: Seagull Books.

———. 2008b. 'Three Narratives on Modernity in a Colonial Metropolis: Calcutta During the Early Twentieth Century'. In *Of Matters Modern: The Experience of Modernity in Colonial and Post-Colonial South Asia*, edited by Debraj Bhattacharya, pp. 242–69. Kolkata: Seagull Books.

Bhattacharya, Krishna Chandra. 1984. 'Svaraj in Ideas'. *Indian Philosophical Quarterly*, 11(4): 281–93.

Bhattacharya, Malini. 2003. '*Gora* and *The Home and the World*: The Long Quest for Modernity'. In *Rabindranath Tagore's Home and the World: A Critical Companion*, edited by P. K. Datta, pp. 127–42. New Delhi: Permanent Black.

Bhattacharya, Sabysachi. 2005. *The Mahatma and the Poet: Letters and Debates between Gandhi and Tagore, 1915–1941*. New Delhi: National Book Trust.

———. 2011. *Rabindranath Tagore: An Interpretation*. New Delhi: Viking, Penguin Books.

Boehmer, Elleke. 1995. *Colonial and Postcolonial Literature*. Oxford: Oxford University Press.

———. 2002. *Empire, the National, and the Postcolonial 1890–1920*. Oxford: Oxford University Press.

Borko, Božidar. 1926. 'Rabindranath Tagore u Zagrebu' (Rabindranath Tagore in Zagreb). *Jutro*, 7(265).

Bose, Buddhadeva. 1994 [1962]. *Tagore: Portrait of a Poet*. Calcutta: Papyrus.

Bose, Neilesh. 2011. 'Muslim Modernism and Trans-Regional Consciousness in Bengal, 1911–1925: The Wide World of Samyabadi'. *South Asia Research*, 31(3): 231–48.

Bose, Sugata. 2006. *A Hundred Horizons: The Indian Ocean in the Age of Global Empire*. Cambridge (Massachusetts): Harvard University Press.

Bose, Sugata, and Ayesha Jalal. 2003. *Modern South Asia: History, Culture, Political Economy*. New Delhi: Oxford University Press.

Bošnjak, Branimir. n.d. *Proizvodnja života* (Production of Life). Zagreb: Stvarnost.

Bradbury, Malcolm, and James McFarlane. 1991. 'The Name and Nature of Modernism'. In *Modernism: A Guide to European Literature 1890–1930*, edited by Malcolm Bradbury and James McFarlane, pp. 19–55. London: Penguin Books.

Brazzoduro, Gino. 1984. 'Kosovel, Our Contemporary'. *Le livre slovène*, 22 (2/3): 61–9.

Brennan, Timothy. 1997. *At Home in the World: Cosmopolitanism Now*. Cambridge: Harvard University Press.

———. 2002. 'Postcolonial Studies between the European Wars: An Intellectual History'. In *Marxism, Modernity and Postcolonial Studies*, edited by Crystal Bartolovich and Neil Lazarus, pp. 185–203. Cambridge: Cambridge University Press.

———. 1989. 'Cosmopolitans and Celebrities'. *Race & Class*, 31: 1–19.

Brooks, David. 2008. 'Srečko Kosovel: Life and Poetry'. In *The Golden Boat*, by Srečko Kosovel, translated by Bert Pribac and David Brooks, assisted by Teja Brooks Pribac, pp. 1–15. Cambridge: Salt Publishing.

Broomfield, J. H. 1968. *Elite Conflict in a Plural Society: Twentieth-Century Bengal*. Berkeley: University of California Press.

Bürger, Peter. 1992. 'On the Problem of the Autonomy of Art in Bourgeois Society'. In *Art in Modern Culture: An Anthology of Critical Texts*, edited by Francis Frascina and Jonathan Harris, pp. 51–63. The University of Michigan: Phaidon.

Butler, Judith, Ernesto Laclau, and Slavoj Žižek. 2000. *Contingency, Hegemony, Universality: Contemporary Dialogues on the Left*. London, New York: Verso.

Cattaruzza, Marina. 1992. 'Slovenes and Italians in Trieste, 1850–1914'. In *Comparative Studies on Government and Non-dominant Ethnic Groups in Europe 1890–1940*, edited by Max Engman, F. W. Carter, A. C. Hepburn, and C. G. Podey, vol. VIII, pp. 189–217. Darthmouth: New York University Press.

Čelešnik, Milan. 1927. 'Rabindranath Tagore pri nas' (Rabindranath Tagore in our country). *Ženski svet*, 5(2): 50.

Cenčič, Mira. 2004. 'Življenjsko okolje Srečka Kosovela' (Living environment of Srečko Kosovel). *Primorska srečanja*, 277(8): 8–12.

Césaire, Aimé. 1972. *Discourse on Colonialism*, translated from French by Joan Pinkham. New York: Monthly Review Press.

———. 2001. *Notebook of a Return to the Native Land*, translated from French by Clayton Eshleman and Annette Smith. Middletown, Connecticut: Wesleyan University Press.

Chakrabarty, Dipesh. 2007. *Provincializing Europe: Postcolonial Thought and Historical Difference*. Princeton: Princeton University Press.

Chakravarty, Bikash. 1998. 'Introduction'. In *Poets to a Poet, 1912–1940: Letters from Bridges, Rhys, Yeats, Sturge Moore, Trevelyan and Pound to Rabindranath Tagore*, edited by Bikash Chakravarty, pp. 1–55. Calcutta: Visva-Bharati.

Chakravarty, Radha. 2013. *Novelist Tagore: Gender and Modernity in Selected Texts*. New Delhi: Routledge.

Chakravarty, Sudeshna. 2013. 'Rabindranath and the Bengal Partition of 1905: Community, Class and Gender'. In *Tagore: At Home in the World*, edited by Sanjukta Dasgupta and Chinmoy Guha, pp. 152–69. New Delhi: Sage Publications.

Chandra, Sudhir. 1992. *The Oppressive Present: Literature and Social Consciousness in Colonial India*. New Delhi: Oxford University Press.

———. 1999. *The Oppressive Present: Literature and Social Consciousness in Colonial India*. New Delhi: Oxford University Press.

Chatterjee, Bhabatosh. 1996. *Rabindranath Tagore and Modern Sensibility*. Delhi: Oxford University Press.

Chatterjee, Partha. 1993 [1986]. *Nationalist Thought and the Colonial World: A Derivative Discourse?* London: Zed Books.

———. 1999 [1994]. *The Nation and its Fragments: Colonial and Postcolonial Histories*. New Delhi: Oxford University Press.

———. 2002. 'The Nationalist Resolution of the Women's Question'. In *Recasting Women: Essays in Colonial History*, edited by Kumkum Sangari and Sudesh Baid , pp. 223–53. New Delhi: Kali for Women.

———. 2003. '*Rabindrik nation ki?*' [What is Tagore's nation?] Puja edition of *Baromas*, 25: 1–23. Calcutta [the text was translated for my personal use by Hana Basu].

———. 2004. '*Rabindrik nation prasange aro du-char katha*' [A few more words about Tagore's nation]. *Baromas*. Calcutta [the text was translated for my personal use by Hana Basu].

Chatterjee, Partha. 2010. *Empire and Nation: Selected Essays*. New York: Columbia University Press.

Chatterjee, Partha. 2011. 'Tagore's Non-Nation'. In *Lineages of Political Society: Studies in Postcolonial Democracy*, pp. 94–126. New York: Columbia University Press.

Chaudhuri, Amit. 2001. 'Introduction'. In *The Picador Book of Modern Indian Literature*, edited by Amit Chaudhuri, pp. xvii–xxxiv. London: Picador.

———. 2008. *Clearing a Space*. Oxford: Peter Lang.

———. 2012. *On Tagore: Reading the Poet Today.*. New Delhi: Viking, Penguin Books India.

Chaudhuri, Nirad C. 1987. *Thy Hand, Great Anarch! India, 1921–1952*. London: Chatto & Windus.

Chaudhuri, Rosinka. 2002. *Gentlemen Poets in Colonial Bengal: Emergent Nationalism and the Orientalist Project*. Kolkata: Seagull Books.

Cheah, Pheng, and Bruce Robbins (eds) 1998. *Cosmopolitics: Thinking and Feeling beyond the Nation*. Minneapolis: University of Minnesota Press.

Childs, Peter, and Patrick Williams. 1997. 'Lines of Resistance'. In *An Introduction to Post-Colonial Theory*, edited by Peter Childs and Patrick Williams, pp. 26–64. Hall: Harvester Wheatsheaf.

Chomsky, Noam. 1999. *Profit over People*. New York: Seven Stories Press.

Choudhuri, Indra Nath. 2013. 'The Other and the Self: Tagore's Concept of Universalism'. In *Tagore: At Home in the World*, edited by Sanjukta Dasgupta and Chinmoy Guha, pp. 104–24. New Delhi: Sage Publications.

Clarke, J. J. 1997. *Oriental Enlightenment: The Encounter between Asian and Western Thought*. London: Routledge.

Clifford, James. 1992. 'Traveling Cultures'. In *Cultural Studies*, edited by Lawrence Grossberg, Cary Nelson and Paula A. Treichler, pp. 96–116. New York: Routledge.

Cohen, Joshua (ed.). 1996. *For Love of Country: Debating the Limits of Patriotism*. Boston: Beacon.

Collins, Michael. 2012. *Empire, Nationalism and the Postcolonial World: Rabindranath Tagore's Writings on History, Politics and Society*. London and New York: Routledge.

Cox, John K. 2009. *Slovenia: Evolving Loyalties*. New York: Routledge.

Črnič, Aleš. 2008. 'Indian Religious Ideas and Practices in Slovenia'. In *Indian Studies: Slovenian Contributions*, edited by Lenart Škof, pp. 81–108. Kolkata: Sampark.

Das, Sisir Kumar. 1986. 'Tagore: A Victim of Translatedation'. *The Indian Literary Review*, 4(1): 71–80.

———. 1994. 'Introduction', in *EW* 1, pp. 9–42.

Das Gupta, Ashin. 2003. 'The Changing Renaissance of Recent History'. In *Exploring Emotional History: Gender, Mentality and Literature in the Indian*

Awakening, edited by Rajat Kanta Ray, pp. 327–39. New Delhi: Oxford University Press.

Das Gupta, Uma. 1982/3. 'A Cultural Nationalism'. *Visva-Bharati Quarterly*, 48(1–4): 376–85.

———. 1991. 'Rabindranath Tagore on Rural Reconstruction: The Shriniketan Programme, 1921–41'. In *Purabi: A Miscellany in Memory of Rabindranath Tagore 1941–1991*, edited by Krishna Dutta and Andrew Robinson, pp. 127–41. London: The Tagore Centre UK.

———. 2004. *Rabindranath Tagore: A Biography*. New Delhi: Oxford University Press.

———. 2006. 'Rabindranath Tagore and Modernity'. In *Tagore and Modernity*, edited by Krishna Sen and Tapati Gupta, pp. 1–11. Kolkata: Dasgupta.

———. 2009. 'Tagore's Ideas of Social Action and the Sriniketan Experiment of Rural Reconstruction, 1922–41'. *University of Toronto Quarterly*, 77(4): 992–1004.

Das Gupta, R. K. 2003. *Vedanta in Bengal*. Kolkata: The Ramakrishna Mission Institute of Culture.

Dasgupta, Subrata. 2006. *The Bengal Renaissance: Identity and Creativity from Rammohun Roy to Rabindranath Tagore*. Delhi: Permanent Black.

———. 2011. *Awakening: The Story of the Bengal Renaissance*. Noida: Random House India.

Dasgupta, Sanjukta. 2013. 'Bengali at Home, English in the World: Bilingual Tagore'. In *Tagore: At Home in the World*, edited by Sanjukta Dasgupta and Chinmoy Guha, pp. 173–84. New Delhi: Sage Publications.

Datta, Pradip Kumar. 2003. 'Bangla Sahitya and the Vicissitudes of Bengali Identity in the Latter Half of the Nineteenth Century'. In *Mastering Western Texts: Essays on Literature and Society*, edited by Sambudha Sen, pp. 220–40. Delhi: Permanent Black.

Dayal, Samir. 2007. 'Repositioning India: Tagore's Passionate Politics of Love'. *Positions*, 15(1): 165–207.

Djurić, Dubravka. 2003. 'Radical Poetic Practices: Concrete and Visual Poetry in the Avant-garde and Neo-avant-garde'. In *Impossible Histories: Historical Avant-gardes, Neo-avant-gardes, and Post-avant-gardes in Yugoslavia, 1918–1991*, edited by Dubravka Djurić and Miško Šuvaković, pp. 64–95. Cambridge (Massachusetts): The MIT Press.

Dović, Marijan. 2005. 'The Canonisation of an "Absent" Author', translated from Slovene by Katarina Jerin. In *Kosoveleova poetika=Kosovel's Poetics*, edited by Janez Vrečko, Boris A. Novak, and Darja Pavlič, pp. 205–13. Ljubljana: Slovensko društvo za primerjalno književnost.

During, Simon. 1990. 'Literature—Nationalism's other? The case for revision'. In *Nation and Narration*, edited by Homi K. Bhabha, pp. 138–53. London and New York: Routledge.

Dutt, Somjit. 2001. 'A Foreign Shine and Assumed Gestures: The Ersatz Tagore of the West'. Available at http://www.parabass.com/rabindranath/articles/pSomjit1.html, accessed 26 September 2013.

Dutta, Krishna, and Andrew Robinson. 2003. *Rabindranath Tagore: The Myriad-Minded Man*. New Delhi: Rupa & Co.

Dutta-Roy, Sonjoy. 2001. *(Re)Constructing the Poetic Self: Tagore, Whitman, Yeats, Eliot*. New Delhi: Pencraft International.

Dyson, Ketaki Kushari. 1996. *In Your Blossoming Flower-Garden: Rabindranath Tagore and Victoria Ocampo*. Calcutta: Sahitya Akademi.

———. 2001. 'Rabindranath Tagore and his World of Colours'. Available at http://www.parabaas.com/rabindranath/articles/pKetaki2.html, accessed 5 March 2015.

———. 2003. 'Introduction'. In *I Won't Let You Go*, by Rabindranath Tagore, translated by Ketaki Kushari Dyson, pp. 15–69. New Delhi: Universal Books Stall Publishers' Distributors (UBSPD).

Dyson, Ketaki Kushari, and Sushobhan Adhikary. 1997. *Ronger Rabindranath: Rabindranather Sahitye o Chitrakalay Ronger Byabahar*. Calcutta: Ananda Publishers.

Easthope, Anthony. 1999. *Englishness and National Culture*. London: Routledge.

Ellman, Richard. 1973. *Yeats: The Man and the Masks*. London: Faber and Faber.

Erzetič, Manca. 2010. *Neevropski vplivi na poezijo Srečka Kosovela: vpliv Rabindranatha Tagoreja na poezijo Srečka Kosovela* (Non-European influences on the poetry of Srečko Kosovel: the influence of Rabindranath Tagore on the poetry of Srečko Kosovel). Undergraduate thesis, University in Nova Gorica, Faculty for Humanities.

Fanon, Frantz. 1986 [1952]. *Black Skin, White Masks*, translated by Charles Lam Markmann. London: Pluto Press.

———. 1963 [1961]. *The Wretched of the Earth*, translated by Constance Farrington. New York: Grove Press.

Flaker, A. 1982. *Poetika osporavanja: Avangarda i književna ljevica* (Poetics of resistance: Avant-garde and the literary left). Zagreb: Školska knjiga.

———. 1985. 'Slikarstvo z besedami' (Painting with words). *Sodobnost*, 33(1): 72–7.

Fleming, K. E. 2000. 'Orientalism, the Balkans, and Balkan Historiography'. *The American Historical Review*, 150(4): 1218–33.

Flora, Guiseppe. 2008. 'Tagore and Italy: Facing History and Politics'. *University of Toronto Quarterly*, 77(4): 1025–57.

Florit, Eugenio. 1957. 'Preface'. In *The Selected Writings of Juan Ramón Jimenez*, by Juan Ramon Jimenez, translated by H. R. Hays, edited by Euengio Florit, pp. xiii–xxxvi. New York: Farrar, Straus and Giroux.

Folejewski, Zbigniew. 1980. *Futurism and Its Place in the Development of Modern Poetry: A Comparative Study and Anthology*. Ottawa: University of Ottawa Press.

Foster, R. F. 1998. *W. B. Yeats: A Life, I: The Apprentice Mage 1865-1914*. Oxford: Oxford University Press.

Gandhi, Leela. 1998. *Postcolonial Theory: A Critical Introduction*. New Delhi: Oxford University Press.

———. 2006. *Affective Communities: Anticolonial Thought, Fin-de-Siècle Radicalism, and the Politics of Friendship*. Durham: Duke University Press.

———. 2007. 'Postcolonial Theory and the Crisis of European Man'. *Postcolonial Studies*, 10(1): 93-110.

Gellner, Ernest. 1983. *Nations and Nationalism*. London: Blackwell.

Ghosh, Parimal. 2008. 'Critique of the Bhadralok and the Bhadralok Critic'. In *Of Matters Modern: The Experience of Modernity in Colonial and Post-colonial South Asia*, edited by Debraj Bhattacharya, pp. 271-303. Kolkata: Seagull Books.

Ghosh, Shohini. 2003. 'Passionate Involvement: Love and Politics in Satyajit Ray's *Ghare Baire*'. In *Rabindranath Tagore's Home and the World: A Critical Companion*, edited by P. K. Datta, pp. 82-106. New Delhi: Permanent Black.

Ghosh, Sisirkumar. 2005. *Rabindranath Tagore*. New Delhi: Sahitya Akademi.

Gibson, Nigel, C. 2003. *Fanon: The Postcolonial Imagination*. Cambridge: Polity Press.

Goldsworthy, Vesna. 1998. *Inventing Ruritania: The Imperialism of the Imagination*. New Haven: Yale University Press.

Grahor, Ivo. 1968. *Življenje in smrt* (Life and death). Ljubljana: Cankarjeva založba.

———. 2004 [1931]. 'Srečko Kosovel: Izbrane Pesmi'. In *Srečko Kosovel: Ikarjev Sen; Dokumenti/Rokopisi/Pričevanja* (Srečko Kosovel: Icarus' Dream; Documents/Manuscripts/Testimonies), edited by Aleš Berger and Ludwig Hartinger, pp. 229-30. Ljubljana: Mladinska knjiga.

Grdina, Igor. 2013. 'Med pesmimi, opusom in zbranim delom', in Srečko Kosovel *Zbrane pesmi* (Collected poems), edited by Neža Zajc, pp. 1132-71. Ljubljana: Študentska založba.

Gspan, Alfonz. 1974. *Neznani Srečko Kosovel; Neobjavljeno gradivo iz pesnikove zapuščine ter kritične pripombe h Kosovelovemu Zbranemu delu in Integralom* (The Unknown Srečko Kosovel; Unpublished Materials from the Poet's Literary Estate and Some Critical Remarks to Kosovel's Collected Works and Integrals). Special edition of *Prostor in čas*, 5(8-12), Ljubljana.

Hallward, Peter. 2001. *Absolutely Postcolonial: Writing between the Singular and the Specific*. Manchester: Manchester University Press.

Hamburger, Michael. 1996. *The Truth of Poetry: Tensions of Modernist Poetry since Baudelaire*. London: Anvil Press Poetry.

Hametz, Maura. 2005. *Making Trieste Italian, 1918-1954*. Woodbridge: Boydell Press.

Haq, Kaiser. 2005. 'Travel Writings of Rabindranath Tagore'. In *Return to Postmodernism: Theory, Travel, Autobiography*, edited by Stierstorfer, pp. 365-74. Heidelberg: Universitätsverlag Winter.

Harlow, Barbara. 1987. *Resistance Literature*. New York: Methuen.

Harrison, Nicholas. 2003. *Postcolonial Criticism: History, Theory and the Work of Fiction*. Cambridge: Polity.

Hatcher, Brian A. 2006. 'Remembering Rammohan: An Essay on the (re) emergence of modern Hinduism'. *History of Religions*, 46(1): 50-80.

———. 2008. *Bourgeois Hinduism, or the Faith of the Modern Vedantists: Rare Discourses from Early Colonial Bengal*. New York: Oxford University Press.

———. 2011. 'Father, Son and Holy Text: Rabindranath Tagore and the Upanishads'. *The Journal of Hindu Studies*, 4: 119-34.

Hay, Stephen, N. 1962. 'Rabindranath Tagore in America'. *American Quarterly*, 14(3): 439-63.

Hobsbawm, E. J. 1992. *Nations and Nationalism since 1780: Programme, Myth, Reality*. Cambridge: Cambridge University Press.

———. 1995. *Age of Extremes: The Short Twentieth Century, 1914-1991*. London: Abacus.

Hogan, Patrick Colm. 2000. *Colonialism and Cultural Identity: Crisis of Tradition in the Anglophone Literatures of India, Africa and the Caribbean*. Albany: State University of New York Press.

———. 2003. 'Introduction'. In *Rabindranath Tagore: Universality and Tradition*, edited by Patrick Colm Hogan and Lalita Pandit, pp. 9-23. Cranbury: Associated University Presses.

———. 2004. *Empire and Poetic Voice: Cognitive and Cultural Studies of Literary Tradition and Colonialism*. Albany: State University of New York Press.

Hough, Graham. 1991. 'The Modernist Lyric'. In *Modernism: A Guide to European Literature, 1890-1930*, edited by Malcolm Bradbury and James McFarlane, pp. 312-22. London: Penguin Books.

Hurwitz, H. M. 1964. 'Ezra Pound and Rabindranath Tagore'. *American Literature*, 36(1): 53-63.

Ilijić, Stjepko. 1926. 'Rabindranath Tagore i fašizam' (Rabindranath Tagore and Fascism). *Obzor*, LXVII, no. 305: 2-3.

Innes, Lyn. 2002. 'Orientalism and Celticism'. In *Irish and Postcolonial Writing: History, Theory, Practice*, edited by Glenn Hooper and Colin Graham, pp. 142-56. Houndmills: Palgrave.

Ivbulis, Viktors. 1999. *Tagore: East and West Cultural Unity*. Calcutta: Rabindra Bharati University.

Jain, Jasbir. 2006. *Beyond Postcolonialism: Dreams and Realities of a Nation.* Jaipur: Rawat Publications.

Jameson, Fredric. 1986. 'Third-World Literature in the Era of Multinational Capitalism'. *Social Text*, no. 15: 65–88.

Jeffares, A. Norman. 1961. *The Poetry of W. B. Yeats.* London: Edward Arnold.

Jelen, Marija Ravbar. 2004. 'Kosovelova domačija' (Kosovel's homestead). *Primorska srečanja*, no. 273: 38–41.

Jelnikar, Ana. 2008. 'Yeats's (Mis)Reading of Tagore: Interpreting and Alien Culture'. *University of Toronto Quarterly*, 77(4): 1005–24.

———. 2011. 'Turning "East": Orientalist Variations on Tagore from the "Eastern Corner of Europe"'. In *Rabindranath Tagore: A Timeless Mind: Commemorating the 150th Birth Anniversary of Rabindranath Tagore*, edited by Amalendu Biswas, pp. 165–77. London: The Tagore Centre UK, 2011.

———. 2012. 'Tagore's Universalist Sparks: A Creative Approach'. In *Tagore: At Home in the World*, edited by Sanjukta Dasgupta and Chinmoy Guha, pp. 291–304. New Delhi: Sage Publications.

———. 2014a. 'Yugoslavia and Its Successors'. In *Rabindranath Tagore: One Hundred Years of Global Reception*, edited by Imre Bagha and Martin Kämpchen, pp. 275–95. New Delhi: Orient Blackswan.

———. 2014b. 'Srečko Kosovel and Rabindranath Tagore: Universalist Hopes from the Margins of Europe'. In *The Internationalist Moment: South Asia, Worlds, and World Views 1917–39*, edited by Ali Raza, Franziska Roy, and Benjamin Zachariah, pp. 188–228. Los Angeles, London, New Delhi, Singapore, Washington DC: Sage Publications.

Johnson, R. 1965. 'Juan Ramon Jiménez, Rabindranath Tagore and "La Poesía Desnuda"'. *The Modern Language Review*, 60(4): 534–46.

Jovanovski, Alenka. 2005. 'Kosovel's "Cons" Poems: An Uneasy Balance', translated from Slovene by Ana Jelnikar. In *Kosoveleova poetika=Kosovel's Poetics*, edited by Janez Vrečko, Boris A. Novak, and Darja Pavlič, pp. 225–38. Ljubljana: Slovensko društvo za primerjalno književnost.

Juvan, Marko. 2005. 'Srečko Kosovel and the Hybridity of Modernism', translated from Slovene by Katarina Jerin. In *Kosoveleova poetika=Kosovel's Poetics*, edited by Janez Vrečko, Boris A. Novak, and Darja Pavlič, pp. 189–99. Ljubljana: Slovensko društvo za primerjalno književnost.

———. 2008. 'National and Comparative Literary Histories in Slovenia: Their Histories, Current Status, and Prospects'. *Slovene Studies*, 30(1): 25–38.

Kämpchen, Martin. 1999. *Rabindranath Tagore in Germany: Four Responses to a Cultural Icon.* Shimla: Indian Institute of Advanced Study.

———. 2013. 'Rabindranath Tagore and Germany: An Overview'. In *Tagore: At Home in the World*, edited by Sanjukta Dasgupta and Chinmoy Guha, pp. 15–24. New Delhi: Sage Publications.

Kaviraj, Sudipta. 2003. 'The Two Histories of Literary Culture in Bengal'. In *Literary Cultures in History: Reconstructions from South Asia*, edited by Sheldon Pollock, pp. 503–65. Berkeley: University of California Press.

Knotková-Čapková, Blanka. 2013. 'Studying Rabindranath Thakur within the Czech Bengali Studies'. In *Tagore: At Home in the World*, edited by Sanjukta Dasgupta and Chinmoy Guha, pp. 215–29. New Delhi: Sage Publications.

Kodrič, Ravel. 2011. 'Listkarstvo in politična invektiva med pobudniki Kosovelovega duhovnega in pesniškega zorenja' ('Feuilleton and Political Invective as Sources of Kosovel's Spiritual and Poetical Coming of Age'), *Primerjalna književnost*, 34(1): 81–116.

Komelj, Miklavž. 2014. 'Kosovel, Lenin in smrt' (Kosovel, Lenin and death). *Literatura*, 26: 279–80, 94–142.

Kopf, David. 1969. *British Orientalism and the Bengal Renaissance: The Dynamics of Indian Modernization, 1773-1835*. Calcutta: Firma K. L. Mukhopadhyay.

———. 1988. *The Brahmo Samaj and the Shaping of the Modern Indian Mind*. New Delhi: Archives Publishers Pvt. Ltd.

Kos, Janko. 1986. 'Slovenska literatura in zgodovinska avantgarda' (Slovene literature and the historical avant-garde), *Slavistična revija*, 3: 247–58.

Kos, Matevž. 2003. *Poskusi z Nietzschejem: Nietzsche in Ničejanstvo v slovenski literaturi* [Attempts with Nietzsche: Nietzsche in Slovenian literature]. Ljubljana: Slovenska matica.

———. 2004. 'Kako brati Kosovela?' (How to Read Kosovel?) In *Srečko Kosovel: Izbrane pesmi* [Srečko Kosovel: selected poems], edited by Matevž Kos, pp. 129–65. Ljubljana: Mladinska knjiga.

Kosovel, Stano. 1971. 'Srečko Kosovel med Ljubljano in Trstom' (Srečko Kosovel between Ljubljana and Trieste). In *Srečko Kosovel v Trstu* (Srečko Kosovel in Trieste), by Srečko Kosovel, Stano Kosovel, Boris Pahor, and Milko Bambič, pp. 11–22. Trieste: Zaliv.

Košuta, M. 2004. 'Srečko Kosovel in Carlo Curcio: romarja v nedosegljivo' ('Srečko Kosovel and Carlo Curcio: Pilgrims of the Unattainable'). In *Slovenski jezik in literatura v evropskih globalizacijskih procesih* (Slovene language and literature in European globalization processes), edited by Marko Jesenšek, pp. 176–83. Ljubljana: slavistično društvo Slovenije.

Kralj, Lado. 1986. *Ekspresionizem* (Expressionism), Literarni leksikon, študije 30. Ljubljana: DZS.

———. 1988. 'Kosovelov konstruktivizem: kritika pojma' (Kosovel's Constructivism: A Critique of the Term). *Primerjalna književnost*, 9(2): 29–44.

Krečič, Peter. 1986. 'Slovene Artistic Avant-Garde and Art Criticism'. In *Slowenische historische Avantgarde/Slovene Historical Avant-Garde*, edited by Aleš Erjavec, pp. 85–97. Ljubljana: Aesthetic Society/Gessellschaft für Ästhetik.

Krečič, Peter. 1989. *Slovenski konstruktivizem in njegovi evropski okviri* [Slovenian constructivism and its European framework]. Maribor: Obzorja.

———. 1999. *Avgust Černigoj.* Ljubljana: Nova Revija.

———. 2004. *Avgust Černigoj, Srečko Kosovel in Konstruktivizem* (Avgust Černigoj, Srečko Kosovel and constructivism), *Primorska srečanja*, year 28, (273): 24–7.

Kripalani, Krishna. 2001 [1986]. *Tagore: A Life.* New Delhi: National Book Trust.

———. 2007. 'Modern Literature'. In *The Illustrated Cultural History of India*, edited by A. L. Basham, pp. 276–98. New Delhi: Oxford University Press.

Kristeva, Julia. 1993. *Nations without Nationalism*, translated by Leon S. Roudiez. New York: Columbia University Press.

Kumar, Siva R. 1999. 'Modern Indian Art: A Brief Overview'. *Art Journal*, 58(3): 14–21.

Kundu, Kalyan, Sakti Bhattacharya, and Kalyan Sircar (eds). 2000. *Imagining Tagore: Rabindranath and the British Press (1912–1941)*. Calcutta: Sahitya Samsad.

Laclau, Ernesto. 1992. 'Universalism, Particularism, and Question of Identity'. *The Identity in Question*, 61: 83–90.

Lago, M. Mary. 1972. 'Introduction'. In *Imperfect Encounter: Letters of William Rothenstein and Rabindranath Tagore 1911–1941*, edited by Mary M. Lago, pp. 1–24. Cambridge, MA: Harvard University Press.

Lal, Ananda. 2001. 'Introduction to Tagore's Plays'. In Tagore 2001j, pp. 3–87.

Larsen, Neil. 2000. 'Imperialism, Colonialism, Postcolonialism'. In *A Companion to Postcolonial Studies*, edited by Henry Schwarz and Sangeeta Ray, pp. 28–52. London: Blackwell Publishers.

Lazarus, Neil. 1993. '(Re)Turn to the People: Ngũgĩ wa Thiong'o and the Crisis of Postcolonial African Intellectualism'. In *The World of Ngũgĩ wa Thiong'o*, edited by Charles Cantalupo, pp. 1–25. Trenton: Africa World Press.

———. 1999. *Nationalism and Cultural Practice in the Postcolonial World.* Cambridge: Cambridge University Press.

Lazarus, Neil, Steven Evans, Anthony Arnove, and Anne Menke. 1995. 'The Necessity of Universalism'. *Differences: A Journal of Feminist Cultural Studies*, 7(1): 75–145.

Legiša, L. 1969. 'Ekspresionizem in novi realizem' (Expressionism and new realism). In *Zgodovina slovenskega slovstva* (The history of Slovene letters), edited by L. Legiša and Alfonz Gspan, pp. 420–48. Ljubljana: Slovenska Matica.

Lelyveld, David. 1993. 'The Fate of Hindustani: Colonial Knowledge and the Project of a National Language'. In *Orientalism and the Postcolonial*

Predicament, edited by C. A. Breckenridge and Peter van der Veer, pp. 23–32. New Delhi: Sahitya Akademi.

Lokar, Janko. 1914. 'Lanska tekmeca za Noblovo književno nagrado' (Last year's rivals for the Nobel Prize). *Slovan*, 12(6): 242–7.

Lukacs, John. 2002. *At the End of an Age*. New Haven: Yale University Press.

Luthar, Oto. 2008. 'From the Habsburg Monarchy to the Kingdom of Yugoslavia'. In *The Land Between: A History of Slovenia*, edited by Oto Lutha, pp. 367–442. Frankfurt am Main: Peter Lang.

MacNeice, Louis. 1967. *The Poetry of W. B. Yeats*. London: Faber and Faber.

Mahalanobis, Prasanta, Chandra. 1985. 'Rabindranath Tagore the Humanist'. *Prasanga Rabindranath*, pp. 1–20, Calcutta: Shrimoki Amed Kotrik.

Malcomson, Scott L. 1998. 'The Varieties of Cosmopolitan Experience'. In *Cosmopolitics: Thinking and Feeling beyond the Nation*, edited by Pheng Cheah and Bruce Robbins, pp. 265–89. Minneapolis: University of Minnesota Press.

Malik, Kenan. 2002. 'All Cultures are Not Equal'. Available at https://www.marxists.org/subject/africa/malik/not-equal.htm (accessed 26 November 2014).

Manela, E. 2007. *The Wilsonian Moment: Self-determination and the International Origins of Anti-colonial Nationalism*. New York: Oxford Unviersity Press.

Margolin, Victor. 1997. *The Struggle for Utopia: Rodchenko, Lissitzky, Moholy-Nagy; 1917–1946*. Chicago: University of Chicago Press.

Masud, S. A. 1988. 'Tagore on Human Values'. In *Rabindranath Tagore and the Challenges of Today*, edited by Bhudeb Chaudhuri, pp. 74–82. Simla: Indian Institute of Advanced Study.

Mazrui, Alamin. 1993. 'Language and the Quest for Liberation in Africa: The Legacy of Frantz Fanon'. *Third World Quarterly*, 14(2): 351–63.

McCourt, John. 2001. *The Years of Bloom: James Joyce in Trieste, 1904–1920*. Dublin: The Lilliput Press.

McFarlane, James.1991. 'The Mind of Modernism'. In *Modernism: A Guide to European Literature 1890–1930*, edited by Malcolm Bradbury and James McFarlane, pp. 71–93. London: Penguin Books.

McLeod, John. 2000. *Beginning Postcolonialism*. Manchester: Manchester University Press.

Mehta, Linn, Cary. 2004. 'Poetry and Decolonization: Tagore, Yeats, Senghor, Cesaire and Neruda, 1914–1950'. PhD thesis, Columbia University.

Mehta, Pratap Bhanu. 2000. 'Cosmopolitanism and the Circle of Reason'. *Political Theory*, 28(5): 619–39.

Melik, Vasilij. 1995. *Slovenci 1848–1918: razprave in članki* (The Slovenes 1848–1918: papers and articles). Ljubljana: Založba Litera.

Metcalf, Barbara D., and Thomas R. Metcalf. 2010. *A Concise History of Modern India*, 2nd ed. Cambridge: Cambridge University Press.

Micić, Ljubomir, and Branko Ve Poljanski. 1926. 'Lettre Ouverte a Rabindranath Tagore'. *Zenit*, 6(43): 17–20.

Miesel, Victor, H. 2003. 'Introduction'. In *Voices of German Expressionism*, edited by Victor H. Miesel, pp. 1–12. London: Tate Publishing.

Miller, David, and Stephen Watts (eds). 2003. *Music While Drowning: German Expressionist Poems*. London: Tate Publishing.

Mirza, Gail Anne. 1977. 'The Hindu Concept of Pure Consciousness in the Poetry of Juan Ramon Jimenez, Rabindranath Tagore, and W. B. Yeats: A Comparative Study'. PhD thesis, State University of New York at Binghamton.

Mislej-Božič, Nadja. 2004. 'Pravili so mu Pilat; Pogovor z Dragico Sosič' [They called him Pilate: In conversation with Dragica Sosič]. *Primorska srečanja*, 273: 51–7.

Mishra, Pankaj. 2012. *From the Ruins of Empire: The Revolt against the West and the Remaking of Asia*. London: Allen Lane, Penguin Books.

Mitra, Priti Kumar. 2009. *The Dissent of Nazrul Islam: Poetry and History*. New Delhi: Oxford University Press.

Mitter, Partha. 2007. *The Triumph of Modernism: India's Artists and the Avant-Garde, 1922–1947*. London: Reaktion Books.

———. 2008. 'Interventions: Decentering Modernism: Art History and Avant-Garde Art from the Periphery'. *Art Bulletin*, 90: 531–47.

Moritsch, Andreas. 1992. '"Slovenes" and "Germans" in Klagenfurt and Ferlach in Southern Carinthia, 1850–1940'. In *Comparative Studies on Government and Non-Dominant Ethnic Groups in Europe, 1890–1940*, vol. VIII, edited by Max Engman, F. W. Carter, A. C. Hepburn, and C. G. Podey, pp. 159–83. Darthmouth: New York University Press.

Morris, Jan. 2001. *Trieste and the Meaning of Nowhere*. Cambridge, MA: Da Capo Press.

Mukherjee, Meenakshi. 2001. 'Introduction'. In *Gora*, by Rabindranath Tagore, translated by Sujit Mukherjee, pp. ix–xxiv. New Delhi: Sahitya Akademi.

Mukherjee, Sujit. 1981. *Translation as Discovery and Other Essays*. New Delhi: Allied Publishers.

Mukhopadhyay, Amartya. 2013. '"Bhinnatā" of "Nations": Tagore's Search in Nationalism, "Bhāratvarṣīya Samāj" and Beyond'. In *Tagore: at Home in the World*, edited by Sanjukta Dasgupta and Chinmoy Guha, pp. 125–52. New Delhi: Sage Publications.

Munda, Jože. 1978. 'Tagore pri nas' (Tagore in Slovenia). In *Rabindranath Tagore*, edited by Janko Moder, pp. 479–82. Nobelovci 7, Ljubljana: Cankarjeva založba.

Musil, Robert. 1995. *The Man without Qualities*, vol. I, translated from German by Sophie Wilkins. New York: Vintage International.

Nandi, S. K. 1999. *Art and Aesthetics of Rabindranath Tagore*. Calcutta: The Asiatic Society.

Nandy, Ashis. 1983. *The Intimate Enemy: Loss and Recovery of Self under Colonialism*. Delhi: Oxford University Press.

———. 2002. *Time Warps: Silent and Evasive Pasts in Indian Politics and Religion*. New Brunswick, NJ: Rutgers University Press.

———. 2005a. *At the Edge of Psychology: Essays in Politics and Culture*. New Delhi: Oxford University Press.

———. 2005b. *The Illegitimacy of Nationalism: Rabindranath Tagore and the Politics of Self*. New Delhi: Oxford University Press.

———. 2005c. 'Sati: A Nineteenth-Century Tale of Women, Violence and Protest'. In *At the Edge of Psychology: Essays in Politics and Culture*, pp. 1–31. New Delhi: Oxford University Press.

Novak, Bogdan C. 1970. *Trieste, 1941–1954: The Ethnic, Political, and Ideological Struggle*. Chicago: University of Chicago Press.

Novak, Boris, A. 2004. 'Kosovel: A Great Poet but a Poor Prosodist', translated from Slovene by Ana Jelnikar. In *Kosovelova poetika=Kosovel's Poetics*, edited by Janez Vrečko, Boris A. Novak, and Darja Pavlič, pp. 133–44. Ljubljana: Slovensko društvo za primerjalno književnost.

Nussbaum, Martha. 1996. 'Patriotism and Cosmopolitanism'. In *For Love of Country: Debating the Limits of Patriotism*, edited by Joshua Cohen, pp. 3–17. Boston: Beacon.

———. 2006. 'Education and Democratic Citizenship: Capabilities and Quality Education'. *Journal of Human Development and Capabilities*, 7(3): 385–95.

———. 2007. *The Clash Within: Democracy, Religious Violence and India's Future*. Harvard: Harvard University Press.

O'Connell, Joseph T. 2011. 'Tracing Vaishnava Strains in Tagore'. *The Journal of Hindu Studies*, 4: 144–64.

O'Connell, Joseph T., and Kathleen M. O'Connell. 2008. 'Introduction: Rabindranath Tagore as "Cultural Icon"'. *University of Toronto Quarterly*, 77(4): 961–70.

———(eds). 2009. *Rabindranath Tagore: Reclaiming a Cultural Icon*. Kolkata: Visva-Bharati.

O'Connell, Kathleen M. 2002. *Rabindranath Tagore: The Poet as Educator*. Kolkata: Visva-Bharati.

———. 2003. 'Siksar Herfer: Education out of Whack'. In *Rabindranath Tagore: Universality and Tradition*, edited by Patrick Colm Hogan and Lalita Pandit, pp. 65–83. Cranbury: Associated University Presses.

Ocvirk, Anton. 1964. 'Opombe' [Notes]. In *CW* 1, pp. 413–505.

Ocvirk, Anton. 1973. 'Srečko Kosovel in njegova pesem' (Srečko Kosovel and his poem). In *Zlati čoln* (The Golden Boat) by Srečko Kosovel, pp. 115–24. Ljubljana, Trst: Državna založba Slovenije, Založništvo tržaškega tiska.

———. 1974. 'Opombe' [Notes]. In *CW* 2, pp. 553–718.

———. 1977. 'Opombe' [Notes]. In *CW* 3/1, pp. 967–1248.

———. 2003. 'Srečko Kosovel in konstruktivizem' (Srečko Kosovel and constructivism). In *Integrali '26*, 2nd ed., pp. 5–112. Ljubljana: Cankarjeva založba.

Osojnik, Iztok. 2012. 'Politična resnica Kosovelove avantgardne konstruktivistične poezije' (The political truth about Kosovel's avantgarde constructivist poetry). In *Kalejdoskop: izbrane pesmi/ wiersze wybrane*, by Srečko Kosovel, translated by Karolina Bucka Kustec, pp. 53–67. Kulturno-umetniško društvo Police. Dubove, Mikołów: Instytut Mikołowski.

Pacheiner-Klander, V. 2008. 'Karol Glaser in Anton Ocvirk: Two Mediators of Indian Literature to Slovenia'. In *Indian Studies; Slovenian Contributions*, edited by Lenart Škof, pp. 49–61. Kolkata: Sampark.

Pahor, Boris. 1971. 'Srečko Kosovel v Trstu' (Srečko Kosovel in Trieste). In *Srečko Kosovel v Trstu* (Srečko Kosovel in Trieste), by Srečko Kosovel, Stano Kosovel, Boris Pahor, and Milko Bambič, pp. 23–44. Trieste: Zaliv.

Pal, Prasanta Kumar. 2003. *Rabindra jiboni*, vol. 9. Kolkata: Ananda Publishers.

Pandit, Lalita. 1995. 'Caste, Race, and Nation'. In *Literary India: Comparative Studies in Aesthetics, Colonialism and Culture*, edited by Patrick Colm Hogan and Lalita Pandit, pp. 207–33. New York: State University of New York.

Paternu, Boris. 1984. 'Problemi ekspresionizma kot orientacijskega modela' (Problems of expressionism as an orientation model). In *Obdobje ekspresionizma v slovenskem jeziku, književnosti in kulturi*, vol. 2, edited by Franc Zadravec, pp. 41–67. Ljubljana: Univerza Edvarda Kardelja.

———. 1985. 'Kosovelova faza slovenskega pesniškega modernizma' (Kosovel's phase within the Slovenian poetic modernism). *Slavistična revija*, 33(2): 247–57.

Pejčić, Jovan. 1988. 'Rabindranath Tagore u Beogradu' (Rabindranath Tagore in Belgrade), *Kulture Istoka*, 5(15): 66–8.

Perloff, Marjorie. 2003. *The Futurist Moment: Avant-Garde, Avant Guerre, and the Language of Rupture*. Chicago and London: University of Chicago Press.

Petrović, Svetozar. 1955. 'Jugoslaveni i Indija' (Yugoslavs and India). *Republika*, 11(1): 382–400.

———. 1970. 'Tagore in Yugoslavia'. *Indian Literature*, 13(2): 5–29.

Pirjevec, Jože. 1994. 'Italian Politcs towards the Slovenes from 1915 to 1994'. *Slovene Studies*, 15(1–2): 63–73.

Pirjevec, Marija. 1993. 'Kosovel, Bartol, Pahor—trije tržaški avtorji v francoščini' (Kosovel, Bartol, Pahor—Three Triestine Authors in French). *Dialogi*, 6/7: 129–35.

———. 1995. 'Narodnost in Nacionalizem v razmišljanju Srečka Kosovela' (Nationhood and nationalism in the thought of Srečko Kosovel). *Primorska Srečanja*, nos 170–1: 442–4.

———. 1997. *Dvoje Izvirov slovenske književnosti* (Two sources of Slovenian literature). Ljubljana: Slovenska Matica.

Pizzi, Katia. 2001. *A City in Search of an Author: The Literary Identity of Trieste*. London: Sheffield Academic Press.

———. 2005. '"Quale Triestinità": Voices and Echoes from Italian Trieste'. In *Kosovelova poetika=Kosovel's Poetics*, edited by Janez Vrečko, Boris A. Novak, and Darja Pavlič, pp. 239–49. Ljubljana: Slovensko društvo za primerjalno književnost.

Pobozniak, Tadeusz. 1961. 'Tagore in Poland'. In *Rabindranath Tagore: A Centenary Volume 1861–1961*, pp. 348–55. New Delhi: Sahitya Akademi.

Poddar, Arabinda. 2004. *Tagore: The Political Personality*. Kolkata: Indiana.

Pogačnik, Jože. 1984. 'Slovenski konstruktivizem' (Slovenian constructivism). In *Obdobje ekspresionizma v slovenskem jeziku, književnosti in kulturi*, edited by Franc Zadravec, vol. 2, pp. 155–83. Ljubljana: Univerza Edvarda Kardelja.

———. 1989. *Twentieth Century Slovene Literature*, translated from Slovene by Anne Čeh. Ljubljana: Slovene Writer's Association.

Pollock, Sheldon. 2000. 'Cosmopolitan and Vernacular in History'. *Public Culture* 12(3): 591–625.

Poniž, Denis. 2004. 'Kosovelovo in Kocbekovo pesniško svetovljanstvo' (Kosovel's and Kocbek's poetic cosmopolitanism). *Nova Revija*, 23(269): 330–43.

Porter, Dennis. 1994 [1983]. 'Orientalism and Its Problems'. In *Colonial Discourse and Post-Colonial Theory: A Reader*, edited by Patrick Williams and Laura Chrisman, pp. 150–61. New York and London: Harvester Wheatsheat.

Puchner, Martin. 2005. *Poetry of the Revolution: Marx, Manifestos, and the Avant-Gardes*. Princeton: Princeton University Press.

Purkayastha, Bandana. 2003. 'Contesting the Boundaries between Home and the World: Tagore and the Construction of Citizenship'. In *Rabindranath Tagore: Universality and Tradition*, edited by Patrick Colm Hogan and Lalita Pandit, pp. 49–65. Cranbury: Associated University Presses.

Radhakrishnan, Manju, and Debasmita Roychowdhury. 2003. "'Nationalism is a Great Menace": Tagore and Nationalism'. In *Rabindranath Tagore: Universality and Tradition*, edited by Patrick Colm Hogan and Lalita Pandit, pp. 29–40. Cranbury: Associated University Presses.

Radice, William. 1994. 'Introduction'. In *Selected Short Stories*, translated by William Radice, pp. 1–28. London: Penguin Books.

Radice, William. 2003a. 'Tagore's Poetic Greatness'. Available at www.parabaas. com/rabindranath/articles/pRadicee.html, 17 July 2014.

———. 2003b. 'Tagore and the Nobel Prize'. In *Poetry and Community: Lectures and Essays, 1991–2001*, pp. 201–15. Delhi: D. C. Publishers.

———. 2012. 'Introduction'. In *Gitanjali: Song Offerings*, by Rabindranath Tagore, translated by William Radice, pp. xv–lxxxvi. New Delhi: Penguin Books.

Ray, Rajat Kanta. 2001. *Exploring Emotional History: Gender, Mentality and Literature in the Indian Awakening*. New Delhi: Oxford University Press.

Raychaudhuri, Tapan. 1999. *Perceptions, Emotions, Sensibilities: Essays on India's Colonial and Post-colonial Experiences*. New Delhi: Oxford University Press.

———. 2002. *Europe Reconsidered*. 2nd edition. New Delhi: Oxford University Press.

———. 2007. 'The Western Impact: Bondage or Catalyst'. In *Tagore and Modernity*, edited by Krishna Sen and Tapati Gupta, pp. 1–17. Kolkata: Dasgupta.

Raza, Ali, Franziska Roy, and Benjamin Zachariah. 2014a. 'Introduction: The Internationalism of the Moment—South Asia and the Contours of the Interwar World'. In *The Internationalist Moment; South Asia, Worlds, and World Views 1917–39*, edited by Ali Raza, Franziska Roy, and Benjamin Zachariah, pp. xi–xii. Los Angeles, London, New Delhi, Singapore, Washington DC: Sage Publications.

———. (eds). 2014b. *The Internationalist Moment: South Asia, Worlds, and World Views 1917–39*. Los Angeles, London, New Delhi, Singapore, Washington DC: Sage Publications.

Robbins, Bruce. 1997. 'Comparative Cosmopolitanisms'. In *Cosmopolitics; Thinking and Feeling Beyond the Nation*, edited by Pheng Cheah and Bruce Robbins, pp. 246–64. Minneapolis: University of Minnesota Press.

Robinson, Andrew. 1989. *The Art of Rabindranath Tagore*. London: André Deutsch.

Rojc, Tatjana. 2005. *Pogledi na nove razsežnosti slovenskega pesništva od Prešerna do Kosovela* (Perspectives on the new dimensions of poetry from Prešeren to Kosovel). Gorica: Goriška Mohorjeva družba.

Rojc, Tatjana. 2008. 'Prelom dvajsetih let: Srečko Kosovel in njegovi sodobniki' (The twenties shift: Srečko Kosovel and his contemporaries). In *Mon Cher Ami: Dragi Srečko ... Neobjavljena pisma Srečku Kosovelu* (Mon Cher Ami: Dear Srečko ... Unpublished Letters to Srečko Kosovel), edited by Tatjana Rojc, pp. 259–93. Gorica: Goriška Mohorjeva Družba.

Rolland, Romain. 2002 [1924]. *Mahatma Gandhi*, translated from French by Catherine D. Groth. New Delhi: Rupa & Co.

Roy, Pabitrakumar. 2002. *Rabindranath Tagore*. New Delhi: Munshiram Manoharlal

Rudolf, Branko. 1958. 'Spremna beseda in opombe' (Foreword and notes). In *Spevi* by Rabindranath Tagore, translated from Slovene by Alojz Gradnik, pp. 83–92. Ljubljana: Mladinska knjiga.

Rusinow, Dennison. 2003. 'The Yugoslav Idea before Yugoslavia'. In *Yugoslavism: Histories of a Failed Idea 1918–1992*, edited by Dejan Djokić, pp. 11–26. London: Hurst & Company.

Saha, Poulomi. 2013. 'Singing Bengal into a Nation: Tagore the Colonial Cosmopolitan?' *Journal of Modern Literature*, 36(2): 1–24.

Said, E. W. 1995 [1978]. *Orientalism*. Harmondsworth: Penguin.

———. 1994. *Culture and Imperialism*. London: Vintage.

———. 2001. 'Nationalism, Human Rights and Interpretation'. In *Reflections on Exile and Other Literary and Cultural Essays*, pp. 411–35. London: Granta Books.

———. 2004. *Humanism and Democratic Criticism*. New York: Palgrave Macmillan.

Šalamun-Biedrzycka, Katarina.1972. *Anton Podbevšek in njegov čas* (Anton Podbevšek and his times). Maribor: Nova obzorja.

Šmitek, Zmago. 1986. *Klic daljnih svetov: Slovenci in neervopske culture* (Call of far-away worlds: Slovenes and non-European cultures). Ljubljana: Založba Borec.

——— (ed.). 2011. *Southern Slavs and India: Relations in Oral Tradition*. Kolkata: Sampark.

Sarkar, Sumit. 1973. *The Swadeshi Movement in Bengal 1903–1908*. New Delhi: People's Publishing House.

———. 2002. 'Nationalism and "Stri-Swadhinata": The Contexts and Meanings of Rabindranath's *Ghare-Baire*'. In *Beyond Nationalist Frames: Relocating Postmodernism, Hindutva, History*, pp. 112–53. Delhi: Permanent Black.

———. 2005 [1990]. 'Calcutta and the 'Bengal Renaissance''. In *Calcutta: The Living City, Volume I: The Past*, edited by Sukanta Chaudhuri, pp. 95–105. New Delhi: Oxford University Press.

Sarkar, Susobhan Chandra. 1970. *Bengal Renaissance and Other Essays*. New Delhi: People's Publishing House.

Sarkar, Tanika. 2001. *Hindu Wife, Hindu Nation: Community, Religion, and Cultural Nationalism*. New Delhi: Permanent Black.

———. 2003. 'Many Faces of Love: Country, Woman, and God in the Home and the World'. In *Rabindranath Tagore's Home and the World: A Critical Companion*, edited by P. K. Datta, pp. 27–44. New Delhi: Permanent Black.

Sartori, Andrew. 2008. *Bengal in Global Concept History: Culturalism in the Age of Capital*. Chicago and London: University of Chicago Press.

Scherber, Peter. 1991. 'Regionalism versus Europeanism in Kosovel'. *Slovene Studies: Journal of the Society for Slovene Studies*, 13(2): 155–65.

Sen, Amartya. 1996. *On Interpreting India's Past*. Calcutta: The Asiatic Society.

———. 2005a. 'Foreword'. In *Selected Letters of Rabindranath Tagore*, edited by Krishna Dutta and Andrew Robinson, pp. xvii–xxv. Cambridge: Cambridge University Press.

———. 2005b. *The Argumentative Indian: Writings on Indian Culture, History and Identity*. London: Penguin Books.

———. 2006. *Identity and Violence; The Illusion of Destiny*. London: Allen Lane.

Sen, Amrit. 2013. 'Tagore, Travel and *Tirtha*'. In *Tagore: At Home in the World*, edited by Sanjukta Dasgupta and Chinmoy Guha, pp. 75–96. Los Angeles, London, New Delhi, Singapore, Washington DC: Sage Publications.

Sen, Nabaneeta. 1966. 'The Foreign Reincarnation of Rabindranath'. *The Journal of Asian Studies*, 25(2): 275–86.

Sen, Sudhir. 1989. 'Tagore's Ideal of Social and Economic Development: Realizing them on a Global Scale in a Revolutionary Age'. In *Rabindranath Tagore in Perspective: A Bunch of Essays*, edited by Nemai Sadhan Bose, pp. 14–40. Calcutta: Visva-Bharati.

Sinha. Mrinalini. 1995. *Colonial Masculinity: The 'Manly Englishman' and the 'Effeminate Bengali' in the Late Nineteenth Century*. Manchester, UK: Manchester University Press.

Sluga, Glenda. 2001. *Difference, Identity, and Sovereignty in Twentieth-Century Europe: The Problem of Trieste and the Italo-Yugoslav Border*. New York: State University of New York Press.

Som, Reba. 2009. *Rabindranath Tagore: The Singer and His Song*. New Delhi: Penguin/Viking.

Šrimf, Franc. 1981/82. 'Srečko Kosovel in Tagore' (Srečko Kosovel and Tagore). *Jezik in slovstvo*, 27(4): 121–3.

Stolte, Carolien. 2014. 'Uniting the Oppressed Peoples of the East: Revolutionary Internationalism in an Asia inflection'. In *The Internationalist Moment: South Asia, Worlds, and World Views 1917–39*, edited by Ali Raza, Franziska Roy, and Benjamin Zachariah, pp. 56–85. Los Angeles, London, New Delhi, Singapore, Washington DC: Sage Publications.

Szabolcsi, Miklós. 1971. 'Avant-Garde, Neo-Avant-Garde, Modernism: Questions and Suggestions'. *New Literary History*, 3(1): 49–70.

Tagore, Rathindranath. 2003 [1958]. *On the Edges of Time*, 2nd ed. Kolkata: Visva-Bharati.

Tagore, Saranindranath. 2006. 'Tagore—History and the Problem of Modernity'. In *Tagore and Modernity*, edited by Krishna Sen and Tapati Gupta, pp. 12–22. Kolkata: Dasgupta.

Tagore, Saranindranath. 2008. 'Tagore's Conception of Cosmopolitanism: A Reconstruction'. *University of Toronto Quarterly*, 77(4): 1070–84.

Talbot, Ian. 2000. 'Nation Building in India: Ideas and Institutions'. In *India and Pakistan*, pp. 163–95. London: Arnold.

Taoua, Phyllis. 2002. *Forms of Protest: Anti-Colonialism and Avant-Gardes in Africa, the Caribbean, and France*. Portsmouth. N.H.: Heinemann.

Taylor, Charles. 1992. *Multiculturalism and the Politics of Recognition: An Essay*. Princeton: Princeton University Press.

Terseglav, Franc. 1921. 'Ghandi (*sic.*)'. *Slovenec*, 3/12/1921, no. 275, p. 2.

Thiong'o, Ngũgĩ, wa. 1993. *Moving the Centre: The Struggle for Cultural Freedoms*. London: James Currey.

Thompson, E. P. 1991. 'Introduction'. In Tagore 1991a, pp. 1–16.

———. 1998. *Alien Homage: Edward Thompson and Rabindranath Tagore*. New Delhi: Oxford University Press.

Thompson, Edward. 1992 [1948]. *Rabindranath Tagore: Poet and Dramatist*. New Delhi: Oxford University Press

Todorova, Maria 1997. *Imagining the Balkans*. New York: Oxford University Press.

Tokarz, Bożena. 2004. 'Univerzalizem v Kosovelovi poeziji (Vesolje in pesniško doživetje celote)'. (Universalism in Kosovel's poetry [Cosmos and the poetic experience of the whole]). In *Slovenski jezik in literatura v evropskih globalizacijskih procesih* (Slovene language and literature in European globalization processes), edited by Marko Jesenšek, pp. 166–75. Ljubljana: slavistično društvo Slovenije.

———. 2005. 'The Idea behind the Integrals in Kosovel's Poetry', translated from Slovene by Ana Jelnikar. In *Kosovelova poetika=Kosovel's Poetics*, edited by Janez Vrečko, Boris A. Novak, and Darja Pavlič, pp. 163–73. Ljubljana: Slovensko društvo za primerjalno književnost.

———. 2013. *Med destrukcijo in konstrukcijo; O poeziji Srečka Kosovela v kontekstu konstruktivizma* (Between destruction and construction: On poetry of Srečko Kosovel in the context of constructivism), translated from Polish by Primož Čučnik. Ljubljana: Literarno-umetniško društvo Literatura.

Tötösy de Zepetnek, Steven. 2002. 'Comparative Cultural Studies and the Study of Central European Culture'. In *Comparative Central European*

Culture, edited by Steven Tötösy de Zepetnek, pp. 1–32.West Lafayatte: Purdue University Press.

Trivedi, Harish. 1992 [1948]. 'Introduction'. In *Rabindranath Tagore: Poet and Dramatist* by Edward Thompson, pp. a1–a39. New Delhi: Oxford University Press.

———. 1995. *Colonial Transactions: English Literature and India*. Manchester: Manchester University Press.

Troha, Vera. 1988. 'O Kosovelu in italijanskemu futurizmu' (On Kosovel and Italian Futurism). *Primerjalna književnost*, 11(2): 1–14.

———. 1993. *Futurizem* (Futurism). Literarni leksikon, študije 40, Ljubljana: DZS.

Van Biljert, Victor A. 2003. 'The Ethics of Modernity in Indian Politics: Past and Present'. *Journal of Human Values*, 9(1): 53–64.

Van Biljert, Victor, A. 2009. 'Tagore's Vision of the Indian Nation: 1900–1917'. In *Rabindranath Tagore: Reclaiming a Cultural Icon*, edited by Joseph T. O'Connell, and Kathleen M. O'Connell, pp. 46–63. Kolkata: Visva-Bharati.

Velikonja, Mitja. 2003. 'Slovenia's Yugoslav Century'. In *Yugoslavism: Histories of a Failed Idea 1918–1992*, edited by Dejan Djokić, pp. 84–99. London: Hurst & Company.

Verginella, Marta. 2005. 'Mit o Slovenskem Trstu' (Myth about the Slovenian Trieste)'. *Zbornik prispevkov v počastitev 75-letnice prog. Sergia Tavana*, pp. 91–104. Nova Gorica: Goriški muzej.

Vinaver, Stanislav. 1926. 'Pesnikova misija u svetu' (Poet's Mission in the World). *Vreme* 16/10/1926, p. 5.

Viswanathan, Gauri. 1989. *Masks of Conquests: Literary Study and British Rule in India*. New York: Columbia University Press.

Voranc, Prežihov. 2014. 'At Doberdob'. In *No Man's Land: Writings from a World at War*, , translated by Ana Jelnikar, and Stephen Watts, edited by Pete Ayrton, pp. 168–75. London: Serpent's Tail.

Vrečko, Janez. 1985. 'Kosovel med Integrali in Konsi' (Kosovel between the Integrals and Kons poems). *Sodobnost*, 33(1): 64–72.

———. 1986. *Srečko Kosovel: slovenska zgodovinska avantgarda in zenitizem* (Srečko Kosovel: Slovenian Historic Avant-Garde and Zenitism). Maribor: Znamenja.

———. 1999. 'Labodovci, pilotovci, konstrukterji, konsisti in tankisti'. *Slavistična revija*, no. 1: 179–98.

———. 2002. 'Kosovel, kraški poet in avantgardist' (Kosovel, Karst Poet and Avant-Gardist). In *Kons* by Srečko Kosovel, translated by Jolka Milič. pp. 13–17. Trst/Trieste: Tržaška knjigarna/Libreria Triestina.

———. 2004. 'Trdovratne zmote o Kosovelovem pesniškem opusu' (Persistent mistakes about Kosovel's poetic opus). In *Slovenski jezik in literatura v evropskih globalizacijskih procesih* (Slovene language and literature in European globalization processes), edited by Marko Jesenšek, pp. 147–57. Ljubljana: slavistično društvo Slovenije.

———. 2005. 'Srečko Kosovel and the European Avant-Garde', translated from Slovene by Katarina Jerin. In *Kosovelova poetika=Kosovel's Poetics*, edited by Janez Vrečko, Boris A. Novak, and Darja Pavlič, pp. 175–87. Ljubljana: Slovensko društvo za primerjalno književnost.

Vrečko, Janez. 2011. *Srečko Kosovel: Monografija* (Srečko Kosovel: A monograph). Ljubljana: Založba ZRC SAZU.

Wachtel, Andrew, B. 1998. *Making a Nation, Breaking a Nation: Literature and Cultural Politics in Yugoslavia*. Stanford: Stanford University Press.

———. 2003. 'Ivan Meštrović, Ivo Andruić and the Synthetic Yugoslav Culture of the Interwar Period'. In *Yugoslavism: Histories of a Failed Idea 1918-1992*, edited by Dejan Djokić, pp. 238–51. London: Hurst & Company.

Webb, Adam, K. 2008. 'The Countermodern Moment: A World-Historical Perspective on the Thought of Rabindranath Tagore, Muhammad Iqbal, and Liant Shuming'. *Journal of World History*, 19(2): 189–212.

Werbner, Pnina. 2006. 'Vernacular Cosmopolitanism'. *Theory, Culture & Society*, 23(2–3): 496–8.

Whitford, Frank. 1991. *Bauhaus*. New York: Thames and Hudson.

Wilcox, John, C. 1983. '"Naked" versus "Pure" Poetry in Juan Ramón Jiménez, with Remarks on the Impact of W. B. Yeats'. *Hispania*, 6(4): 511–22.

Williams, Louise Blakeney. 2007. 'Overcoming the "Contagion of Mimicry": The Cosmopolitan Nationalism and Modernist History of Rabindranath Tagore and W. B. Yeats'. *American Historical Review*, 112(2): 69–100.

Williams, Raymond. 1961. *The Long Revolution*. New York: Penguin Books.

———. 1989. *The Politics of Modernism: Against the New Conformists*. London: Verso.

Wilson, Rob. 1998. 'A New Cosmopolitanism Is in the Air: Some Dialectical Twists and Turns'. In *Cosmopolitics: Thinking and Feeling Beyond the Nation*, edited by Pheng Cheah, and Bruce Robbins, pp. 351–62. Minneapolis: University of Minnesota Press.

Wolf, Michaela. 2000. 'The Third Space in Postcolonial Representation'. In *Changing the Terms: Translating in the Postcolonial Era*, edited by Sherry Simon and Paul St-Pierre, pp. 127–45. Ottawa: University of Ottawa Press.

Wolff, Larry. 1994. *Inventing Eastern Europe: The Map of Civilization on the Mind of the Enlightenment*. Stanford: Stanford University Press.

Yeats, W. B. 1985. *The Collected Poems of W. B. Yeats*. London: Macmillan.

Young, Robert. 1990. *White Mythologies: Writing History and the West*. London/New York: Routledge.

———. 2003. *Postcolonialism: A Very Short Introduction*. Oxford: Oxford University Press

Zachariah, Benjamin. 2008. 'Residual Nationalism and the Indian (Radical?) Intellectual on Indigenism, Authenticity and the Colonizer's Presents'. In *Of Matters Modern: The Experience of Modernity in Colonial and Postcolonial South Asia*, edited by Debraj Bhattacharya, pp. 330–59. Kolkata: Seagull Books.

Zachariah, Benjamin. 2011. *Playing the Nation Game: The Ambiguities of Nationalism in India*. New Delhi: Yoda Press.

———. 2013. 'Postcolonial Theory and History'. In *The SAGE Handbook of Historical Theory*, edited by Nancy Partner and Sarah Foot, pp. 378–96. Los Angeles, London, New Delhi, Singapore, Washington DC: Sage Publications.

Zadravec, Franc (ed.). 1966a. *Pot skozi noč: izbor iz slovenske futuristične in ekspresionistične lirike* (Path through the night: Selection from Slovenian futurist and expressionist lyrics). Ljubljana: Mladinska knjiga.

———. 1966b. 'Konstruktivizem in Srečko Kosovel' (Constructivism and Srečko Kosovel). *Sodobnost*, 14(1–2): 1248–56.

———. 1966c. 'Futurizem in ekspresionizem v slovenski poeziji' (Futurism and expressionism in Slovenian poetry). In *Pot skozi noč: izbor iz slovenske futuristične in ekspresionistične lirike* (Path through the night: Selection from Slovenian futurist and expressionist lyrics), edited by Franc Zadravec, pp. 93–138. Ljubljana: Mladinska knjiga.

———. 1974. 'Položaj slovanskih, romanskih in germanskih literature pri Slovencih v obdobju med 1918 in 1941' (The status of Slavic, Romance and Germanic literatures with Slovenes in the period between 1918 and 1941). In *X. Seminar slovenskega jezika, literature in kulture, 1.–13. Julija 1974*, edited by Tine Logar, pp. 73–90, Ljubljana: Univerza v Ljubljani, Filozofska fakulteta.

———. 1984. *Obdobje ekspresionizma v slovenskem jeziku, književnosti in kulturi*, vol. 2. Ljubljana: Univerza Edvarda Kardelja.

———. 1986. *Srečko Kosovel 1904–1926*. Koper, Trst: Monografija.

Zep, Ira G. 1991. 'Tagore as Ferryman'. In *Rabindranath Tagore: American Intepretations*, edited by I. G. Zepp, pp. 9–16. Calcutta: Writer's Workshop.

Žižek, Slavoj. 2014. *Trouble in Paradise: From the End of History to the End of Capitalism*. London: Allen Lane.

Župančič, Oton. 1914. 'Rabindranath Tagore'. *Slovan*, 12(6): 31–2.

Index

About the Author

Ana Jelnikar is a research associate at the Research Centre of the Slovenian Academy of Sciences and Arts in Ljubljana, Slovenia. She earned her PhD from School of Oriental and African Studies (SOAS), University of London. As a literary translator (and editor) she has a number of publications to her name including *Look Back, Look Ahead: Selected Poems of Srečko Kosovel* (co-translated with Barbara Siegel Carlson, 2010), Meta Kušar's *Ljubljana* (co-translated with Stephen Watts, 2010). She is also one of the two founders of the annual *Golden Boat International Poetry Translation Workshop* in Slovenia and the translator of the first Slovenian edition of C. G. Jung's *Man and His Symbols*.